GLOBAL ISSUES

NUCLEAR NONPROLIFERATION

GLOBAL ISSUES

NUCLEAR NONPROLIFERATION

Phillip Margulies

Foreword by Sharon Squassoni

Carnegie Endowment for International Peace

Viva Books

New Delhi | Mumbai | Chennai | Kolkata | Bangalore | Hyderabad | Kochi | Guwahati

First Indian Edition 2010

VIVA BOOKS PRIVATE LIMITED

- 4737/23 Ansari Road, Daryaganj, New Delhi 110 002
  E-mail: vivadelhi@vivagroupindia.net, Tel. 42242200
- 76, Service Industries, Shirvane, Sector 1, Nerul, Navi Mumbai 400 706
  E-mail: vivamumbai@vivagroupindia.net, Tel. 27721273, 27721274
- Jamals Fazal Chambers, 26 Greams Road, Chennai 600 006
  E-mail: vivachennai@vivagroupindia.net, Tel. 28290304, 28294241
- B-103, Jindal Towers, 21/1A/3 Darga Road, Kolkata 700 017
  E-mail: vivakolkata@vivagroupindia.net, Tel. 22836381, 22816713
- 7, Sovereign Parl: Apartments, 56-58, K. R. Road, Basavanagudi, Bangalore 560 004
  E-mail: vivabangalore@vivagroupindia.net, Tel. 26607409, 26607410
- 101-102 Mughal Marc Apartments, 3-4-637 to 641, Narayanguda, Hyderabad 500 029
  E-mail: vivahyderabad@vivagroupindia.net, Tel. 27564481, 27564482
- First Floor, Bee.. Towers, SRM Road, Kaloor, Kochi 682 018, Kerala
  E-mail: vivakochi@vivagroupindia.net, Tel: 0484-2403055, 2403056
- 232, GNB Road, Beside UCO Bank, Silpukhuri, Guwahati 781 003
  E-mail: vivaguwahati@vivagroupindia.net, Tel: 0361-2666386

www.vivagroupindia.com

Published by arrangement with

Facts on File, Inc.
132 West 31st Street
New York 10001
USA

ISBN 978-81-309-1423-7

Published by Vinod Vasishtha for Viva Books Private Limited, 4737/23, Ansari Road, Daryaganj, New Delhi-110 002. Printed and bound by Anand Sons, Delhi - 110 092.

CONTENTS

Foreword

Nuclear weapons are ultimate weapons. They are thought to deter military attack because the destruction they would wreak is unthinkable. The world hopes that they are weapons of last resort, while those involved in their development and deployment create scenarios and target lists for use. People worry that in the world's most troubled regions, conventional crises could lead inadvertently to nuclear war.

Even for the established nuclear powers—the United States, Russia, China, France, and the United Kingdom—nuclear weapons have not solved their military problems. As Phillip Margulies points out in this volume, "Though the United States remains the world's greatest military and economic power, it faces the future with a more restricted sense of its ability to influence events beyond its borders, including its ability to curb the proliferation of nuclear weapons."

In the last decade, three states have tested nuclear weapons; the United States went to war with one state that it believed was developing weapons of mass destruction; and many fear that Iran may be the next to acquire nuclear weapons. Since the September 11, 2001, terrorist attacks on the United States, concern has grown about the possibility that terrorists might one day seek to acquire and use nuclear weapons to cause even greater destruction. Moreover, the discovery in 2003 that Pakistani scientist A. Q. Khan secretly had been selling key equipment and technology for enriching uranium—material that can be used in nuclear reactor fuel or in nuclear weapons—to Iran, Libya, and North Korea has made many skeptical that proliferation can be controlled. Whether the Khan network had additional customers is not entirely clear, since the United States has not been able to question Dr. Khan directly.

Sixty years after they were first developed, nuclear weapons do not appear to be closer to extinction. While there is widespread agreement on the threat nuclear weapons pose to humanity, there is also tacit agreement on the perception that they confer prestige and power upon those who possess them. Until the nuclear weapon states move decisively to eliminate their arsenals, nuclear weapons will continue to be attractive to states seeking to enhance their prestige.

While eventual elimination of nuclear weapons will reduce the threat that terrorists might gain access to such weapons, efforts are required now to strengthen physical protection and accounting of nuclear material that could be used in nuclear weapons, and also of radioactive material that could be used in so-called dirty bombs. Some progress has been made, but more needs to be done.

Nuclear proliferation is not an easy topic, even for the most expert policy analysts. Phillip Margulies has written a clear narrative of why nuclear weapons were developed, the threat they pose, and the attempts that have been made to slow their proliferation. This volume in many respects takes the mystery out of nuclear weapons and why countries want to have them, which is a good starting point for students.

Part I of the volume covers the background and theory of nuclear weapons development and control, from the dawn of the atomic age and its idealistic attempts to create international control of nuclear weapons and the nuclear fuel cycle through the current dilemmas facing the international community over India, Pakistan, Israel, North Korea, and Iran. After an introduction to the scope of the problem, chapter 2 explores the U.S.-Soviet nuclear weapons competition during the cold war as the context for other states developing nuclear arsenals, as well as the impetus for strategic arms control agreements. The practice of nuclear weapons policy under the George W. Bush administration is explored in detail in this chapter. In chapter 3, "Global Perspectives," the author summarizes the development of nuclear weapons in regions of concern: South Asia, the Middle East, and East Asia. He charts the motivations and capabilities of India, Pakistan, Israel, Iran, and North Korea.

The remaining sections provide resources for students of nuclear proliferation, including an annotated bibliography, a list of organizations involved in countering proliferation, a glossary, and a compendium of relevant U.S. and international historical documents. The compendium gives a flavor of the historical debate that is critical to understanding the context and controversy surrounding nuclear weapons' development, while the up-to-date resources will facilitate further in-depth study of the topic.

Whether the world succeeds or fails in limiting the spread of nuclear weapons is critical for this generation and those to come. Decisions about major international agreements, imposition of sanctions, the desirability of conducting air strikes on the territory of certain countries, and, ultimately, whether to go to war have hinged on assessments of whether some countries seek nuclear weapons. Nuclear nonproliferation has been a critical component of U.S. foreign policy for more than six decades and until nuclear weapons are abolished, it will remain so.

What is more, the U.S. government spends about $55 billion annually on nuclear security—maintaining nuclear weapons to deter others from attacking us, cleaning up the nuclear mess from decades of producing nuclear weapons, securing our nuclear facilities from attack, and helping reduce the threat posed by nuclear weapons and nuclear materials overseas. While this may be a drop in the bucket compared to the U.S. defense budget, it is a sizable amount and deserves scrutiny by the American taxpayer. Is the U.S. federal government spending the right amount of resources on the right problems? Understanding why and how to slow proliferation will help inform the public about the choices their government is making—from efforts in diplomacy, intelligence, and export controls to international laws and treaties and military actions. Ultimately, the bold and fateful choices that states may make—whether to give up nuclear weapons for good, develop them in secret, brandish them openly, or possibly even use them—rest on calculations of what their citizenry will bear.

—Sharon Squassoni
Senior Associate, Nonproliferation Program
Carnegie Endowment for International Peace

List of Acronyms

ABM—antiballistic missile

BJP—Bharatiya Janata Party

CIA—Central Intelligence Agency

CTBT—Comprehensive Test Ban Treaty

CTR—Cooperative Threat Reduction

DMZ—demilitarized zone

HE—high explosives

HEU—highly enriched uranium

IADA—International Atomic Development Authority

IAEA—International Atomic Energy Agency

ICBM—intercontinental ballistic missile

KGB—Committee for State Security (Kormitet Gosudarstvennoy Bezopasnosti)

MIRV—multiple independently targeted reentry vehicle

MTCR—Missile Technology Control Regime

NATO—North Atlantic Treaty Organization

NGO—nongovernmental organizations

NSG—Nuclear Suppliers Group

SAC—Strategic Air Command

SDI—Strategic Defense Initiative, byname Star Wars

SLBM—submarine-launched ballistic missiles

SORT—Strategic Offensive Reduction Treaty

START I—Strategic Arms Reduction Talks I

START II—Strategic Arms Reduction Talks II

List of Acronyms

TNT—trinitrotoluene

UNAEC—United Nations Atomic Energy Commission

USAEC—United States Atomic Energy Commission

USSR—Union of Soviet Socialist Republics

V-2 rocket—Vergeltungswaffe 2

WHO—World Health Organization

WMD—weapons of mass destruction

PART I

At Issue

1

Introduction

THE THREAT OF NUCLEAR PROLIFERATION

The Swedish chemist Alfred Nobel hoped that dynamite, which he invented in 1867, would make war so terrible that nations would be forced to settle their disputes peacefully. "Perhaps my factories will put an end to war sooner than your congresses," he once boasted.[1] He would probably have admitted his mistake if he had lived to see the 20th century's two "total" wars, in which the rules for distinguishing between civilians and soldiers were ignored and all the tools of modern technology were used to manufacture death on an unprecedented scale. War did become more terrible than ever before, but instead of turning away from it in horror, nations practiced it more ruthlessly, sure that their very existence was at stake.

World War II, which caused the deaths of 50 million people, concluded with two new inventions that raised war's potential destructiveness to previously undreamed of levels. The first was the atomic bomb, the immediate ancestor of today's thermonuclear weapons. The second was the V-2 rocket, the prototype of today's intercontinental ballistic missiles (ICBMs), which can send nuclear warheads across the world in half an hour.

Up to and including the atomic bomb—dropped in 1945 on Japan—nations have always made use of major advances in weaponry, and arms races have always led to war. If this pattern holds true with nuclear weapons, human civilization is in jeopardy. These observations have haunted the debate among scientists, generals, and politicians ever since the opening of the atomic age.

The stakes have continued to rise as new countries have acquired nuclear arms: the United States in 1945, the Soviet Union in 1949, England in 1952, France in 1960, China in 1964, Israel sometime in the 1960s, India in 1974, Pakistan in 1998, and North Korea in 2006.

Brief History of Nuclear Proliferation

BEGINNING OF THE ATOMIC AGE

The nuclear age began with a race in which the United States sought to develop nuclear weapons before its enemy did. Ironically, the race had only one participant, at least to begin with.

In the 1930s, breakthroughs in nuclear physics alerted a handful of scientists to the possibility of inventing an atomic bomb. Several of these scientists, including Leo Szilard (1898–1964), Edward Teller (1908–2003), and Eugene Wigner (1902–95), had come to live in America in flight from the rise of fascism in Europe. Their first thought, after realizing that an atomic bomb could be built, was that Adolf Hitler's Germany had the know-how to build one. For the Nazis to be in sole possession of such a powerful weapon would be intolerable. So, in the summer of 1939, Szilard, Teller, and Wigner decided to persuade the American government to develop the bomb first.

They asked Albert Einstein (1879–1955) to assist them in making their case. Contrary to popular legend, Einstein did not himself come up with the idea for the atomic bomb (his words on learning that a nuclear chain reaction could be used to make a bomb were, "I never thought of that,"), but he agreed to use his fame to help the relatively obscure group of exiled physicists get the U.S. government's attention.[2] Einstein signed a letter that Szilard had written, addressed to President Franklin D. Roosevelt (1882–1945). The letter spoke of the future peacetime benefits of atomic energy and of its potential as a weapon.

Since they did not want to sound like utopian dreamers, the physicists did not mention their other hopes for the bomb. "We realized," Eugene Wigner wrote later, "that, should atomic weapons be developed, no two nations would be able to live in peace with each other unless their military forces were controlled by a higher authority. We realized that these controls, if they were effective enough to abolish atomic warfare, would be effective enough to abolish also all other forms of war. The hope was almost as strong a spur to our endeavors as was our fear of becoming the victims of the enemy's atomic bombings."[3]

In Wigner's view, the very existence of nuclear weapons would face countries with a dilemma that could be solved only by creating a world government.

Szilard, Teller, and Wigner were right about the possibility of making the bomb, and they were right to think that it would change the world. History has proved them to be mistaken on several other points, however. Though scientists in Hitler's Germany did put their talents at the service of the state, developing such military novelties as jet fighter aircraft, unmanned aircraft, and the V-2 rocket, they did not engage in a crash nuclear weapons program, as the United States did.[4] The United States and its allies defeated Germany without the help of the atomic bomb. Then, in the 60-plus years since their invention, the existence of nuclear weapons has not led to world government, nor has it led, so far, to nuclear war. Instead, it has led to tense standoffs, nuclear arms races, and a vast industry of nuclear weapons systems.

At the order of U.S. president Harry S. Truman (1884–1972), on August 6, 1945, an atomic bomb was dropped on Hiroshima, a Japanese industrial city with a population of around 280,000 civilians and 43,000 soldiers. On August 9, a second atomic bomb was dropped on Nagasaki, another major Japanese city. Both cities were virtually destroyed. An estimated 340,000 Japanese eventually died from the combined effects of the blast and radiation.[5] In a radio broadcast on August 15, the Japanese emperor Hirohito (1901–89) told his people that they must "endure the unendurable" and surrender on allied terms.[6]

The Soviet dictator Joseph Stalin (1879–1953) immediately called a meeting, including the People's Commissar of Munitions Boris L. Vannikov and one of the country's leading nuclear physicists, Igor Vasilyevich Kurchatov (1903–60), later known as the "father of the Soviet atom bomb."

> *A single demand of you, comrades. Provide us with atomic weapons in the shortest possible time. You know that Hiroshima has shaken the whole world. The equilibrium has been destroyed. Provide the bomb—it will remove a great danger from us.*[7]

With Stalin's inevitable decision, the nuclear arms race now had two participants.

The scientists who had suggested developing the atomic bomb to counter a German bomb program—a program that turned out not to exist—were dismayed by the destruction of Hiroshima and Nagasaki not only because they considered its use immoral but because they believed it would make a postwar nuclear arms race inevitable. Leo Szilard called the use of the bomb on Japan "one of the greatest blunders of history."[8] In 1946, a group of guilt-ridden nuclear physicists founded the *Bulletin of the Atomic Scientists,* a magazine best known for the "doomsday clock" on its covers—an image of a clock face, its hands indicating a time a few minutes from midnight. "World government is our only hope for survival," wrote Edward Teller in 1948 in the pages of the *Bulletin.*[9]

THE COLD WAR PROMOTES "VERTICAL" PROLIFERATION

The United States and the Soviet Union emerged from the war as its two great victors, mutually suspicious and representing opposing ideologies. Each had its allies, and each sought the allegiance of the newly independent countries that were forming with the break-up of the colonial empires of Great Britain, France, Japan, the Netherlands, Belgium, and Italy. Assuming that the future would resemble the recent past, it became commonplace for people to speak of "World War III," and to say that it would be an "atomic war" between the United States and the Soviet Union. Early efforts to contain the spread of nuclear weapons failed due to the deep mistrust between the United States and the Soviet Union.

On August, 29, 1949, the USSR exploded its first atomic bomb. American aircraft detected atmospheric evidence of the secret test, and on September 23, Truman announced publicly that the Soviets had broken America's nuclear monopoly. Only four months later, at the beginning of 1950, Truman made a further announcement. Upping the ante in the great nuclear poker game, the United States was developing "the so-called hydrogen or super-bomb." Probably the Soviets had already made the decision to develop their own hydrogen bomb.[10]

The United States detonated "Mike," the world's first thermonuclear weapon, or hydrogen bomb, at Enewetak Atoll in the Marshall Islands on November 1, 1952. The force of the explosion was 10.4 megatons, or 10.4 million tons of TNT, 500 times more powerful than the bomb dropped on Nagasaki.[11] The Soviets tested a hydrogen bomb less than a year later. From then until the late 1980s, the nuclear arms race only gathered momentum.

Mutual fear and hostility between the East (the Soviets and their allies) and the West (the Americans and their allies) led to an increase in the number and types of nuclear weapons and their delivery systems—a process now called *vertical nuclear proliferation*—and to the spread of nuclear weapons to more and more countries—*horizontal nuclear proliferation*. By 1970, the nuclear weapons possessed by each side numbered in the tens of thousands—over 26,000 warheads in the United States alone and over 11,000 in the Soviet Union.[12] There were hydrogen bombs on aircraft ready to be dropped on enemy targets; there were guided missiles in underground silos aimed at enemy cities, factories, and military installations; there were missiles on nuclear submarines; and there were thousands of "tactical" nuclear weapons able to be launched in the form of artillery shells in Europe. Later, both countries added MIRVs (Multiple Independently Targeted Reentry Vehicles) to their missiles, multiplying the number of warheads that a missile could deliver after it was launched, and each introduced another leg of its nuclear armory in the form of missiles and warheads mounted on mobile launchers in constant motion on the ground. Any one of the systems had the potential to kill hundreds of millions of people, depopulating the enemies' countries and poisoning the atmosphere of the Earth. By 1986, the number of warheads possessed by both sides exceeded 60,000.[13]

Why did the Soviets and the United States make so many bombs? There is no single answer to that question, for throughout the cold war arms race, military planners disagreed about the purpose of the weapons and the ways in which they might be used.

The primary justification for the size of the buildup was *deterrence*: The possession of so many weapons would prevent an attack by making it clear that no matter who won the war, the enemy would regret beginning it. The reason the goal of deterrence led to a race to be ahead in bombs was that in a nuclear war the bombs themselves would be military targets. A country with a small number of bombs—small by comparison with the enemy's—might not be able to launch its own after a surprise attack. It would have no "second strike capability." The other side would therefore have a "first strike capability." This very possibility might encourage a surprise attack; if you thought war was inevitable and that being the first to attack was the best way of ensuring your own people's survival, would it not be your duty to do it? Large overlapping nuclear weapons systems were meant to assure that neither side could knock out the other's nuclear capability with a first strike, so long as neither side got too far ahead in bombs. With the secrecy that surrounded nuclear weapons, it was difficult to be sure, so each side kept building more weapons.

In addition, some analysts believed that having more nuclear weapons than a potential enemy gave one side an advantage in international political disputes. This was another incentive to keep building bombs.

Finally, from the beginning, many politicians in the United States reasoned that the Soviet economy was inherently weak; they would be unable to keep up, and if they tried, they would collapse. Some historians believe that this actually happened, though not until decades after it was first predicted, when the Soviet Union finally broke apart in 1991.

THE MILITARY-INDUSTRIAL COMPLEX AND THE NUCLEAR ARMS RACE

There were also nonstrategic reasons for the buildup, as was hinted by U.S. president Dwight D. Eisenhower (1890–1969) in his January 17, 1961, farewell address, when he said the American people must "guard against the acquisition of unwarranted influence, whether sought or unsought, by the military-industrial complex."[14] Weapons manufacturers profited from the growth of the nuclear arsenals and related systems, military forces gained prestige, and politicians benefited when money and jobs flowed to their constituents. As these interests grew in size, their influence on government increased.

The military-industrial complex, though surely a significant influence on decisions concerning nuclear weapons, is not omnipotent. Military budgets do get cut from time to time, military bases close, and the ultimate outcome of the cold war shows that arms reduction is possible. In the late 1980s, the United States and the Soviet Union agreed to reduce their nuclear arsenals, and since the breakup of the Soviet Union in 1991, Russia and the United States have continued to reduce them sharply. Current levels are in the thousands instead of the 10s of thousands.[15]

THE COLD WAR PROMOTES HORIZONTAL NUCLEAR PROLIFERATION

In addition to promoting vertical proliferation, the buildup of arms, the cold war led to horizontal proliferation, the spread of nuclear weapons to new countries. NATO, an alliance between the United States and the democracies of Western Europe, was created in 1949 to deter an attack on Europe from the Soviet Union; it stood ready to battle the forces of the Soviets and their Eastern European allies (the Warsaw Pact), who, it was feared, might overrun Western Europe in a lightning attack. NATO's military problem was that the Soviet Union and its allies, with their vast conventional (that is, nonnuclear) forces, was next to Europe, while the United States was an ocean away. In a war of tanks, aircraft, artillery, and infantry, the Warsaw Pact could have overwhelmed NATO in days, before the United States could bring in the bulk of its own armed forces. To redress this imbalance, NATO deployed up to 7,000 "tactical," or short-range, nuclear weapons in Europe and announced that it would use them if necessary in reply to a conventional attack by Warsaw Pact forces.[16] This decision put nuclear weapons in the hands of many military commanders of various nationalities, though in theory they were American weapons and the launch of a nuclear weapon would have required the cooperation of an American commander.[17]

The conventional superiority of Warsaw Pact forces to NATO forces was one reason why the U.S. military planners were not eager to "ban the bomb" and regarded antinuclear demonstrators as dupes of the Soviet Union. Total nuclear disarmament would have given a major military advantage to the communists. (Besides, the Soviet Union opposed on-site inspections of its weapons facilities, and without such inspections, arms agreements would have been difficult to monitor.)

Feeling threatened by the Warsaw Pact and believing that possession of nuclear weapons was the key to great power status in the modern world, Europe's advanced industrial powers moved swiftly to develop their own nuclear weapons, independently of the United States.

England, which had done some of the primary research on the development of the atomic bomb in the 1930s and 1940s, produced its first atomic weapon in 1952. In 1960, France became the world's fourth nuclear power, detonating a large atomic device in the Sahara.

After the Soviet Union, the West's greatest cold war antagonist was mainland China, which became a Communist country in 1949. Though China's chairman Mao Zedong (1893–1976) derided the military significance of nuclear weapons, calling the bomb "a paper tiger," China exploded its first atomic bomb in 1964 and its first hydrogen bomb about a year and a half later. China's motivation for developing a bomb was probably to deter an attack and to prevent it from being threatened with nuclear weapons, as the United States tended to do during international crises during the 1950s and 1960s. (The threats were made indirectly, in the form of assertions intended to reach the ears of the Chinese leadership and in deployments during times of crisis of planes or artillery capable of delivering nuclear warheads. They are described in McGeorge Bundy's history of U.S. nuclear decision-making, *Danger and Survival*.)[18] At first, the Soviet Union assisted China with its nuclear program; by the time China had nuclear weapons, however, they were probably meant to deter its neighbor, the Soviet Union, as much as its supposed ideological enemy, the United States.

Cuba, though it never possessed the scientific or industrial capability to manufacture nuclear weapons, became a location for nuclear warheads in 1962, when Soviet premier Nikita Khrushchev (1894–1971) installed nuclear-armed medium-range ballistic missiles on the Caribbean island. After a tense standoff that may have brought the world to the brink of all-out nuclear war, the weapons were removed.[19]

A final nuclear state that may be said to have arisen from the tensions of the cold war is North Korea, an impoverished, secretive Communist dictatorship that has been in a standoff with South Korea since the early 1950s. The 1991 breakup of the Soviet Union did nothing to affect North Korea's isolation and paranoia. North Korea tested its first nuclear weapons in 2006.

NUCLEAR PROLIFERATION OUTSIDE THE COLD WAR CONTEXT

The struggle of the superpowers was not the only conflict capable of causing nuclear proliferation. Israel, India, and Pakistan acquired nuclear weapons because of security concerns independent of the cold war, concerns that did not end with the breakup of the Soviet Union.

Israel

Ever since the state of Israel was created in 1948 over the objections of virtually every other country in the Middle East, the Arab-Israeli conflict has been simmering, repeatedly breaking out into open war. Some time in the 1960s, Israel developed nuclear weapons as its ultimate insurance against a combined attack by its enemies. It is difficult to say exactly when Israel became a nuclear weapons state, because Israel has never conducted a nuclear weapons test. The Israeli government officially claims not to have nuclear weapons, while hinting broadly that it really does possess them. In 1986, the *Sunday Times* of London reported Israel could have "at least 100 and as many as 200 nuclear weapons of varying destructive power."[20]

India and Pakistan

When India gained independence from the British Empire in the late 1940s, it split up into two nations, the Islamic country of Pakistan and the much larger, multiracial, and multireligious country of modern India. Though India's independence movement is famous for its nonviolence, the breakup of India and Pakistan was marked by terrible bloodshed: Some estimate the number of Muslims and Hindus killed in sectarian violence at 1 million in addition to some 6 million refugees. The two countries have fought three wars since then and are engaged in a continual struggle over the province of Kashmir, which is predominantly Islamic in religion but is a part of India. Historically, India has feared conflict not only with Pakistan, its neighbor to the west, but also China, its neighbor to the north.

During the 1950s and 1960s, India acquired a great deal of nuclear know-how, in part thanks to its participation in international programs intended to promote the peaceful uses of nuclear energy. On May 18, 1974, India conducted a successful test that the Indian government described as a "peaceful nuclear explosion." During the 1980s, India added to its nuclear capability with research on thermonuclear weapons (hydrogen bombs), an effort that culminated in five tests of nuclear weapons in 1998. Pakistan replied a few weeks later by conducting five nuclear tests of its own, thereby becoming the first Islamic nation to have nuclear weapons.

NUCLEAR PROGRAMS THWARTED

Iraq

The Iraqi dictator Saddam Hussein (1935–2006) was very interested in acquiring powerful weapons systems. After the 1991 Gulf War, begun when Iraq invaded its neighbor Kuwait, the country's secret nuclear weapons program was eliminated as part of the peace settlement imposed on Iraq. Other countries, particularly the United States, suspected Iraq of reviving the program. While inspections conducted under UN auspices turned up no convincing evidence that Iraq had a viable nuclear weapons program, Saddam Hussein's systematic attempts to make things difficult for the inspectors seemed very suspicious to European and American leaders. In 2003, while the UN inspection team asked for more time to complete its work, the U.S. government invaded Iraq on the pretext that Saddam Hussein was developing nuclear weapons, as well as chemical and biological weapons, and might give them to terrorists. A thorough search after the invasion showed no evidence of nuclear, chemical, or biological weapons in Iraq.[21]

Libya

Libya, a country long considered a "rogue state" by the United States, announced in 2003 that it had decided to stop trying to acquire nuclear weapons and cooperate with international bodies that were attempting to control the spread of WMD. As a gesture of good faith, Libya revealed a great deal about a secret network headed by Dr. A. Q. Khan, the scientist who had guided Pakistan's nuclear weapons program. In this way, the world learned that Dr. Khan (supposedly without the Pakistani government's knowledge, though this seems highly unlikely) had been secretly supplying nuclear weapons technology to Libya, Iran, North Korea, and perhaps others.[22] The revelations about the Khan network heightened Iran's nuclear ambitions.

STATES THAT HAVE GIVEN UP NUCLEAR WEAPONS OR NUCLEAR WEAPONS PROGRAMS

Encouragingly, Libya and Iraq are not the only states that have turned around on the road to nuclear weapons development. The former Soviet republics of Belarus, Kazakhstan, and Ukraine, which inherited nuclear weapons following the Soviet Union's 1991 collapse, subsequently returned their nuclear weapons to Russia and signed the Nuclear Nonproliferation Treaty (NPT) as nonnuclear weapon states. South Africa, which secretly developed a small number of nuclear weapons in the 1970s and 1980s, dismantled them and joined the NPT in 1991. Argentina and Brazil shelved nuclear weapons programs in the early 1990s; Romania abandoned its nuclear weapons program in 1989; and Algeria, which was thought in the early 1990s to have developed a nuclear weapon, signed the NPT in 1993. Australia, Canada, Japan, and South Korea are not nuclear weapons states despite possessing nuclear knowhow. In western Europe (with the exceptions of France and Great Britain), several countries with advanced technical capability are not nuclear weapons states.

What Nuclear Weapons Can Do

Nuclear weapons pose many different kinds and degrees of danger. Between the 1950s and the end of the cold war, Americans became accustomed to imagining the worst case, the universal destruction that would result from unlimited nuclear war between the United States and the Soviet Union, each assisted by their nuclear-armed allies. Though this prospect is much less immediate now that the cold war has ended, it is worth considering because it is possible that proliferation will spark new arms races and lead countries to build vast nuclear arsenals once again.

The thermonuclear weapons that the United States and the Soviet Union began deploying in the 1950s are far more powerful than the weapons that killed hundreds of thousands in Hiroshima and Nagasaki. In the rough calculation most often used to compare the power of the bombs, the Hiroshima bomb had an energy of 12.5 kilotons, the equivalent of 12,500 tons of the chemical explosive TNT, while a typical strategic thermonuclear bomb has an explosive force of 1 megaton, the equivalent of 1,000,000 tons of TNT, or 80 Hiroshima bombs. To put it another way, a 2-megaton bomb would have an explosive power equal to all the bombs dropped in World War II.[23] In 1982, at the height of the nuclear arms race between the Soviet Union and the United States, the world contained around 50,000 explosive nuclear warheads, together possessing, as the author Jonathan Schell put it, "the explosive yield of roughly twenty billion tons of TNT, or one million six hundred thousand times the yield of the bomb that was dropped by the United States on the city of Hiroshima. . . ."[24]

In a war in which the United States and the Soviet Union had used all their forces against each other's military installations, factories, and cities, each side would have run out of targets long before it had run out of bombs. Schell notes, "substantially the whole human construct in the United States would be vaporized, blasted or otherwise pulverized out of existence." A 1983 study for the WHO concluded that 1.1 billion people would be killed outright in a nuclear war involving the United States, the Soviet Union, Europe, China, and Japan. Another 1.1 billion would suffer serious injury and radiation sickness for which medical help would be unavailable due to a breakdown of society.[25]

Nuclear weapons have many ways to kill. The fireball of a 1-megaton nuclear explosion would grow to two miles across and set off massive secondary fires. "Anyone caught in the open within 9 miles of ground zero would receive third-degree burns and would probably be killed; closer to the explosion, people would be charred and killed instantly. From Greenwich

Village up to Central Park, the heat would be great enough to melt metal and glass."[26] Nuclear explosions have electromagnetic effects that disrupt communications and in modern society would immediately cause chaos, thwarting rescue efforts and making military defenses ineffective. Nuclear explosions create radioactive debris that can continue to poison and kill people for months after the initial blast—this is the "fallout," to escape which people in the 1950s and 1960s were advised to build shelters stocked with several months' worth of food. Nuclear explosions introduce radioactive isotopes into the environment, where they enter the food chain and cause cancer, sterility, and birth defects. Even a few nuclear explosions set off in populated areas during a "limited" nuclear war could cause millions of deaths immediately and create the conditions for mass starvation due to the destruction of a country's agriculture. Wind and water, which do not respect national boundaries, would carry poisonous radiation to neighboring countries.

All of the planets' living things would probably be affected by an all-out nuclear war using tens of thousands of weapons; how severely is uncertain. It is possible the ozone layer of the Earth, which protects plants and animals from harmful radiation from space, would be destroyed. A 1983 *Science* article suggested that dust raised by nuclear explosions, combined with the spread of smoke in the atmosphere from nuclear-started fires, could absorb sunlight, lowering the temperature of the Earth by between 1° and 5° C. The resulting nuclear winter would last for months and destroy many species by starvation.[27] Some studies have cast doubt on the severity of the temperature change that might be caused, but the theory has neither been confirmed nor discredited.

NUCLEAR WEAPONS V. WMD

It has become common in the last decade for journalists, politicians, and diplomats to speak of nuclear weapons as belonging to a larger category of WMD that includes biological and chemical weapons. The implication is that these weapons have a moral and practical equivalency: They are alike in that they should never be used, and special efforts should be made to restrict access to them. This category has its uses. Certainly, people interested in arms control should keep it in mind that human ingenuity is a moving target and that technology may one day produce other threats to human life of the same order of magnitude as nuclear weapons—a new plague, for example, that would travel swiftly through an unprotected population.

Still, as things stand today, the dangers posed by nuclear weapons and other WMD are of a different order. The scale of the potential humanitarian disaster these weapons threaten is not the same. Neither are the military calculations they provoke.

Nuclear weapons can destroy a city of millions in a matter of minutes, or destroy much of the world in an afternoon. No other weapon can do that. When the United States invaded Iraq in 1990 and again in 2003, U.S. soldiers drilled with gas masks to protect them from the expected chemical attacks, which fortunately never came. If the United States had believed that Iraq already had nuclear weapons and missiles capable of delivering them to Washington, D.C., or New York City, the military situation would have been different, and the United States would probably not have invaded Iraq. A difference that has such an important effect on U.S. foreign policy and world history is worth remembering.

PEACEFUL NUCLEAR POWER GENERATION AND NUCLEAR WEAPONS

Nuclear energy has an ambiguous place in the history of nuclear proliferation. In the late 1940s and early 1950s, nuclear energy seemed to promise a utopia—a world of virtually free energy, a world of such plenty that there would be no war. Those prospects seem much more distant today, but other developments have continued to make the promise of nuclear power important. Worldwide demand for energy is greater than ever; unlike coal and oil, nuclear energy does not produce greenhouse gases and so does not contribute to global warming; with proper safeguards it does not contribute to air pollution; it can be produced anywhere; its sale does not put money into the pockets of the governments of problematic regimes such as the Republic of Iran; the supply of it cannot be cut off by the interruption of a pipeline; its production does not threaten animal habitats; and it is a potentially limitless renewable resource, while the supply of coal and oil will eventually run out.

Nuclear power generation has its drawbacks, however. Accidents at nuclear power generating facilities could spread toxic radiation. Nuclear power generation produces waste that may be poisonous for thousands of years. Most worrying of all, the technology that produces nuclear power has always been closely related to the technology of nuclear bomb making; a nation that acquires the know-how to build nuclear reactors and make nuclear fuel goes a long way toward acquiring the know-how to build nuclear weapons. The radioactive isotopes used by and produced in nuclear power generation can be used for a slow nuclear reaction that generates heat to run turbines, or they can be concentrated (in the process called uranium enrichment), then slammed together abruptly by high explosives to reach critical mass in a bomb.

POTENTIAL FOR NUCLEAR WAR

During the cold war, military analysts devoted a great deal of time to discussing the conditions that could lead to nuclear war. These nuclear scenarios remain relevant today.

Escalation

In a war between two nuclear weapons states, both sides might at first confine themselves to conventional weapons, recognizing that a nuclear war would lead to unacceptable damage for both countries. But as defeat loomed, the side that was losing might break the nuclear taboo in a desperate attempt to change the course of the war. In a fight to the death, how can you refrain from using your most powerful weapons?

Concern about escalation is one reason that the United States has never yet made use of so-called tactical, or battlefield, nuclear weapons, and why their proposed deployment is considered controversial today. Used to destroy well-shielded weapons or against an enemy command post in a deep underground bunker, a tactical nuclear weapon might be considered merely one step above an assault on the same target with conventional explosives, but it would cross a line that has not been crossed since 1945.

Escalation could work in another way: A country with nuclear weapons might pledge to protect a less-well-armed country, then at a later date be drawn into a war as a result. Networks of alliances make it possible for small wars to become large ones, as they ultimately did in World Wars I and II. A war between nonnuclear weapons states could become a war between nuclear weapons states.

Preemptive War/Preventive War

The principal danger, one that the cold war's vast accumulations of nuclear weapons were supposed to prevent (by making the option suicidal), was a deliberate surprise nuclear attack. Presuming that the leaders on both sides were sane, the likeliest motivation for a surprise attack would be *preemptive war.* During an international crisis, leaders might feel that a war was just a matter of time, and the advantage would lie with the side that attacked first. Under such circumstances, leaders might consider themselves irresponsible not to launch the first nuclear strike—it would simply be the logical thing to do. U.S. and Soviet leaders considered this option a number of times, especially in the early 1960s, when Soviet premier Nikita Khrushchev and U.S. president John F. Kennedy (1917–63) faced each other, each determined to show toughness and not to be the first to blink during international crises centering on control of the German city of Berlin and on Khrushchev's decision to place nuclear missiles in Cuba.

A country could also make a decision to wage *preventive war*—to begin a war even when attack did not seem imminent to prevent a potential enemy from becoming strong enough to pose a threat. This might seem like the right thing to do when there was a temporary imbalance between the nuclear forces of two countries, and the generals in the stronger country advised its leaders that it would be best to strike while the chance of victory was greater. During the late 1940s and early 1950s, the United States was well ahead of the Soviet Union in nuclear arms, and U.S. leaders did consider using nuclear weapons to crush the Soviet Union before it became capable of destroying the United States. During that brief period, the Soviet Union might not have been able to use its nuclear weapons to retaliate; the Soviets lacked a credible (that is, convincing) second strike capability. Presidents Truman and Eisenhower each decided against this option—Truman because the people of the United States would abhor it, Eisenhower because it would make the rest of the world fear and loathe the United States.[28]

As new countries acquire nuclear weapons, their neighbors already armed with nuclear weapons will be faced repeatedly with the decision of whether to engage in preventive war, especially during the period when the new nuclear weapons state has a primitive nuclear force without a credible second strike capability.

Unauthorized Use

The 1964 movie *Dr. Strangelove,* which dares to find humor in the nuclear dilemma, suggests another way that nuclear war might begin: In the film, an insane American general, convinced that the communists are using fluoridation to sap his people's "purity of essence," orders atomic bombers under his command to attack the Soviet Union. Though *Dr. Strangelove* is a satire, unauthorized use of nuclear weapons by a crazy or insubordinate commander is a very real danger whose likelihood mounts as more countries possess nuclear weapons. The United States, fortunately, has a long tradition of military subordination to civilian control. The U.S. military has never decided on its own to start a war; it has never tried to take control of the government. There is no evidence that a U.S. military commander has ever attempted to launch or explode a nuclear weapon without authorization. Outside the United States, however, the military overthrow of civilian governments is common. Such an occurence would be especially worrying in a country that had nuclear weapons.

The Soviet Union, shortly before it broke up, underwent an attempted coup d'état during which Soviet premier Mikhail Gorbachev (1931–   ) was kidnapped. When the Soviet Union did break up in 1991, no one in the United States could be quite sure who was in charge of the Soviet nuclear weapons. The risk of unauthorized use may be especially high in a country undergoing a revolution or a country whose civilian government is weak.

Accidental Use

It is also possible that a nuclear war could be started by accident. During times of tension, the United States and the Soviet Union would put their nuclear arsenals on "high alert," ready to launch on short notice at the sign of a surprise attack from the enemy. An attack could begin at the push of a button, and buttons can be pushed in error. Since an accidental nuclear missile launch or explosion would be perceived by the other side as an attack, it could trigger an unintended nuclear war, a war caused by a technical problem.

Opportunities for a new sort of nuclear miscalculation arose when the United States and the Soviet Union put into place sensitive computerized systems designed to keep either country from being caught napping. Potentially, war could have resulted from a false alarm due to a malfunction of these early warning systems. If these systems were not sensitive enough, they might fail to respond to an attack. But the more sensitive they were, the more prone they were to see an attack where there was none. There were many errors and close calls during the cold war. For example, in October 1960, shortly after the United States had installed its Ballistic Missile Early Warning System, U.S. radar detected a nonexistent ballistic missile attack. Luckily, other radar checking the same areas gave conflicting information, and it was concluded the first radar was malfunctioning.

On November 9, 1979, U.S. missile crews received warning of an all-out nuclear attack from the Soviet Union—an error that resulted when a training tape was mistakenly loaded into a computer. In this case, U.S. leaders checked data from early warning satellites, which had detected no missile launch, and realized their mistake.

According to former CIA director James Woolsey, the U.S. early warning system once mistook a rising moon for a Russian ICBM attack. Experts decided the data could not be true because, at the time, Soviet premier Nikita Khrushchev was in the United States.

These are just a few of many known incidents, and since nuclear matters are shrouded in secrecy, we will never know how many close calls there actually were. Though they are now only footnotes to history, the fact that these near disasters could occur in the world's most well-run, tightly controlled nuclear weapons system has important implications for nuclear proliferation.[29]

Nuclear Terrorism

Long before the 9/11 attacks promoted terrorism to the top of the list of international security threats, governments worried what terrorists might do with nuclear weapons. Several terrorist groups, including Osama bin

Laden's al-Qaeda network, are known to have attempted to acquire nuclear weapons.

A country seeking to hide its own complicity in a nuclear attack might give a nuclear weapon to terrorists. This possibility was used by the United States as a justification for the invasion of Iraq in 2003. Alternatively, terrorists might steal a nuclear weapon from a nuclear weapons state that had a poor security system. The likeliest scenario involving nuclear proliferation and terrorism is that terrorists might obtain radioactive fissile materials and combine them with conventional explosives to create a "dirty bomb," causing widespread panic and radioactive contamination. These dangerous materials are far more plentiful and under much less strict control than are nuclear weapons; they are easier to obtain on the black market. Though a dirty bomb is not a nuclear weapon and would not kill vast numbers of people, it would be a very effective device for spreading panic and disrupting society.[30]

It should be said, however, that while nuclear weapons proliferation increases the chances of terrorists obtaining fissile materials for a dirty bomb, so does peaceful nuclear power development, because the fissile materials used in power generation and produced as a by-product of nuclear power could also be used to create a dirty bomb. A terrorist group could cause even more damage with a well-targeted attack that used conventional explosives to destroy a nuclear power facility.

THE SPECIAL DANGERS POSED BY NEW NUCLEAR WEAPONS STATES

The arsenals of new nuclear weapons states such as India, Pakistan, Israel, and North Korea are much smaller than those of the United States and Russia, so the threats they pose are different. In addition to the possibility that hostile states might give a bomb or radioactive materials to terrorists, there is the concern that use of nuclear weapons by a small country might trigger a war between the nuclear superpowers, either by the superpowers taking sides in a smaller conflict or the superpowers mistaking the source of the attack.

Although the number of warheads involved is not enough to threaten humanity with extinction, a nuclear war between the nuclear states of India and Pakistan or between Israel and a nuclear Iran could also cause a number of deaths exceeding those in any previous war. Radiation and fallout from a war between minor nuclear weapons states could poison the environment in neighboring countries.

In addition, the world's smaller nuclear arsenals may not always remain small. The economies of China and India are developing quickly; they may one day be able to support large nuclear establishments. If Japan, which has one of the world's leading economies, decided to arm itself, it could develop a large nuclear arsenal and an advanced missile technology very quickly. The fears and ambitions that have led countries to acquire nuclear weapons in the first place may one day propel them into nuclear arms races similar to the U.S.-Soviet arms race of the cold war; 30 years from now, if the spread of nuclear weapons is unchecked, the temporary roll-back of the early 1990s may be lost. The world of 2040 might be a world in which not just two countries, but several countries, or over a dozen countries, have the ability to unleash a full-scale nuclear war, a world in which there are not "only" 50,000 warheads but hundreds of thousands of warheads.

NUCLEAR OPTIMISTS: WE SHOULD WELCOME THE SPREAD OF NUCLEAR WEAPONS

Nevertheless, perhaps these dire predictions will not come to pass even if nuclear proliferation continues. Perhaps they are based on a misunderstanding of the global strategic realities that nuclear weapons create.

Some analysts maintain that nuclear weapons have actually promoted international peace and stability and that therefore nuclear nonproliferation efforts are misguided. This view is put forward by few thinkers in the realist school of international relations. Realists maintain that leaders and organizations behave in their own rational self-interest, especially when it comes to questions of survival, and our policies should be based on this assumption.

In the more than 60 years since 1945, there have been many wars, some of them causing millions of deaths, but World War III has not occurred. This is a very striking contrast from the first half of the 20th century, with its two world wars. In *The Spread of Nuclear Weapons,* Columbia University political science professor Kenneth M. Waltz argues that we owe these six decades of peace, "if peace is defined as the absence of general war among the major states of the world,"[31] largely to the existence of nuclear weapons. "Weapons and strategies change the situation of states in ways that make them more or less secure," Waltz points out. "If weapons are not well suited for conquest, neighbors have more peace of mind. We should expect war to become less likely when weaponry is such as to make conquest more difficult. . . ."

Waltz lists several ways in which nuclear weapons reduce the chance of war:

- Leaders know that war between nuclear weapons states may escalate from conventional war into nuclear war, so the state that begins a war with a nuclear weapons state risks its own destruction or at least very grave damage to itself. "States are not likely to run major risks for minor gains."

- The dangers of nuclear warfare are well known, making states less likely to blunder into war for lack of information.
- The deterrent power of nuclear weapons removes the need of land for strategic purposes, in the past a major motivation for wars of conquest. "A country with a [nuclear] deterrent strategy does not need territory as much as a country relying on conventional defense."
- Nuclear deterrence, though it does not eliminate all conflict between nuclear armed countries, prevents them from threatening each other's vital interests, since each country knows that another country would use nuclear weapons only when its survival was at stake.

The wars of the last 60 years have occurred in countries not armed with nuclear weapons. And when the United States and the Soviet Union fought their proxy wars, they fought them in places far from the centers of their vital interests, places like Indochina and Africa. They did not fight in Europe, where East and West shared a long border. They competed, but they were careful not to threaten each other's survival.

Waltz's argument is not a new version of Alfred Nobel's overoptimistic views about dynamite. The point is not that nuclear weapons make war too terrible to wage for humanitarian reasons, but that nuclear weapons make war clearly unprofitable, thereby reducing the likelihood that rational leaders will begin wars. This means that Waltz's views depend on the rationality of leaders of nuclear weapons states, and he undertakes to demonstrate that even the most erratic and bloodthirsty leaders—such as Idi Amin, former dictator of Uganda, and Muammar al-Qaddafi of Libya—have behaved rationally when faced with strong foes; they did not start wars with states that had the power to destroy them. Even Hitler, Waltz maintains, would have been stopped in 1939 by the prospect of certain ruin for Germany—and if he had not been, his generals would have refused to obey him, as they apparently did near the war's end when he ordered that they use poison gas against the Allied armed forces.

Waltz doubts that the acquisition of nuclear weapons by small countries will lead to nuclear arms races similar to those between the United States and the Soviet Union, because small countries cannot afford large arsenals and because their security does not demand it—a few bombs are enough to deter attack; more does not improve their position. He believes that the spread of nuclear weapons, even if unopposed, is likely to occur slowly and involve a handful of states rather than many. "Many states feel fairly secure living with their neighbors. Why should they want nuclear weapons?"

To the argument that nuclear weapons may be more dangerous in the possession of a state that is unstable or undergoing a civil war, Waltz remarks that it is hard to comprehend "why, in an internal struggle for power, the contenders would start using nuclear weapons. Who would they aim at? . . . Those who fear the worst have not shown how [internal power struggles] might lead to the use of nuclear weapons."

As for nuclear accidents, Waltz argues that a state will do whatever is necessary to prevent them, since the state's survival depends on it, and he maintains that while small nuclear states may have less elaborate systems to prevent accidents, they also have smaller arsenals that are easier to control. Finally, he says, small nuclear states, even so-called rogue states, would not supply terrorists with a bomb because the risk that their complicity would be discovered would be too great.

NUCLEAR PESSIMISTS: WE SHOULD FEAR THE SPREAD OF NUCLEAR WEAPONS

Nuclear pessimists, such as political scientist Scott D. Sagan, who debates Waltz in the pages of *The Spread of Nuclear Weapons,* agree that nuclear war is irrational and would not benefit anyone. The problem, as the pessimists see it, is that not everyone is a realist; neither every leader nor every state can be expected to behave rationally. The fact that they do not is shown, Sagan believes, both by history and by analysis of the nature of decision making in organizations. For the nuclear pessimists, it is not so much the Amins, Qaddafis, and Hitlers that pose the problem, it is the organizations that all leaders, good or evil, rely on to achieve their aims.

Because it is difficult to get people to work together and agree on goals, organizations have a limited, "bounded" rationality. The choices that organizations make are the end product of internal power struggles; they are not necessarily the best choices. Organizations rely heavily on routines and standard operating procedures; they are slow to adapt to changing conditions. They are short-sighted—they translate objectives into short-term goals and tend to lose sight of the ultimate objective. Strong organizations are blind to outside criticism, because when the members are highly loyal, they tend to dismiss ideas that come from outside the organization (but if the members are more open-minded, they are less loyal, weakening the organization). Organizations often maximize their own power and importance rather than serving the goal for which the organization is formed—for example, the army may be reluctant to give up a weapons system that has become obsolete for fear its budget will be cut and it will lose prestige relative to the air force.

These basic flaws in organizations limit the rationality of governments and military establishments. Democracies suffer from them just as much as dictatorships and can behave just as irrationally. Authoritarian regimes, though, do have a special problem: They are unduly influenced by their armed forces. In some nations, the army is almost indistinguishable from the state; in others, the army is not fully under civilian control, and from time to time it may stage a coup d'état. This fact may make nuclear war more likely because military organizations tend to see everything as a military problem. To a person whose only tool is a hammer, everything looks like a nail, so militarized regimes are more likely to make war.

How, specifically, might these weaknesses of organizations lead to nuclear war if nuclear weapons spread to many countries? Scott D. Sagan suggests that they will lead to errors in meeting three basic requirements of nuclear deterrence: First, states must not wage preventive nuclear war during the period when a rival state seems weak enough to be crushed with impunity. Second, nuclear weapons states must have credible second strike capabilities, so their rivals will not be tempted to destroy them with a first strike. Third, nuclear weapons systems must not be prone to accidents or unauthorized use.

There Is a High Risk That New Nuclear Weapons States Will Resort to Preventive War

Addressing the first requirement of deterrence, Sagan points out that military people have a bias toward preventive war. It is, after all, a military solution; it is what military leaders understand. In the United States during the 1940s and 1950s, the idea of preventive nuclear war was consistently suggested by military leaders. Fortunately, civilian authorities said no. In a militarized state, the military solution might prevail, and nuclear weapons might be used.

New Nuclear Weapons States May Fail to Build a Credible Second Strike Capability

Organizational weaknesses may also prevent new nuclear states from developing nuclear forces with a credible second strike capability, without which, opposing nuclear states may be tempted to wage preemptive or preventive war. To show how likely this is, Sagan points to many instances in the cold war in which military leaders resisted or prevented improvements necessary to maintain a credible second strike capability. In the United States, the SAC gave a low priority to the deployment of ICBMs, and the navy resisted the deployment of SLBMs. Each branch resisted these improvements because the ideas for them came from outside the organizations and did not fit with a narrow conception of their missions—the SAC to fly planes, the navy to use submarines against enemy ships. If the military had had its way, America's second strike capability would have been impaired.

In the Soviet Union and China, similar problems actually did hinder and delay achievement of credible second strike capabilities. In the Soviet Union, the military's addiction to strict routines and procedures made it easy for U.S. spy planes to spot (and target) Soviet nuclear facilities, which always looked the same from the air. Crude errors by the Soviet navy made it possible for the United States to crack the code of the Soviets' underwater communication system in the early 1970s and to know the location of every Russian ballistic missile submarine.[32] Military and bureaucratic confusions also delayed China's achievement of survivable nuclear forces.

Nuclear Proliferation Increases the Chance for Nuclear Accidents and Unauthorized Use

There are many reasons to be pessimistic about the ability of new nuclear states to avoid nuclear accidents and unauthorized use in the future. Even in the United States, there have been many close calls and false alarms that might have led to the onset of nuclear war; in a new, poor nuclear weapons state with a less well-equipped, less professional force, nuclear accidents and unauthorized use are more likely to occur.

In 1991, when UN weapons inspectors looked at the Iraq nuclear program, they found that the crude bomb the Iraqis were planning to build would have been likely to go off by accident. "The design calls for cramming so much weapon-grade uranium into the core . . . that the bomb would inevitably be on the verge of going off—even while sitting on the workbench."[33] If a bomb went off by accident, the explosion might be mistaken for the result of an enemy nuclear attack, and it could lead to a "counterattack" and nuclear war. It might even lead automatically to the implementation of the country's nuclear war fighting plan.

New nuclear states may also fear a "decapitation attack," an attack that would eliminate the head of state or disrupt command and control at the outset of a war. To prepare for this contingency, they may delegate the decision to use nuclear weapons to local commanders. This would make mistaken use of the weapons much more likely. The political unrest and instability could also lead to accidental use of nuclear weapons, Sagan suggests.[34]

Though Sagan does not mention this, unrest could also lead to unauthorized use. As the bomb passes from hand to hand, it may come under the control of a fanatic who is not motivated by self-interest as Kenneth Waltz defines it but views this moment of power as the opportunity to wage holy war against absolute evil.

SOLUTIONS

A History of Nuclear Nonproliferation

Nuclear nonproliferation, the effort to contain the spread of nuclear weapons, has a history only a little briefer than the history of the weapons themselves. The first attempts, in the late 1940s and early 1950s, to reach international agreements that would limit the spread of nuclear weapons failed completely; they were a prelude to the greatest arms race in human history. Later efforts have had mixed results. Some countries have discontinued their nuclear weapons programs or been persuaded not to acquire nuclear arms, while a few have continued down the nuclear road—some of these despite signing nonproliferation treaties. This mixed result leaves room for argument over whether the NPT has been effective, and U.S. policy makers do argue heatedly about it. The debate matters a great deal, since momentous decisions are based on it. What should the United States do to guarantee its own security? Should it try to strengthen existing treaties, or should it rely for its security on other methods, such as missile defense systems or war against suspected violators (as in the case of Iraq)? The entire history is worth examining for what it reveals about possible solutions to the problem and for the challenges that all such attempts will face.

THE BARUCH PLAN, 1946: PUT THE UNITED NATIONS IN CHARGE OF THE BOMB

The United States's first plan for nuclear nonproliferation was the boldest and most sweeping ever proposed. For a brief period in 1946, the utopian hopes that Eugene Wigner did not dare mention in 1939—hopes for international control of atomic energy—were taken seriously at the highest levels of the U.S. government. On Truman's order, a series of reports were prepared by scientists and managers who had helped develop the atomic bomb. These reports became the basis for a proposal delivered to the UN's IAEA by America's first UN representative, Bernard Baruch (1870–1965), on June 14, 1946.[35]

Baruch suggested that atomic energy be put into the hands of an IADA controlled by the UN. This organization would have a total monopoly on the materials needed to make bombs. It would have two main jobs. On the one hand, it would provide nuclear technology for power generation and other peaceful uses to countries that needed it. On the other hand, it would exercise tight control over the technology and the materials that were needed both for energy and weapons production. It would conduct inspections to see if countries were cheating, that is, preparing to produce nuclear weapons. Countries suspected of trying to build weapons would be subject to severe punishment, probably including military action against them by other nations under UN auspices. To make this threat credible, Baruch suggested that actions taken by the IADA not be subject to a veto by members of the UN Security Council. This would have been a major exception to the UN charter, under which the UN could authorize military action only if there were no objection by any of the permanent members on the Security Council: the Soviet Union, the United States, Britain, China, and France.

The Soviet Union rejected the Baruch Plan; Soviet representatives said that the proposal was just a ruse by the United States to retain its monopoly on nuclear weapons. This objection had some basis, since according to the Baruch plan, the United States would give up its weapons to the IADA only *after* the IADA had established inspections and control over nuclear activities in the Soviet Union. From the Soviet point of view, the United States and the Soviets were like two strangers in a room. One had a gun in his hand, and the other one just might have a gun in his pocket. The man with the gun in his hand—the United States—was promising to put down his gun, but only after the other man—the USSR—proved that he was not armed.

Perhaps changes could have made the Baruch plan acceptable to both sides. For example, since the Soviets did not have the bomb yet, the United States could have agreed to give its weapons to the IADA when inspections began, not afterward. But the United States, as the only country with the bomb, was in no mood to compromise. The Baruch plan was presented to the Soviets as a take-it-or-leave-it proposition, and it went nowhere.[36] The Soviet Union's subsequent position on nuclear weapons was to call for an absolute ban on them, but without any inspections to ensure compliance, an unrealistic position that U.S. leaders dismissed as propaganda.[37]

In retrospect, the Baruch Plan failed because neither the Soviet Union nor the United States had the will to reach a serious arms agreement; there was no follow-up on the initial proposal. In the United States, most politicians and most of the public felt that the United States should take advantage of its position of strength as the only nuclear power and that, in any case, the Soviets could not be trusted to honor agreements. A few years later, the imbalance of conventional forces between NATO and the Warsaw Pact made the United States unwilling to give up its nuclear weapons even if the other side would as well.

The Soviet Union, for its part, had a highly secretive, totalitarian government, dead set against any treaty that required inspections of its military facilities. Its leaders were deeply suspicious of U.S. motives and decided that the only reliable counter to U.S. nuclear superiority was to catch up.

ATOMS FOR PEACE, 1954: PUT THE UNITED NATIONS IN CHARGE OF FISSILE MATERIALS

In early 1952, Truman established a panel of consultants to study the threat posed by the nuclear arms race. Chaired by J. Robert Oppenheimer (1904–76), who had led the team that created the first atomic bomb, the panel warned that if matters continued on their present course, both sides would soon be able to destroy each other. Soon both the Soviets and the United States would "each have a clear-cut capacity to do very great damage to the other, while each will be unable to exert that capacity except at the gravest risk of receiving similar terrible blows in return. . . . "There is likely to be a point in our time when the Soviet Union has 'enough' bombs, no matter how many more we ourselves may have."[38]

Concerned primarily with the mounting numbers of bombs possessed by the two superpowers, the panel made two main suggestions: First, the United States should publicize the strength of its own nuclear arsenal and its estimates of the strength of the Soviet arsenal; to avoid mistakes, the Soviets should know what the United States had, and they should know that the United States knew what they had. Second, the panel advised that the Americans and the Soviets must find a way to "get a reduction in the size of [nuclear] stockpiles . . . such that neither side need fear a sudden knockout from the other."

In July 1953, the Soviets tested their first hydrogen bomb. Learning that a single such bomb could destroy New York City, the new U.S. president, Eisenhower, sought a new international initiative that would encourage the United States and the Soviets to reduce their stockpiles of nuclear weapons. Eisenhower called his proposal the Atoms for Peace program. The United States and the Soviet Union would each contribute a certain amount of fissile materials to a UN agency ultimately the IAEA, established in 1957, which would store and protect the material from being stolen while devising "methods whereby this fissionable material would be allocated to serve the peaceful purposes of mankind."[39] Eisenhower hoped that as time went on, the United States and the Soviet Union could contribute more and more fissile materials to the program, which would be the basis for later serious arms negotiations between the United States and the Soviet Union.

Atoms for Peace was Eisenhower's attempt to jump-start a stalled arms agreement process. To make a beginning, Atoms for Peace did not ask for much. It avoided items that the Soviets had found unacceptable before (such as elaborate on-site inspections, putting weapons in the hands of an international agency, or strict punishment for noncompliance), and it gave the rest of the world an incentive for pushing the superpowers into an agreement (help with nuclear power generation).

Thanks to the strong support it generated among nonnuclear weapons states, Atoms for Peace eventually went into effect. Unfortunately, it did not do what it was intended to do. The Soviets, at the beginning, had objected that Eisenhower's plan would actually lead to nuclear proliferation—other nations participating in the program would gain the know-how and materials they needed to make bombs—and, in retrospect, the Soviets were right. But at the time, the United States was more worried about vertical proliferation than horizontal proliferation, and the design of the Atoms for Peace program reflected this concern. The United States did address concern over the spread of nuclear weapons to other countries: As originally proposed to the IAEA, the program contained strong safeguards that would prevent participants in the program from using the materials produced in power generation from being diverted to the use of bombs. These safeguards were opposed by several other countries. In its eagerness to get an agreement, the United States dropped the safeguards, hoping that somehow they could be put back later. They were not put back.

By the late 1950s, it was clear that Atoms for Peace would also fail to lead to arms reduction agreements between the United States and the Soviets. On the contrary, the two countries were busy amassing their awesome planet-poisoning arsenals and putting them on the tips of ground-launched and submarine-launched missiles, nor was the program effective in reducing the spread of nuclear weapons.[40]

THE NUCLEAR NONPROLIFERATION TREATY, 1968: INCENTIVES TO ABANDON THE QUEST FOR NUCLEAR WEAPONS

In the late 1950s, U.S. policy was the chief immediate cause of horizontal nuclear proliferation. To counter the Warsaw Pact's conventional military superiority over NATO, the United States was deploying nuclear weapons in Europe and relaxing its rules for transferring nuclear technology to its allies. In 1958, the U.S. Congress amended the 1945 Atomic Energy Act to permit the transfer of weapons materials, design information, and parts to nations that had "made substantial progress in the development of nuclear weapons."[41] Both the United States and the Soviet Union were conducting hundreds of nuclear weapons tests in the atmosphere, causing damage to the environment.

Smaller nations now began to worry that a conflict involving the new nuclear weapons states would lead to war between the superpowers, with devastating effects for the innocent bystanders. In 1959, Irish foreign minister Frank Aiken offered to the UN General Assembly a proposal to limit the spread of nuclear weapons. Admitting that it was "hardly realistic" to expect an agreement on the abolition of nuclear weapons any time soon, he argued, "what we can do is to reduce the risks which the spread of these weapons involves for this generation, and not to hand on to our children a problem even more difficult to solve than that with which we are now confronted."[42]

Aiken's proposal was eventually refashioned into the Nuclear Nonproliferation Treaty (NPT), which was passed at the Conference of the Eighteen-Nation Committee on Disarmament in 1968. As is common with treaties, its intentions were changed somewhat along the way. The NPT was a compromise, with the concerns of different parties written into it. Nonnuclear nations were not convinced that they had nothing to lose by renouncing nuclear weapons. They asked in return for guarantees and incentives. These guarantees and incentives weakened the treaty, but they did not render it useless.

Unlike earlier nonproliferation agreements, the NPT has probably slowed the spread of nuclear weapons, but exactly how much is in dispute. To understand the NPT's strengths and weaknesses, it helps to consider its provisions in detail. Some of the treaty's 11 articles address its primary purpose; others make the treaty palatable to the nonnuclear states and in so doing provide loopholes that can enable nations to creep slowly toward the ability to make nuclear weapons.

The first three articles address the treaty's primary aim of slowing the spread of nuclear weapons. Article I pledges nuclear weapons states not to help nonnuclear weapons states acquire nuclear weapons or the technology to make nuclear weapons, directly or indirectly. Article II pledges other states not to seek such assistance and not to manufacture "or otherwise acquire" the weapons. Article III pledges the nonnuclear weapons states to submit to a system of safeguards to ensure that fissionable materials are not diverted from peaceful uses to the manufacture of weapons.

Then this same article provides its signers with a loophole destined to be invoked repeatedly over the years: "The safeguards required by this article shall be implemented in a manner designed to comply with Article IV of this Treaty, and to avoid hampering the economic or technological development of the Parties or international cooperation in the field of peaceful nuclear activities. . . ."

Article IV contains a large incentive for the nonnuclear weapons states that sign the treaty. Its first paragraph defends their "inalienable right of all the Parties to the Treaty to develop research, production and use of nuclear energy for peaceful purposes without discrimination and in conformity with Articles I and II of this Treaty." The second paragraph obliges the other parties, especially the nuclear weapons states, to help the NPT signatories with the development of nuclear energy for peaceful purposes.

Article V pledges signatories to share any potential benefits of "peaceful applications of nuclear explosions." According to Article VI, nuclear states are obligated to pursue negotiations to cease the nuclear arms race and ultimately reach general and complete nuclear disarmament.

The remaining five articles are technical, asserting that signers are free to sign other, regional treaties to limit nuclear weapons, describing the rules for amending, signing, and ratifying the NPT, and the conditions for withdrawing from it, and scheduling a review conference to be held 25 years after it went into effect in 1970.

France, despite being one of the nuclear states under the terms of the NPT, did not sign the treaty until 1992; South Africa, which pursued nuclear weapons allegedly with the help of Israel, did not sign it until 1991; Brazil did not sign until 1998; and Cuba signed in 1995 but did not ratify until 2002. India, Pakistan, and Israel have refused to sign the NPT. Some NPT signatories, such as Libya, Iraq, North Korea, and Iran have violated its provisions.[43]

The biggest weakness of the treaty, aside from the fact that some states did not sign it, is that under its provisions on nuclear energy development, states can get very close to the ability to produce nuclear weapons. Arguably, it provides cover for countries to manipulate the rules to become nuclear states and then to withdraw from the treaty and complete the process.

The 25-year review conference that was written into the NPT was held in 1995. The consensus of most parties, especially of the nonnuclear weapons states, was that the NPT had been effective in containing nuclear proliferation, but the nuclear weapons states had not done enough to meet their obligations under Article VI of the treaty. The nuclear weapons states had certainly not disarmed, and though by 1995 there had been significant arms reductions by the United States and the republics of the former Soviet Union, the United States and Russia were both engaged in modernization of their nuclear weapons forces and did not seem to be on the road to nuclear disarmament.[44]

Mixed Results of the NPT

Whether the NPT has been a success or failure is a glass half-full/half-empty dispute. Detractors point to North Korea and Iran, states whose acquisition or imminent acquisition of nuclear weapons threatens both their own regions and the United States, for both are extremely hostile to the United States. Defenders argue that NPT has *slowed* the spread of nuclear weapons and should be strengthened to make it better. Thomas

Graham, Jr., the Clinton administration's special ambassador for nuclear disarmament issues, argues for this glass half-full view:

> *For more than thirty years, the Nuclear Non-Proliferation Treaty has been a bulwark against [the spread of nuclear weapons]. Because of the NPT, the international community has thus far been largely successful in preventing the spread of nuclear weapons. The predictions made during the Kennedy administration that as many as twenty-five to thirty nations would have nuclear weapons integrated into their arsenals by the end of the 1970s did not come true, thanks to the NPT. The International Atomic Energy Agency reports that, while many nations now possess the technological capabilities to produce nuclear weapons, only a handful have crossed the nuclear threshold.*[45]

Some critics argue that the NPT has not been read properly, and its provisions have not really been enforced: The United States should lead the world in opposing large "peaceful" nuclear projects that help states develop technology that can be used for nuclear weapons. Henry D. Sokolski, the hawkish head of the Nonproliferation Policy Education Center (NPEC), advocates greater suspicion and more aggressive actions:

> *We should view additional large civilian nuclear projects—including nuclear power and desalinization plants, large research reactors, and regional fuel-cycle centers—as illegitimate under the Nuclear Nonproliferation Treaty if they are not privately financed or approved after an open international bidding process against less risky alternatives.*[46]

EXPORT CONTROL GROUPS: NSG AND MTCR

Article III.2 of the NPT pledges signers of the treaty not to export special equipment and materials necessary to the manufacture of nuclear weapons to nonnuclear weapons states except under special IAEA safeguards. In the early 1970s a group of representatives from 15 nuclear supplier states held a series of meetings in Vienna, meetings chaired by Professor Claude Zangger of Switzerland, in order to help implement this aspect of the treaty, to determine just what "equipment and materials" should be restricted and to establish the procedures under which their sale would be restricted or permitted. The Zangger Committee, as this group has come to be called, was the first of the export control groups and is still in existence. It maintains and updates a list of equipment and materials that may be exported only under IAEA safeguards, often called the "trigger list" because an item's presence on the list triggers the requirement for safeguards.

In 1974, India, which had not signed the NPT, announced that it had tested a "peaceful nuclear explosion." Deciding the NPT by itself was not enough to slow the spread of nuclear weapons, the United States led an effort to get states with advanced nuclear technology to restrict their exports of special nuclear materials and nuclear technology. In the late 1970s, the key nuclear supplier nations, which included not only nuclear weapons states but states with advanced nuclear power generation technology, formed an organization called the NSG and agreed to a set of guidelines for restricting sales of technology and materials that might be used for nuclear weapons. The agreement helped plug important holes in the NPT, since it prohibited the export of nuclear technology by France, which had not signed the NPT and was not a member of the Zangger Committee. Like the NPT, though, the NSG permits exports of safe nuclear technology. There are currently 45 members of the NSG. Though the Zangger Committee and the NSG obviously have goals in common, their methods and membership are different, and their overlapping efforts support each other.

The capacity to deliver nuclear weapons by means of ballistic missiles obviously multiplies the danger presented by a nuclear weapons state. However, like nuclear technology, missile technology has a peaceful use—it can assist space exploration and the launch of satellites. So in the mid-1980s another export control organization, the MTCR, was formed; its technologically advanced members agreed not to export missile technology above a certain threshold to countries likely to use it for aggressive military purposes. The MTCR did permit the export of missile technology and hardware transfers for nonmilitary satellites, aircraft, and small short-range tactical missiles (which were presumably defensive).

The NSG and the MTCR both address an important nonmilitary cause of nuclear proliferation, which is that the sale of weapons technology is very profitable. Not only arms manufacturers, but the states in which arms manufacturers are based, can be enormously tempted by the short-term gains of selling weapons systems—or technology that can easily be used in weapons systems—to a country that does not have the ability to produce such systems on its own. Practically all the arms with which industrially backward countries around the world bristle—the weapons with which they kill millions of their neighbors and oppress their own people—are produced by factories in the United States, western Europe, Russia, and China.

REGIONAL NONPROLIFERATION TREATIES

Groups of states have also made separate agreements to create "nuclear-free zones" in their regions. The Treaty of Tlatelolco, originally signed in 1967, is intended to accomplish this for Latin America and the Caribbean. Every country in the region has signed this treaty.[47] Parties to the treaty agree not to acquire or permit the presence of nuclear weapons on their territory. The Treaty of Rarotonga, signed in 1985, establishes a nuclear free zone in the South Pacific. In 1996, 43 African nations signed the Pelindaba Treaty, creating a nuclear weapon–free zone in Africa. As of 2007, 51 of the 53 eligible signatories have signed the treaty, although only eight have ratified it. (However, South Africa, the African nation that came closest to building a bomb, is among those who have ratified the treaty). In 1995, the Treaty of Bangkok created a nuclear weapons–free zone in Southeast Asia; the treaty went into force in 1996. Only one nuclear weapons state, China, has signed the protocols to this treaty, which prohibits the threat or use of nuclear weapons within the zone.

COMPREHENSIVE TEST BAN TREATY

Nuclear weapons states conduct nuclear weapons tests to make sure their warheads work, to demonstrate their power to potential enemies, and to give their own military leaders confidence that the weapons are not duds. The testing creates radioactive material that continues to be dangerous for thousands of years after the initial explosion. It damages the environment and the health of all living things and has been linked to increased cancer rates. The worst effects are caused by atmospheric testing. In 1963, in the first really effective arms agreement of the cold war, the United States, the Soviet Union, and 101 other states signed the Limited Test Ban Treaty, forbidding nuclear testing in the Earth's atmosphere, in space, and underwater.

Underground testing continued, however, over the objections of most nonnuclear states. After the end of the cold war, and as the 1995 review of the NPT approached, international pressure built for the United States and the states of the former Soviet Union to reach an agreement banning all nuclear testing. The ban was resisted by the military establishments in the United States and Russia as well as by nuclear weapons laboratories for whom this is a bread-and-butter issue. The treaty was adopted by the UN General Assembly on September 10, 1996. As of 2007, 41 of the 44 required states have signed the treaty (North Korea, India, and Pakistan have not signed), and 34 have ratified it, including Russia in 2000. In 1999 the U.S. Senate rejected President Clinton's request for its consent to ratify the treaty.

UN SECURITY COUNCIL RESOLUTION 1540—PREVENT NUCLEAR TERRORISM

The attacks of 9/11 raised fears that the world faced a new age of terrorism: Before the 1990s, virtually all terrorist acts were conducted on a small scale for relatively specific objectives. But al-Qaeda's attacks have been of a different order. They are meant to kill as many people as possible: It is known that its leaders are seeking nuclear weapons, and there is little doubt that they would use them if they could. In response to this emerging threat, in April 2004 the UN adopted UN Security Council Resolution 1540. This resolution requires that all states adopt and enforce "appropriate, effective" laws and measures, such as export controls, to prevent nonstate actors, that is, terrorists, from acquiring WMD and related delivery vehicles. Under the resolution, states must also impose controls and safeguards on sensitive materials that could be used to develop such weapons.

Other Strategies for Nuclear Nonproliferation

Beyond international agreements such as the NPT, export controls, and the creation of regional nonnuclear zones, there are several other strategies to slow the spread of nuclear weapons. The major nonproliferation treaties, because they all involve several countries, are usually referred to as "multilateral" agreements. Nonproliferation strategies involving agreements between two countries are called "bilateral."

Among the commonest bilateral approaches to nonproliferation, the United States and other countries can offer economic incentives to reward nonproliferators, and they can attempt to punish proliferators with economic sanctions. They can offer embattled states various security alternatives so that they can protect themselves without recourse to nuclear weapons. They can attempt to defuse the political tensions in regional hot spots where states' fears or ambitions tempt them to acquire nuclear weapons.

CARROTS AND STICKS: ECONOMIC INCENTIVES AND SANCTIONS

An industrialized nation can attempt to use its advantages as a technological leader and large economy to influence other states, offering technical and financial assistance—*incentives*—to states that agree to forgo nuclear weapons. The United States has often pursued this policy. Countries can punish—impose *sanctions* on—proliferators by withdrawing the benefits of trade and assistance, a strategy that is most effective when enforced through multilateral agreements or the UN.

Incentives and sanctions are both important parts of nonproliferation efforts. However, both are difficult to apply properly. In the donor states, incentives cost taxpayers money. When they take the form of assistance with nuclear power generation (as they often have, ever since the Atoms for Peace program), incentives can backfire by helping countries develop nuclear weapons.

Economic sanctions can be applied not only to countries seeking to acquire nuclear weapons, but to the suppliers, the corporations in the countries assisting the would-be nuclear weapons state. Economic sanctions often face opposition within the country that imposes the sanctions as industries lose business as a result. In the United States, the states in which these industries reside are represented by senators and members of Congress, who may see to it that bills imposing sanctions are watered down to serve the short-term interests of their constituents. When strong sanctions are imposed despite opposition, they may simply drive would-be nuclear proliferators into the arms of economic competitors who *will* do business with them. That is why, usually, sanctions are more effective as part of multilateral agreements.

The details of economic sanctions imposed by the United States take the form of acts of Congress, such as the Iran Nonproliferation Act of 2000, which prohibit specific categories of trade with the countries sanctioned.

IMPROVE REGIONAL SECURITY OR PROVIDE SECURITY ALTERNATIVES

The states that have acquired nuclear weapons have all had something in common: They have all been countries with an especially high fear of invasion or attack. The United States and the Soviet Union were international competitors, and war between them seemed likely; NATO forces armed themselves against invasion from the Soviet Union; China armed itself from fear of the United States and the Soviet Union; Israel feared its neighbors; India and Pakistan feared each other; and North Korea faces threats from South Korea and the United States. Countries in relatively peaceful regions have little incentive to develop nuclear weapons. So actions that reduce regional tensions and make war less likely will remove incentives to develop nuclear weapons.[48] Even while regional issues are unresolved and tensions remain high, the international community could discourage proliferation by providing states with some other guarantee that they will not be invaded—either a pledge to defend them or improved conventional military forces.

DISCOURAGE PROLIFERATION BY PUTTING COUNTRIES UNDER OUR NUCLEAR UMBRELLA

When a country gets nuclear weapons, its neighbors may want to acquire them to protect themselves from intimidation or attack. Proliferation can be slowed by providing such friendly nations with a nuclear guarantee—if they are attacked, one of the nuclear weapons states will use its weapons against their attackers, as the United States probably would have if the Warsaw Pact had attacked NATO during the cold war.

Two problems beset this method of stopping nuclear proliferation. On one hand, such a guarantee could lead to a "1914" scenario, an escalation of a small war into a big one through a system of alliances and guarantees, such as happened at the beginning of World War I. On the other hand, because nuclear war is so terrible, such a guarantee might not be credible in the first place. During the cold war, it was often said that Great Britain and France developed their own nuclear capabilities because they could not be sure that "In case of a nuclear exchange . . . the U.S. [would] sacrifice New York, Chicago, and Los Angeles for Paris, London, and Berlin"[49] Why should Japan believe that the United States would sacrifice New York for Tokyo?

SHOULD THE U.S. DISCRIMINATE BETWEEN GOOD AND BAD PROLIFERATORS?

Henry D. Sokolski of the NPEC has advocated an approach that "distinguished between progressive and hostile illiberal regimes, something no previous nonproliferation regime has done" and noted that "Over the last decade American and allied presidents have endorsed the idea that expanding the number of democratic nations is critical to international security. What is required now is to make U.S. and allied nonproliferation policy an integral part of this larger understanding."[50] Writers at the libertarian think tank the Cato Institute also take the view that proliferation should be imposed selectively, going so far as to compare current nonproliferation policy to gun control regulation, which they also oppose.

> *America's current nonproliferation policy is the international equivalent of domestic gun control laws, and exhibits the same faulty logic. Gun control laws have had little effect on preventing criminal elements from acquiring weapons. Instead, they disarm honest citizens and make them more vulnerable to armed predators. The nonproliferation system is having a similar perverse effect. Such unsavory states as Iran and North Korea are well along on the path to becoming nuclear powers while their more peaceful neighbors are hamstrung by the Nuclear Nonproliferation Treaty from countering those moves.*[51]

The view that nuclear weapons are good in some hands and bad in others was reflected in the nonproliferation policies of the George W. Bush (1946–) administration, but in ways that seem to have dismayed Sokolski. George W. Bush and his secretary of state Condoleezza Rice gave their blessing to nuclear initiatives by India, a democratic country, and gave the back of their hand (with unimpressive effect) to attempts to get nuclear arms by North Korea and Iran. The Bush administration used the suspicion that Iraq was again attempting to acquire nuclear weapons as one of its reasons to invade Iraq in 2003. This suspicion proved to have been false and based on very weak evidence.

It should also be said that discriminating between "good" and "bad" proliferators is unconvincing to much of the world. The view of who is good and who is bad changes quickly, and not just away from American shores. To the degree that the United States discriminates between different proliferators, its fairness is doubted.

DISCOURAGE PROLIFERATION BY SHARING MISSILE DEFENSE TECHNOLOGY

The United States and other nations have been attempting since 1946 to find a technological answer to the challenge posed by the combination of nuclear weapons and ballistic missiles. At various times, the answer has been sought in ABMs (defensive guided missiles accurate enough to hit incoming missiles); space-based X-ray lasers (weapons based on satellites that will be able to observe missile launches from space and instantly knock them out with the help of supercomputers and a harmless, albeit treaty-breaking outer-space thermonuclear explosion); missiles with thermonuclear warheads that will get close to incoming weapons while they are still outside the atmosphere and explode near them, causing them to detonate prematurely; and the use of many other systems.

The SDI (nicknamed "Star Wars" by its critics), introduced during the administration of Ronald Reagan (1911–2004), is the best-known missile defense program. Missile defense was also promoted under both Bush administrations, and it receives strong support from political conservatives and aerospace industry executives. In a 2006 article published by the NPEC, Boeing executive Mitchell Kruger, who as a Senate aid helped draft the National Missile Defense Act of 1999, recommended sharing of missile defense technology with friendly countries as an answer to nuclear and missile proliferation.

Opponents of missile defense regularly make three basic points. First, if the missile defense systems worked, they would be destabilizing to nuclear deterrence because they would be seen as giving their possessor a first strike capability (I can attack you and rely on my missile defense to protect me). Reagan acknowledged this criticism in his first speech on missile defense in 1983:

> *I clearly recognize that defensive systems have limitations and raise certain problems and ambiguities. If paired with offensive systems, they can be viewed as fostering an aggressive policy, and no one wants that.*

> *But with these considerations firmly in mind, I call upon the scientific community in our country, those who gave us nuclear weapons, to turn their great talents now to the cause of mankind and world peace, to give us the means of rendering these nuclear weapons impotent and obsolete.*[52]

While these phrases elegantly managed the transition to the next paragraph of the president's speech, they did not actually answer the question they raised, nor did any other part of the speech answer it. Critics of missile defense would argue that it has never been adequately answered.

Second, critics say, missile defense systems are a recipe for a renewed arms race, since countries will make more bombs and missiles to guarantee that some will get through defenses. And third, so far, they do not work and show no good promise of ever working because improvements in defense will always be matched by improvements in offense; there is no reason to think that offense will not continue to maintain its impressive lead forever. After half a century of trying, missile defense systems have never been practical for any purpose except to break existing agreements and to provide jobs for scientists and engineers.

Advocates of missile defense point out that all military systems must undergo failure before they achieve success and see the handful of successful tests as grounds for optimism. Surely we can expect this technology, like all others, to get better over time. Perhaps it will remain impractical against a massive attack by an enemy like the cold war Soviet Union, but what about the attack of just one or a few missiles from a "rogue state" that behaves irrationally? North Korea does not have the capability of building thousands of warheads and missiles, just a few—a functional missile defense program could defend against those few.

Opponents point out that the current strategic situation is temporary and say that advocates overlook the unintended consequences of missile defense development. A system might be developed to counter an attack from North Korea, but China and Russia would have to take account of it, so it would promote an arms race with those countries. If we share missile defense technology, it would promote arms races between small nuclear weapons states, and it would destabilize their own nuclear deterrence.

PARADOXES OF NUCLEAR DETERRENCE: OFFENSE IS DEFENSE, DEFENSE IS OFFENSE

Advocates of missile defense, who also tend to be proponents of "limited nuclear war," ridicule the balance of terror on which nuclear deterrence is based. Former CIA chief James Woolsey has quoted a sardonic summary of the logic: "Offense is defense. Defense is offense. Weapons that kill people are good. Weapons that kill weapons are bad."[53]

These phrases do sound strange, and they do reflect the ideas of deterrence embodied in many arms control agreements, so it may help to translate them. "Offense is defense" means that believers in deterrence think nuclear weapons are not useful as offensive weapons—their main purpose is to prevent others from attacking you. The saying that the best offense is a good defense is not only a cliché, it is a truism: virtually everyone believes it. "Defense is offense" means that deployment of a missile defense system may be interpreted by the enemy as preparation for nuclear war, because if it worked it might give its possessors a first-strike capability. "Weapons that kill people are good" means that nuclear weapons targeting populations promote deterrence and make nuclear war less likely. "Weapons that kill weapons are bad" means that deployment of missile defenses or weapons targeting the enemies' nuclear facilities may be seen to express an intention to fight and win a nuclear war and may therefore make nuclear war more likely—in fact, it may tempt both sides to make a preemptive strike.

The nuclear age faces us with strange choices. The important question is not whether these statements that sum up the logic of nuclear deterrence are absurd, but whether they are true.

---

[1] Frederick W. Haberman, Editor, *Nobel Lectures, Peace 1951–1970.* Amsterdam: Elsevier Publishing Company, 1972. Quoted in "Office of the United Nations High Commissioner for Refugees—Nobel Lecture" at http://nobelprize.org/nobel_prizes/peace/laureates/1954/refugees-lecture.html.

[2] Richard Rhodes. *The Making of the Atomic Bomb.* New York: Simon & Schuster, 1986, pp. 291–317.

[3] Eugene Wigner. "Are we making the transition wisely?" *Saturday Review,* November 17, p. 28.

[4] Rhodes. p. 405. Rhodes quotes Hitler's adviser Albert Speer: "On the suggestion of the nuclear physicists we scuttled the project to develop an atom bomb . . . after I had again queried them about deadlines and been told that we could not count on anything for three or four years." On the same page, Rhodes quotes the German nuclear physicist Werner Heisenberg's article in *Nature* in 1947, saying German scientists "were spared the decision as to whether or not they should aim at producing atomic bombs."

[5] Rhodes. pp. 734, 740.

[6] Rhodes. p. 744.

[7] David Holloway. "Entering the Nuclear Arms Race: The Soviet Decision to Build the Atomic Bomb, 1939–45." *Social Studies of Science* II (1981): pp. 159–97.

[8] Rhodes. p. 735.

[9] Edward Teller. "Comments on the 'draft of a world constitution'" *Bulletin of the Atomic Scientists,* July, 1948, p. 204. In time, distrust of the Soviet Union would change Teller's

mind. He would put his faith in technology intended to make the United States omnipotent. He later became known as "the father of the hydrogen bomb," and he was one of the scientists who persuaded Ronald Reagan of the need for the controversial Strategic Defense Initiative ("Star Wars").

[10] McGeorge Bundy. *Danger and Survival.* New York: Vintage Books, 1988, p. 197. Bundy's book examines the top-level decision making at key turning points of the U.S.-Soviet nuclear arms race.

[11] NuclearFiles.org. "Timeline of the Nuclear Age."

[12] Bundy. p. 319.

[13] "NRDC: Nuclear Data—Table of USSR/Russian Nuclear Warheads, 1949–2002." Available online. URL: http://www.nrdc.org/nuclear/nudb/datab10.asp. "NRDC: Nuclear Data—Table of US Nuclear Warheads, 1949–2002." Available online. URL: http://www.nrdc.org/nuclear/nudb/datab9.asp. Accessed November 17, 2007.

[14] Public Papers of the Presidents. Dwight D. Eisenhower, 1960, pp. 1,035–1,040

[15] Nathan E. Busch. *No End in Sight: The Continuing Menace of Nuclear Proliferation.* Lexington, Ky.: University Press of Kentucky, 2004, p. 38.

[16] Thomas Graham, Jr. *Common Sense on Weapons of Mass Destruction.* Seattle & London: University of Washington Press, 2004, pp. 63–64.

[17] Busch. p. 46.

[18] Bundy. pp. 239, 279–281. "We have the authority of Eisenhower himself for the view that a deliberate threat of nuclear war was decisive in ending the Korean War," Bundy writes (239). At the time of the Quemoy-Matsu crisis with China in 1955—an argument over islands claimed by Nationalist China and Red China—Eisenhower was publicly asked whether the US would use tactical nuclear weapons in a general war in Asia and replied "I see no reason why they shouldn't be used just exactly as you would use a bullet or anything else." In his memoirs Eisenhower said that he had hoped his answer "would have some effect in persuading the Chinese Communists of the strength of our determination." (279). During a second flare-up of the dispute over Quemoy-Matsu, Bundy says, the U.S. positioned air and naval forces on and near Quemoy that were known to possess nuclear weapons and deployed howitzers that were known to be capable of delivering nuclear warheads. Bundy believes these nonverbal nuclear threats were effective in making Red China back down. (279–281).

[19] Bundy. pp. 391–462.

[20] Bundy. p. 507.

[21] Graham. p. 14.

[22] Graham. p. 57.

[23] Carl Sagan. "The Nuclear Winter," *Science*, Dec. 1983, p. 1,283. www.cooperative individualism.org/sagan_nuclear_winter.html. Retrieved January 4, 2007.

[24] Jonathan Schell. *The Fate of the Earth.* New York: Knopf, 1982, p. 3.

[25] Sagan.

[26] Johnathan Schell. *The Fate of the Earth* and *The Abolition.* Stanford, Calif.: Stanford University Press, 2000. p. 48.

[27] Sagan.

[28] Scott D. Sagan and Kenneth N. Waltz. *The Spread of Nuclear Weapons: A Debate Renewed.* New York: W.W. Norton, 2003, pp. 56–59. "During both the Truman and Eisenhower administrations, senior U.S. military officers seriously advocated preventive war options and, in both cases, continued favoring such ideas well after civilian leaders ruled against them."(56).

[29] Busch. p. 58.

[30] Busch. pp. 12–13.

[31] Sagan and Waltz. The following quotations and the presentation of Waltz's views are based on chapter 1, "More May Be Better," pp. 3–45.

[32] Sagan and Waltz, p. 68. "The organization failures of the Russian military that led to this problem read more like the Keystone Cops than the KGB. The Soviets failed to encrypt many messages sent through an underwater communications cable in the Sea of Okhotsk to the missiles submarine base at Petropavlovsk, figuring that such protected waters were safe from US spying activities. To make matters worse, they gave away the location of the 'secret' communications cable by posting a sign at the beach telling local fisherman [sic] 'do not anchor, cable here.'"

[33] Busch, p. 242.

[34] Scott D. Sagan's explanations of the limited rationality of organizations and its dire implications for nuclear proliferation are given in Sagan and Waltz, pp. 46–87.

[35] Henry D. Sokolski. *Best of Intentions: America's Campaign Against Strategic Weapons Proliferation.* Westport, Conn.: Praeger, 2001, pp. 13–21.

[36] Bundy. pp. 155–196.

[37] Bundy. p. 198.

[38] Sokolski. p. 26.

[39] "United States 'Atoms for Peace' Proposal: Address by President Eisenhower to the General Assembly, December 8, 1953." In U.S. Department of State, *Documents on Disarmament, 1945–59,* vol. 2, p. 399.

[40] The discussion of Atoms for Peace is based on Sokolski, pp. 25–33.

[41] Sokolski. p. 41.

[42] Quoted in Fighting Proliferation Chapter 1 "What Does the History of the Nuclear Nonproliferation Treaty Tell Us about Its Future?" Henry Sokolski. http://fas.org/irp/threat/fp/b19ch1.htm.

[43] Sokolski discusses the genesis of the NPT and the tension between its various provisions on pp. 39–56.

[44] "FAS Weapons of Mass Destruction. Nuclear Nonproliferation Treaty (NPT) Chronology." www.fas.org/nuke/control/npt/chron.htm. Retrieved January 4, 2007.

[45] Graham. pp. 51–52.

[46] Henry D. Sokolski. "Nuclear 1914: The Next Big Worry." In Henry Sokolsi, ed., *Taming the Next Set of Strategic Weapons Threats.* Carlisle, Pa.: Strategic Studies Institute, 2006.

[47] "Treaty of Tlatelolco." Available online at http://www.opanal.org/opanal/Tlatelolco/P-Tlatelolco-i.htm.

[48] Forsberg et. al. p. 73.

[49] John Lewis Gaddis. *Strategies of Containment: A Critical Appraisal of Postwar American National Security.* New York: Oxford University Press, 1982. Quoted in "Nuclear Files: Key Issues: Nuclear Weapons: History: Cold War: Strategy: Massive Retaliation." Available online at http://www.nuclearfiles.org/menu/key-issues/nuclearweapons/history/cold-war/strategy/strategy-massive%20retaliation.htm.

[50] Sokolski. *Best of Intentions,* p. 111.

[51] Ted Galen Carpenter. "Not All Forms of Nuclear Proliferation Are Equally Bad." Available online. URL: http://www.cato.org/pub_display.php?pub_id=2886.

[52] http://www.presidentialrhetoric.com/historicspeeches/reagan/nationalsecurity.html.

[53] James Woolsey in the foreword to Sokolski, *Best of Intentions,* pp. ix–x.

2

Focus on the United States and Russia

From 1949 to the present day, the United States and the Soviet Union (later Russia) have been the two major nuclear weapons states. For much of that time, they have also seemed to be the two most likely to have a nuclear war with each other. Several of the most important nuclear arms agreements to date have been bilateral agreements between the two nuclear superpowers, treaties designed either to reduce the likelihood of nuclear war or to slow or reverse the nuclear arms race that had raised the risks of war to such terrifying heights.

In 1963, recoiling from the tense nuclear standoffs of the early 1960s, the leaders of the United States and the Soviet Union signed the Hotline Agreement. Establishing close communications links between the leaders of the two nations, the Hotline Agreement was the first of a series of treaties designed to reduce the likelihood that the superpowers would have to use their nuclear arsenals, whether through error or the lack of means to conduct last-minute diplomacy. Later treaties of this type included the 1973 Prevention of Nuclear War Agreement (a rather vague but welcome statement of good intentions) and the 1987 agreement to establish Nuclear Risk Reduction Centers.

Two treaties signed in 1972, both intended to restrain the growth of the U.S. and Soviet arsenals, were the outcome of a long negotiation process that historians now call SALT I, short for Strategic Arms Limitations Talks I (the Roman numeral distinguishes it from a later series of talks, known as SALT II). One of the two SALT I agreements was the Antiballistic Missile Treaty (ABM), which limited each side to two antiballistic missile sites with 100 interceptors each—reduced to one site each in 1974. The second of the SALT I treaties, the Interim Agreement, froze the total number of ballistic missile launchers for a five-year period. Both sides agreed to continue adherence to the treaty in 1977. Unfortunately, the Interim Agreement permitted both the United States and the Soviet Union to "MIRV" their missiles, that is, to arm each ballistic missile with MIRVs. As the acronym hints, a MIRVed missile, when it nears the foe, sends out several smaller missile each armed with a nuclear warhead. One ballistic missile thereby achieves the result of several missiles hitting several targets. The MIRV technology, which had been developed in the 1960s, enabled both parties to evade the intended effects of the Interim Agreement, which counted delivery vehicles, not warheads.

The SALT II treaty, signed in 1979, limited the number of strategic (that is, long-range) nuclear delivery vehicles to 2,400, to be reduced to 2,250 by 1982. It also addressed the loophole of MIRVed missiles, limiting MIRVed launchers to a total of 1,320 and specifying the number of warheads on each type of launcher—10 on ICBMs and 14 on SLBMs. Though the terms of SALT II left both sides with the ability to destroy each other's societies and cause mass species extinction, the U.S. Senate saw it as too favorable to the Soviet Union and never ratified it. In 1986, the United States announced that it would no longer abide by the agreement.

With the possible exception of the 1972 ABM treaty, none of these bilateral nuclear arms control agreements significantly restrained the growth of the superpowers' arsenals, much less reduced them. Then, in 1987, there came a historic breakthrough: Diplomatic teams under the direction of President Ronald Reagan and Soviet leader Mikhail Gorbachev negotiated the Intermediate Range Nuclear Forces (INF) Treaty, which prohibited the existence and production of intermediate- and short-range missiles. For the first time since the advent of nuclear weapons, an entire class of them was eliminated, and not merely to make room for some new, improved, and more deadly weapons system. The restriction of the treaty to short- and medium-range missiles meant that its main effects were felt in Western Europe. The agreement proved that nuclear arms reductions were possible.

In 1991, as the Soviet Union was in the process of disintegrating, leaders of the nuclear powers signed the Strategic Arms Reduction Treaty (START, now known as START I), which limited each side to 6,000 deployed nuclear warheads.[1] START II, signed by U.S. president George H. W. Bush and Russian president Boris Yeltsin in 1993, banned the use of MIRVs on ICBMs. Russia subsequently withdrew from this agreement, which never went into force.

With these arms control treaties, Armageddon became a more remote possibility, but the collapse of the Soviet Union created new nuclear proliferation problems: the poorly guarded bombs and fissile materials left over from the Soviet Empire and of great interest to terrorists, and the possibility that unemployed Russian nuclear scientists would sell their services to foreign dictators. The United States and Russia have met these challenges with a group of special programs collectively entitled Cooperative Threat Reduction (CTR) to improve the security of Russian nuclear assets and provide civilian employment for Russian scientists.

After 9/11, leaders in the United States began to emphasize a new threat, that rogue states such as Iraq, Iran, or North Korea would give nuclear weapons or other WMD to terrorists. The Bush administration, which took office in 2001, suggested that this threat may call for military action to prevent rogue states from acquiring nuclear weapons. Using this logic, in 2003 the United States invaded Iraq. Though the United States claimed that it was turning to military action only as a last resort, U.S. allies such as France and Germany were unconvinced. They saw a trigger-happy United States using nonproliferation as an excuse to reshape the Middle East by force. After the invasion, it looked as if the critics were right: No WMD and no nuclear program were found in Iraq.

Today, as the most powerful nation in the world with the largest military force, the United States sees itself as having a special mission to stem the spread of nuclear weapons. Critics, however, see the United States as a culprit in nuclear proliferation, willing to sell nuclear materials and know-how to nations it sees as friendly, refusing to vow that it will not be the first to use nuclear weapons, promoting an ineffective and destabilizing missile defense technology, and maintaining an aggressive military posture that only makes states such as Iran and North Korea rush to acquire nuclear weapons faster as insurance against U.S. invasion.

END OF THE COLD WAR

The road toward the historic nuclear treaties of the late 1980s and early 1990s had taken many detours. The results were in many ways quite unexpected. They occurred only after the U.S. president who participated in them had a remarkable change of heart.

When Reagan became president in 1981, he believed that previous arms agreements such as the 1972 ABM Treaty and the Interim Agreement (renewed in 1979) had permitted the Soviets to acquire a dangerous lead in the nuclear arms race, and he called for a $180-billion nuclear buildup. Though he went through the motions of continuing the nuclear arms limitations talks begun by his predecessors, he did not seem to expect them to lead anywhere. He said that communists could not be trusted to keep treaties. A 1982 secret national security decision directive[2] leaked to the *New York Times* revealed a new U.S. military plan—to win a "protracted nuclear war." Many people in the United States and Western Europe feared that

Reagan, who called the Soviet Union "an evil empire," intended to start such a war.

The Soviet spy agency, the KGB, thought so as well. In 1983, this belief nearly led to disaster. In November of that year, NATO conducted a military exercise in which they simulated the procedures for the release of nuclear weapons. The Soviets, informed by their agents of the approaching exercise, took it for the real thing and considered the option of striking first before the NATO missiles were launched. Fortunately, they decided to put their forces on alert and wait.

Soon afterward, William Casey, the director of the CIA, told Reagan by what a thin margin World War III had just been avoided. Reagan was shocked. To him, the good intentions of the United States were self-evident; he had not considered that the Soviets might fear a surprise nuclear attack from the United States. In his second term as president, Reagan actively pursued serious arms reductions with the Soviet Union.

The new Soviet leader, Gorbachev, was also eager to negotiate major arms reductions. Both the Soviet economy and its political system were moribund, and Gorbachev was ready to take radical steps to reform them. Reagan and Gorbachev overcame decades of mutual distrust to sign a sweeping arms agreement, setting the pattern for the sharp arms reductions that were negotiated after each of them left office.

Gorbachev's reforms came too late to save the Soviet system. Between 1989 and 1991, in a series of mostly bloodless revolutions, the Soviet satellite states that had been part of the Warsaw Pact repudiated communism. At the same time, the various republics that made up the Soviet Union began to assert their independence. At the end of 1991, the Soviet Union broke apart. Later agreements involving the arsenals of the former Soviet Union were negotiated between U.S. presidents and the presidents of the Russian Federation.

ARMS REDUCTION AGREEMENTS AFTER THE COLD WAR

As of 2007, the last major nuclear arms agreement between the United States and Russia was the Strategic Offensive Reduction Treaty (SORT), signed in 2002 by U.S. president George W. Bush and Russian president Vladimir Putin. The agreement is often referred to as the "Moscow Treaty." Under the terms of the treaty, the United States and Russia will reduce their deployed offensive nuclear forces to 1,700–2,200 strategic warheads apiece by December 31, 2012. At the time Bush and Putin signed the agreement, the target warhead level was roughly equivalent to a cut of two-thirds in the deployed forces for each side.[3] However, the treaty lacked the timelines and verification and implementation measures of previous strategic arms control agreements, and it did not call for the destruction of any warheads or delivery vehicles.

Agreements like these are surely an improvement from the late 20th century, when tens of thousands of nuclear weapons were ready for launch on a minute's notice. Still, critics charge, they fail to take advantage of a historic opportunity to ban nuclear weapons or limit them to a handful incapable of causing global catastrophe. The number of weapons Russia and the United States would deploy even after the 2012 reductions would still be far greater than either country needs for protection. No one is threatening the survival of the United States or the Russian Federation; the only purpose their nuclear arsenals serve is to intimidate other countries, and even for that purpose they are ineffective, as Iran and North Korea, for example, proceed with their nuclear weapons programs. Nor have these agreements fulfilled the promise of the Nuclear Nonproliferation Treaty (NPT), in which nuclear weapons states pledged to make serious movement toward nuclear disarmament.

Further, the treaties are extremely deceptive, looking better to a public that neglects to read the fine print. For example, SORT's limits on deployed weapons ends on the day that it is supposed to be achieved. The treaty says that the United States and Russia must each reduce their strategic weapons to below 2,200 by the end of 2012, but it leaves them free to begin building them up again immediately afterward.

And they could build them up again almost overnight. The agreement calls only for a reduction of weapons that are *deployed*; it does not count warheads that are stockpiled—stored separately from ICBMs, SLBMs, and long-range bombers. No warheads or delivery vehicles need to be destroyed as part of the SORT reduction process. The START I agreement between the USSR and the United States, which limited the number of delivery vehicles—ICBMs, and SLBMs—that each side could own and arranged for the destruction of the excess delivery vehicles, is due to expire in 2009, three years before the date in 2012 when SORT's targets are supposed to have been reached and the agreement simultaneously expires. (In December 2001, after the United States withdrew from the ABM Treaty, Russia withdrew from the START II agreement, which thus never went into force.) Though Russia and some of America's European allies have expressed a desire to replace START I with another agreement before it expires, or at least extend it past 2009, the United States under George W. Bush has been uninterested.

In 2003, when SORT went into force, Russian army general Andrey Nikolayev, chairman of the state Duma's committee on defense, noted that the treaty allowed for the fitting of multiple warheads to its missile systems. "We could not do this before. Now we have legal clearance for it." He went on to say, "if the USA develops an [antiballistic missile] system which substantially affects our security, Russia will undoubtedly take commensurate steps, even including withdrawal from the SORT treaty. The ratification law makes provision for this."[4]

As of 2005, according to *Arms Control Today*, the United States had 5,968 strategic warheads, more than 1,000 operational tactical weapons, and approximately 3,000 reserve strategic and tactical warheads; Russia, 4,978 strategic warheads, approximately 3,500 operational tactical warheads, and

Strategic Nuclear Arms Control Agreements

	SALT I	SALT II	START I	START II	SORT
Deployed Warhead Limit	Limited Missiles, Not Warheads	Limited Missiles and Bombers, Not Warheads	6,000	3,000–3,500	1,700–2,200
Deployed Delivery Vehicle Limit	U.S.: 1,710 ICBMs & SLBMs; USSR: 2,347 ICBMs & SLBMs	2250	1,600	Not Applicable	Not Applicable
Status	Expired	Never Entered into Force	In Force	Never Entered into Force	In Force
Date Signed	May 26, 1972	June 18, 1979	July 31, 1991	January 3, 1993	May 24, 2002
Date Entered into Force	October 3, 1972	Not Applicable	December 5, 1994	Not Applicable	June 7, 2003
Implementation Deadline	Not Applicable	December 31, 1981	December 5, 2001	December 31, 2007	December 31, 2012
Expiration Date	October 3, 1977	December 31, 1985	December 5, 2009	December 5, 2009	December 31, 2012

Source: Based on Arms Control Association. "U.S.-Soviet/Russian Arms Control," June 2002. Available online. URL: www.armscontrol.org/act/2002_06/factfilejune02.asp. Accessed July 11, 2007.

more than 11,000 stockpiled strategic and tactical warheads. Though relations between the United States and Russia are not hostile enough to fuel an arms buildup on the scale of the cold war, existing treaties between them would not prevent a rapid return to their old ways.

RUSSIA

The New Nuclear Threat in Russia

NEW DANGERS POSED BY THE SOVIET UNION'S COLLAPSE

Osama bin Laden has declared the acquisition of nuclear weapons a "religious duty," and documents found in al-Qaeda hideouts in Afghanistan include crude designs for nuclear weapons as well as blueprints of nuclear power plants in the United States. Other terrorist groups, including the Japanese end-of-the-world cult Aum Shinrikyo, are also believed to have sought to obtain nuclear weapons and fissile material.[5] There is little doubt that some terrorists would love to get their hands on nuclear weapons or, failing that, on nuclear fissile material to help them make a "dirty bomb." The likeliest place for such a group to obtain WMD is at present in the former Soviet Union, a place with so much ill-guarded nuclear material that it has been called the "Home Depot" of terrorists.[6]

One consolation for the despotic nature of the Soviet government was that its nuclear weapons and nuclear materials were under strict centralized control. Nuclear facilities of all kinds were well maintained, making thefts by outsiders highly unlikely; the people who dealt with nuclear materials were well paid, patriotic, and closely watched by the secret police, making an "inside job" unlikely as well. This all changed with the breakup of the Soviet Union. One nuclear weapons state immediately became four: Belarus, Kazakhstan, Russia, and Ukraine. Even more worrying, the struggling Russian economy left many nuclear installations poorly guarded and soldiers and officials underpaid, angry, and in a position to sell something valuable to an international black market. As one analyst summed up the problem, "A security system designed for a single state with a closed society, closed borders, and well-paid, well-cared-for nuclear workers has been splintered among multiple states with open societies, open borders, desperate, underpaid nuclear workers, and rampant theft and corruption."[7]

In view of the chaos in Russia following the breakup of the Soviet Union and the weakness of the Soviet economy in the 1990s, it seems a wonder that terrorists have *not* yet exploded a nuclear weapon. Certainly, we cannot be sure that they do not have one or at least sufficient nuclear material for a dirty bomb. In September 2000, Russian prime minister Mikhail Kasayanov admitted knowing of 21 attempts to steal registered nuclear materials between 1991 and 1999. It seems likely that some thefts were successful and either not discovered or not reported by Russian officials.

SECURING AND GUARDING NUCLEAR MATERIALS IN THE FORMER SOVIET REPUBLICS

In 1991, the year the Soviet Union was dissolved, U.S. senators Sam Nunn and Richard Lugar sponsored a bill allocating $400 million of Defense Department funds to aid the former Soviet republics (including Russia itself) with the "transportation, storage, safeguarding, and destruction of nuclear weapons [and with] the prevention of weapons proliferation."[8] Nunn and Lugar's bill gradually evolved into the CTR, a series of programs, carried out in cooperation between the United States and these former Soviet Republics. The program was difficult to negotiate, in part because the Russian government and the agencies in charge of its nuclear materials were reluctant to admit that there was any problem with security in the first place; to do so, as they saw it, amounted to an admission of incompetence.

The CTR program and related efforts on the part of the United States to assist the former Soviet republics in maintaining nuclear safety have faced immense challenges and met with varying success:

- In the 1990s, the CTR helped Russia improve the security of its nuclear weapons during transportation, when nuclear weapons were brought from Belarus, Kazakhstan, and Ukraine back to Russia and the weapons were moved to a smaller number of sites within Russia. The U.S. government provided Russia with "armored blankets" and "supercontainers" to protect warheads during shipment, equipment to improve security for nuclear weapons railcars, and guard railcars. This assistance may not have been fully adequate to the task, however. According to the Russian nonproliferation journal *Yaderny Kontrol,* in 1997, Russian military units had only 17 percent of the cargo trucks they needed for transportation of nuclear weapons.[9] Fortunately, with the consolidation of Russia's nuclear forces achieved by now, these special transportation security needs are no longer as great as they were in the 1990s.
- As time went on, the CTR devoted a greater portion of its efforts to improving security at Russian storage facilities, helping Russia design computer tracking systems for warheads, providing software for evaluating potential weaknesses at storage sites, and supplying fences and sensors.[10]

- Meanwhile, another agreement between the United States and Russia simplified the security problems posed by the weapons grade, highly enriched uranium (HEU) that, thanks to arms reduction agreements, was no longer needed for weapons. In accordance with the 1993 Highly Enriched Uranium Purchase agreement, the United States undertook to purchase 500 metric tons of Russia's weapons grade HEU; the HEU would then be "blended down," or mixed with natural uranium to eliminate its weapon usability and be used as commercial reactor fuel. By 2004, 175 metric tons of Russian HEU, or the equivalent of approximately 7,000 nuclear warheads, had been eliminated under this program.[11]
- The two countries also established the Material Protection, Control, and Accounting program, a major effort to improve the security of Russia's fissile material, and they signed an accord to build a secure Russian storage facility for fissile materials.[12]
- Starting in 1993, nuclear scientists in Russia and the United States, who enjoyed a greater degree of mutual trust than their counterparts in their respective governments, led an effort of their own to improve Russian nuclear security. Eventually, working through the U.S. Department of Energy, the U.S. and Russian scientists worked to trouble-shoot problems at Russian storage facilities and to institute systems that would make them secure. Some of the new systems introduced, such as the use of bar codes, tamper-proof seals, and video surveillance cameras and alarm systems, seem very elementary, suggesting that security beforehand must have been very relaxed.[13]

THE PROLIFERATION THREAT OF RUSSIA'S UNEMPLOYED NUCLEAR SCIENTISTS

Ultimately, knowledge, not uranium or plutonium, is the most important ingredient in nuclear weapons production. So the greatest danger posed by the reduction of Russia's nuclear arsenal may be the large number of nuclear weapons scientists who have been left idle, with no alternative use for their abilities. Russian scientists, engineers, and workers with special expertise in nuclear weapons and missile systems would be in great demand in states such as Iran and North Korea that want to become nuclear weapons states. Russian expertise would make a more permanent contribution to these states' nuclear ambitions than Russian uranium or plutonium.

According to a 2003 article in *Arms Control Today,* "The downsizing of WMD production plants and related infrastructure will continue to displace thousands of scientists and workers skilled in the details of weapon design, manufacture, and maintenance." The Russian government has tried to divert some of this talent to commercial projects, but such efforts have not been particularly successful.[14]

Nuclear Policy in Russia

It seems that despite the reduction of Russia's nuclear forces and the decrease in tensions with the United States, Russia relies more than ever on its nuclear forces for safety. In fact, its nuclear stance is in some senses more aggressive than it was during the cold war. Russia is no longer ringed by captive Eastern European buffer states or the buffer of some of the republics that broke away from the Soviet Union. It has a much smaller, weaker, less-well-funded conventional armed forces than it had during the cold war. Thus, Russia relies on its nuclear forces to deter attack.

On January 17, 2000, Vladimir Putin, then acting president of the Russian Federation, signed into law a new national security strategy that lowered the threshold on the first use of nuclear weapons. According to the Russian strategy, nuclear weapons could be used to oppose any attack, nuclear or conventional, if other efforts failed to repel the aggressor and allowed the first use of nuclear arms "in case of a threat to the existence of the Russian Federation." The new Russian strategic doctrine stated, "The Russian Federation must have nuclear forces capable of delivering specified damage to any aggressor state or a coalition of states in any situation." This strategy is clearly not a step in the direction of nuclear disarmament—rather, it makes deterrence based on nuclear weapons the cornerstone of Russia's defense.[15]

Currently, Russia has little to fear from its neighbors, and the likelihood of war is very small. When Russia wants to exert pressure on its neighbors, it seems to prefer using its immense oil and gas resources, hinting that it will withdraw them from countries whose policies it dislikes. It is important to remember, though, that international politics does not stand still. In the past, Russia has had a fractious relationship with its neighbor China, which is also a nuclear weapons state. Russia and the United States still differ on many issues, including Iran. If the United States were to attack Iran to prevent it from becoming a nuclear weapons state, it would have to deal with the reaction of Russia.

Russia as Nuclear Proliferator

Today Russia takes advantage of its experience in nuclear matters to earn revenue and exercise political influence through sales of advanced conventional weapons technology and nuclear technology (in theory for peaceful purposes) to other countries. Russia has been especially active in meeting the conventional weapons and nuclear desires of Iran, an oil-rich, Islamic fundamentalist state regarded with great suspicion by the United States and its European allies. The Russian government claims that it only supplies "defensive" weapons to Iran, but what is a defensive weapon? Probably all weapons could be called defensive, and improved defenses supplied from abroad could certainly help a country conduct an aggressive military strategy with its own homegrown weapons.

Russia is helping to build nuclear reactors in Iran and has agreed to supply Iran with reactor fuel. Defending these moves, Russia points out that the arrangements require that spent reactor fuel be returned to Russia, reducing the risk that plutonium (useful in making weapons) could be separated from the fuel in Iran. Russia contends that the reactors will not pose a proliferation risk because they will operate under NPT safeguards. Under NPT provisions, the IAEA would be able to monitor Iran's declared nuclear activities to ensure they were not diverted to military uses; under a 2003 protocol that Iran signed, the IAEA could also detect clandestine nuclear activities—signed only after Iran was found to have built secret nuclear facilities in violation of its NPT commitments. Since Iran has a history of attempting to conduct such suspicious activities in secret and is suspected of wanting to become a nuclear weapons state, these deals caused widespread criticism in the United States and Europe.[16]

In early 2005, insisting they were for "defense only," Russia reached an agreement to sell Iran 29 surface-to-air missiles. This deal, too, was criticized in the United States. It was also roundly criticized in Israel, which regards Iran as a grave threat to its existence.

In July 2006, the United States imposed sanctions on Russia's state-run military export agency, Rosoboronexport, and on the Russian warplane maker Sukhoi for exporting military hardware to Iran; the United States maintained that the exports violated the Iran Nonproliferation Act[17] signed into U.S. law in March 2000. The Iran Nonproliferation Act calls for sanctions against countries that export "destabilizing numbers and types of advanced conventional weapons" to Iran as well as on exporters of lethal military equipment to state sponsors of terrorism. The sanctions would take the form of stopping exports of U.S. technology and high-tech services and denying the sanctioned countries licenses to use American technology. Russia could face these U.S. sanctions depending on the types of weapons it sells to Iran.

Phrases such as "destabilizing numbers and types of advanced conventional weapons" leave a great deal of room for interpretation. Both the Clinton and second Bush administrations, anxious to have good relations with Russia, have been reluctant to impose sanctions. The United States lifted sanctions imposed on Rosoboronexport and Sukhoi in November 2006 during negotiations concerning Russia's entry into the World Trade Organization. Soon afterward, Russia denied reports that it had gone ahead with the sale of antiaircraft missiles and a few weeks later confirmed the reports.[18]

Whether these antiaircraft missiles promote nuclear proliferation is a matter of interpretation; the missiles will be deployed around Iran's nuclear reactors. They are probably intended to defend these reactors against attack by the United States or Israel.

UNITED STATES

Nuclear Policy Under the Second Bush Administration

The 2000 election of George W. Bush as president brought into national office a group of decision makers who considered the previous administration weak on defense and believed they had a mandate to remake the U.S. armed forces to meet the challenges of the new century. The new administration's thinking with respect to nuclear weapons was embodied in a Nuclear Posture Review presented to Congress in December 2001. Though the report was "classified" (secret), it was leaked to the media, something that tends to happen quickly when controversial documents are presented to U.S. politicians.

For those favoring nuclear arms reduction and possible abolition, the Bush administration's review was dismaying. It foresaw new roles for nuclear weapons, and it seemed to blur the lines between nuclear and conventional forces. For example, the report suggests that the forces that carry conventional "global strikes" be merged with nuclear forces. Under this plan, an ICBM might contain either nuclear warheads or conventional explosives. Critics object that until it landed, an enemy would have no way of knowing what sort of warhead the ICBM contained, so if such a missile were used against a nuclear weapons state it might initiate a nuclear counterstrike. Worse, a conventional ICBM attack against a "rogue state" such as Iran or North Korea might be misunderstood as a preemptive nuclear strike against neighboring Russia or China, leading to nuclear retaliation against the United States.

The report also envisioned an increased role for small, "low-yield," nuclear weapons, intended to destroy hardened targets such as underground bunkers for commanders or weapons that could not be effectively reached by conventional explosives. Critics fear that the use of such weapons would break the taboo that has prevented nuclear war since 1945. Nuclear weapons would eventually become a part of the war planning of many nations, and future wars could easily escalate from bunker busting nuclear weapons to the use of strategic nuclear weapons.[19]

A more recent U.S. military planning document, the March 2005 Doctrine for Joint Nuclear Operations, written under the direction of the chairman of the Pentagon's Joint Chiefs of Staff, went even further in calling for "integrating conventional and nuclear attacks" to "ensure the most efficient use of force and provide US leaders with a broader range of [nuclear and conventional] strike options to address immediate contingencies. Integration of conventional and nuclear forces is therefore crucial to the success of any comprehensive strategy. This integration will ensure optimal targeting, minimal collateral damage, and reduce the probability of escalation."[20]

In contrast to the 1995 version of the Doctrine for Joint Nuclear Operations, the 2005 doctrine called for using nuclear weapons in response to a threat or use of "weapons of mass destruction"—that is, nuclear weapons would be used to counter biological or chemical weapons or perhaps even the threat of those weapons, or in a preventive war against a state that was developing nuclear weapons but did not have them yet.[21] In a paragraph discussing the 2001 Nuclear Posture Review, which provided the thinking behind the new nuclear doctrine, the Doctrine for Joint Nuclear Operations stated that states "armed with WMD will likely test US security commitments to its allies and friends. In response, the US needs a range of capabilities to assure friends and foe alike of its resolve. A broader array of capability is needed to dissuade states from undertaking diplomatic, political, military, or technical courses of action (COAs) that would threaten US and allied security. US forces must pose a credible deterrent to potential adversaries who have access to modern military technology, including WMD and the means to deliver them."[22]

With its refusal to limit the role of nuclear weapons to a deterrent against an attack on the United States or its major allies, the revised doctrine aroused a storm of criticism when it appeared on the Internet in March 2005; it was removed on September 11, 2005. In December of that year, seven senators and nine representatives, all Democratic Party members, addressed an open letter to President Bush expressing alarm at the revised doctrine and arguing that "this effort to broaden the range of scenarios in which nuclear weapons might be contemplated is unwise and provocative."[23]

Amid this criticism, the new doctrine was cancelled in February 2006. It remains important because it provides a window to one school of thought among policy makers, one that strongly influenced Ronald Reagan during his first term and George W. Bush during both terms. This school seeks to redefine nuclear weapons as normal instruments of warfare. It presents itself as a plea for more humane nuclear weapons designed for military targets. As Secretary of Defense Donald Rumsfeld put it in an April 2005 appearance before the Senate Armed Services Panel, "The only thing we have is very large, very dirty, big nuclear weapons. It seems to me studying it [the Robust Nuclear Earth Penetrator, a proposed "bunker buster" tactical nuclear weapon] makes all the sense in the world."[24] Facing strong opposition in Congress, the Bush administration ultimately dropped its proposals for funding research for the Robust Nuclear Earth Penetrator.[25]

The American Congress and the American people balk at the idea of using nuclear weapons as normal instruments of war. The American people have never been in full agreement with their military planners on the subject of nuclear weapons, however. This gap is reflected in the difference between the statements American presidents make regarding nuclear weapons in speeches and the United States's position on nuclear weapons in its official papers and statements to foreign diplomats. From Truman onward in speeches that receive widespread coverage, most American presidents have said that a nuclear war would have no winners. Our government's official stance, however, has always been that we claim the right to be the first to use nuclear weapons in some future conflict. Even today, as in the days when NATO faced the Warsaw Pact, the United States has refused to adopt a "no first use policy"—that is, to state officially that it will not be the first to use nuclear weapons in a future conflict.

9/11 AND PREVENTIVE WAR

A little more than a year after the terrorist attacks of September 11, 2001, the Bush administration announced changes in its general military planning. On September 20, 2002, the administration issued a new National Security Strategy (NSS) that broadened the conditions under which the United States might engage in a war.

In the past, the United States, like all other countries, has claimed the right to defend itself and to engage in "preemptive war," to launch an attack on another country when it judges that an attack from that country is imminent. It is not necessary, according to internationally accepted norms and the laws of war, to wait for enemy forces to land on your territory or the enemy's bombs to explode on your soil for you to be justified in launching your own forces. The enemy's mobilization with an obvious intent to attack is enough.

"Preventive war," however, is not permitted under international law. A country would be waging preventive war if it judged that in a few years, its neighbor would pose a threat and decided to strike now while the enemy was still relatively weak. The Bush administration's 2002 National Security Strategy received widespread attention and criticism because, while it did not use the words *preventive war*, it redefined what it called "preemption" to include what had previously been called preventive war. Pointing to the emergence of a new class of countries it called "rogue states," the NSS asserted that the possibility that rogue states might supply terrorists with WMD, including nuclear weapons, made it necessary for the United States to act in advance to deal with "emerging" threats.

> *The United States will not use force in all cases to preempt emerging threats, nor should nations use preemption as a pretext for aggression. Yet in an age where the enemies of civilization openly and actively seek the world's most destructive technologies, the United States cannot remain idle while dangers gather.*[26]

The United States could not afford to wait for terrorists to strike, said the NSS, nor could it easily predict a terrorist strike like 9/11. The next attack might come in the form of a nuclear weapon or other WMD supplied to terrorists by a rogue state such as Iran, Iraq, or North Korea. These new circumstances create a "compelling case for taking anticipatory actions to defend ourselves, even if uncertainty remains as to the time and place of the enemy's attack."

Other parts of the NSS made more traditional points about the need for international cooperation to resolve conflicts and combat nuclear proliferation. The assertion of the United States's right to act militarily against "emerging threats," however, was the new element among the many policies announced in the document, and it received the widest attention and criticism.

Critics pointed out that there is nothing, except the threat of force by other nations, to prevent countries from using "preemption as a pretext for aggression." Analysts for the Brookings Institution, an independent research institute, argued that the new policy "reinforces the image of the United States as too quick to use military force and to do so outside the bounds of international law and legitimacy."

> *This can make it more difficult for the United States to gain international support for its use of force, and over the long term, may lead others to resist U.S. foreign policy goals more broadly, including efforts to fight terrorism.... Advocating preemption warns potential enemies to hide the very assets we might wish to take preemptive action against, or to otherwise prepare responses and defenses.*[27]

WAR TO PREVENT IRAQ FROM ACQUIRING WMD

In 2003, the administration took its new strategic thinking to its logical conclusion with the invasion of Iraq, a country with a repellent government, but one that posed no immediate threat to the United States. At the time of the U.S. invasion of Iraq, no one outside Iraq, and perhaps no more than a handful of people *in* Iraq, knew the real state of that country's effort to develop WMD. Iraq's dictator, Saddam Hussein, had certainly possessed some very dangerous weapons at one time and hoped to acquire more, including nuclear weapons. He had been forced to accept intrusive UN weapons inspections in Iraq as part of the settlement of the first Gulf War, which ended in 1991. Inspection teams were charged with finding Iraq's illegal nuclear, chemical, and biological weapons programs and seeing to it that they were dismantled under UN supervision. After doing everything he could to deceive and thwart their efforts, Saddam Hussein expelled the UN inspectors at the end of 1998. Soon afterward, in an operation called Desert Fox, the United States and Britain bombed sites in Iraq suspected of being involved in weapons production.

Because Saddam Hussein had played a shell game with the weapons inspectors, however, experts in the field of weapons proliferation were uncertain if Iraq's WMD had been eliminated. It was assumed, based on the dictator's treatment of the inspectors, that he would try to reconstitute his weapons programs as soon as he could. "We know that Saddam Hussein pursued weapons of mass murder even when inspectors were in his country," said President George W. Bush in a speech to the UN General Assembly on September 12, 2002. "Are we to assume that he stopped when they left?" Calling Saddam Hussein's regime "a grave and gathering danger," Bush said that "to assume this regime's good faith is to bet the lives of millions and the peace of the world in a reckless gamble."[28]

U.S. spy agencies attempted to gain information on Saddam Hussein's presumed weapons programs. The evidence was based on dubious sources—a key informant on Iraq's nuclear program had been given the code name "Curve Ball" by U.S. intelligence operatives unconvinced of his truthfulness. Vice President Dick Cheney, however, spoke as if there were no doubts: "We now know that Saddam Hussein has resumed his efforts to acquire nuclear weapons," he asserted in a speech in August 2002, and on September 8 on the TV program *Meet the Press* he said that he knew "with absolute certainty" that Saddam Hussein was buying equipment to build a nuclear bomb.[29]

At the end of 2002, facing a threatened invasion, Saddam Hussein permitted UN weapons inspectors into Iraq again. The UN team's head,

Dr. Hans Blix, insisted that with time—a matter of "months"—his inspectors could determine the truth, but the United States insisted that Hussein was deceiving the inspectors and the only solution now was war.

After the March 2003 American invasion, with the upbeat name Operation Iraqi Freedom, succeeded in eliminating the country's regular armed forces, U.S. inspectors failed to find the weapons whose existence had been used to justify the war. On January 28, 2004, David Kay, head of the Iraqi Survey Group charged with finding the WMD, told Congress, "We were almost all wrong." Saddam Hussein had no chemical, biological, or nuclear weapons, nor had he the means to make them.[30]

Though the United States achieved a quick victory over Iraq's armed forces, the United States turned out to be unprepared to deal with the insurgency that followed the invasion or to stabilize Iraq, which subsequently descended into a state of protracted civil war. Four years later, the preventive war against Iraq looked like a terrible mistake. More than 100,000 Iraqis had been killed, a few American soldiers were being killed every day, and the country had become a training ground for exactly the sort of Islamic fanatics who had perpetrated the 9/11 attacks.

For good or ill, one effect of Operation Iraqi Freedom has been to make another war in the name of nonproliferation less likely in the near future. With the example of Iraq before them, the people of the United States are in no mood for a war to keep nuclear weapons out of the hands of Iran or to take them away from the North Koreans. In fact, it is possible that it was only the failure of America's military policies in Iraq that prevented the United States from moving on to a preventive war with Iran. In 2005, when success in Iraq still seemed possible, the *New Yorker* and the *Washington Post* reported that plans for an Iran invasion were being discussed within the Bush administration. By 2007, public disenchantment with the war in Iraq made military action against Iran seem far less likely, though tensions between the United States and Iran remained high.

MILITARY CONTRACTORS CONTINUE TO INFLUENCE NUCLEAR WEAPONS DECISIONS

Each year around $40 billion, approximately 10 percent of the annual U.S. defense budget, is spent on nuclear weapons. Thanks to mergers and acquisitions that have consolidated the U.S. defense industry, this money goes to a smaller group of corporations than ever before. These defense contractors have a great deal of money to spend on public relations campaigns to convince the public and politicians of the need for their services; they are also very important to the economic health of the states in which their manufacturing is located. The loss of a major defense contract can result in a regional depression. That is why, historically, not only stockholders but union leaders and workers have favored policies that lead to big defense contracts. Senators and congressmembers in California, Virginia, Texas, Florida, and Arizona, states in which defense industries are concentrated, all have a strong motive to support big nuclear defense budgets. Big defense budgets are good for their states, and it is all too easy to believe that what is good for your state is good for the country and the world.

MISSILE DEFENSE PROGRAM

Since the 1980s, political conservatives in the United States have tended to favor the development of missile defense, while liberals have disparaged it. Missile defense programs received support and funding under Reagan and his successor, George H. W. Bush. They received much less support under Clinton, who sometimes said missile defenses might offer protection against attacks from rogue states but did not show much interest in large outlays of money for these programs. George W. Bush, who took office in 2001, returned to greater support of missile defense, taking steps to deploy missile defense systems that were still in the development stage. In December 2001, Bush went further than his predecessors in officially withdrawing from the 1972 U.S.-Russian Anti-Ballistic Missile Treaty (ABM). "I have concluded the ABM treaty hinders our government's ability to develop ways to protect our people from future terrorist or rogue-state missile attacks," Bush announced. "Defending the American people is my highest priority as commander in chief and I cannot and will not allow the United States to remain in a treaty that prevents us from developing effective defences."

With the cold war over and the U.S. withdrawal from the ABM treaty long expected, the Russian government did not regard U.S. withdrawal from the treaty as a hostile act, and the Russian response was muted. Russian prime minister Putin called the withdrawal from the treaty "annoying" but said the United States was wi hin its rights.[31] Perhaps the Russians welcomed the move, for on the day after the United States withdrew from the ABM treaty, Russia announced that it was pulling out of the 1993 START II nuclear arms treaty. START II had banned the use of MIRVs on ICBMs. So, among other effects, Russian withdrawal from START II had the effect of permitting the Russians to continue using multiple warheads, or MIRVs (multiply targeted reentry vehicles) .

Spending on missile defense rose throughout the first five years of the Bush administration. President George W. Bush's request on behalf of missile defense for the fiscal year 2007, submitted in February 2006, was $11.2 billion, the administration's highest ever.[32] The administration has promoted not only the development of missile defense but the sharing of this technology with allies.

In November 2006, the Democrats gained a majority in both houses of Congress. Their victory was widely attributed to public disenchantment with George W. Bush's foreign policy. These changes may affect the prospects for missile defense technology, since Democrats are usually less enthusiastic about missile defense, and the new lawmakers have pledged to control spending. In May 2007, the House of Representatives voted to cut a relatively small amount—a little less than $764 million—from the approximately $9 billion the Bush administration had proposed to spend on missile defense in the following year. Among the funds cut were $160 million that had been slated for the construction of missile defenses in Poland. This part of the program was the one the Russians liked least.

United States as Nuclear Proliferator

Every nuclear weapons state has at some time or other contributed to nuclear proliferation. The United States is certainly no exception, and a case could easily be made that it has been the worst culprit, since its cold war strategy was to place nuclear weapons on its allies' territory. During the cold war, the United States deployed nuclear weapons in 27 different global locations, including 18 countries and U.S.-controlled territories.[33]

President Eisenhower approved extensive nuclear deployments in the Pacific, totaling about 1,600 weapons on Japan, Okinawa, Guam, the Philippines, South Korea, and Taiwan. Although Japan's nonnuclear policy of not possessing, not producing, and not introducing nuclear weapons had been in effect since 1959, nuclear weapons were indeed stored in Japan until 1965. Claims of Japan's nuclear-free status by Japanese leaders were technically correct, if not wholly truthful, since the bombs stored on Japan's main island lacked plutonium and/or uranium cores. Meanwhile, complete warheads and whole bombs were kept on U.S. Navy ships offshore of Sasebo and Yokosuka. The United States also stored nuclear weapons on Chichi Jima and Iwo Jima, two Pacific islands that the United States tried to avoid giving back to Japan.

CONCLUSION

In the 1990s, the United States enjoyed a period of extraordinary leadership. It was the world's sole nuclear superpower, with a conventional military force far ahead of the nearest competitor. Critics say that its leaders failed to use the nation's great advantages to meet their obligations under the Nuclear

Nonproliferation Treaty. There are no do-overs in history, so we will never know whether the United States lost an opportunity to denuclearize the world.

The historic opportunity came to an abrupt end in the early 2000s, when a terrorist attack shocked the nation into a willingness to support a military policy that, by the end of the decade, looked short sighted. Though the United States remains the world's greatest military and economic power, it faces the future with a more restricted sense of its ability to influence events beyond its borders, including its ability to curb the proliferation of nuclear weapons.

---

[1] Ray Perkins, Jr, *The ABCs of the Soviet-American Nuclear Arms Race.* Pacific Grove, Calif.: Brook/Cole Publishing, 1991.

[2] NSDD-13. Quoted in Ronald E. Powaski, *Return to Armageddon.* New York: Oxford University Press, 2000, p. 16.

[3] Wade Boese. "U.S. Reports on Nuclear Treaty Implementation." *Arms Control Today,* December 2006. http://www.armscontrol.org/act/2006_12/NuclearTreaty.asp. Retrieved January 4, 2007.

[4] Nuclearfiles.org. Project of the Nuclear Age Peace Foundation. Timeline of the Nuclear Age, 2003. http://www.nuclearfiles.org/menu/timeline/2000/2003.htm.

[5] Busch, p. 11.

[6] Henry L. Stimson Center. "Cooperative Nonproliferation Program: Preventing the Spread of Nuclear, Biological, and Chemical weapons." www.stimson.org/ctr/?SN=CT20050223775. Retrieved January 4, 2007.

[7] Matthew Bunn. *The Next Wave: Urgently Needed New Steps to Control Warheads and Fissile Materials.* Carnegie Endowment for International Peace and Harvard University, 2000, p. 10.

[8] Busch, p. 124.

[9] Busch, p. 114.

[10] Busch, p. 114.

[11] Kenneth N. Luongo and William E. Hoehn III. "Reform and Expansion of Cooperative Threat Reduction,," *Arms Control Today,* June 2003. http://www.armscontrol.org/act/2003_06/luongohoehn_june03.asp. Retrieved January 4, 2007.

[12] Busch, p. 124.

[13] Busch, pp. 125–127.

[14] Luongo and Hoehn, op. cit.

[15] "WMD 411 Chronology—2000." NTI. http://www.nti.org/f_wmd411/2000.html.

[16] Paul Kerr. "Russia, Iran Sign Deal to Fuel Nuclear Reactor" *Arms Control Today,* November 2006. www.armscontrol.org/act/2006_11/RussiaIran.asp. Retrieved January 21, 2001.

[17] "Russia's arms exporter denies reported missile supplies to Iran" RIA Novosti Russian News & Information Agency. http://en.rian/ru/russia/20061125/55985161.html. Retrieved January 21, 2007.

[18] Yaakov Katz and Herb Keinon. "Israel Warns Russia on Iran Arms Sale." *The Jerusalem Post.* Jan. 17, 2007. www.jpost.com/servlet/Satellite?pagename=JPost/JPArticle/ShowFull&cid=116746774535. Retrieved January 21, 2007.

[19] Robert S. Norris, Hans M. Kristensen, and Christopher E. Paine. *"Nuclear Insecurity: A Critique of the Bush Administration's Nuclear Weapons Policies."* The Natural Resources Defense Counsel, September 2004.

[20] Doctrine for Joint Nuclear Operations. p. JP 3-12-13. www.nukestrat.com/us/jcs/JCS_JP3-12_05draft.pdf. Retrieved January 4, 2007.

[21] Walter Pincus. "Pentagon Revises Nuclear Strike Plan." *Washington Post,* September 11, 2005, A1.

[22] Doctrine for Joint Nuclear Operations, I-4.

[23] Congresswoman Ellen O. Tauscher, 10th District, Calif., December 2,2005 press release, "Rep. Tauscher Cautions Against Aggressive Nuclear Policy." www.nukestrat.com/us/jcs/JP_Congress120205.pdf. Retrieved January 4, 2007.

[24] Ibid.

[25] Lawrence S. Wittner, "Why Bush Abandoned the Plan for New Nukes," Massachusetts in Peace Action. 10/31/05. www.masspeaceaction.org/no_new_nukes.htm. Retrieved January 4, 2007.

[26] The National Security Strategy of the United States, September 2002, p . 19. www.whitehouse.gov/nsc/nss5.html. Retrieved January 4, 2007.

[27] Michael E. O'Hanlon, Susan E. Rice, and James B. Steinberg. "Policy Brief #113, The New National Security Strategy and Preemption." December 2002, The Brookings Institution. www.brook.edu/comm/policybriefs/pb113.pdf. Retrieved January 4, 2007.

[28] President George W. Bush's Speech to the United Nations General Assembly, September 12, 2002. In Craig R. Whitney, ed., *The WMD Mirage: Iraq's Decade of Deception and America's False Premise for War.* New York: Public Affairs, 2005, pp. 13–14.

[29] Whitney, p. 5.

[30] Whitney, p. 175.

[31] BBC News, Thursday, 13 December 2001, 18:17 GMT. "America Withdraws from ABM Treaty." news.bbc.co.uk/2/hi/americas/1707812.stm. Retrieved March 8, 2007.

[32] Wade Boese. "Missile Defense Spending Soars to New Heights." *Arms Control Today,* March 2006. www.armscontrol.org/act/2007_01-02/index.asp. Retrieved March 8, 2007.

[33] "Nuclear Files: Timeline of the Nuclear Age: 1999." Available online. URL: http://www.nuclearfiles.org/menu/timeline/1990/1999.htm. Accessed November 16, 2007.

3

Global Perspectives

SOUTH ASIA

History of the Conflict

The region of South Asia consists of seven independent nations and one territory of the United Kingdom, all located on or near the Indian subcontinent. The list includes three of the most populous countries in the world—the Republic of India, with 1.1 billion inhabitants; the Islamic Republic of Pakistan, with 169 million; and the People's Republic of Bangladesh, with 147 million—as well as some of the least populous, such as the Republic of Maldives, with 329,000 inhabitants. Together, the inhabitants of South Asia represent about a fifth of the world's population; it is one of the most densely populated places on Earth.

Afghanistan, which lies to the northwest, is not technically a part of South Asia but is an important neighbor with close links and historical ties to Pakistan. In the late 1990s, Afghanistan was under the control of an Islamic fundamentalist group called the Taliban, which let al-Qaeda make the country its base of operations. In 2002, after the September 11 attacks, the United States helped an Afghan rebel group overthrow the Taliban. Al-Qaeda's leader, Osama bin Laden, probably fled from Afghanistan to neighboring Pakistan, where apparently he is sheltered by friendly tribesmen in areas the Pakistani government does not control.[1]

South Asia contains two of the world's nine nuclear weapons states, India and Pakistan. India exploded its first nuclear device in 1974 and followed up in May 1998 with a series of five nuclear weapons tests. Pakistan responded to India's five nuclear weapons tests with five of its own at the end of the same month. The entry of India and Pakistan into the "Nuclear Club" is regarded as the greatest failure to date of the international effort to counter the spread of nuclear weapons. That these two particular countries should be nuclear weapons states is particularly worrisome because they have fought

South Asia at a Glance

COUNTRY	POPULATION (MILLIONS, JULY 2008 EST.)	AREA (SQ. KM)	MAJOR RELIGIOUS GROUPS	OFFICIAL LANGUAGE	FORM OF GOVERNMENT	YEAR FOUNDED/ INDEPENDENCE
India	1,148	3,287,590	Hindu (81%) Muslim (12%) Christian (2.3%) Sikh 1.9%	Hindi and 14 others	Parliamentary democracy	1947
Pakistan	168	803,940	Muslim (97%)	Urdu	Military dictatorship	1947
Bangladesh	154	144,000	Muslim (88%) Hindu (11%)	Bengla	Parliamentary democracy	1971
Nepal	30	147,181	Hindu (80.6%) Buddhist (10.7%) Muslim (4.2%) Kirant (3.6%)	Nepali	Parliamentary monarchy	1923
Sri Lanka	21	65,610	Buddhist (68%) Hindu (18%) Muslim (8%) Christian (7%)	Singalese, Tamil	Parliamentary democracy	1947
Bhutan	.7	18,147	Buddhist (75%) Hindu (15%)	Dzongkha	Monarchy	1949
Maldives	.4	298	Muslim (100%)	Dhivehi	Republic	1965
British Indian Ocean Territory		60		English	Territory of the United Kingdom	1965

three major wars with each other since their creation in 1947 and are engaged in a bitter and violent territorial dispute in Kashmir, in which religion and terrorism play roles. Pakistan and India share a long border, the distances between the principal cities of the two countries are short, and the warning either side would get of a nuclear attack would be brief.

There are other reasons to regret the nuclear capabilities of India and Pakistan. While India has a stable government and a history of strong civilian control of the military, Pakistan has a history of political instability, coups d'état, and nuclear proliferation. A substantial minority of the Pakistani population are extreme Islamic fundamentalists. It is not easy to be certain who will control Pakistan's nuclear weapons in the future, who might have a finger on the button, and who might be given a bomb or bomb-making material. But above all, it is the continuing tensions between two states newly armed with nuclear weapons that led U.S. president Bill Clinton to describe South Asia as "the most dangerous place on Earth."

ORIGINS OF INDIA AND PAKISTAN AND THEIR CONFLICT

The modern states of India and Pakistan came into existence in 1947. Great Britain, exhausted and bankrupt after World War II, had decided to leave the colonial possession it had dominated since the 18th century. British India's last viceroy, Lord Louis Mountbatten (1900–79), was given the job of managing India's transition to independence in January 1947.

By that time, India's independence movement had split along religious lines into two major parties. The largest, the Indian National Congress (INC), was dominated by Hindus, who were the majority of India's very diverse population. The smaller party was the Muslim League, formed by Muslims who feared discrimination as a minority in an independent India. At different times, the Muslim League sought different means of protecting the rights of Muslims in the state that would come after independence; its primary demand was for specific constitutional protection for the Muslim minority in the future Indian state. As independence neared, however, the two sides found it difficult to compromise. Mountbatten came up with a two-state solution. The part of India that had been ruled directly by Great Britain would be divided into two large countries—India, with a multireligious, largely Hindu population, and Pakistan, with a predominantly Muslim population. Due to the distribution of the Muslim population, Pakistan would consist of two noncontiguous states, East Pakistan and West Pakistan. In addition, each of the several "princely states," South Asian states that Britain had ruled indirectly through their own monarchial governments, would decide for themselves whether to join India or Pakistan.[2]

The great Indian independence leader Mohandas K. Gandhi (1869–1948) disagreed with partition, and he was not alone in his opposition to it. When Mountbatten announced it in a radio broadcast on June 3, 1947, in New Delhi, there was widespread rioting. The partition plan nevertheless proceeded; India and Pakistan became independent on August 14, 1947. Two days later, when the boundaries of the new nations were announced, civil war broke out, which led to the mass migration of between 10 and 15 million Hindus, Muslims, and Sikhs, "the biggest and bloodiest peacetime mass migration in history," according to one historian.[3] Estimates of the number of people who died during this process range between 200,000 and 1 million, with 500,000 being the likeliest figure. Some of this violence amounted to what we would now call "ethnic cleansing," an effort to frighten people away with terror, but it went further, since people were attacked even while they were fleeing. Both Hindus and Muslims engaged in acts of extraordinary brutality, including systematic rape and mutilation. Women of the opposing group were tattooed or branded with the words "Pakistan Zindabad" (Long Live Pakistan) or "Hindustan Zindabad" (Long Live India)."[4] Such acts created an enduring legacy of hatred between the people of the two new nations.

Historians disagree about the causes of the enmity between Hindus and Muslims in India and Pakistan. Some see an inevitable cultural conflict that was bound to erupt when the British left the scene; others blame the British Empire's policy of "divide and rule" for treating Muslims and Hindus unequally and encouraging mutual suspicions. After the creation of the two countries, differences continued to be exacerbated by the disputes over territory, especially in Kashmir, and by Pakistan's fear of India, which had a much larger population and greater resources of all kinds. The cold war, too, contributed to the tensions. During the cold war, India sought to make itself into a socialist democracy and accepted a great deal of Soviet technical and military assistance while in theory remaining neutral—or, as Indians preferred to put it, "nonaligned,"—in the Soviet-U.S. competition. The United States, which suspected India of sliding into the Soviet orbit, formed a military alliance with Pakistan, seeking to make it into a bulwark against Soviet influence in South Asia.

India has the constitution of a representative, parliamentary democracy. Such constitutions do not always correspond to the reality of a country's politics, but Indian democracy has been genuine for most of the years since it was adopted in 1950; the exception was the period 1975–77, when Prime Minister Indira Gandhi (1917–84) used emergency powers to crack down on her political opponents. Even these two years of emergency rule, during which civil rights were suspended and the opposition jailed, were initiated by a civilian leader rather than a group of generals, as in all too many other countries, and it was ended voluntarily by Indira Gandhi herself. The military has never made policy in India, and the country has been free of the military coups that often plague developing nations. India's founders believed that religion and ethnic identity could not be the basis for an Indian state, since the country's population was so diverse. Only 81 percent of the population are Hindu; even following partition, fully 12 percent are Muslim (the remainder include Christians, Sikhs, Buddhists, Jains, and Parsis). There are 15 official languages; English is not one of them, yet it is the primary language spoken nationwide and widely used in business, science, and politics.[5]

Pakistan, in contrast to India, is a state based on religious and ethnic unity, growing out of Muslims' desires not to suffer discrimination as a minority in India, yet this unity has proven elusive, for Pakistan's ethnic and linguistic diversity is as great as India's. Members of Pakistan's several ethnic minorities grow up speaking their own languages, such as Punjabi, Pashto, Sindhi, or Siraiki. Pakistan's official national language, Urdu, is the first language of less than 8 percent of its inhabitants. The domination of the largest ethnic group, the Punjabis, arouses resentment in the other groups. Some Pakistani leaders have attempted to use Islam as a means of uniting the nation, but this is a rather dangerous strategy for Pakistan: Although 97 percent of Pakistanis today are Muslim, they practice different forms of Islam.[6]

For almost all of its history, Pakistan has been a politically unstable country; periods of civilian rule have alternated with periods during which the military has taken power. The loyalty of major Pakistani institutions to the central government is uncertain. There are mountainous tribal regions where the central government cannot impose its will. In 1971, East Pakistan, helped by India, broke away and became the separate country of Bangladesh. This conflict, Pakistan's third war with India, further increased the insecurity and repressiveness of Pakistan's government. Its outcome—the loss of a vast chunk of Pakistan's territory—was a key reason for Pakistan's decision to acquire nuclear weapons.

THE INDIA-PAKISTAN WARS

The conflict that would become Pakistan's first war with India broke out in July 1947 in Kashmir, a geographically vast, predominantly Muslim area with a long history of amicable relations between its Hindus and Muslims. Kashmir was one of the "princely states," whose governments were supposed to choose between India and Pakistan. The maharaja of Kashmir was a Hindu, while the population was predominantly Muslim; the maharaja hoped for Kashmir to become an independent state. Muslim rebels tried to take over the country so that it would join Pakistan. Soon, troops from Pakistan and

India intervened, each determined that Kashmir would be a part of their new state. In October 1947, the maharaja formally agreed to the accession of Kashmir to India, a legal change that was not accepted either by Pakistan or by the rebels. The war continued until a January 1949 cease-fire arranged by the UN Security Council. By then, India occupied about two-thirds of the territory, including Kashmir's best land and most of its natural resources. Pakistan occupied the remaining third.

War between India and Pakistan broke out again in 1965 after a series of skirmishes along the 1949 cease-fire line. Fighting spread quickly and escalated into a full-scale war in which the armies penetrated deep into their neighbors' territories and occupied each other's land. This territory was exchanged when the war formally ended in 1966; no progress had been made in resolving the Kashmir issue. To this day, Pakistan and India each claim the entirety of Kashmir.

The third war between India and Pakistan was the Bangladesh War of 1971, in which India aided the independence movement of East Pakistan, which chafed under the political and economic dominance of West Pakistan. India won a decisive victory in this war, and East Pakistan became the independent nation of Bangladesh. Kanishkan Sathasivam, the author of *Uneasy Neighbors,* a 2005 study of the mutual relationships of India, Pakistan, and the United States, believes that the 1971 war continues to influence the policies of the Pakistani government and the psychology of its people, and he cites several reasons. The loss deeply wounded Pakistan's national pride at the same time it reduced Pakistan's size in population and territory. Pakistan, already small by comparison with India, became smaller still. Furthermore, Pakistanis began to suspect that India wanted to destroy Pakistan entirely, perhaps by causing other Pakistani provinces to rebel and declare independence. This belief is "a core element of Pakistan's post-1971 national psychology," in Sathasivam's view. The war undermined Pakistan's very reason for being, since Bangladesh was a Muslim country in South Asia that had opted out of Pakistan, supposedly the South Asian state for Muslims.[7]

Additionally, the war influenced Pakistan's nuclear ambitions by making Pakistanis feel that outside alliances would not help them when they most needed it:.

> *Pakistan emerged from the 1971 war with a tremendous sense of victimization and bitterness over what it considered to have been betrayal and abandonment by its major ally, the United States. . . . To add to this "betrayal" by the United States, China had not aided Pakistan to any significant extent in the war. This bitterness contributed greatly to Paki-*

stan's subsequent single-minded pursuit of nuclear weapons, its political and military elites having resolved never again to rely on alliances, and explains why Pakistan resolutely rejected any and all entreaties by Washington during the late 1980s and 1990s to keep Pakistan from walking down the nuclear path.[8]

INDIA'S AND PAKISTAN'S NUCLEAR PROGRAMS

India began its nuclear research program in its first year after independence. From the beginning, the goal of the program was ambiguous. Its main purpose was the pursuit of cheap energy. But it also quietly aimed at giving India the ability to produce nuclear weapons.

India's first prime minister, Jawaharlal Nehru (1889–1964), had a worldwide reputation as an apostle of peace who had worked with Mahatma Gandhi. As the first head of state of a country that had gained its independence through the practice of nonviolence, Nehru did not want to be associated with a plan to acquire the most terrible weapons in existence. On the other hand, he knew that the technology for nuclear energy and nuclear weapons went together, and he was no pacifist in Mahatma Gandhi's sense—if nuclear weapons were needed for India's survival, he wanted India to have them. In 1948, the Indian government established an Indian Atomic Energy Commission. Nehru's words at the time expressed the double-sided nature of India's pursuit of atomic power:

> *We are now facing an atomic age. . . . If we have to remain abreast in the world as a nation which keeps ahead of things, we must develop this atomic energy quite apart from war. . . . Of course, if we are compelled as a nation to use it for other purposes, possibly no pious sentiments of any of us will stop the nation from using it that way.*[9]

Two-edged comments like this have always characterized Indian leaders' statements about nuclear weapons. In 1966, Indian prime minister Indira Gandhi echoed Nehru's remarks, acknowledging that nuclear expertise would be useful for bomb making should it be necessary: "We are building up our atomic power. Of course, we are using it for peaceful purposes; but in the meantime we are increasing our know-how and other competence."[10]

In the 1950s, India's own research program grew faster with help from Atoms for Peace, U.S. president Eisenhower's nonproliferation program, which was designed to provide countries with the means to develop nuclear energy in exchange for a promise not to manufacture nuclear weapons. In the 1960s, building on the industrial base and technologies it had already acquired on its own and through Atoms for Peace, India purchased equipment that would help it to separate plutonium, usable for a bomb.

By the time the Nuclear Nonproliferation Treaty (NPT) was being drafted in 1968, India was so far along in nuclear development that signing the treaty would have meant dismantling much of its program. After much debate in the country's parliament, India refused to sign. On May 18, 1974, India announced that it had conducted a "peaceful nuclear explosion." International reaction to India's test was surprisingly mild, far different from the recent reactions to North Korea's and Iran's nuclear programs. In private talks, U.S. secretary of state Henry Kissinger reportedly told Indira Gandhi "something to the effect of 'Congratulations. You did it, you showed you could build nuclear weapons. You have the bomb. Now what do we do to keep it from blowing up the world?'" France congratulated India. Japan expressed "regret," and Sweden said it was unfortunate but blamed the nuclear weapons states for not progressing toward the disarmament promised in the NPT. The Soviet Union expressed mild concern, and China did not react at all. Canada, which had supplied India with the nuclear reactor it had used to get plutonium for its bomb, regarded India's bomb as a betrayal of trust and froze all assistance for two nuclear reactors that were then under construction in India with Canadian help. The harshest criticism came from Pakistan's prime minister Zulfikar Ali Bhutto (1928–79), who called the explosion a "fateful development" and said that Pakistan was "determined not to be intimidated" and would never give in to "nuclear blackmail."[11] Pakistan had made plans to acquire nuclear weapons in 1972, after its 1971 defeat and the loss of Bangladesh. It announced in October 1974 that it would master the entire nuclear fuel cycle (enabling it to produce bomb making material), and on October 18 it signed an agreement with a French firm to construct a plutonium reprocessing plant in Chashma, Pakistan. Daniel Patrick Moynihan, U.S. ambassador to India, had anticipated Pakistan's response. In May 1974, after India's "peaceful" nuclear test, he told Indira Gandhi:

> *India has made a huge mistake. Here you were the No.1 hegemonic power in South Asia. Nobody was No. 2 and call Pakistan No. 3. Now in a decade's time, some Pakistani general will call you up and say I have four nuclear weapons and I want Kashmir. If not, we will drop them on you and we all meet in heaven. And then what will you do?*[12]

After this start, India's nuclear weapons program slowed down. Many influences combined to put a break on development. One important factor was stepped-up international efforts to halt nuclear proliferation in the late

1970s. Nuclear weapons states had formed an organization called the Nuclear Suppliers Group (NSG) in 1975 and agreed to restrict sales of nuclear weapon technology to states that did not already have the bomb. These agreements were imperfect—India did acquire nuclear materials and technology from abroad—but they slowed down the process. The United States and other nations used diplomacy and the threat of sanctions to dissuade India and Pakistan from developing nuclear weapons. When intelligence agencies began reporting that India and Pakistan probably had nuclear weapons, other nations tried to persuade India and Pakistan not to take the fateful next step of testing the weapons and declaring themselves to be nuclear weapons states.

The Indian nuclear weapons program grew slowly during this period. There was little money to spare for nuclear weapons, which were a low priority for the Indian people. As Moynihan had pointed out, a nuclear arms race between India and Pakistan would not be to India's benefit. Thus, almost two and a half decades passed between the 1974 test and India's 1998 tests. In the 1980s, India developed its own brand of ballistic missile capable of reaching targets in Pakistan and China. Pakistan also developed and tested ballistic missiles.

INDIA'S MOTIVE FOR BUILDING THE BOMB

Why did India develop the bomb? Analysts disagree about the reasons. The controversy is worth exploring since we must understand the reasons nuclear weapons spread if their spread is to be prevented. The usual explanation, based on the order in which nuclear weapons were achieved in the region, is a sort of domino effect: China developed nuclear weapons out of fear of its nuclear neighbor Russia, India developed nuclear weapons out of fear of China, and Pakistan developed nuclear weapons out of fear of India.

George Perkovich, author of *India's Nuclear Bomb: The Impact on Global Proliferation* (1999), disagrees with this view, which he identifies with the "realist" school of international relations. While Pakistan's quest for the bomb is explainable by realist considerations, Perkovich says, India's motivations had more to do with the Indian public's desire to see India possess the symbols of "great power" status, nuclear weapons being one of them. Though national security needs certainly influenced the many decisions that led India down the nuclear road, these decisions were also influenced by many other factors such as

> *the perception that nuclear capabilities symbolize India's achievement of scientific-technical prowess and national sovereignty and establish India's membership in the aristocracy of nuclear states who set the*

standards of international rank. India also perceives the U.S.-led nonproliferation regime as a racist, colonial project to deny India the fruits of its own labor and the tools of its own security.[13]

It is a complicated question, and by choosing facts selectively a convincing case could be made to prove either conclusion. Against the realist position, it is certainly true that India's real security would have been greater if neither India nor Pakistan had nuclear weapons, and many statements by Indian leaders show that national pride played a part in India's decision to develop them. Though China had nuclear weapons targeting India, the likelihood that they would be used was very small. Other countries have had nuclear neighbors without acquiring nuclear weapons.

On the other hand, India's problems with Pakistan were deep and intractable. They are enough to provide a "realist" explanation for the development of nuclear weapons by both countries. India would have a realist motive to have nuclear weapons if Pakistan had them, and after the Bangladesh war, it was very likely that Pakistan would try to develop nuclear weapons. Pakistanis felt that their country's survival was threatened, and they knew Pakistan could not defeat India in a conventional war. For Pakistan, nuclear weapons seemed to make sense as an insurance against attack or intimidation by India; with or without India's nuclear program, Pakistan was likely to attempt to acquire nuclear weapons or develop them on their own.

Thus, though India's nuclear program came first, the decision to move from a nuclear capability to nuclear weapons was made under the assumption that Pakistan would eventually have nuclear weapons. In fact, the two countries, recognizing they were in a nuclear arms race, discussed controlling the race in the early 1990s. Both sides were aware that each might be tempted to attack the other's nuclear facilities; in 1992 they exchanged lists of the facilities as a preparation for an agreement not to attack them.[14]

These considerations pushed India down the nuclear path. But why did India conduct nuclear tests exactly when it did? It could have conducted them years earlier or years later. In 1998, however, an ultranationalist party, the Bharatiya Janata Party (BJP), held the balance of power in the nation's parliament. The Indian public was beginning to be dissatisfied with the BJP; the BJP's leadership was seen as weak and disorganized. The BJP hoped to change that image with a defiant move to let India finally announce itself as a nuclear weapons state.

INDIA AND PAKISTAN CONDUCT TWIN NUCLEAR TESTS

And so, 24 years after its first "peaceful nuclear explosion" in 1974, India shocked the world by testing three nuclear weapons on May 11, 1998. One of the tests was reportedly of a thermonuclear weapon. Two days later it conducted two more tests. Polls in India showed that the Indian public overwhelmingly approved of the tests, as the BJP leadership had hoped. In Washington, D.C., the Clinton administration was dismayed and angry, not only at the tests themselves, but because they had been given no warning of them, either publicly or privately.

At the month's end, on May 26, 1998, as an obvious reply to India, Pakistan detonated five nuclear devices in a single day. "Today, we have settled a score," Pakistan's prime minister, Nawaz Sharif (1949–), declared over national television.

It was India's turn to be shocked. Politicians in India's opposition parties accused the government of unleashing a nuclear arms race; India's prime minister, Atal Behari Vajpayee (1929–), told them that faced with this outside threat they must show unity. One opposition leader, S. Jaipal Reddy, nevertheless pointed out what India had lost by turning its rivalry with Pakistan into a nuclear rivalry: "India had a decisive military edge over Pakistan. We must remember that an atom bomb is a great equalizer. With this test, the edge that India had has been wiped out."[15]

The U.S. Congress imposed economic sanctions on India and Pakistan, blocking an assortment of loans and credits to their governments and banning the export to India or Pakistan of technology that could be used to make nuclear weapons or missiles. However, President Clinton asked Congress to give him the power to rescind some of these sanctions in exchange for concessions from either India or Pakistan. From Clinton's point of view, it was unrealistic to believe that India or Pakistan would dismantle their nuclear weapons programs. The aim of diplomacy should be to contain the damage, to prevent an all-out nuclear arms race between India and Pakistan. Clinton attempted without success to get the two nations to sign the CTBT. Congress, under pressure from the U.S. Farm lobby, rolled back some of the sanctions within months.

In 1999, India and Pakistan once again came close to war over Kashmir; Pakistani forces, together with Kashmiri militants based in Pakistan, crossed into the Indian side of the Line-of-Control and battled with Indian forces for several weeks. They were finally driven back by Indian forces with the help of diplomatic pressure from the United States. Kanishkan Sathasivam points out that India chose not to pursue the Pakistani forces beyond the Line-of-Control, and notes:

> *This unwillingness on the part of India to carry the battle across the LoC seemed to reinforce Pakistan's belief that no matter the level of provocation, India would not go so far as to risk full-blown war with Pakistan.*[16]

Clearly, the possession of nuclear weapons was a much greater help to Pakistan than it was to India.

2002: THE MOST DANGEROUS YEAR

The 9/11 attacks caused immediate changes in the relationship between the United States and both India and Pakistan. As the United States was preparing for war in Afghanistan, both India and Pakistan agreed to an unprecedented degree of cooperation with the United States. India allowed its territory to be used as a base for U.S. air strikes on Afghanistan, something that would have been inconceivable through most of modern India's history. Pakistan's military dictator, Pervez Musharraf (1943–), was in a particularly difficult position: Pakistan was one of only three countries that had officially recognized the Taliban regime in Afghanistan, who were known to have provided a safe haven to Osama bin Laden and his terrorist organization, al-Qaeda. Powerful and potentially violent forces within Pakistan would likely attempt to unseat Musharraf if he now helped the United States defeat the Taliban. Nevertheless, Musharraf chose to cooperate with the United States. In the meantime, the United States lifted all that remained of the sanctions that had been imposed on India and Pakistan after their nuclear weapons tests.

While much of the world's attention was fixed on Afghanistan, India and Pakistan came close to war. Using the tactics that were becoming popular with Islamic rebels all over the world, Kashmiri militants began to conduct suicide attacks against Indian military and civilian targets. On December 13, 2001, five Islamic terrorists armed with guns attacked the Indian parliament in New Delhi, killing seven people (none of them politicians) and injuring 18 others before being killed themselves. Indians saw the attack as a Pakistani plot to eliminate India's leadership and prepared for war. More than half a million Indian troops were mobilized along the 1,300-kilometer India-Pakistan border. The Indian chief of staff announced that his forces were "fully ready" for all-out conventional war with Pakistan.[17]

India has an overwhelming conventional military superiority to Pakistan; this imbalance increases the danger that a conventional war between India and Pakistan would escalate to nuclear war. Pakistan, feeling that its survival was threatened, might deploy nuclear weapons at a very early stage of such a war.[18]

Fortunately, the India-Pakistan war of 2002 never took place, and in 2003 the two sides agreed to a cease-fire along their mutual border, including the Line-of-Control in Kashmir. Though neither country has signed the CTBT, India and Pakistan have agreed in high level talks with each other not to conduct further nuclear tests for the foreseeable future. Both countries have tested ballistic missiles since 2002; to avoid the danger of a missile launch being mistaken for an attack, they have an agreement to warn each other beforehand of missile tests.

UNITED STATES PLEDGES NUCLEAR ASSISTANCE TO INDIA

In a further relaxation of its nuclear policy toward India, in 2005 the United States agreed to supply India with civilian nuclear technology and conventional military equipment. In return, India agreed to place some civilian nuclear facilities, but not its nuclear weapons program, under international monitoring and to refrain from further nuclear weapons tests. The deal was criticized as an abandonment of nonproliferation policies. Critics pointed out that even though the materials would go only to India's nuclear power reactors, the effect would be to free up more uranium for India's nuclear weapons. An article in *Foreign Policy* objected to the deal as a further erosion of the NPT.

> *The NPT is based on a central bargain: Existing weapon states agree to disarm gradually, and cooperate on nuclear energy issues with nonnuclear weapon states, who, in return, give up their right to have nuclear weapons. The deal now on the table breaks the fragile balance of the treaty's bargain. It permits nuclear cooperation with India—a state in possession of nuclear weapons not recognized by the NPT—without requiring India to accept nonproliferation conditions or make the concessions that apply to nearly all other states. This exceptionalism built into the deal would create a dangerous double-standard and reverse longstanding U.S. nonproliferation policy. It also infuriates neighboring Pakistan, which pressed the United States for a similar deal in March [2006], only to receive the cold shoulder.*[19]

Henry Sokolski of the Nonproliferation Policy Education Center favors a certain amount of exceptionalism, a policy that "distinguished between progressive and hostile illiberal regimes."[20] Nevertheless, he, too, believed that the current U.S. deal with India weakens the NPT. In a May 26, 2006, debate posted online by the Council on Foreign Relations, Sokolski argued:

> *Article I of the Non-Proliferation Treaty (NPT) currently obliges the United States not to help a state's military nuclear efforts in any way if that state did not have a bomb before 1968.... it's the rules. Violate them, as the United States is proposing to do by giving India access to foreign uranium, settle for the meager nonproliferation commitments*

India has offered so far, and the nuclear rules will only be weakened even further.[21]

Defenders of the agreement pointed out that India, Pakistan, and Israel are already nuclear weapons states outside the NPT system. "In some ways, the nonproliferation system has already lost its virginity," said Teresita Schaffer, director of the South Asia program at the Center for Strategic and International Studies, in reply to Sokolski. She pointed out that the head of the IAEA, France, Britain, and Russia all support the U.S. deal with India. One reason they do, she said, "is that for the past thirty years, India has kept its nuclear commitments and has not exported its nuclear goods or know-how."

As of November 2007, the United States's deal with India was still being debated. The U.S. Congress had yet to approve it.

PAKISTAN AS A PROLIFERATOR

In December 2003, when the United States's had ousted the Taliban from Afghanistan and was preparing for war in Iraq, Libya's dictator, Muammar al-Qaddafi (1942–)—a sponsor of international terrorism since the 1970s whose country has long been on the United States's list of "rogue states"—decided that it would be better to work with the United States than against it. His government announced that henceforth Libya would stop trying to acquire nuclear weapons and cooperate with international nonproliferation efforts. As part of its cooperation, Libya revealed something very useful and at the same time rather awkward for the United States. It revealed that for some time Libya and other "rogue states," including Iran and North Korea, had been receiving nuclear weapons technology from a network run by Dr. Abdul Qadeer Khan, the father of Pakistan's nuclear weapons program. Dr. Khan was perhaps the most honored and admired man in Pakistan.

As the news of the A. Q. Khan network filtered out to the public, India accused Pakistan of being a major proliferator of nuclear weapons, especially to North Korea. The Pakistani government denied it. "All our [nuclear] assets are under strict control," Musharraf asserted on September 25, 2003. "I can guarantee they will not fall in the wrong hands."[22]

On February 4, 2004, Dr. Khan admitted on Pakistani television that during the past two decades he had secretly provided North Korea, Libya, and Iran with crucial technological and intellectual building blocks for making nuclear weapons. Insisting that he had done all this on his own, without the knowledge of Pakistan's government, Khan apologized to the people of

Pakistan for what he had done. He was pardoned by Pakistani president Musharraf shortly afterward.

Could A. Q. Khan really have passed on secret information without the knowledge or permission of his government? The United States preferred to take Pakistan's word for it. In 2004 and for some years afterward, Pakistan would be a key ally in the United States's effort to prevent the Taliban from retaking control of Afghanistan, and it would not help to displease or destabilize its government. President Bush, in a speech given later the same month, praised the work of U.S. intelligence agencies in cracking the case but did not discuss to what extent the Pakistani government might have assisted the Khan network; nor did he criticize President Musharraf's decision to pardon Dr. Khan. To do so would have triggered U.S. sanctions against Pakistan.

Nevertheless, U.S. officials have stated they would not seek to engage in nuclear cooperation with Pakistan because of its poor proliferation record. Pakistan is still seeking such a deal.

How To Respond When Nonproliferation Fails

The graduation of India and Pakistan to the status of nuclear weapons states raises a host of questions for students of nonproliferation. Will the NPT unravel because it has been flouted by these two countries that never signed it? Or can it be shored up and patched up, perhaps by bringing India and Pakistan partway into it. Would doing that be seen as a reward for bad behavior, leading other states to imitate India and Pakistan, or simply an exercise of realism that recognizes the unique security situation of these two countries?

Indians believe that as a modernizing country with more than a billion people, a country that has acted responsibly—not supported terrorism, not exported its technology to "rogue states"—they deserve to be among the handful of countries that possess nuclear weapons. But if India has nuclear weapons on those grounds, on what grounds should Pakistan have them, which is a smaller country, is suspected of supporting terrorists in Kashmir, and has shared nuclear technology with Iran and North Korea, but faces a nuclear threat in India? Should there be a different policy for India and Pakistan?

What is the most useful response for the United States, its allies, and the world in general when, despite our best efforts, nuclear weapons spread to new countries? Should the response be tough or soft? Should the new nuclear weapons states be punished through sanctions, or is it too late for sanctions to change anything? Should the United States make piecemeal concessions to would-be nuclear weapons states in exchange for specific agreements giving something back, such as agreement to permit IAEA inspections or some guarantee to limit the export of nuclear materials and technology? Should the United States. fight the spread of nuclear weapons whenever and wherever they appear, or should it concentrate on fighting the spread of nuclear weapons to states that might threaten U.S. interests?

Whatever the ultimate answers to these questions, the case of India and Pakistan is a reminder that the spread of nuclear weapons is always a gradual process. India and Pakistan with nuclear capabilities are not as dangerous as India and Pakistan with weapons deployed and aimed at each other's cities. India and Pakistan each with a handful of deployed nuclear weapons are still not as dangerous as India and Pakistan each bristling with hundreds of warheads. The effort to counter a given nation's weapons' program does not end when it announces the explosion of a bomb.

THE MIDDLE EAST

History of the Conflict

The Middle East, as the term is generally used today, consists of Bahrain, Egypt, Iran, Iraq, Israel, Jordan, Kuwait, Lebanon, Oman, Qatar, Saudi Arabia, Syria, Turkey, the United Arab Emirates, and Yemen as well as the lands currently occupied by Israel, which one day may make up the Palestinian state. It is home tc around 352 million people, a little under 6 percent of the world's population. With the exception of Iran, Turkey, and Israel, the majority of the people in these states are Arabic speaking. With the exception of Israel, the majority religion is Islam.

The American people know the Middle East as a place where oil comes from and where, coincidentally or not, a lot of its troubles originate: The United States has fought two wars in the Middle East in 15 years; the Middle East was the birthplace of the 9/11 hijackers who considered it their "religious duty" to attack the United States; it is the location of the cruel and seemingly endless Israeli-Palestinian conflict; it is home to Iran, whose citizens, with the encouragement of their leaders, chant "Death to America;" its governments for the most part are undemocratic; it abounds in kings and dictators; the boundaries of some of its states, drawn at the ends World Wars I and II, are in dispute; and it is in the throes of an Islamic fundamentalist movement, whose more fanatical adherents are also often violent and who want to replace the region's secular regimes with Islamic governments. Millions of Americans hold it as an article of faith that the battle of Armageddon will begin there sometime soon.[23]

The Middle East at a Glance

COUNTRY	POPULATION (MILLIONS, JULY 2008 EST.	AREA (SQ. KM)	MAJOR RELIGIOUS GROUPS	OFFICIAL LANGUAGE	FORM OF GOVERNMENT	YEAR FOUNDED/ INDEPENDENCE
Egypt	82	1,001,449	Muslim (90%) Christian (10%)	Arabic	Republic (authoritarian)	1922
Turkey	72	783,562	Muslim (99%)	Turkish	Parliamentary democracy	1919
Iran	66	1,648,195	Muslim (98%)	Persian	Theocracy with some democracy	Modern Iran: 1906 Revolution: 1979
Iraq	28	438,317	Muslim (97%)	Arabic	Parliamentary democracy	1932
Saudi Arabia	28	2,149,690	Muslim (by law, all citizens must be Muslim)	Arabic	Absolute monarchy	1926
Yemen	23	527,968	Muslim (99%)	Arabic	Republic	1990
Syria	20	183,885	Muslim (90%) Christian (10%)	Arabic	One-party dictatorship	1946
Israel	7	20,770	Jewish (76%) Muslim (16%) Christian (2%)	Hebrew; Arabic	Parliamentary democracy	1948
Jordan	6	92,342	Muslim (92%) Christian (6%)	Arabic	Constitutional monarchy	1950

(continued)

The Middle East at a Glance *(continued)*

COUNTRY	POPULATION (MILLIONS, JULY 2008 EST.	AREA (SQ. KM)	MAJOR RELIGIOUS GROUPS	OFFICIAL LANGUAGE	FORM OF GOVERNMENT	YEAR FOUNDED/ INDEPENDENCE
United Arab Emirates	4.6	83,600	Muslim (62%) Hindu (25%) Christian (8.5%) Buddhist (4%)	Arabic	Constitutional monarchy	
Lebanon	3.9	10,452	Muslim (56%) Christian (40%)	Arabic	Parliamentary democracy, with confessionalism	1942
Qatar	.9	11,437	Muslim (93%)	Arabic	Monarchy	1971
Oman	2.7	119,498	Muslim (87.5%) Hindu (5.6%)	Arabic	Absolute monarchy	1971
Kuwait	2.6	17,818	Muslim (85%)	Arabic	Costitutional Monarchy	1961

It is no wonder that the thought of the spread of nuclear weapons in the Middle East obsesses policy makers in Washington, D.C. Neither is it surprising that some governments in the Middle East have sought nuclear weapons as a source of safety and influence in a dangerous neighborhood.

The Middle East's tangled politics are further complicated by the fact that Russia, the United States, and Europe consider the region vital to their strategic interests and have been meddling in its affairs for more than a century and a half. The very term *Middle East* was coined by a military theorist, Alfred Thayer Mahan, in 1902 to draw attention to the importance of the Persian Gulf and the Suez Canal for naval power and thus for trade and war—whoever controlled this region controlled the world, said Thayer.[24] Though the Middle East had once been home to the world's most advanced civilizations, its people had been left behind by the Industrial Revolution. By the middle of the 19th century, the region's economies, armies, and governments were unable to compete with those of Europe. Since Thayer's time, the region's oil resources have provided outsiders with an additional motive to influence Middle Eastern politics.

U.S. intervention has often been crucial in the Middle East, a fact bitterly resented in the region. To highlight some of the best-known interventions:

- **Saudi Arabia.** The support of U.S. oil companies and U.S. governments has kept the Saud family in power in oil-rich Saudi Arabia. Although the United States imports only about 11 percent of its oil from Saudi Arabia, Saudi cooperation helps keep world oil prices in check, which is helpful to the United States.
- **Iran.** In 1953, when a popularly elected Iranian leader named Mohammed Mossadegh nationalized Iran's oil industries, the U.S. CIA intervened to overthrow him and to restore Shah Reza Pahlavi (1919–80), who had fled the country after falling out with Mossadegh, to the Iranian throne.[25] This U.S. intervention is one reason why the revolutionary Islamic regime that ousted the shah in 1979 calls the United States the "Great Satan."
- **Israel.** The United States, which strongly supports the state of Israel, is seen in the Middle East as the only country capable of forcing Israel to make concessions that would allow for the establishment of a Palestinian state. Those in the Middle East who do not accept Israel's existence see it as a puppet or proxy of the United States. Those who accept Israel's existence but want to see an end to the Israeli-Palestinian conflict blame the United States for not achieving a solution.

- **Iraq.** In the 1980s, the administration of Ronald Reagan supplied Saddam Hussein's Iraq with weapons to help it in its war with Iran. In 1991 and again in 2003, the United States went to war in Iraq.
- **Libya.** In 1986, American planes attacked Tripoli, the capital of Libya, and other targets in Libya, killing at least 100 people. The attacks were launched in retaliation for a Libyan-sponsored terrorist attack on Americans.

As of 2007, only one state in the Middle East, Israel, had nuclear weapons. Iraq and Libya had formerly had nuclear weapons programs, both of which have been dismantled. Iran is believed to be actively seeking the capability of making nuclear weapons. Since Iran is, at least in theory, committed to exporting its revolution, is a supporter of terrorism, and is regarded with suspicion by its neighbors, its ambition to achieve nuclear capability is both understandable and worrying for the peace of the region.

ISRAEL

Modern Israel was created in 1948 as a Jewish state by a vote of the UN; its creation was the culmination of a political movement called Zionism. In the late 1800s, Zionists decided that a country of their own was the best answer to the history of persecution and anti-Semitism the Jews had experienced as a dispersed people in Christian Europe and the Islamic Middle East.

Zionism was a secular movement. The first Zionists considered establishing a Jewish state in North America or sub-Saharan Africa, to which Jews have no historical or religious ties. They quickly found, however, that there was only one place that could fire the imaginations of their fellow Jews. That place was the ancient biblical homeland of Israel, or Palestine as it was then called, a strip of dry land that in the 1800s was under the rule of the decaying Ottoman Empire. Over the course of several decades, as the Ottoman Empire disintegrated and Palestine fell under the control of Great Britain, Zionists continued to buy land in Palestine, to colonize it, and to build the institutions of a state. The murder of 6 million European Jews during World War II created new militancy among Zionists, who used violence and in some cases terrorism to drive the British out of the country. Britain turned the matter over to the UN, which voted to divide the land into two adjacent states, one for Jews and one for Palestinian Arabs.

The region's Arab states rejected the plan and attacked Israel in 1948. As an outcome of the war that followed, Israel emerged with a much larger territory than it had been granted by the UN, three quarters of a million Palestinians fled or were driven from their homes, and the remainder of the territory intended for the new Arab state was annexed by Jordan. Millions of

Jews from Europe, the Middle East, and Russia emigrated to Israel, which in the half century since has proved itself a viable, though beleaguered, state.

The region's Arab countries remained hostile to Israel. In 1967, the armies of Egypt, Syria, and Jordan, with additional troops supplied by Iraq, Saudi Arabia, and Kuwait, massed for an attack on Israel, a mobilization that may have been intended as a bluff. Greatly outnumbered in men and arms, Israel launched a preemptive strike. By the war's end, six days later, Israel controlled vast stretches of its neighbors' territories.

This "Six-Day War" of 1967 marked a turning point in the modern history of the Middle East for several reasons. The humiliating defeat of the modernizing, secular Arab states made Arab intellectuals look to Islamic fundamentalism as a way to unify and strengthen their people.[26] Palestinian nationalists, with a new level of support from Arabs, began to hijack planes and kill Israeli civilians in a campaign that succeeded in publicizing their grievances and made terrorism look good to future generations of Arabs and non-Arabs in the Middle East. In the mid-1970s, after another war with Egypt and Syria, Israel returned most of Egypt's territory in exchange for peace and recognition but retained control over several other territories. These include the whole of Jerusalem (Israel had held only West Jerusalem before 1967; East Jerusalem, because it is the location of sites holy to Judaism, Christianity, and Islam, is a dangerous political flashpoint); the Golan Heights (Syrian territory); the Gaza Strip (formerly Egyptian territory); and the land between the River Jordan and the official boundary of Israel, usually called the "West Bank." Most fatefully of all, Israel began to build settlements on the West Bank and the Gaza Strip, territory inhabited by millions of Palestinian Arabs.

Israel's long conflict with the Palestinian Arabs has been marked on both sides by racism, myth making, and a tendency to demonize the enemy. Palestinian "suicide bombers" blow themselves up in an attempt to kill as many Israeli civilians as they can. Israel replies with attacks on Palestinian towns, attacks in which Palestinian civilians are killed. Opinion polls taken in Israel and among Palestinians show that the majority of both populations favor a "two state solution" in which a Palestinian state is established on the West Bank and the Gaza Strip, yet their leaders have shown themselves unable to make the hard decisions needed to bring about this solution.

The Israeli Nuclear Program

Israel embarked on a nuclear weapons program in its earliest years as a state, hunting in the Negev desert for uranium reserves, which failed to materialize. In 1952, the country created an Israeli Atomic Energy Commission, whose chairman asserted that an Israeli bomb was the best way to assure "that we shall never again be led as lambs to the slaughter."[27] In the 1950s, with the help of French nuclear technicians, Israel built a nuclear reactor and a chemical reprocessing plant capable of turning the reactor's products into fissile material usable for weapons.

The Israeli nuclear program was conducted in secret, outside the supervision of the IAEA of the UN; though there is no doubt that Israel has nuclear weapons, experts disagree as to when it first had them and how many it has possessed at any given time. It is believed that by 1967, Israel had two nuclear weapons, which Israel's prime minister Levi Eshkol (1895–1969) ordered ready for use during the Six-Day War.[28] The following year, a report by the U.S. CIA concluded that Israel had begun to produce nuclear weapons. The country has had in excess of 100 nuclear weapons at least since the 1980s.[29]

Israel clearly means for its neighbors to know that it has nuclear weapons—they would be useless as a deterrent otherwise—but its policy has been to maintain officially that it is a nonnuclear state and to keep the exact number of weapons it possesses a secret. In 1986, when a former Israeli nuclear worker named Mordechai Vanunu revealed details about the Israeli nuclear weapons program to a British newspaper, he was regarded as a traitor by most Israelis; Vanunu was led into a trap by Israeli intelligence and sentenced to 18 years of imprisonment. According to former Israeli prime minister Shimon Peres (1923–), who testified for the prosecution at Vanunu's trial, "A certain amount of secrecy must be maintained in some fields. The suspicion and fog surrounding this question are constructive, because they strengthen our deterrent."[30]

Israel has not signed the NPT. It is attached to its nuclear deterrent, even though it has the strongest conventional force in the region. It is interesting and perhaps important to examine the effect of Israel's nuclear deterrent in the light of political scientist Kenneth M. Waltz's theories regarding the effects of the possession of nuclear weapons on war. Nuclear weapons did not prevent the Egyptian attack on territories held by Israel during the 1973 Yom Kippur War. However, that attack, though very damaging to Israel's armed forces, was not directed against Israel's core territories; it did not threaten Israel's survival. Since 1973, Israel has endured incursions by irregular fighters, attacks by suicide bombers, and rockets fired into its territory from Lebanon and Iraq, but there has been no invasion of Israel since 1973.

Israel is also not a signatory to the Missile Technology Control Regime, and it maintains one of the largest, if not the largest, ballistic missile programs in the Middle East. Israel's missile program, like its nuclear program, is secret; even the exact names of its missiles are in dispute.

The United States has said very little on the subject of Israel's nuclear weapons while objecting heatedly to nuclear weapons programs in Libya, Iraq, and Iran and demanding international action on them. Other states in the region regard this position as the height of hypocrisy. Israel used a program of peaceful nuclear power generation as a cover for the development of nuclear weapons. Since Israel has not signed the NPT, its nuclear weapons program does not violate the treaty. Otherwise it did exactly what Iran is accused of doing. Israel, however, has not called for the destruction of Iran, while the president of Iran has said that Israel should be "wiped off the map."[31]

In December 2003, the head of the IAEA, Egyptian Mohamed ElBaradei, told the Israeli newspaper *Haaretz* that the IAEA operated under the assumption that Israel had nuclear weapons. He urged Israel to sign the NPT, agree to inspections, and disarm, saying that Israel's nuclear capability did not enhance the country's capability, since it only made other Middle Eastern countries feel threatened. It seems unlikely, however, that Israel would disarm voluntarily in the absence of a comprehensive Middle East peace agreement, including official recognition of Israel by other countries in the region.[32]

IRAN

Iran, also called Persia in the West, was home to more than one of the great empires of the ancient world. Much of its culture and folkways, such as the covering of women's faces, were practiced in Persia thousands of years ago. Iran is also a new, revolutionary state. In 1979, the modernizing but autocratic shah Reza Pahlavi, son of the founder of modern Iran, was overthrown in a popular revolution. Many segments of Iranian society, both secular and religious, fundamentalist and Marxist, had been discontented with the rule of the shah, who had kept control only through ruthless use of the army and secret police. A 76-year-old Muslim cleric, Ayatollah Ruholla Khomeini (1902–89), was the spiritual leader of the revolt, and he soon showed extraordinary political talents in shaping the fluid revolutionary conditions. Khomeini played his allies against each other and consolidated his power as the ruler of an Islamic fundamentalist state.

Khomeini believed—and persuaded most of the Iranian people to agree—that the Koran as administered by Islamic clerics should be the law of the land, as supposedly it had been in the days of the Prophet. Since he was the supreme Islamic cleric in the country, Khomeini had authority greater than the president, prime minister, and elected parliament of Iran. Khomeini and his followers declared that all other current regimes of Islamic countries were corrupt and un-Islamic and therefore deserved to be overthrown. He declared his opposition to Israel, reversing the position of Iran under the shah, who had been tacitly, though not publicly, an ally of Israel. When militants stormed the U.S. embassy in Tehran, taking 50 U.S. hostages, Khomeini did nothing to stop them, though the action violated international diplomatic norms. The United States in response declared Iran an international outlaw; Khomeini had already denounced the United States as the Great Satan.[33]

Iran's religious establishment continued to consolidate its authority during Iran's eight-year war with Iraq, which invaded Iran in 1980. The Iraq-Iran conflict, during which the region's Arab states as well as the United States supplied Iraq with arms, pulled Iranians together. Dissent was stifled, as it often is in time of war. The struggle with Iraq was seen as a war of survival, though Iran continued to fight it long after Saddam Hussein's armed forces had been beaten back and Saddam was ready to make peace. It was during this war that Khomeini and his clerics developed an Islamic justification for suicide, which traditionally had been thought to be condemned by the Koran. Khomeini sent teenage boys, nearly all under 15 years old, to walk across minefields in advance of his armies, deliberately sacrificing their lives. Each little martyr had been given a plastic key to heaven to hang around his neck so he would be motivated with a guarantee of salvation. Whatever their effect on the war and on public opinion in Iran, such acts of fanaticism made outsiders question the rationality of Iran's leadership.

After Khomeini's death in 1989, Iran's religious establishment remained in power but pursued a milder policy aimed at normalizing relations with the West. Iranian officials have stated that they do not want Iran to remain an outlaw state, and many of their actions support this contention. However, its leaders are compelled to uphold the ideology of the Islamic revolution, which is the theoretical basis of their power. In this, Iran's predicament is similar to that of other revolutionary regimes such as the French Republic in the 18th century and Russia after 1917. As one analyst puts it, "Normalization and routinization of foreign policy necessitates jettisoning revolutionary claims, which are believed to be an intrinsic part of the regime's legitimacy. The revolutionary impulse competes with a detached pragmatism and often subverts it."[34]

Isolation

Even before its revolutionary leaders declared all the other regimes in the region to be illegitimate, Iran had an uneasy relationship with its neighbors, with whom it has many intractable differences. The Iranians are not Arabs—the name *Iran* ("Land of the Aryans") reflects this, for it refers to the fact that Iranians are Aryans; their language, Persian, is Indo-European rather than

Semitic. Ethnically and linguistically, Iranians belong to a minority in the Middle East.

In religion as well, Iranians are in the minority. Most of the people are adherents of the Shia sect of Islam rather than the Sunni sect, to which the vast majority of the approximately 1.2 billion Muslims around the world belong. Only in Iran, Iraq, Bahrain, and Lebanon do Shiites outnumber Sunnis, and until recently Iraq's minority Sunnis were in control of that country. As Iraq's civil war shows, Shiites and Sunnis can be fierce enemies. When Afghanistan became an Islamic fundamentalist state under the Taliban in the late 1990s, there was mutual hostility between Iran and Afghanistan, though they were both revolutionary Islamic regimes: The Taliban were Sunnis. Thus, even if all the secular states of the Middle East were to be overthrown by Islamic revolutions, Iran could be surrounded by enemies—indeed, its isolation would be more acute, since religion would be an even stronger influence on foreign policy.

Though neither its revolution nor its survival is threatened, Iran seeks greater influence in the Middle East. Its people and its leaders feel it is entitled to leadership as a country with great oil wealth, a large, relatively well-educated population, a strategic location between the Middle East and the Indian subcontinent, and a potentially strong industrial base. Yet it is denied this leadership by its Arab neighbors, and as of 2003 it found itself flanked by the armed forces of the United States, in Afghanistan to the east and Iraq to the west.

Friends and Technology Suppliers: Russia and China

Isolated in the Middle East, sworn enemy of the United States, and viewed by Europe with suspicion, Iran has sought a strategic relationship with Russia. Since the early years of Khomeini's revolution, Iran has had a tacit agreement with Russia: Iran refrained from exporting its revolution to the Soviet Union (an officially atheist state containing many millions of Muslims), and in exchange the USSR gave Iran arms and technology. This relationship continued after the collapse of the Soviet Union.

Iran seeks warm relations with China as well. It regards China as a rising power in Asia, and it looks to cooperation with an Asian power as a counterweight to Europe and the United States. China, for its part, has shown itself eager to profit by sales of its technology and to build commercial relationships all over the world without respect to religion or ideology.

In recent years both Russia and China have supplied Iran with nuclear technology over the objections of Europe and the United States. Yet neither Russia nor China really wants Iran to have nuclear weapons, and neither country wants to go so far as to upset their own relationship with the United States.

Iran's Claims and the World's Suspicions

Iran claims that it is developing nuclear power for its own energy needs now and in the future. It is doing so, say Iran's leaders, because it has a right to nuclear technology under the terms of the NPT, which it has signed, and because nuclear know-how is a characteristic of a modern, forward-thinking state. Iran's leaders say that other countries, particularly the United States and Europe's nuclear weapons states, want to deny Iran nuclear know-how in order to keep Iran backward. Iran insists that it has no intention of acquiring nuclear weapons. As proof, Iranian officials cite a fatwa (Islamic judicial ruling) issued in August 2005 by Ayatollah Ali Khamenei (successor to Khomeini) banning nuclear weapons. In a 2004 interview with the Arab news network *Al-Jazeera,* Hassan Rowhani, then secretary of Iran's Supreme National Security Council and in charge of Iran's nuclear program, asserted that Iran also had pragmatic reasons to forswear WMD, including nuclear weapons:

> *Our decision not to possess weapons of mass destruction is strategic because we believe that these weapons will not provide security for Iran. On the contrary, they will create big problems. Iran exerted huge efforts during the past few years to build bridges of confidence with the states of the region. We absolutely do not want to blow up those bridges by mobilizing our resources to produce weapons of mass destruction. We are confident that our possession of these weapons will force these countries to seek the support of big powers. Consequently, national security will worsen. This will not serve our national security.*[35]

This explanation sounds plausible. It is true that if Iran broke or withdrew from the NPT and announced that it possessed nuclear weapons, it would undermine its efforts to achieve trust as a responsible international citizen and might drive its neighbors into the arms of the "big powers," perhaps even the United States. It is also true that Khamenei's fatwa against WMD carries some weight, since Iran is an Islamic republic whose leaders derive their legitimacy from the claim that they are subservient to Islamic law. Perhaps they would pay a price for disregarding the fatwa.

Nevertheless, few people outside Iran, and perhaps only a minority of people within Iran, doubt that Iran seeks the capability of making nuclear weapons. For one thing, the kind of nuclear capacity that Iran says it wants to acquire would bring it within months of the ability to make a bomb. Iran maintains that it has the right and need to master the full nuclear fuel cycle, giving it self-sufficiency in all aspects of the peaceful use of nuclear energy, from mining uranium to plutonium reprocessing. If it had this capability, it would be able to produce nuclear weapons, and there is no plausible economic or commercial reason for achieving it; Iran is a country low in uranium reserves, and it would actually be more economical for Iran to buy enriched uranium than to buy uranium and then enrich it, as it seems to intend to do. Thus, Iran could generate nuclear power and meet its energy needs without mastering the full nuclear fuel cycle—it could purchase nuclear fuel as other countries do and would thereby avoid all the international suspicion and anger its nuclear policies have aroused. Shahram Chubin, an analyst for the Carnegie Endowment for International Peace, notes several objections to Iran's argument.

> *First, even states like Sweden, which has ten [nuclear] reactors, do not feel the need for enrichment facilities and instead buy their fuel on the open market, which is less expensive. Second, even . . . possessing the full fuel cycle, Iran will remain dependent on imports of uranium because it lacks adequate indigenous supplies. Third, with reference to increased domestic energy consumption, the problem for Iran is the growing demand for gasoline, not electricity. Iran's domestic consumption of heavily subsidized and thus wasted gasoline is costly and growing in line with the population. Therefore, nuclear power plants, which produce electricity, will not begin to address this demand (Iran's vast indigenous gas reserves are discounted from the equation).*[36]

Further, when Iranian leaders talk about their nuclear programs, they appear to expect benefits from it that the possession of additional energy resources and scientific prestige could not supply—but which some people think nuclear weapons do supply. Ali Larijani, who had replaced Rowhani as secretary of Iran's Supreme National Security Council, said in 2005, "They [the United States] are also concerned that if Iran acquires nuclear technology the situation in the region will be altered."

History of Nuclear Deception and Stalling of the IAEA

Suspicions about Iran's supposedly peaceful nuclear program are also based on systematic deceptions practiced by Iran's government. Iran's nuclear power program was started in 1957, under the shah, as part of the Atoms for Peace program and later continued under the terms of the NPT. Since 1979, it has been conducted under conditions of secrecy, and Iran has concealed much of its nuclear activities from the IAEA.

In September 2002, photographs taken from commercial satellites showed major new nuclear sites in Iran; they were facilities that Iran had not reported to the IAEA and that were obviously constructed in a way to conceal their size and importance. One of the facilities was a uranium enrichment site. While it was not technically a violation of the NPT for Iran to build a uranium enrichment site, it was certainly very suspicious for Iran to build one in secret. The IAEA insisted that Iran permit inspections of its secret nuclear facilities under construction. The United States accused Iran of seeking the ability to make nuclear weapons and demanded that Iran cooperate with IAEA inspections.[37]

The discovery that Iran had been building secret nuclear facilities and concealing nuclear material and experiments occurred at a time when Iran's leaders felt unusually vulnerable to outside pressure, particularly from the United States. The United States had just toppled the Taliban regime in Afghanistan, putting U.S. armed forces on Iran's northeastern border, and it evidently intended to invade Iraq, which would put it on Iran's western border. Not only the United States, but the European Union and, with much less urgency, Russia and China were suspicious of Iran's nuclear ambitions. Under those circumstances, Iran's leaders began a period of reluctant compliance with IAEA inspections of its nuclear facilities. Iran's cooperation was always grudging and partial, aimed at giving as little ground as possible without causing an international crisis and endangering the country's growing economic ties to other countries, especially Europe. In December 2003, Iran signed an Additional Protocol to the NPT, which would allow IAEA enhanced access and information, but as of this writing the Iranian parliament has not ratified the agreement. Iran voluntarily implemented the protocol from 2004 to 2006.

Iran became less cooperative in 2005. By that time, the United States had become bogged down in Iraq. U.S. credibility had declined with proof that Saddam Hussein had no WMD—the United States had made false claims about Iraq, why should the world believe U.S. claims about Iran? Iran's government was rolling in money thanks to a high international price for oil, its main source of revenue, and Iranian elections had put a new, ultranationalist government in charge. The new president, Mahmoud Ahmadinejad (1956–), replaced the head of Iran's Supreme National Security Council, pragmatist Hassan Rowhani, with a hard-liner, Ali Larijani. "If Iran becomes atomic Iran," Larijani told a group of Iranian Revolutionary Guard Corps commanders in 2005, "no longer will anyone dare challenge it, because they would have to pay too high a price."[38] In August 2005 Iran announced that it was resuming uranium enrichment activities.

In a speech given on October 26, 2005, in Tehran, Ahmadinejad declared that the state of Israel should be "wiped off the map." Though it is common for states in the Middle East to take the side of the Palestinians and oppose Israeli policies, Ahmadinejad's comments and others like them are more extreme than it is usual for Middle Eastern leaders to make in public; apart from raising fears of what Iran would do if it had nuclear weapons, the speech showed a reckless indifference to world opinion that seemed like a throwback to the Iran of the 1980s.

In February 2006, the IAEA, citing Iran's obstructionist tactics and history of concealment, referred the case of Iran to the UN Security Council. This was a move that Iran's earlier cooperation with IAEA inspections had taken pains to avoid, but now Iran was defiant. After the Security Council issued a statement expressing "serious concern" about Iran's nuclear program, Ayatollah Ali Khamenei called the Security Council "a paper factory for issuing worthless and ineffective orders" and added that Iran would "resist any pressure and threat. . . ."[39]

U.S. Response to Iran's Nuclear Program

The U. S. government has no doubt that Iran intends to acquire the capability of making nuclear weapons as well as the capability of delivering them to distant targets with the use of ballistic missiles. Shahram Chubin notes that the United States has five overlapping choices available to it in its confrontation with Iran's nuclear ambitions:

- **Prevention.** Using sanctions and export controls to delay the program
- **Containment.** Freezing the program at a certain level
- **Rollback or Reversal.** Using threats, military strikes, and perhaps invasion to get Iran to abandon its nuclear ambitions
- **Regime Change.** Removing the regime by force, as the United States did in Iraq
- **Co-option.** Accepting the inevitability of Iran's acquisition of nuclear weapons and attempting to make it a responsible nuclear weapons state

In the interest of prevention, the United States has used unilateral sanctions, punishing Iran for seeking nuclear weapons by limiting American commercial involvement with the country, as well as "secondary sanctions," which are sanctions on countries that trade with Iran. Since they have hurt the Iranian economy, these sanctions have probably helped delay the development of Iran's nuclear program, but obviously they have not stopped it. Chubin observes that Iran has found these sanctions "painful but not unbearable," and their effect is limited by the fact that Iranian leaders see the United States as permanently hostile to Iran; they do not believe that a change in nuclear policy would result in the lifting of the sanctions. High oil prices in the 2000s, which have helped boost the income of oil-producing countries, further reduce the impact of sanctions on Iran's economy.

The preferred goal of the United States toward Iran's nuclear program has been rollback, with an implied threat of military action, and the preferred method since at least mid-2003 has been regime change. The Bush administration has maintained that the United States cannot deal with an unrepresentative and repressive government (though historically the United States has dealt with many such governments and continues to do so; China and Pakistan are among the current examples). "Focus on the regime's tyranny, its loathsome human rights record, and its controlled elections is a constant refrain," notes Chubin.

> *U.S. policy toward Iran is characterized by a special antipathy going beyond distrust or the legacy of past events such as the hostage crisis and Beirut bombings. For a certain category of Americans, Iran is the very embodiment of evil, more so than North Korea or even Iraq. . . .* [40]

The U. S. government has repeatedly accused Iran of aiding insurgents in Iraq, and in early 2007 it began to give greater publicity to these charges.

International Response

The story of Iran's quest for nuclear weapons—or at least for the capability to produce nuclear weapons—and the international response to that quest is making headlines as this book is being written. The story is unfolding so rapidly that what is written on this page will undoubtedly be outstripped by events. As of spring 2007, the United States and its ally the United Kingdom were involved in what is best described as a cold war with Iran. In late 2006 and early 2007, the United States persuaded its partners on the UN Security Council to adopt two resolutions, one calling on Iran to suspend uranium enrichment and nuclear fuel reprocessing. The second resolution gave Iran 60 days to comply or face sanctions that included restraints on all shipment of weapons to and from Iran. Iran's president reacted with an expression of contempt for the Security Council. "Using the Security Council as an instrument, the enemies of Iran want to prevent the progress of the Iranian nation," Ahmadinejad said at a rally in Iran. "But the Security Council today has no legitimacy among world nations." He added, "If all of you gather and also invite your ancestors from hell, you will not be able to stop the Iranian nation."[41]

Each member of the Security Council has its own distinct relationship with Iran, which colors its response to the threat of Iran as a nuclear weapons state. The Iranian revolution has traditionally been very hostile to the United Kingdom, and the United Kingdom has tended to side with the United States, taking a tough stance that has left open the threat of war. U.S-led wars in the Middle East are extremely unpopular with French and German voters, and these countries' governments, while favoring strong sanctions against Iran's nuclear programs, have avoided threats of military action against Iran. In 2006, France's president Jacques Chirac suggested in an interview that the world might just have to learn to live with a nuclear Iran, then quickly retracted his comments, which were not in accordance with official French policy. France's new president, Nicholas Sarkozy, has advocated tougher sanctions against Iran if it does not comply with Security Council demands. During the negotiations that led to the 2006 and 2007 Security Council resolutions against Iran, French and German diplomats strove to persuade Russia and China to agree to stronger sanctions against Iran.

Russia and China have in the past sought strong commercial relationships with Iran and are disinclined to regard this good economic partner as a threat to world peace. Probably neither China nor Russia wants Iran to have nuclear weapons, but they have consistently been reluctant to impose strong sanctions on Iran.

China has growing energy needs and is actively seeking new sources of oil around the world. In 2006, as controversy over Iran's nuclear research program intensified, China's state-owned Petroleum and Chemical Corporation announced a deal with Iran to develop a new oil field and purchase natural gas from Iran. Since the 1990s, Russia has assisted Iran in the building of a large nuclear reactor in Bushehr. The United States has never been happy with Russia's nuclear assistance to Iran, and it has been an irritant in U.S.-Russian relations. In July 2007, Russia announced that it would delay the completion of the reactor, giving a nonpolitical reason for the decision—the Iranians were behind on their payments. Some analysts interpret the announcement as a face-saving way for Russia to revise its policy on Iran's nuclear development. Tension surrounding Iran's nuclear quest eased somewhat with the release of the November 2007 United States National Intelligence Estimate. Dramatically reversing earlier judgments, the new NIE concluded that Iran had stopped its nuclear weapons program in 2003 and had not restarted it. However, the report found that Iran was continuing to enrich uranium and would have enough nuclear material to make a nuclear weapon by around the middle of the next decade.

Northeast Asia at a Glance

COUNTRY	POPULATION (MILLIONS, JULY 2008 EST.	AREA (SQ. KM)	MAJOR RELIGIOUS GROUPS	OFFICIAL LANGUAGE	FORM OF GOVERNMENT	YEAR FOUNDED/ INDEPENDENCE
People's Republic of China	1,330	9,569,960	Nonreligious (59%) Traditional Beliefs (33%) Buddhist (6%) Muslim (1.4%)	Mandarin Chinese	Socialist republic (single-party state)	Ancient China: 1766 B.C.E. As PRC: 1949
Japan	127	377,873	Professing both Shintoism and Buddhism (84%)	Japanese	Constitutional monarchy (parliamentary democracy)	Traditional: 660 B.C.E. Meiji Constitution: 1890
South Korea	49	99,646	No preference (46.5%) Christian (14%) Buddhist (11%)	Korean	Democracy	1948
North Korea	23	120,540	Religious practices discouraged	Korean	Hereditary dictatorship	1948
China (Taiwan)	23	35,801	Professing Buddhism, Confucianism, and Taoism (93%) Christianity (4.5%)	Mandarin Chinese	Democracy	1949

NORTHEAST ASIA

Taken together, the countries of Japan, the People's Republic of China, the Republic of China (Taiwan), North Korea, and South Korea constitute Northeast Asia, the home of more than 1.5 billion people, just under a fourth of the world's population. It is the one region in the world where nuclear weapons have actually been used, twice in the month of August 1945. Northeast Asia was controlled by outsiders in the 1800s and endured several decades of war and revolution during the 20th century. In recent decades, rapid economic growth has reached every country in the region except the one that causes the most worry, North Korea.

Today Northeast Asia is changing fast. In the near future, its population increase can be expected to produce social turmoil among its people, greater competition for world resources from its businesses, and a desire for greater influence on world affairs among its governments.

Two states in the region have nuclear weapons. One is mainland China. It has had them for many years, but it has not shown much desire to increase its arsenal, nor has it tended to threaten its neighbors with them. China's nuclear restraint is probably due to the fact that it faces no threats to its survival: Weak and fragmented at the beginning of the 20th century, China is now a strong state with a population of 1.3 billion and a $185 billion trade surplus with the United States. It does not need to brandish nuclear weapons to throw its weight around. The leaders of China have pulled off a remarkable feat. They have managed to retain power at home during a transition from a planned economy to a market economy while retaining the political system of communism and single-party rule. China's government is undemocratic and does not tolerate dissent, but for the moment the vast majority of its people seem to be content to enjoy a better life than their parents did.

The region's other nuclear state is North Korea, a "rogue state" that is isolated, highly secretive, and belligerent and one of the few remaining states that operates on a Soviet-style command economy. North Korea probably has only a few small atom bombs, and the rest of the world hopes to persuade it to build no more and perhaps to get rid of the ones it has. If it does not, the immediate threat that North Korea poses to Americans would be small compared with its threat to spur nuclear proliferation among its neighbors, South Korea and Japan, who have the means and the know-how to build large nuclear arsenals but who, so far, have lacked the motive.

History of the Conflict

North Korea is half of the historical Korea, a country that existed as a single nation from the seventh century until 1945. Korea grew up in the shadow of

China, its mighty neighbor to the west, and had a relationship of rivalry and occasional conflict with Japan, its island neighbor to the east. In 1905, as an outcome of the Russo-Japanese War, Japan occupied part of Korea, and five years later Japan annexed the entire country. For 35 years, Japan tried to remake Korea into its own image, leaving a legacy of resentment; Koreans remember the Japanese occupation as a series of insults to national honor. Outsiders see a more complex reality. The Japanese committed war crimes in Korea, but some believe that Japan's modernization program helped Korea in the long term. Commercial relationships with Japan have fueled South Korea's current prosperity.[42]

In August 1945, after the United States dropped an atomic bomb on Hiroshima and it was clear the war with Japan would soon be over, the Soviet Union invaded Japanese-occupied Korea. It was an opportunistic move, but the United States did not object, thinking Russian help might still be needed to deal with Japanese die-hards fighting on the Asian mainland. This resistance did not materialize, and in hindsight the U.S. acceptance of Russian control in northern Korea looks like a historic blunder. The United States and the Soviet Union agreed to a temporary division of Korea into two occupation zones, one administered by the Russians north of the 38th parallel (a line across the approximate middle of the Korean Peninsula) and another administered by the United States south of the 38th parallel. The division has lasted 62 years. Neither country recognizes the other's legitimacy. Both lay claim to the entire Korean Peninsula.

With the blessing of the Soviets, northern Korea became the People's Republic of Korea, a Communist state, under a former guerilla fighter named Kim Il Sung (1912–94). Southern Korea became the Republic of Korea, with a government that was for many years corrupt and undemocratic, though much less repressive than the totalitarian government of Kim Il Sung. It is common to refer to the countries as simply North Korea and South Korea. In 1950, North Korea attacked South Korea, beginning a war that ultimately involved the United States and China, causing between 1.3 and 3.5 million deaths, including around 36,000 Americans, and many more casualties.

The war ended in a stalemate that persists. On the 2.5 mile-wide DMZ positioned roughly at the 38th parallel, the most heavily armed border in the world, a million soldiers of North Korea face 700,000 South Korean and 37,000 U.S. troops.[43] There are many ties between the people on both sides of the line. The Korean people expect one day that their country will be reunified, but sharp differences in the political and economic systems of North and South Korea will make that hard to achieve.

ORWELLIAN STATE

If we view the fate of the two Koreas as a test of the relative merits of communism and capitalism, capitalism has won a decisive victory. South Korea, after rocky decades of corrupt military dictatorships, is now a thriving democracy. North Korea is a failed state. Unable to feed its own people without charity from abroad, it pours its resources into its armed forces. The government controlled media, when not assuring the people that they live in a paradise, blame the United States for the country's poverty. During the Korean War, U.S. bombs flattened the North Korean capital of Pyongyang and destroyed North Korea's industrial and agricultural infrastructure. Outside observers, however, attribute the failure of North Korea to its centrally planned economy, totalitarian political institutions, and incompetent leadership.

Under Kim Il Sung and his son Kim Jong Il (1942–), who succeeded him, North Korea became a highly regimented society with a broken economy, dependent on aid from the Soviet Union and the People's Republic of China. Writers often use the word *Orwellian* to describe the country, and the word fits perfectly. Like the citizens of Oceania in George Orwell's novel *1984*, the people of North Korea are lied to constantly. They live in want and are told they are prosperous; they endure rigid social and political controls and are told they are free. They know that their closest acquaintances may be government informers. In the capital city of Pyongyang, loudspeakers blare political slogans such as "Long Live the Revolutionary Sovereignty of Laborers and Farmers Led by Kim Jong Il!" The North Korean workday begins with a 30-minute reading session during which the editorials in the party newspapers are studied.[44] Citizens are divided into three political classes—loyal, wavering, or hostile—which determine what food they eat, what job they do, and whether they attend a university. "Hostile" includes the descendants of perceived enemies of the state and all minority religious groups. North Korean elections are a totalitarian ritual: 100 percent of the citizens vote, and the "Dear Leader" Kim Jong Il is elected with 100 percent of the vote.

The state controlled media built a personality cult around Kim Il Sung, expunging all records of human failings or error from his biography, giving him credit for whatever achievements North Korea can boast of (the chief of these being the supposed defeat of the United States in the Korean War), and referring to him in terms that made him little less than a god. At Kim Il Sung's death in 1994, he was for all practical purposes deified, and the mantle of infallibility fell on his pampered, temperamental son Kim Jong Il.

ECONOMIC COLLAPSE AT THE END OF THE COLD WAR

The end of the cold war left North Korea out on a limb. With the withdrawal of aid from the Soviet Union and the reduction of aid from China, North Koreans suffered a severe drop in the standard of living. In the 1990s, North Korea's ruinous agricultural and trade policies led to famines during which between 500,000 and 3 million North Koreans died of starvation (the government's secretiveness makes estimates difficult). Between 100,000 and 300,000 North Koreans fled to northeastern China.[45] Since that time, North Korea has depended on foreign aid and assistance from international nongovernmental aid organizations (NGOs) to feed its people and heat their homes in the winter.

The donors who contribute this aid face grim choices: The North Korean government spends money on its bloated military establishment that it could spend on food, so in a sense, this charity supports the North Korean military and helps keep North Korea's repressive government in power. Recent experience teaches that even with its people starving, North Korea's government would continue to support its military first. The North Korean people are hostages to their ugly government, and to withdraw aid is to let the hostages die.

North Korea's economic collapse is an important reason for the criminal international behavior that leads North Korea to be branded a "rogue state." The North Korean government needs money to fund its nuclear program, to pay off its top military leaders, and to pay its spies overseas. To generate this money, the government maintains a network of trading companies under the name Division 39, which conducts such illegal activities as counterfeiting U.S. money (North Korean $100 bills are reportedly among the best forgeries in the world), drug cultivation, drug running, and money laundering.[46] North Korea has also earned money exporting missiles to countries such as Iran and is believed to have shared its nuclear know-how with Iran and Iraq.

Programs like Division 39 are especially worrisome in the light of North Korea's nuclear capabilities. While it would clearly be suicidal for North Korea to launch a nuclear attack on the United States or even to invade South Korea, a nuclear North Korea, desperate for cash, might sell its nuclear weapons to whoever would pay. Perhaps, for the right price, North Korea might sell a nuclear device to terrorists.

NORTH KOREA'S NUCLEAR PROGRAM

The North Korean government says that its nuclear program is defensive; history as well as logic support its claim, without making North Korea's possession of these weapons desirable. During the 1950–53 war, U.S. president Harry S. Truman and U.S. president Dwight D. Eisenhower each at different times threatened to use the atomic bomb against North Korea. Later the United States deployed a wide array of nuclear weapons in South Korea, all aimed at North Korea. While these weapons were eventually withdrawn, South Korea had its own nuclear program that North Korea had to worry about. South Korea abandoned its nuclear weapons program in the 1970s but has the capability to produce nuclear weapons. Furthermore, South Korea was protected by the United States's "nuclear umbrella," that is, it was U.S. policy that nuclear weapons might be used against North Korea if it attacked South Korea.

It is not surprising, then, that North Korea has been seeking nuclear weapons since the end of the Korean War. In the mid-1950s, the Soviet Union helped North Korea with nuclear research, training its physicists in Moscow. Later China helped train North Korean physicists as well. In the 1960s, the Soviets installed a nuclear reactor in Yongbyon, North Korea, and another one in the same location in the 1980s. Although North Korea joined the IAEA in 1974 and signed the NPT in 1985, and North Korea has a genuine need for nuclear power, many aspects of North Korea's nuclear program were suspicious, particularly from the 1980s on. Neither of the reactors at Yongbyon was connected to North Korea's electricity grid, raising concerns that power generation was not their real purpose. The second reactor the Soviets gave North Korea had the capacity to produce weapons-usable plutonium, needed for atomic bombs; it was similar to the reactors pursued by India and Israel to make their bombs.

In the 1990s, North Korea tried to buy two more nuclear reactors from the Soviet Union, but by this time the Soviet leader, Mikhail Gorbachev, was insisting on cash payment. North Korea could not afford to pay. China, noting that North Korea's nuclear program seemed to have a military purpose, withdrew its technical support of the program and stopped transferring nuclear technology to North Korea. North Korea looked elsewhere for resources and began trading its nuclear know-how as well as funds from Division 39 with countries such as Pakistan that were working toward a nuclear weapons capability. By the late 1980s, the Japanese and South Korean press were reporting that North Korea was capable of reprocessing plutonium into weapons-grade material.

Meanwhile, in the 1980s, North Korea was busy acquiring missiles that could deliver warheads to far-away targets. North Korea acquired SCUDs (tactical ballistic missiles originally developed by the Soviet Union) from Egypt, and with help from Iran, North Korean engineers copied the designs and built on them to develop missiles with a 310-mile range, which the country started to manufacture on a large scale in the early 1990s. Next it developed long-range missiles, with a range of 850 to 1,240 miles, and a possible capability of 3,500 miles, putting them within striking distance of Alaska or Hawaii.[47] In 1993, deserted by its former allies the USSR and China, who had both recognized South Korea, Kim Il Sung apparently felt that he had nothing to lose, and North Korea announced that it would withdraw from the NPT.

International Response

CLINTON'S RESPONSE: THE AGREED FRAMEWORK

With the CIA guessing in 1993 that North Korea had already produced enough plutonium "for one, and possibly two, nuclear weapons" by the late 1980s, both the U.S. Congress and U.S. president Bill Clinton became alarmed, but choices were limited. UN sanctions against North Korea would probably be opposed by China, South Korea, and Japan and in any case would not have much effect against a poor country that had very little trade with the outside world—sanctions would only make the North Korean people suffer more. Preemptive strikes would be even more unpopular internationally and would be in violation of international law. They might also lead to disaster for the United States and for all Koreans. Clinton's advisers believed that an air attack on North Korea's nuclear facilities would lead to a full-scale war between the United States and North Korea.

Senior officials of the Clinton administration were weighing these options when they learned that former president Jimmy Carter (1924–) had taken it upon himself to negotiate with Kim Il Sung's government. According to Clinton's Secretary of Defense William Perry: "Well, we were literally in the process of giving the briefing to [President Clinton], laying out the three alternative options, when the call came in from President Carter [in North Korea who] said that he had talked with Kim Il Sung and that Kim Il Sung had told him that he was prepared to stop the program at Yongbyon if the United States was prepared to offer him a light-water reactor, an alternative kind of nuclear reactor."

Further negotiations with the North Korean government led to the deal known as the Agreed Framework, under which the North promised to freeze and eventually dismantle its graphite-moderated reactors and related facilities in exchange for alternative energy supplies and eventually, normalization of political and economic relations with the United States. Under this deal, the United States would withdraw the threat of preemptive military action and begin to establish trade and diplomatic relations with North Korea. Further, the United States would arrange for the construction of two light water reactors in North Korea, to be completed in 2003, replacing the two Soviet reactors and supplying North Korea with enough heavy fuel to replace the energy lost by abandoning the Soviet reactors. (Light water reactors are suitable for nuclear power generation but less so for plutonium production.) In return, the North Koreans would dismantle the Soviet reactors, dispose of the nuclear fuel rods, and remain in the NPT, and the IAEA would return to conduct inspections. The Clinton administration, which had pledged to balance the U.S. budget, was particularly pleased that according to the agreement South Korea and Japan would pay most of the cost of the new light water reactors, which would be constructed by the Korean Energy Development Organization.

Clinton's negotiating team hoped that the Agreed Framework would ultimately lead to a reunification of Korea under the South Korean government (much as East Germany had recently reunited with West Germany, on West German terms). But both the U.S. Congress and the South Korean government were unhappy with the deal. Critics regarded it as a giveaway to the North Koreans, one that put the United States in the position of guaranteeing the sovereignty and security of North Korea's brutal government. North Korea had threatened the world with nuclear weapons and been rewarded for it.

Since the failure of the Agreed Framework is often used to back up arguments that only the threat of force will work against North Korea, it is important to note that none of the participants kept their part of the bargain. During the late 1990s, Japan and South Korea were in the throes of the East Asian financial crisis; funding of the nuclear power project became bogged down in delays and arguments over its terms. The construction of the light-water reactors fell far behind schedule. The United States promised oil shipments to North Korea but delivered them very erratically.

In the late 1990s, U.S. conservatives, who had won control of Congress, were more sure than ever that the North Koreans were calling the shots, blackmailing the United States, and being bought off by the Clinton administration. Conservatives saw a series of quid pro quos between the United States and North Korea as simply "rewarding" North Korea for bad behavior:

- After testing a ballistic missile in August 1998, North Korea agreed to cancel another launch in exchange for a U.S. agreement to lift certain trade restrictions.
- In exchange for permitting an inspection of one of North Korea's nuclear sites, the United States agreed to send extra food shipments.
- In late 1999, North Korea agreed to a moratorium on further long-range missile tests, and in return the United States lifted some of its economic sanctions.
- In a subsequent meeting concerning missiles, Kim Jong Il's negotiators demanded that the United States provide $1 billion annually to North Korea if North Korea halted its missile exports.

Critics of Clinton's policy noted that Kim was demanding larger and larger concessions from the United States. To the critics, Kim Jong Il was a dictator similar to Adolf Hitler; engagement was appeasement, and these deals were a series of little "Munichs" (that is, they resembled the notorious deal in which British prime minister Neville Chamberlain permitted Adolph Hitler to annex Czechoslovakia, which only made Hitler greedier and stronger). Clinton, however, remained committed to a policy of engagement. He sent Secretary of State Madeleine Albright to meet with North Korean officials in Pyongyang in 2000.[48] Initially, South Korean officials also criticized the Clinton administration for giving too much and getting too little from North Korea. However, the South Korean attitude changed with the election of South Korean president Kim Dae Jung (1925–), who served from 1998 to 2002 and also pursued a policy of engagement with North Korea. During Kim Dae Jung's term in office, summit meetings were held between the two Koreas, South Korean tourists visited North Korea, and there were reunions for families separated since the Korean War. Kim Dae Jung's administration called his attempt at easing relations the "Sunshine Policy." South Korean advocates of the Sunshine Policy desire a slow increase in economic, cultural, and diplomatic relations between the two Koreas. They see an improvement in North Korean living standards as a necessary prerequisite to reunification. Though they want the country to be reunified under the South Korean government, they want to avoid a sudden collapse of the North Korean government.[49]

BUSH DECLARES THAT NORTH KOREA IS PART OF THE AXIS OF EVIL

There were two sharply different schools of thought on North Korea within the administration of George W. Bush, who became president of the United States in 2001. Members of the State Department, led by Secretary of State Colin Powell, favored a continued policy of engagement. More conservative members of the administration, who included Secretary of Defense Donald Rumsfeld and powerful Vice President Dick Cheney, thought that the United States had made too many concessions to North Korea, and it was time to get tough.

Initially, Secretary of State Colin Powell signaled that the new administration planned to continue Clinton's policies toward North Korea. He was undercut by the president, who favored a hard line that soon became harder. The U.S. position in 2001 prior to 9/11 was that North Korea would be given a chance to live up to its part of the Agreed Framework, but there would be no further negotiations and no concessions from the United States. The ball was in Kim Jong Il's court. When South Korea's president, Kim Dae Jung, visited the United States in March asking Bush to support his Sunshine Policy, Bush showed himself cool to the idea. The terrorist attacks of September 11 empowered the hardliners in the Bush administration, and very soon the "ball in their court" hardened to a veiled threat of military action.

In a January 29, 2002, State of the Union address, Bush declared that Iraq, Iran, and North Korea together posed an unacceptable threat to the safety of the world. "States like these, and their terrorist allies, constitute an axis of evil, arming to threaten the peace of the world. By seeking weapons of mass destruction, these regimes pose a grave and growing danger. They could provide these arms to terrorists, giving them the means to match their hatred. They could attack our allies or attempt to blackmail the United States. In any of these cases, the price of indifference would be catastrophic."[50]

During World War II, the term *axis* referred to the fascist alliance of Japan, Italy, and Germany. If by using this phrase, Bush meant that the three states, which all were seeking nuclear weapons, formed a political alliance, he was obviously wrong; Iraq and Iran were mutually hostile states whose hatred for the United States was not enough to unite them. All three states had distinctly different ideologies and interests—they did not form an alliance. However, the Axis of World War II is also known for another characteristic: They had the reputation of a group with whom it was futile to negotiate—the Axis understood only force. So by using it, when it had no other application, Bush seemed to suggest that negotiating with these enemies would be pointless. Bush's use of the word *evil* also suggests a rejection of diplomacy.

Without explicitly declaring war on the three nations named, the president hinted at a preventive war: "We will not wait on events while dangers gather." A year later, the United States invaded Iraq, undoubtedly making the leadership and people of Iran and North Korea wonder if they were next.[51]

CRISIS

In summer 2002, U.S. intelligence found increasing evidence that North Korea was attempting to procure equipment to enrich uranium. In response, the United States suspended fuel oil shipments to North Korea. U.S. officials said they would not talk to North Korea again until North Korea had dismantled the enrichment program and permitted outsiders to verify that they had done so.[52] In December, North Korea expelled the IAEA inspectors. On January 9, 2003, 10 years after its first threat to withdraw from the NPT, North Korea again announced that it was leaving the treaty, calling the United States's bluff while the United States was busy preparing to go to war in Iraq; the war began in March 2003 and would keep the United States busy for a longer period of time than the Bush administration anticipated. In February

2003, North Korea announced that it had restarted its "research reactor." Military analysts calculated that at this time North Korea could possess enough plutonium for one or two bombs; its arsenal could grow to about eight warheads by the end of the year.[53]

The United States's choices with respect to North Korea were now even narrower than those it had faced in 1993. War (probably beginning with extensive air strikes on North Korea's nuclear facilities) would still be costly, and now it would interfere with U.S. plans to invade Iraq. China and Russia were still not ready to impose sanctions on North Korea, arguing that sanctions were unlikely to make Kim Jong Il relinquish his only international bargaining chip, his nuclear weapons program. The United States had said it would not negotiate, and to change its mind now would make the United States look soft.

THE SIX-PARTY TALKS

To avoid the appearance of speaking to North Korea directly, between 2003 and 2007 the United States engaged with several other nations in a series of "Six-Party Talks" held in Beijing, China. The six participants were North Korea, South Korea, the United States, China, Russia, and Japan. The United States and Japan demanded that North Korea completely and verifiably dismantle its nuclear weapons program and insisted that this be done before any aid was given to North Korea. South Korea, China, and Russia preferred a step-by-step approach in which North Korea would be rewarded for various steps taken in the direction of nuclear disarmament. North Korea itself demanded that the United States make some concessions first. It wanted assurance that the United States would not try to overthrow the North Korean government by force, the light water reactors promised it under the Agreed Framework, diplomatic relations with the United States, and the lifting of U.S. financial and trade sanctions on North Korea. In effect, North Korea was asking for the same guarantees already agreed to back in the early 1990s as a part of the Agreed Framework.

For almost three years, the Six-Party Talks made little progress. In October 2006 North Korea tested a nuclear weapon and declared itself a nuclear weapons state. Perhaps this was an attempt to jump-start the talks, in the hope that a demonstration of military capability would win concessions from the United States and the United Nations.

On October 3, 2006. North Korea announced that it intended to conduct an underground test of a nuclear device. China and Russia joined other members of the UN Security Council in a resolution urging North Korea not to do so, saying the test would "jeopardize peace, stability and security in the region and beyond."[54] On October 6, North Korea announced that the test had been completed, and on October 11 the United States said that it believed the test had taken place (seismographs used to detect underground nuclear explosions indicated that this one was weaker than expected, and there was speculation that the bomb might have been a "fizzle" or a fake, using conventional explosives). Earlier that year, North Korea had conducted a series of missile tests, reminding the world that it had the means of sending nuclear warheads to distant destinations.

On October 14, 2006, the UN Security Council condemned the nuclear test and voted to impose sanctions on North Korea: At the insistence of Russia and China, however, military force was not among the threats. The sanctions forbade the sale or transfer to North Korea of material that could be used to make nuclear, biological, and chemical weapons or ballistic missiles, banned international travel to North Korea, and froze the overseas assets of people associated with North Korea's weapons programs. The resolution also authorized all countries to inspect cargo going in and out of North Korea to detect illicit weapons.[55]

At the beginning of the next month, at China's urging, North Korea announced that it would return to the Six-Party Talks, which resumed after a year's adjournment. The new round of talks led to an agreement. This was probably due to several changes in conditions: North Korea had created a crisis atmosphere by detonating a nuclear weapon; the Security Council had imposed tough sanctions on North Korea; the United States was stalled in Iraq, making it unready for war with North Korea; and, finally, the U.S. public had become deeply disenchanted with George W. Bush's foreign policy, which, in their judgment, had not fulfilled its promise of providing greater safety and security to the people of the United States. The Bush administration needed a foreign policy victory.

On the issue of North Korea, the balance of power within the administration shifted to the State Department, headed by Secretary of State Condoleezza Rice. After years of unyielding tough talk on behalf of the United States, Rice began to dangle carrots before North Koreans; she suggested that one day, if North Korea proved cooperative, this "rogue state" might be permitted to join the Asia-Pacific Economic Forum (a group of 21 Asian Pacific countries that includes both the United States and the former U.S. enemy Vietnam).[56]

In the talks themselves, the United States made several concessions it had not made earlier, essentially agreeing to the step-by-step approach advocated by China and Russia—providing North Korea with emergency energy assistance, renewing diplomatic relations, and agreeing to bilateral (U.S.-North Korean) talks in exchange for rather limited North Korean concessions—North Korea shutting down its Yongbyon nuclear facilities and agreeing to limits on its production of plutonium. The agreement did not require North Korea to abandon its existing nuclear weapons and postponed many issues for later negotiations.[57] U.S. relations with North Korea were back on the "something for you, something for me" basis of the Clinton years; progress would be slow and frustrating and the outcome uncertain.

CONCLUSION

Throughout the 1990s, hard-line conservatives in the United States expressed frustration with piecemeal approaches to nuclear nonproliferation, approaches such as the Agreed Framework, which they saw as rewarding and bribing proliferators. With control of the White House and both houses of Congress and the solid backing of the American people, after 2001 conservatives were able to give their ideas a decisive trial. In word and actions, the Untied States said in effect that the era of Mr. Nice Guy was over and a new sheriff was in town. Over the objections of its traditional international allies, the United States invaded Iraq in the name of nuclear proliferation. The Untied States made short work of Iraq's armed forces and toppled Saddam Hussein's brutal regime.

If that success had lasted, if weapons of mass destruction had been found, if the United States had succeeded in pacifying the country and remaking it into a democracy or even into a dictatorship friendly to the United States, the hardliners would have been justified, and their methods would have been applied to North Korea and Iran. Perhaps, as conservatives hoped, the mere threat of force would have been sufficient. History, however, took a different course. At the moment, it certainly seems as though force and the threat of force have had a fair trial. They have reduced the international prestige of the United States and set back the cause of nuclear nonproliferation. If that cause is to be furthered in the future, it will be accomplished through the murky, inglorious, imperfect processes of politics and diplomacy.

---

[1] Brian Ross. "CIA Rushing Resources to Bin Laden Hunt." *ABC News: The Blotter.* March 5, 2007. http://blogs.abcnews.com/theblotter/2007/03cia_rushing_res.html. Retrieved March 8, 2007.

[2] John McLeod. *The History of India.* Westport, Conn.: Greenwood Press, 2002, pp. 97–98, p. 18, pp. 121–127.

[3] J. Sri Raman. *Flashpoint: How the U.S., India and Pakistan Brought Us to the Brink of Nuclear War,* Monroe, Maine; Common Courage Press, 2004, p. 29.

[4] Raman, p. 31.

[5] Kanishkan Sathasivam. *Uneasy Neighbors: India, Pakistan and US Foreign Policy.* Hampshire, England: Ashgate Publishing, 2005, pp. 20–21.

[6] Ian Talbot. *Pakistan: A Modern History.* New York: Palgrave MacMillan, 2005, p. 29.

[7] Sathasivam, pp. 6–11 for India and Pakistan wars and discussion of effect of Bangladesh war.

[8] Sathasivam, pp. 10–11.

[9] Raj Chengapa. *Weapons of Peace: The Story of India's Quest to be a Nuclear Power.* New Delhi: HarperCollins Publishers India, 2000, p. 79.

[10] George Perkovich. *India's Nuclear Bomb: The Impact on Global Proliferation.* Berkeley: University of California Press, 1999, p. 119.

[11] Perkovich, pp. 183–186.

[12] Perkovich, p. 186.

[13] Perkovich, p. 7.

[14] Perkovich, p. 324.

[15] Perkovich, p. 434.

[16] Sathasivam, p. 13.

[17] Sathasivam, p. 14.

[18] Sathasivam, p. 160.

[19] Thomas Graham, Jr. Leonor Tomero, and Leonard Weiss. "Think Again: U.S.-India Nuclear Deal." *Foreign Policy,* posted July 2006. www.cfr.org/publication/10731/usindia_nuclear_deal.html. Retrieved March 8, 2007.

[20] Sokolski, *Best of Intentions,* p. 111.

[21] Henry Sokolski and Teresita Schaffer. "The U.S.-India Deal: The Right Approach?" May 26, 2006, *The Council on Foreign Relations.* www.cfr.org/publication/10731/usindia_nuclear_deal.html.

[22] Karen Yournsih. "India, Pakistan, Trade Barbs Over Nukes." *Arms Control Today.* October 2003. www.armscontrol.org/act/2003_10/IndiaPakistan.asp. Retrieved March 8, 2007.

[23] In an Associated Press–sponsored poll taken at the end of 2006, one in four Americans anticipated that the Second Coming of Jesus Christ would occur in 2007. This belief is commonly found among Christian fundamentalists, those evangelical Christians who contend that the Bible is literally true. According to Revelation, a final battle between the forces of good and evil will occur in a place called Armageddon, probably located in Israel. Many—probably tens of millions—of evangelical Christians in the United States believe that the return of Jesus will be preceded, first, by the "rapture," in which Christians who, like President Bush, have been "born again" through a Christian conversion experience will be lifted into the heavens, and then by a time of "tribulations," which will climax with the violent cleansing of the planet. The battle of Armageddon is expected to be one of the tribulations. Belief in an imminent Second Coming, the rapture, and the tribulations was widespread among U.S. president George W. Bush's political supporters. Critics have suggested that it has had an unfortunate effect on U.S. foreign policy, especially with respect to the Middle East. Since Christian fundamentalists regard an attack on Israel as a desirable fulfillment of prophecy, they tend to favor policies that exacerbate the Arab-Israeli conflict.

[24] Roger Adelson. *London and the Invention of the Middle East: Money, Power, and War, 1902–1922.* New Haven, Conn.:Yale University Press, 1995. pp. 22–23

[25] Peter Mansfield and Nicolas Pelham. *A History of the Middle East, Second Edition.* New York: Penguin, 2003. p. 250.

[26] Fouad Ajami. *The Arab Predicament.* Cambridge: Cambridge Univ Press, 1981.

[27] "Nuclear Weapons—Israel." FAS Weapons of Mass Destruction WMD Around the World. Available online at http://www.fas.org/nuke/guide/israel/nuke/.

[28] http://www.fas.org/nuke/guide/israel/nuke/. Updated January 8, 2007.

[29] BBC News. "Israel's Nuclear Programme." Updated December 22, 2003.

[30] Hannah K. Strange. "How Britain Helped Israel Make the Bomb," *United Press International,* August 4, 2005. Available on-line at http://www.globalsecurity.org/org/news/2005/050804-uk-israel-bomb.htm.

[31] "Ahmadinejad: Wipe Israel Off Map" *Al Jazeera.net.* October 28, 2005. english.aljazeera.net/English/archive/archive?ArchiveId=15816. Retrieved March 8, 2007.

[32] "'Scrap Nuclear Arms' Israel Urged" *BBC New Middle East.* December 12, 2003. news.bbc.co.uk/2/hi/middle_east/3312865.stm. Retrieved March 8, 2007.

[33] Mansfield, p. 329.

[34] Shahram Chubin. *Iran's Nuclear Ambitions.* Washington, D.C.: Carnegie Endowment for International Peace, 2006, p. 14.

[35] Chubin, p. 57.

[36] Chubin, pp. 25–26.

[37] Anthony H. Cordesman and Khalid R. Al-Rodhan. *Iran's Weapons of Mass Destruction: The Real and Potential Threat.* Washington, D.C.: CSIS Press, Center for Strategic and International Studies, 2006, pp. 125–126.

[38] Chubin, p. 33.

[39] Cordesman and Al-Rodhan, p. 153.

[40] Chubin, p. 90.

[41] Colum Lynch. "6 Powers Agree on Sanctions for Iran," *Washingtonpost.com.* Available at http://www.washington post.com/wp-dyn/content/article/2007/03/15/AR2007031500248.html.

[42] Edward A. Olsen. *Korea, The Divided Nation.* Westport, Conn.: Preager Security International, 2005, pp. 51–53.

[43] Paul French. *North Korea: The Paranoid Peninsula—A Modern History.* New York: Zed Books, 2005, p. 3.

[44] French.

[45] French, p. 130.

[46] French, p. 156.

[47] French, pp. 224–227 summarizes the history of North Korea's nuclear program.

[48] French, pp. 201–204 discusses and summarizes Clinton's engagement policy.

[49] Michael O'Hanlon and Mike Mochizuki. *Crisis on the Korean Peninsula: How to Deal with a Nuclear North Korea.* New York: McGraw-Hill, 2003,p. 12.

[50] "Online NewsHour: President Bush's State of the Union—January 29, 2002." Available at http://www.pbs.org/newshour/bb/white_house/sotu2002/sotu_text.html.

[51] www.whitehouse.gov/news/releases/2002/01/20020129-11.html. Retrieved February 22, 2002.

[52] O'Hanlon and Mochizuki, p. 15.

[53] O'Hanlon and Mochizuki, pp. 32-33.

[54] "U.N. Council Presses North Korea to Drop Plans for Nuclear Test" *New York Times,* late edition (East Coast)). New York: October 7, 2006. p. A.3.

[55] Warren Hoge and David E. Sanger. "Security Council Supports Sanctions on North Korea" *New York Times,* late edition (East Coast)). New York: October 15, 2006. p. 1.1.

[56] Helene Cooper and David E. Sanger. "U.S. Signals New Incentives for North Korea." *New York Times,* late edition (East Coast)). New York: November 19, 2006. p. 1.8.

[57] U.S. Department of State. "North Korea—Denuclearization Action Plan: Statement by President Bush on Six Party Talks." www.state.gov/r/pa/prs/ps/2007/february/80479.htm. Retrieved February 22, 2007.

PART II

Primary Sources

4

United States Documents

U.S. NUCLEAR POLICY

The Franck Report (June 11, 1945) (excerpt)

In 1945, the U.S. government asked a committee headed by physicist James Franck to study the likely social and political effects of the atomic bomb. The committee included scientists who had been involved in the Manhattan Project as well as Leo Szilard, who had originally proposed its creation. In a secret report written over a month before the first atomic bomb had been tested, the committee addressed the problems created by the very existence of nuclear weapons. The central observation of the report is made in its preamble, in which the authors state that nuclear weapons present a danger for which there is no technical solution. "This protection can only come from the political organization of the world." The Franck Report advised against using the atomic bomb against Japan, predicting that such an action would launch "a flying start toward an unlimited arms race." It recommended two other options instead: first and best, that the bomb be presented to the world in a technical demonstration—exploded but not on human beings—and its power be put under international control. If the U.S. government found that option unacceptable, the committee suggested that the bomb be kept a secret, permitting the United States to gain an even greater, perhaps unbeatable, lead in the nuclear arms race that would follow.

Report of the Committee on Political and Social Problems Manhattan Project "Metallurgical Laboratory" University of Chicago, June 11, 1945

[. . .]

II. Prospectives of Armaments Race

It could be suggested that the danger of destruction by nuclear weapons can be prevented—at least as far as this country is concerned—by keeping our discoveries secret for an indefinite time, or by developing our nucleonic armaments at such a pace that no other nations would think of attacking us from fear of overwhelming retaliation

The answer to the first suggestion is that although we undoubtedly are at present ahead of the rest of the world in this field, the fundamental facts of nuclear power are a subject of common knowledge. . . .

It may be asked whether we cannot achieve a monopoly on the raw materials of nuclear power. The answer is that even though the largest now known deposits of uranium ores are under the control of powers which belong to the "western" group (Canada, Belgium and British Indies); the old deposits in Czechoslovakia are outside this sphere. Russia is known to be mining radium on its own territory; and even if we do not know the size of the deposits discovered so far in the USSR, the probability that no large reserves of uranium will be found in a country which covers 1/5 of the land area of the earth (and whose sphere of influence takes in additional territory), is too small to serve as a basis for security. . . .

One could further ask whether we cannot feel ourselves safe in a race of nuclear armaments by virtue of our greater industrial potential, including greater diffusion of scientific and technical knowledge, greater volume and efficiency of our skilled labor corps, and greater experience of our management. . . . The answer is that all that these advantages can give us is the accumulation of a larger number of bigger and better atomic bombs—and this only if we produce those bombs at the maximum of our capacity in peace time, and do not rely on conversion of a peace time nucleonics industry to military production after the beginning of hostilities.

However, such a quantitative advantage in reserves of bottled destructive power will not make us safe from sudden attack. Just because a potential enemy will be afraid of being "outnumbered and outgunned," the temptation for him may be overwhelming to attempt a sudden unprovoked blow—particularly if he would suspect us of harboring agressive intentions against his security or "sphere of influence." In no other type of warfare does the advantage lie so heavily with the agressor. He can place his "infernal machines" in advance in all our major cities and explode them simultaneously, thus destroying a major part of our industry and killing a large proportion of our population, aggregated in densely populated metropolitan districts. Our possibilities of retaliation—even if retaliation would be considered compensation for the loss of tens of millions of lives and destruction of our largest cities—will be greatly handicapped because we must rely on aerial transportation of the bombs, particularly if we would have to deal with an enemy whose industry and population are dispersed over a large territory.

If no efficient international agreement is achieved, the race of nuclear armaments will be on in earnest not later than the morning after our first demonstration of the existence of nuclear weapons. After this, it might take other nations three or four years to overcome our present head start, and 8 or 10 years to draw even with us if we continue to do intensive work in this field. This might be all the time we have to bring about the regroupment of our population and industry. Obviously, no time should be lost in inaugurating a study of this problem by experts.

IV. Methods of International Control

We now consider the question of how an effective international control of nuclear armaments can be

Summary

The development of nuclear power not only constitutes an important addition to the technological and military power of the United States, but also creates grave political and economic problems for the future of this country

Nuclear bombs cannot possibly remain a "secret weapon" at the exclusive disposal of this country, for more than a few years. The scientific facts on which their construction is based are well known to scientists of other countries. Unless an effective international control of nuclear explosives is instituted, a race of nuclear armaments is certain to ensue following the first revelation of our possession of nuclear weapons to the world. Within ten years other countries may have nuclear bombs, each of which, weighing less than a ton, could destroy an urban area of more than five square miles. In the war to which such an armaments race is likely to lead, the United States, with its agglomeration of population and industry in comparatively few metropolitan districts, will be at a disadvantage compared to the nations whose population and industry are scattered over large areas.

We believe that these considerations make the use of nuclear bombs for an early, unannounced attack against Japan inadvisable. If the United States would be the first to release this new means of indiscriminate destruction upon mankind, she would sacrifice public support throughout the world, precipitate the race of armaments, and prejudice the possibility of reaching an international agreement on the future control of such weapons.

Much more favorable conditions for the eventual achievement of such an agreement could be created if nuclear bombs were first revealed to the world by a demonstration in an appropriately selected uninhabited area. . . .

Source: U.S. National Archives. Washington D.C.: Record Group 77, Manhattan Engineer District Records, Harrison-Bundy File, folder #76. Available online. URL: http://www.dannen.com/decision/franck.html. Accessed March 23, 2007.

Trinity Test, Eyewitness Account by Cyril S. Smith (July 25, 1945)

The code name Trinity was given to the first atomic bomb test, which was conducted on July 26, 1945, by the United States at a secret location in New Mexico on what is now the White Sands Missile Range. The detonation was equivalent to the explosion of around 20 kilotons of TNT. The witnesses, scientists, engineers, and military personnel who had worked on the project, were proud of their achievement but sobered by its implications. The famous words uttered on the occasion give a good idea of the range of emotions felt by the participants. "The effects could well be called unprecedented, magnificent, beautiful, stupendous and terrifying. No man-made phenomenon of such tremendous power had ever occurred before," wrote General Thomas Farrell. Robert Oppenheimer, the scientific director of the project, remembered a passage from the Bhagavad Gita "I am become Death, the Destroyer of Worlds." Dr. Kenneth Bainbridge, director of the Trinity test, perhaps intended the same thing in less poetic language: "Now we are all sons-of-bitches."

About a week after the test, several eyewitnesses were asked to record their observations and reactions, and this memo from Cyril S. Smith, who was one of the men responsible for the mechanical assembly of the plutonium core, was one of the responses.

DATE: July 25, 1945
TO: Lieutenant Taylor
FROM: C. S. Smith
SUBJECT: Trinity Shot

You requested me to write a brief description of the Trinity shot. Since this took place over a week ago my impressions have undoubtedly been modified very considerably by subsequent discussion and many features have faded from memory.

I was located at the base camp, behind a five foot embankment near the water tanks at T = 0. I was facing away from the shot, somewhat bent down below the top of the bank. In addition, my eyes were partly covered by a welder's glass. For a time estimated as two seconds (though it may have been less) I was watching the ground through the corner of my eye. Even though this was lighted by reflection from the clouds, it was intensely bright and apparently free from color. Since the shot there has been some discussion of the duration of this intense light, but it is definitely my recollection that I opened and closed my eyes several times and waited for the light to decrease in intensity before turning to face the reaction zone directly. Even after the estimated 2 seconds the light was still intense enough to be clearly seen through the welder's glass but there was no direct ball of fire or structure or any symmetry, this part of the phenomenon evidently having ceased.

The appearance of a turbulent gas apparently undergoing combustion was quite surprising. It looked not much different from the film of the 100 ton shot or any large fire, for instance an oil tank fire or the Graf Zeppelin. After another second or two I removed the welder's glass and looked directly. As the main light became less intense, the bluish ionization zone became visible, extending to a diameter almost twice that of the area where there was incandescence. I noticed a dust cloud travelling near the ground, and at some stage (I am not sure whether early or late in the proceedings, but it was definitely illuminated by the shot) I noticed a ring, supposedly of moisture condensed by the rarefaction wave, at a level slightly below the clouds. This ring did not spread, but once formed seemed to remain stationary.

At the instant after the shot, my reactions were compounded of relief that "it worked"; consciousness of extreme silence, and a momentary question as to whether we had done more than we intended. Practically none of the watchers made any vocal comment until after the shock wave had passed and even then the cheers were not intense or prolonged. The elation of most observers seemed to increase for a period of 30 minutes afterwards, as they had a chance to absorb the significance of the achievement.

The rising of the cloud of reaction products to above the cloud level seems to have proceeded rapidly but in a normal fashion. It was noticeable that there were a number of rough projections, indicating high local turbulence. Shortly after the smoke column with its mushroom top was formed, wind currents distorted it into a jagged or corkscrew appearance. There was a dust cloud over the ground, extending for a considerable distance. A cloud, whether of dust or moisture particles, hung close to the ground and slowly drifted east into the hills, persisting for over an hour.

The obvious fact that all of the reaction products were not proceeding upward in a neat ball but were lagging behind and being blown by low altitude winds over the ground in the direction of inhabited areas produced very definite reflection that this is not a pleasant weapon we have produced. Later reflections were on the manner of defense against it and the realization that a city is henceforth not the place in which to live.

I repeat that no attention should be paid to any comment made in this report, since the described events occurred many days ago.

Cyril Stanley Smith
CSS:bc
cc:
Hawkins
File

Source: U.S. National Archives, Record Group 227, OSRD-S1 Committee, Box 82 folder 6, "Trinity." Available online. URL: http://www.dannen.com/decision/smith-cs.html. Accessed March 27, 2007.

Harry S. Truman, Diary (July 25, 1945) (excerpt)

As the ailing Franklin Roosevelt's vice president, Harry Truman knew little of the administration's inner workings or its secrets. In his memoirs, published in 1955, he reported that his first intimation of the existence of the atomic bomb came on the day he assumed the oath of office, on April 12, 1945, when Secretary of War Henry Stimson, asked to speak to him about "a most urgent" topic. "Stimson told me that he wanted me to know about an immense project that was under way—a project looking to the development of a new explosive of almost unbelievable destructive power." (Memoirs, *Vol. 1, p. 10). In July, as news of the successful test of the atomic bomb reached him, Truman was in*

Potsdam, Germany, at a conference in which the U.S. president, British prime minister Winston Churchill, and Soviet premier Joseph Stalin discussed their plans for the postwar world. He mentioned the existence of a highly destructive weapon "casually" to Joseph Stalin on July 24. On the following day, he made the excerpted notation in his diary. Although Truman recorded his belief that the bomb would be used for "military objectives," the majority of the bomb's victims were, in fact, civilians.

> We have discovered the most terrible bomb in the history of the world. It may be the fire destruction prophesied in the Euphrates Valley Era, after Noah and his fabulous Ark.
>
> Anyway we "think" we have found the way to cause a disintegration of the atom. An experiment in the New Mexico desert was startling—to put it mildly. Thirteen pounds of the explosive caused the complete disintegration of a steel tower 60 feet high, created a crater 6 feet deep and 1,200 feet in diameter, knocked over a steel tower 1/2 mile away and knocked men down 10,000 yards away. The explosion was visible for more than 200 miles and audible for 40 miles and more.
>
> This weapon is to be used against Japan between now and August 10th. I have told the Sec. of War, Mr. Stimson, to use it so that military objectives and soldiers and sailors are the target and not women and children. Even if the Japs are savages, ruthless, merciless and fanatic, we as the leader of the world for the common welfare cannot drop that terrible bomb on the odd capital or the new.
>
> He and I are in accord. The target will be a purely military one and we will issue a warning statement asking the Japs to surrender and saves lives I'm sure they will not do that, but we will have given them the chance. It is certainly a good thing for the world that Hitler's crowd or Stalin's did not discover this atomic bomb. It seems to be the most terrible thing ever discovered, but it can be made the most useful . . .

Source: Truman quoted in Robert H. Ferrell. *Off the Record: The Private Papers of Harry S. Truman* (New York: Harper and Row, 1980), pp. 55–56. Available online. URL: http://www.dannen.com/decision/hst-jl25.html. Accessed March 23, 2007.

U.S. President Harry S. Truman Announces the Dropping of the Atomic Bomb on Hiroshima (August 7, 1945)

The first of the two atomic bombs that have been used in warfare was dropped on the Japanese city of Hiroshima on August 6, 1945. The following day, as he was returning from the Potsdam Conference aboard the USS Augusta, *Truman received the message "HIROSHIMA BOMBED . . ." and exclaimed to his staff, "This is the greatest thing in history!" He announced the news in a national radio address excerpted below. In contrast to later explanations of the decision to drop the bomb, which emphasize a desire to save lives that would be lost in the taking of the Japanese home islands in the last stages of the war, Truman's speech to the American people stresses revenge. Reminding his listeners of the attack on Pearl Harbor, Truman says that the Japanese, who started the war, have been "repaid." Though Truman asserted that Hiroshima was a "military base," glossing over the loss of civilian life, a more candid speech might not have made his listeners question his decision. American soldiers were still dying in large numbers—thousands sometimes in a single battle—and the bombing of enemy cities had become a source of satisfaction, not regret, to people on the home front.*

> "Sixteen hours ago an American airplane dropped one bomb on Hiroshima, an important Japanese Army base. That bomb had more power than 20,000 tons of TNT. It had more than 2,000 times the blast power of the British "Grand Slam," which is the largest bomb ever yet used in the history of warfare.
>
> The Japanese began the war from the air at Pearl Harbor. They have been repaid manyfold. And the end is not yet. With this bomb we have now added a new and revolutionary increase in destruction to supplement the growing power of our armed forces. In their present form these bombs are now in production, and even more powerful forms are in development.
>
> It is an atomic bomb. It is a harnessing of the basic power of the universe. The force from which the sun draws its power has been loosed against those who brought war to the Far East. . . .

Source: "Harry S. Truman's Announcement of the Dropping of an Atomic Bomb on Hiroshima, 1945." Available online. URL: http://www.classbrain.com/artteenst/publish/article_99.shtml. Accessed March 23, 2007.

Eisenhower's Atoms for Peace Speech (December 8, 1953)

A state of deep mistrust and mutual fear already existed between the United States and the Soviet Union when Dwight D. Eisenhower assumed office in 1953. Though both the cold war and the U.S.-Soviet nuclear arms race proceeded apace during Eisenhower's eight years as president, he evidently wished things were otherwise, and he began a bold attempt to change them in this speech delivered personally to the UN General Assembly during the end of his first year as president. The proposals Eisenhower put forward in this speech eventually evolved into the Atoms for Peace program. Under Atoms for Peace, nuclear weapons states would help other nations develop nuclear technology in exchange for their acceptance of controls that would make it difficult for them to develop nuclear weapons. A similar bargain would become the basis for the Nuclear Nonproliferation Treaty.

On July 16, 1945, the United States set off the world's first atomic explosion. Since that date in 1945, the United States of America has conducted 42 test explosions.

Atomic bombs today are more than 25 times as powerful as the weapons with which the atomic age dawned, while hydrogen weapons are in the ranges of millions of tons of TNT equivalent.

Today, the United States' stockpile of atomic weapons, which, of course, increases daily, exceeds by many times the explosive equivalent of the total of all bombs and all shells that came from every plane and every gun in every theatre of war in all of the years of World War II.

A single air group, whether afloat or land-based, can now deliver to any reachable target a destructive cargo exceeding in power all the bombs that fell on Britain in all of World War II.

In size and variety, the development of atomic weapons has been no less remarkable. The development has been such that atomic weapons have virtually achieved conventional status within our armed services. In the United States, the Army, the Navy, the Air Force, and the Marine Corps are all capable of putting this weapon to military use.

But the dread secret, and the fearful engines of atomic might, are not ours alone.

In the first place, the secret is possessed by our friends and allies, Great Britain and Canada, whose scientific genius made a tremendous contribution to our original discoveries, and the designs of atomic bombs.

The secret is also known by the Soviet Union.

The Soviet Union has informed us that, over recent years, it has devoted extensive resources to atomic weapons. During this period, the Soviet Union has exploded a series of atomic devices, including at least one involving thermo-nuclear reactions.

If at one time the United States possessed what might have been called a monopoly of atomic power, that monopoly ceased to exist several years ago. Therefore, although our earlier start has permitted us to accumulate what is today a great quantitative advantage, the atomic realities of today comprehend two facts of even greater significance.

First, the knowledge now possessed by several nations will eventually be shared by others—possibly all others.

Second, even a vast superiority in numbers of weapons, and a consequent capability of devastating retaliation, is no preventive, of itself, against the fearful material damage and toll of human lives that would be inflicted by surprise aggression.

The free world, at least dimly aware of these facts, has naturally embarked on a large program of warning and defense systems. That program will be accelerated and expanded.

But let no one think that the expenditure of vast sums for weapons and systems of defense can guarantee absolute safety for the cities and citizens of any nation. The awful arithmetic of the atomic bomb does not permit any such easy solution. Even against the most powerful defense, an aggressor in possession of the effective minimum number of atomic bombs for a surprise attack could probably place a sufficient number of his bombs on the chosen targets to cause hideous damage.

Should such an atomic attack be launched against the United States, our reactions would be swift and resolute. But for me to say that the defense capabilities of the United States are such that they could inflict terrible losses upon an aggressor—for me to say that the retaliation capabilities of the United States are so great that such an aggressor's land would be laid waste—all this, while fact, is not the true expression of the purpose and the hope of the United States.

To pause there would be to confirm the hopeless finality of a belief that two atomic colossi are doomed malevolently to eye each other indefinitely across a trembling world. To stop there would be to accept helplessly the probability of civilization destroyed—the annihilation of the irreplaceable heritage of mankind handed down to us generation from generation—and the condemnation of mankind to begin all over again the age-old struggle upward from savagery toward decency, and right, and justice.

Surely no sane member of the human race could discover victory in such desolation. Could anyone wish his name to be coupled by history with such human degradation and destruction....

These is at least one new avenue of peace which has not yet been well explored—an avenue now laid out by the General Assembly of the United Nations.

In its resolution of November 18th, 1953 this General Assembly suggested-and I quote—"that the Disarmament Commission study the desirability of establishing a sub-committee consisting of representatives of the Powers principally involved, which should seek in private an acceptable solution ... and report on such a solution to the General Assembly and to the Security Council not later than 1 September 1954."

The United States, heeding the suggestion of the General Assembly of the United Nations, is instantly prepared to meet privately with such other countries as may be "principally involved," to seek "an acceptable solution" to the atomic armaments race which over shadows not only the peace, but the very life, of the world.

We shall carry into these private or diplomatic talks a new conception.

The United States would seek more than the mere reduction or elimination of atomic materials for military purposes.

It is not enough to take this weapon out of the hands of the soldiers. It must be put into the hands of those who will know how to strip its military casing and adapt it to the arts of peace.

The United States knows that if the fearful trend of atomic military build up can be reversed, this greatest of destructive forces can be developed into a great boon, for the benefit of all mankind.

The United States knows that peaceful power from atomic energy is no dream of the future. That capability, already proved, is here—now—today. Who can doubt, if the entire body of the world's scientists and engineers had adequate amounts of fissionable material with which to test and develop their ideas, that this capability would rapidly be transformed into universal, efficient, and economic usage.

To hasten the day when fear of the atom will begin to disappear from the minds of people, and the governments of the East and West, there are certain steps that can be taken now.

I therefore make the following proposals:

The Governments principally involved, to the extent permitted by elementary prudence, to begin now and continue to make joint contributions from their stockpiles of normal uranium and fissionable materials to an international Atomic Energy Agency. We would expect that such an agency would be set up under the aegis of the United Nations.

The ratios of contributions, the procedures and other details would properly be within the scope of the "private conversations" I have referred to earlier.

The United states is prepared to under take these explorations in good faith. Any partner of the United States acting in the same good faith will find the United States a not unreasonable or ungenerous associate.

Undoubtedly initial and early contributions to this plan would be small in quantity. However, the proposal has the great virtue that it can be under taken without the irritations and mutual suspicions incident to any attempt to set up a completely acceptable system of world-wide inspection and control.

The Atomic Energy Agency could be made responsible for the impounding, storage, and protection of the contributed fissionable and other materials. The ingenuity of our scientists will provide special safe conditions under which such a bank of fissionable material can be made essentially immune to surprise seizure.

The more important responsibility of this Atomic Energy Agency would be to devise methods where by this fissionable material would be allocated to serve the peaceful pursuits of mankind. Experts would be mobilized to apply atomic energy to the needs of agriculture, medicine, and other peaceful activities. A special purpose would be to provide abundant electrical energy in the power-starved areas of the world. Thus the contributing powers would be dedicating some of their strength to serve the needs rather than the fears of mankind.

The United States would be more than willing—it would be proud to take up with others "principally involved:" the development of plans where by such peaceful use of atomic energy would be expedited.

Of those "principally involved" the Soviet Union must, of course, be one.

I would be prepared to submit to the Congress of the United States, and with every expectation of approval, any such plan that would:

First—encourage world-wide investigation into the most effective peace time uses of fissionable material, and with the certainty that they had all the material needed for the conduct of all experiments that were appropriate;

Second—begin to diminish the potential destructive power of the world's atomic stockpiles;

Third—allow all peoples of all nations to see that, in this enlightened age, the great powers of the earth, both of the East and of the West, are interested in human aspirations first, rather than in building up the armaments of war;

Fourth—open up a new channel for peaceful discussion, and initiate at least a new approach to the many difficult problems that must be solved in both private and public conversations, if the world is to shake off the inertia imposed by fear, and is to make positive progress toward peace. . . .

Source: "Atoms for Peace," address given by Dwight D. Eisenhower before the General Assembly of the United Nations on December 8, 1953. The Eisenhower Center. Available online. URL: http://www.eisenhower.archives.gov/speeches/Atoms_For_Peace_UN_speech.html. Accessed March 23, 2007.

U.S. President Dwight D. Eisenhower Warns the Nation of the "Military—Industrial Complex" (January 17, 1961)

The presidential administration of Dwight D. Eisenhower witnessed and promoted an unprecedented increase in peacetime military spending and with it the growth of military contractors whose principal source of business was the sale of military hardware—tanks, missiles, helicopters, automatic weapons, computer systems, etc.—to a permanently enlarged military force. As Eisenhower noted in his farewell address to the nation, this was a relatively new state of affairs. In earlier eras and earlier conflicts, the government's military needs had been supplied primarily by consumer goods companies who adapted their production to meet a crisis, turning "plowshares into swords" as needed. While Eisenhower believed that the United States confronted a genuine threat in the Soviet Union, making this permanent military buildup necessary, he noted that it created a group of powerful interests with an ominous potential for influencing policy. Not only the military contractors themselves, but their workers and politicians in their home states anxious to bring home "pork" to their constituents had a vested interest in perpetuating this buildup. In other parts of the speech, Eisenhower addresses issues that seem even timelier now than they did in 1961: He reminds his fellow Americans to take care of the environment and not to prefer war to the "frustrations" of diplomacy.

[. . .]

A vital element in keeping the peace is our military establishment. Our arms must be mighty, ready for instant action, so that no potential aggressor may be tempted to risk his own destruction.

Our military organization today bears little relation to that known by any of my predecessors in peacetime, or indeed by the fighting men of World War II or Korea.

Until the latest of our world conflicts, the United States had no armaments industry. American makers of plowshares could, with time and as required, make swords as well. But now we can no longer risk emergency improvisation of national defense; we have been compelled to create a permanent armaments industry of vast proportions. Added to this, three and a half million men and women are directly engaged in the defense establishment. We annually spend on military security more than the net income of all United States corporations.

This conjunction of an immense military establishment and a large arms industry is new in the American experience. The total influence—economic, political, even spiritual—is felt in every city, every State house, every office of the Federal government. We recognize the imperative need for this development. Yet we must not fail to comprehend its grave implications. Our toil, resources and livelihood are all involved; so is the very structure of our society.

In the councils of government, we must guard against the acquisition of unwarranted influence, whether sought or unsought, by the military-industrial complex. The potential for the disastrous rise of misplaced power exists and will persist.

We must never let the weight of this combination endanger our liberties or democratic processes. We should take nothing for granted. Only an alert and knowledgeable citizenry can compel the proper meshing of the huge industrial and military machinery of defense with our peaceful methods and goals, so that security and liberty may prosper together.

Akin to, and largely responsible for the sweeping changes in our industrial-military posture, has been the technological revolution during recent decades.

In this revolution, research has become central; it also becomes more formalized, complex, and costly. A steadily increasing share is conducted for, by, or at the direction of, the Federal government.

Today, the solitary inventor, tinkering in his shop, has been overshadowed by task forces of scientists in laboratories and testing fields. In the same fashion, the free university, historically the fountainhead of free ideas and scientific discovery, has experienced a revolution in the conduct of research. Partly because of the huge costs involved, a government contract becomes virtually a substitute for intellectual curiosity. For every old blackboard there are now hundreds of new electronic computers.

The prospect of domination of the nation's scholars by Federal employment, project allocations, and the power of money is ever present and is gravely to be regarded.

Yet, in holding scientific research and discovery in respect, as we should, we must also be alert to the equal and opposite danger that public policy could itself become the captive of a scientific-technological elite.

It is the task of statesmanship to mold, to balance, and to integrate these and other forces, new and old, within the principles of our democratic system—ever aiming toward the supreme goals of our free society.

V.

Another factor in maintaining balance involves the element of time. As we peer into society's future, we—you and I, and our government—must avoid the impulse to live only for today, plundering, for our own ease and convenience, the precious resources of tomorrow. We cannot mortgage the material assets of our grandchildren without risking the loss also of their political and spiritual heritage. We want democracy to survive for all generations to come, not to become the insolvent phantom of tomorrow.

VI.

Down the long lane of the history yet to be written America knows that this world of ours, ever growing smaller, must avoid becoming a community of dreadful fear and hate, and be instead, a proud confederation of mutual trust and respect.

Such a confederation must be one of equals. The weakest must come to the conference table with the same confidence as do we, protected as we are by our moral, economic, and military strength. That table, though scarred by many past frustrations, cannot be abandoned for the certain agony of the battlefield.

Source: "Eisenhower's Farewell Address to the Nation—January 17, 1961." Available online. URL: http://mcad ams.posc.mu.edu/ike.htm. Accessed March 11, 2007.

President Ronald Reagan's "Star Wars" Speech (March 23, 1983)

On March 23, 1983, at the end of a long televised address on national security, Ronald Reagan introduced his Strategic Defense Initiative (SDI), a proposal to use ground-based and space-based systems to protect the United States from attack by strategic nuclear ballistic missiles. Reagan was deeply uneasy with the balance of terror between the nuclear forces of the United States and the Soviet Union, a military state of affairs summed up by the phrase "mutually assured destruction." He responded enthusiastically to scientific advisers who suggested that with the right investment an antimissile technology could provide a foolproof shield against nuclear attack. If it would work as well as Reagan hoped, such a defensive system would have the effect of putting the nuclear genie back in the bottle. Critics, however, charged that Reagan's proposal was militarily naïve, technically unworkable, and astronomically expensive, for starters. Perhaps worst of all, it was destabilizing. Shields are usually used in combination with swords, and combined with Reagan's other nuclear military programs, SDI might send a message that the United States intended to wage and win a nuclear war. SDI's critics tried to kill it with ridicule, dubbing the program "Star Wars." While SDI never proved itself to be technically feasible, today's missile defense programs are descended from it and still have their advocates.

[. . . .] Now, thus far tonight I have shared with you my thoughts on the problems of national security we must face together. My predecessors in the Oval Office have appeared before you on other occasions to describe the threat posed by Soviet power and have proposed steps to address that threat. But since the advent of nuclear weapons, those steps have been increasingly directed toward deterrence of aggression through the promise of retaliation. This approach to stability through offensive threat has worked. We and our allies have succeederd in preventing nuclear war for more than three decades. In recent months, however, my advisers, including in particular the Joint Chiefs of Staff, have underscored the necessity to break out of a future that relies solely on offensive retaliation for our security.

Over the course of these discussions, I have become more and more deeply convinced that the human spirit must be capable of rising above dealing with other nations and human beings by threatening their existence. Feeling this way, I believe we must throroughly examine every opportunity for reducing tensions and for introducing greater stability into the strategic calculus on both sides. One of the most important contributions we can make is, of course, to lower the level of all arms, and particularly nuclear arms. We are engaged right now in several negotiations with the Soviet Union to bring about a mutual reduction of weapons. I will report to you a week from tomorrow my thoughts on that score. But let me just say I am totally committed to this course.

If the Soviet Union will join with us in our effort to achieve major arms reduction we will have succeeded in stabilizing the nuclear balance. Nevertheless it will still be necessary to rely on the specter of retaliation—on mutual threat, and that is a sad commentary on the human condition.

Wouldn't it be better to save lives than to avenge them? Are we not capable of demonstrating our peaceful intentions by applying all our abilities and our ingenuity to achieving a truly lasting stability? I think we are—indeed, we must!

After careful consultation with my advisers, including the Joint Chiefs of Staff, I believe there is a way. Let me share with you a vision of the future which offers hope. It is that we embark on a progam to counter the awesome Soviet missile threat with measures that are defensive. Let us turn to the very strengths in technology that spawned our great industrial base and that have given us the quality of life we enjoy today.

What if free people could live secure in the knowledge that their security did not rest upon the threat of instant U.S. retaliation to deter a Soviet attack; that we could intercept and destroy strategic ballistic missiles before they reached our own soil or that of our allies?

I know this is a formidable technical task, one that may not be accomplished before the end of this century. Yet, current technology has attained a level of sophistication where it is reasonable for us to begin this effort. It will take years, probably decades, of effort on many fronts. There will be failures and setbacks just as there will be successes and breakthroughs. And as we proceed we must remain constant in preserving the nuclear deterrent and maintaining a solid capability for flexible response. But isn't worth every investment necesary to free the world from the threat of nuclear war? We know it is!

In the meantime, we will continue to pursue real reductions in nuclear arms, negotiating from a position of strength that can be insured only by modernizing our strategic forces. At the same time, we must take steps to reduce the risk of a conventional military conflict escalating to nuclear war by improving our nonnuclear capabilities. America does possess—now—the technologies to attain very significant improvements in the effectiveness of our conventional, nonnuclear forces. Proceeding boldly with these new technologies, we can significantly reduce any incentive that the Soviet Union may have to threaten attack against the United States or its allies.

Honoring Commitments

As we pursue our goal of defensive technologies, we recognize that our allies rely upon our strategic offensive power to deter attacks against them. Their vital interests and ours are inextricably linked—their safety and ours are one. And no change in technology can or will alter that reality. We must and shall continue to honor our commitments.

I clearly recognize that defensive systems have limitations and raise certain problems and ambiguities. If paired with offensive systems, they can be viewed as fostering an aggressive policy and no one wants that.

But with these considerations firmly in mind, I call upon the scientific community in our country, those who gave us nuclear weapons to turn their great talents now to the cause of mankind and world peace: to give us the means of rendering these nuclear weapons impotent and obsolete.

Tonight, consistent with our obligations under the ABM Treaty and recognizing the need for closer consultation with our allies, I am taking an important first step. I am directing a comprehensive and intensive effort to define a long-term research and development program to begin to achieve our ultimate goal of eliminating the threat posed by strategic nuclear missiles. This could pave the way for arms control measures to eliminate the weapons themselves. We seek neither military superiority nor political advantage. Our only purpose—one all people share—is to search for ways to reduce the danger of nuclear war.

My fellow Americans, tonight we are launching an effort which holds the promise of changing the course of human history. There will be risks, and results take time. But I believe we can do it. As we cross this threshold, I ask for your prayers and your support. Thank you, good night and God bless you.

Source: "President Reagan's Strategic Defense Initiative Speech, March 23, 1983." Available online. URL: http://www.fas.org/spp/starwars/offdocs/rrspch.htm. Accessed March 26, 2007.

George W. Bush's "Axis of Evil" Speech (January 29, 2002)

In his 2002 State of the Union speech, delivered soon after the American invasion of Afghanistan, U.S. president George W. Bush named three countries believed to be seeking nuclear weapons and accused of supporting terrorism an "axis of evil," representing a threat to the security of the United States. The countries were Iraq, Iran, and North Korea. It was later reported that Bush's speech writer, David Frum, came up with the phrase "axis of hatred," later changed to "axis of evil." He had been given the assignment of making a very succinct case for overthrowing Iraqi dictator Saddam Hussein. Frum later said that he was inspired by his rereading of Franklin Roosevelt's speech. The foes of the United States in World War II were called the "Axis," and though temporarily allies they really disliked and distrusted one another, as undoubtedly Iraq, Iran, and North Korea did.

For the Bush administration's critics, the parallel seemed far-fetched, and so did the idea that Iraq, Iran, and North Korea constituted a single problem. However, the specter of a nuclear weapons state that also supported terrorism eventually persuaded the mainstream American media that war with Iraq was necessary.

Thank you very much. Mr. Speaker, Vice President Cheney, members of Congress, distinguished guests, fellow citizens: As we gather tonight, our nation is at war, our economy is in recession, and the civilized world faces unprecedented dangers. Yet the state of our Union has never been stronger.

We last met in an hour of shock and suffering. In four short months, our nation has comforted the victims, begun to rebuild New York and the Pentagon, rallied a great coalition, captured, arrested, and rid the world of thousands of terrorists, destroyed Afghanistan's terrorist training camps, saved a people from starvation, and freed a country from brutal oppression.

The American flag flies again over our embassy in Kabul. Terrorists who once occupied Afghanistan now occupy cells at Guantanamo Bay. And terrorist leaders who urged followers to sacrifice their lives are running for their own.

America and Afghanistan are now allies against terror. . . .

Our cause is just, and it continues. Our discoveries in Afghanistan confirmed our worst fears, and showed us the true scope of the task ahead. We have seen the depth of our enemies' hatred in videos, where they laugh about the loss of innocent life. And the depth of their hatred is equaled by the madness of the destruction they design. We have found diagrams of American nuclear power plants and public water facilities, detailed instructions for making chemical weapons, surveillance maps of American cities, and thorough descriptions of landmarks in America and throughout the world.

What we have found in Afghanistan confirms that, far from ending there, our war against terror is only beginning. Most of the 19 men who hijacked planes on September the 11th were trained in Afghanistan's camps, and so were tens of thousands of others. Thousands of dangerous killers, schooled in the methods of murder, often supported by outlaw regimes, are now spread throughout the world like ticking time bombs, set to go off without warning.

Thanks to the work of our law enforcement officials and coalition partners, hundreds of terrorists have been arrested. Yet, tens of thousands of trained terrorists are still at large. These enemies view the entire world as a battlefield, and we must pursue them wherever they are. So long as training camps operate, so long as nations harbor terrorists, freedom is at risk. And America and our allies must not, and will not, allow it.

Our nation will continue to be steadfast and patient and persistent in the pursuit of two great objectives. First, we will shut down terrorist camps, disrupt terrorist plans, and bring terrorists to justice. And, second, we must prevent the terrorists and regimes who seek chemical, biological or nuclear weapons from threatening the United States and the world.

Our military has put the terror training camps of Afghanistan out of business, yet camps still exist in at least a dozen countries. A terrorist underworld—including groups like Hamas, Hezbollah, Islamic Jihad, Jaish-i-Mohammed—operates in remote jungles and deserts, and hides in the centers of large cities.

While the most visible military action is in Afghanistan, America is acting elsewhere. We now have troops in the Philippines, helping to train that country's armed forces to go after terrorist cells that have executed an American, and still hold hostages. Our soldiers, working with the Bosnian government, seized terrorists who were plotting to bomb our embassy. Our Navy is patrolling the coast of Africa to block the shipment of weapons and the establishment of terrorist camps in Somalia.

My hope is that all nations will heed our call, and eliminate the terrorist parasites who threaten their countries and our own. Many nations are acting forcefully. Pakistan is now cracking down on terror, and I admire the strong leadership of President Musharraf.

But some governments will be timid in the face of terror. And make no mistake about it: If they do not act, America will.

Our second goal is to prevent regimes that sponsor terror from threatening America or our friends and allies with weapons of mass destruction. Some of these regimes have been pretty quiet since September the 11th. But we know their true nature. North Korea is a regime arming with missiles and weapons of mass destruction, while starving its citizens.

Iran aggressively pursues these weapons and exports terror, while an unelected few repress the Iranian people's hope for freedom.

Iraq continues to flaunt its hostility toward America and to support terror. The Iraqi regime has plotted to develop anthrax, and nerve gas, and nuclear weapons for over a decade. This is a regime that has already used poison gas to murder thousands of its own citizens—leaving the bodies of mothers huddled over their dead children. This is a regime that agreed to international inspections—then kicked out the inspectors. This is a regime that has something to hide from the civilized world.

States like these, and their terrorist allies, constitute an axis of evil, arming to threaten the peace of the world. By seeking weapons of mass destruction, these regimes pose a grave and growing danger. They could provide these arms to terrorists, giving them the means to match their hatred. They could attack our allies or attempt to blackmail the United States. In any of these cases, the price of indifference would be catastrophic.

We will work closely with our coalition to deny terrorists and their state sponsors the materials, technology, and expertise to make and deliver weapons of mass destruction. We will develop and deploy effective missile defenses to protect America and our allies from sudden attack. And all nations should know: America will do what is necessary to ensure our nation's security.

We'll be deliberate, yet time is not on our side. I will not wait on events, while dangers gather. I will not stand by, as peril draws closer and closer. The United States of America will not permit the world's most dangerous regimes to threaten us with the world's most destructive weapons.

Our war on terror is well begun, but it is only begun. This campaign may not be finished on our watch—yet it must be and it will be waged on our watch.

We can't stop short. If we stop now—leaving terror camps intact and terror states unchecked—our sense of security would be false and temporary.

History has called America and our allies to action, and it is both our responsibility and our privilege to fight freedom's fight.

Source: President Delivers State of the Union Address. Available online. URL: http://www.whitehouse.gov/news/releases/2002/01/20020129-11.html. Accessed March 25, 2007.

IRAQ

National Intelligence Estimate, Iraq's Continuing Program of Weapons of Mass Destruction (October 2002) (excerpts)

A National Intelligence Estimate (NIE) is a document generated as needed by U.S. intelligence agencies summarizing their best judgment on a given issue. The October 2002 NIE regarding Iraq's weapons of mass destruction, was produced in great haste in response to a last-minute request from Congress, which sought a factual basis on which to make the momentous decision of whether to go to war in Iraq. Usually, such documents are highly classified, but sometimes an unclassified summary is prepared. The classified NIE was given to Congress two days before the key vote to go to war. An unclassified summary was also prepared, excerpted below, which was criticized as omitting important details. With what, in hindsight, looks like a selective and overly pessimistic reading of intelligence data concerning Iraq's weapons program, the October 2002 NIE reported that without outside intervention Saddam Hussein would have a nuclear weapon "within this decade." Discussing the flaws in the NIE later on the Public Broadcasting show Frontline, *weapons inspector David Kay (who led the team that determined there were no viable WMD programs in Iraq) called it "a poor job, probably the worst of the modern NIEs." He explained the failure by the "pressure" to produce a policy conclusion in the absence of sufficient information. Critics outside the intelligence community go further: They accuse the NIE's writers of obliging the administration by reaching conclusions that supported the case for war.*

We judge that Iraq has continued its weapons of mass destruction (WMD) programs in defiance of UN resolutions and restrictions. Baghdad has chemical and biological weapons as well as missiles with ranges in excess of UN restrictions; if left unchecked, it probably will have a nuclear weapon during this decade. (See INR alternative view at the end of these Key Judgments.)

We judge that we are seeing only a portion of Iraq's WMD efforts, owing to Baghdad's vigorous denial and deception efforts. Revelations after the Gulf war starkly demonstrate the extensive efforts undertaken by Iraq to deny information. We lack specific information on many key aspects of Iraq's WMD programs.

Since inspections ended in 1998, Iraq has maintained its chemical weapons effort, energized its missile program, and invested more heavily in biological weapons; in the view of most agencies, Baghdad is reconstituting its nuclear weapons program.

- Iraq's growing ability to sell oil illicitly increases Baghdad's capabilities to finance WMD programs; annual earnings in cash and goods have more than quadrupled, from $580 million in 1998 to about $3 billion this year.
- Iraq has largely rebuilt missile and biological weapons facilities damaged during Operation Desert Fox and has expanded its chemical and biological infrastructure under the cover of civilian production.
- Baghdad has exceeded UN range limits of 150 km with its ballistic missiles and is working with unmanned aerial vehicles (UAVs), which allow for a more lethal means to deliver biological and, less likely, chemical warfare agents.
- Although we assess that Saddam does not yet have nuclear weapons or sufficient material to make any, he remains intent on acquiring them. Most agencies assess that Baghdad started reconstituting its nuclear program about the time that UNSCOM inspectors departed—December 1998.

How quickly Iraq will obtain its first nuclear weapon depends on when it acquires sufficient weapons-grade fissile material.

- If Baghdad acquires sufficient fissile material from abroad it could make a nuclear weapon within several months to a year.
- Without such material from abroad, Iraq probably would not be able to make a weapon until 2007 to 2009, owing to inexperience in building and operating centrifuge facilities to produce highly enriched uranium and challenges in procuring the necessary equipment and expertise.

  - Most agencies believe that Saddam's personal interest in and Iraq's aggressive attempts to obtain high-strength aluminum tubes for centrifuge rotors—as well as Iraq's attempts to acquire magnets, high-speed balancing machines, and machine tools—provide compelling evidence that Saddam is reconstituting a uranium enrichment effort for Baghdad's nuclear weapons program. (DOE agrees that reconstitution of the nuclear program is underway but assesses that the tubes probably are not part of the program.)

- Iraq's efforts to re-establish and enhance its cadre of weapons personnel as well as activities at several suspect nuclear sites further indicate that reconstitution is underway.
- All agencies agree that about 25,000 centrifuges based on tubes of the size Iraq is trying to acquire would be capable of producing approximately two weapons' worth of highly enriched uranium per year.

• In a much less likely scenario, Baghdad could make enough fissile material for a nuclear weapon by 2005 to 2007 if it obtains suitable centrifuge tubes this year and has all the other materials and technological expertise necessary to build production-scale uranium enrichment facilities. . . .

Source: Craig R. Whitney, ed. "The National Intelligence Estimate." In *The WMD Mirage: Iraq's Decade of Deception and America's False Premise for War.* New York: PublicAffairs, 2005, pp. 17–19.

The View of the Secretary of State for Intelligence and Research (October 2002) (excerpts)

The National Intelligence Estimate, which was published in response to congressional request for information helpful in deciding whether to authorize the 2003 invasion of Iraq, also contained a minority view, emanating from the State Department. The office of the assistant secretary of state for intelligence and research (INR) put a different construction on the evidence cited in other parts of the report. Though not doubting Saddam Hussein's desire for weapons of mass destruction, the INR found that not enough was known to say it was likely that Iraq had succeeded in reconstituting its prohibited weapons programs.

State/INR Alternative View of Iraq's Nuclear Program

The Assistant Secretary of State for Intelligence and Research (INR) believes that Saddam continues to want nuclear weapons and that available evidence indicates that Baghdad is pursuing at least a limited effort to maintain and acquire nuclear weapons-related capabilities. The activities we have detected do not, however, add up to a compelling case that Iraq is currently pursuing what INR would consider to be an integrated and comprehensive approach to acquire nuclear weapons. Iraq may be doing so, but INR considers the available evidence inadequate to support such a judgment. Lacking persuasive evidence that Baghdad has launched a coherent effort to reconstitute its nuclear weapons program, INR is unwilling to speculate that such an effort began soon after the departure of UN inspectors or to project a timeline for the completion of activities it does not now see happening. As a result, INR is unable to predict when Iraq could acquire a nuclear device or weapon.

In INR's view Iraq's efforts to acquire aluminum tubes is central to the argument that Baghdad is reconstituting its nuclear weapons program, but INR is not persuaded that the tubes in question are intended for use as centrifuge rotors. INR accepts the judgment of technical experts at the U. S. Department of Energy (DOE) who have concluded that the tubes Iraq seeks to acquire are poorly suited for use in gas centrifuges to be used for uranium enrichment and finds unpersuasive the arguments advanced by others to make the case that they are intended for that purpose. INR considers it far more likely that the tubes are intended for another purpose, most likely the production of artillery rockets. The very large quantities being sought, the way the tubes were tested by the Iraqis, and the atypical lack of attention to operational security in the procurement efforts are among the factors, in addition to the DOE assessment, that lead INR to conclude that the tubes are not intended for use in Iraq's nuclear weapon program.

Confidence Levels for Selected Key Judgments in This Estimate

High Confidence

- Iraq is continuing, and in some areas expanding, its chemical, biological, nuclear and missile programs contrary to UN resolutions.
- We are not detecting portions of these weapons programs.
- Iraq possesses proscribed chemical and biological weapons and missiles.
- Iraq could make a nuclear weapon in months to a year once it acquires sufficient weapons-grade fissile material

Moderate Confidence

- Iraq does not yet have a nuclear weapon or sufficient material to make one but is likely to have a weapon by 2007 to 2009. (See INR alternative view, page 84).

Low Confidence

- When Saddam would use weapons of mass destruction.
- Whether Saddam would engage in clandestine attacks against the US Homeland.
- Whether in desperation Saddam would share chemical or biological weapons with al-Qa'ida.

INR's Alternative View:
Iraq's Attempts to Acquire Aluminum Tubes

Some of the specialized but dual-use items being sought are, by all indications, bound for Iraq's missile program. Other cases are ambiguous, such as that of a planned magnet-production line whose suitability for centrifuge operations remains unknown. Some efforts involve non-controlled industrial material and equipment—including a variety of machine tools—and are troubling because they would help establish the infrastructure for a renewed nuclear program. But such efforts (which began well before the inspectors departed) are not clearly linked to a nuclear end-use. Finally, the claims of Iraqi pursuit of natural uranium in Africa are, in INR's assessment, highly dubious.

Source: Craig R. Whitney, ed. "State/INR Alternative View of Iraq's Nuclear Program." In *The WMD Mirage: Iraq's Decade of Deception and America's False Premise for War.* New York: PublicAffairs, 2005, pp. 23–25.

President Bush Addresses the Nation on Iraq (March 27, 2003) (excerpts)

In September 2002, as a coalition consisting mainly of U.S. and U.K. forces prepared to invade Iraq, Saddam Hussein, who had expelled UN weapons inspectors from his county in 1999, agreed to let them back in. On March 7, Hans Blix, the leader of the UN Special Commission that conducted the inspections. asked for more time to continue the work, but the United States insisted that Iraq would only continue to deceive the inspectors and it was necessary to disarm Iraq by force. In the speech excerpted here, the president announced the imminent invasion of Iraq, citing as his justification the threat that Saddam Hussein would give nuclear weapons to terrorists.

My fellow citizens, events in Iraq have now reached the final days of decision. For more than a decade, the United States and other nations have pursued patient and honorable efforts to disarm the Iraqi regime without war. That regime pledged to reveal and destroy all its weapons of mass destruction as a condition for ending the Persian Gulf War in 1991.

Since then, the world has engaged in 12 years of diplomacy. We have passed more than a dozen resolutions in the United Nations Security Council. We have sent hundreds of weapons inspectors to oversee the disarmament of Iraq. Our good faith has not been returned.

The Iraqi regime has used diplomacy as a ploy to gain time and advantage. It has uniformly defied Security Council resolutions demanding full disarmament. Over the years, U.N. weapon inspectors have been threatened by Iraqi officials, electronically bugged, and systematically deceived. Peaceful efforts to disarm the Iraqi regime have failed again and again—because we are not dealing with peaceful men.

Intelligence gathered by this and other governments leaves no doubt that the Iraq regime continues to possess and conceal some of the most lethal weapons ever devised. This regime has already used weapons of mass destruction against Iraq's neighbors and against Iraq's people.

The regime has a history of reckless aggression in the Middle East. It has a deep hatred of America and our friends. And it has aided, trained and harbored terrorists, including operatives of al Qaeda.

The danger is clear: using chemical, biological or, one day, nuclear weapons, obtained with the help of Iraq, the terrorists could fulfill their stated ambitions and kill thousands or hundreds of thousands of innocent people in our country, or any other.

Last September, I went to the U.N. General Assembly and urged the nations of the world to unite and bring an end to this danger. On November 8th, the Security Council unanimously passed Resolution 1441, finding Iraq in material breach of its obligations, and vowing serious consequences if Iraq did not fully and immediately disarm.

Today, no nation can possibly claim that Iraq has disarmed. And it will not disarm so long as Saddam Hussein holds power. For the last four-and-a-half months, the United States and our allies have worked within the Security Council to enforce that Council's long-standing demands. Yet, some permanent members of the Security Council have publicly announced they will veto any resolution that compels the disarmament of Iraq. These governments share our assessment of the danger, but not our resolve to meet it. Many nations, however, do have the resolve and fortitude to act against this threat to peace, and a broad coalition is now gathering to enforce the just demands of the world. The United Nations Security Council has not lived up to its responsibilities, so we will rise to ours.

We are now acting because the risks of inaction would be far greater. In one year, or five years, the power of Iraq to inflict harm on all free nations would be multiplied many times over. With these capabilities, Saddam Hussein and his terrorist allies could choose the moment of deadly conflict when they are strongest. We choose to meet that threat now, where it arises, before it can appear suddenly in our skies and cities. . . .

Source: Craig R. Whitney, ed. "President George W. Bush Addresses the Nation on Iraq." In *The WMD Mirage: Iraq's Decade of Deception and America's False Premise for War.* New York: PublicAffairs, 2005, pp. 166–170.

David Kay's Opening Statement to the Senate Armed Services Committee (January 28, 2004)

The United States had first led a coalition against Iraq in 1991 as part of a mission to counter Iraq's 1990 invasion and occupation of its neighbor Kuwait. As part of the settlement that ended that 1991 war, Iraq and its dictator, Saddam Hussein, were required to allow international weapons inspectors to oversee the destruction of his WMD; he was also forced to agree not to develop new WMD. Though it seems that all or nearly all of the weapons were, in fact, destroyed under UN supervision, Hussein played a cat-and-mouse game with the inspection team, often attempting to thwart and deceive them. In 1998, he expelled the inspection team and defied international demands that he let them return in accordance with the agreements he had signed. Saddam Hussein may have practiced these deceptions and expelled the inspectors in order to prepare to rebuild his WMD capability at a later date, or he may have done these things in order to fool potential rivals in the region, reasoning that the possibility that Iraq had WMD was sufficient to intimidate rivals and deter attack. In any event, he had not been able to rebuild his chemical, biological, or nuclear weapons programs. In the wake of Operation Iraqi Freedom, the Iraqi Survey Group, led by weapons inspector David Kay, hunted for the weapons that had been used to justify the war. Their search failed to supply that justification, as Kay informed the U.S. Senate in January 2004.

Let me begin by saying, we were almost all wrong, and I certainly include myself here.

Senator [Edward] Kennedy knows very directly. Senator Kennedy and I talked on several occasions prior to the war that my view was that the best evidence that I had seen was that Iraq indeed had weapons of mass destruction.

I would also point out that many governments that chose not to support this war—certainly, the French president, [Jacques] Chirac, as I recall in April of last year, referred to Iraq's possession of WMD.

The Germans certainly—the intelligence service believed that there were WMD.

It turns out that we were all wrong, probably in my judgment, and that is most disturbing.

We're also in a period in which we've had intelligence surprises in the proliferation area that go the other way. The case of Iran, a nuclear program that the Iranians admit was 18 years on, that we underestimated. And, in fact, we didn't discover it. It was discovered by a group of Iranian dissidents outside the country who pointed the international community at the location.

The Libyan program recently discovered was far more extensive than was assessed prior to that.

There's a long record here of being wrong. There's a good reason for it. There are probably multiple reasons. Certainly proliferation is a hard thing to track, particularly in countries that deny easy and free access and don't have free and open societies.

In my judgment, based on the work that has been done to this point of the Iraq Survey Group, and in fact, that I reported to you in October, Iraq was in clear violation of the terms of [U.N.] Resolution 1441. Resolution 1441 required that Iraq report all of its activities—one last chance to come clean about what it had.

We have discovered hundreds of cases, based on both documents, physical evidence and the testimony of Iraqis, of activities that were prohibited under the initial U.N. Resolution 687 and that should have been reported under 1441, with Iraqi testimony that not only did they not tell the U.N. about this, they were instructed not to do it and they hid material.

I think the aim—and certainly the aim of what I've tried to do since leaving—is not political and certainly not a witch hunt at individuals. It's to try to direct our attention at what I believe is a fundamental fault analysis that we must now examine.

And let me take one of the explanations most commonly given: Analysts were pressured to reach conclusions that would fit the political agenda of one or another administration. I deeply think that is a wrong explanation.

And like I say, I think we've got other cases other than Iraq. I do not think the problem of global proliferation of weapons technology of mass destruction is going to go away, and that's why I think it is an urgent issue. . . .

Source: Craig R. Whitney, ed. "David Kay's Opening Statement to the Senate Armed Services Committee." In *The WMD Mirage: Iraq's Decade of Deception and America's False Premise for War.* New York: PublicAffairs, 2005, pp. 198–201.

Senate Select Committee on Intelligence Report on the U.S. Intelligence Community's Prewar Intelligence Assessments on Iraq (July 9, 2004)

Following the U.S.-led invasion of Iraq on March 20, 2003, which overthrew Saddam Hussein's government, U.S. weapons inspectors were able to conduct a thorough search for Iraq's WMD. They found little or no evidence of the menacing weapons programs discussed in the 2002 National Intelligence Estimate. The failure to find weapons that had been used to justify an invasion of a sovereign country, an invasion conducted over the protests of UN weapons inspectors who had asked for more time to do their jobs, was a serious embarrassment for the United States and its leaders. On June 20, 2003, Senator Pat Roberts, a Republican and the chairman of the Senate Select Committee on Intelligence, and Senator John D. Rockefeller IV, a Democrat and that committee's vice chairman, announced that the committee would conduct a detailed review of the Iraqi WMD intelligence process. The committee's report, issued on July 9, 2004, identified numerous failures in the intelligence gathering and analysis. The report found that these failures led to the creation of inaccurate materials that misled both government policy makers and the American public. The report of a second phase of the investigation, addressing the way senior policy makers used the intelligence, was published on May 25, 2007. These documents are available online on the Web site of the Senate Select Committee on Intelligence.

Conclusions

Overall Conclusions—Weapons of Mass Destruction

Conclusion 1. Most of the major key judgments in the Intelligence Community's October 2002 National Intelligence Estimate (NIE), Iraq's Continuing Programs for Weapons of Mass Destruction, either overstated, or were not supported by, the underlying intelligence reporting. A series of failures, particularly in analytic trade craft, led to the mischaracterization of the intelligence.

The major key judgments in the NIE, particularly that Iraq "is reconstituting its nuclear program," "has chemical and biological weapons," was developing an unmanned aerial vehicle (UAV) "probably intended to deliver biological warfare agents," and that "all key aspects—research & development (R&D), production, and weaponization—of Iraq's offensive biological weapons (BW) program are active and that most elements are larger and more advanced than they were before the Gulf War," either overstated, or were not supported by, the underlying intelligence reporting provided to the Committee. The assessments regarding Iraq's continued development of prohibited ballistic missiles were reasonable and did accurately describe the underlying intelligence.

The assessment that Iraq "is reconstituting its nuclear program" was not supported by the intelligence provided to the Committee. The intelligence reporting did show that Iraq was procuring dual-use equipment that had potential nuclear applications, but all of the equipment had conventional military or industrial applications. In addition, none of the intelligence reporting indicated that the equipment was being procured for suspect nuclear facilities. Intelligence reporting also showed that former Iraqi nuclear scientists continued to work at former nuclear facilities and organizations, but the reporting did not show that this cadre of nuclear personnel had recently been regrouped or enhanced as stated in the NIE, nor did it suggest that they were engaged in work related to a nuclear weapons program.

Source: Craig R. Whitney, ed. "Senate Select Committee on Intelligence Report on the U.S. Intelligence Community's Prewar Intelligence Assessments on Iraq." In *The WMD Mirage: Iraq's Decade of Deception and America's False Premise for War.* New York: PublicAffairs, 2005, pp. 202–203.

NORTH KOREA

Review of United States Policy Toward North Korea: Findings and Recommendations (October 12, 1999)

In November 1998, President Bill Clinton and his national security advisers asked a team led by Dr. William J. Perry to conduct an extensive review of U.S. policy toward the secretive, totalitarian, and economically troubled

Democratic Republic of North Korea. For more than a decade, the primary goal of U.S. policy toward North Korea had been to prevent the country from acquiring nuclear weapons; this had been the special aim of the 1994 "Agreed Framework," a hastily-put-together pact in which the U.S. and other interested parties, including South Korea, committed themselves to providing North Korea with various forms of assistance if North Korea would forgo nuclear weapons development. In 1998, U.S. leaders were also concerned with North Korea's sales of ballistic missiles and nuclear technology, North Korea's support for terrorism, the economic collapse of the country, and the potential results, whether good or disastrous, of the often-anticipated collapse of the North Korean regime. The results of the review were published almost a year later. While history has written new chapters to the story, the report is still of use as a source of information on the North Korean regime and an analysis of U.S. policy toward the country.

The Agreed Framework of 1994 succeeded in verifiably freezing North Korean plutonium production at Yongbyon—it stopped plutonium production at that facility so that North Korea currently has at most a small amount of fissile material it may have secreted away from operations prior to 1994; without the Agreed Framework, North Korea could have produced enough additional plutonium by now for a significant number of nuclear weapons. Yet, despite the critical achievement of a verified freeze on plutonium production at Yongbyon under the Agreed Framework, the policy review team has serious concerns about possible continuing nuclear weapons-related work in the DPRK. Some of these concerns have been addressed through our access and visit to Kumchang-ni.

The years since 1994 have also witnessed development, testing, deployment, and export by the DPRK of ballistic missiles of increasing range, including those potentially capable of reaching the territory of the United States.

There have been other significant changes as well. Since the negotiations over the Agreed Framework began in the summer of 1994, formal leadership of the DPRK has passed from President Kim Il Sung to his son, General Kim Jong Il, and General Kim has gradually assumed supreme authority in title as well as fact. North Korea is thus governed by a different leadership from that with which we embarked on the Agreed Framework. During this same period, the DPRK economy has deteriorated significantly, with industrial and food production sinking to a fraction of their 1994 levels. The result is a humanitarian tragedy which, while not the focus of the review, both compels the sympathy of the American people and doubtless affects some of the actions of the North Korean regime.

An unrelated change has come to the government of the Republic of Korea (ROK) with the Presidency of Kim Dae Jung. President Kim has embarked upon a policy of engagement with the North. As a leader of great international authority, as our ally, and as the host to 37,000 American troops, the views and insights of President Kim are central to accomplishing U.S. security objectives on the Korean Peninsula. No U.S. policy can succeed unless it is coordinated with the ROK's policy. Today's ROK policy of engagement creates conditions and opportunities for U.S. policy very different from those in 1994.

Another close U.S. ally in the region, Japan, has become more concerned about North Korea in recent years. This concern was heightened by the launch, in August 1998, of a Taepo Dong missile over Japanese territory. Although the Diet has passed funding for the Light Water Reactor project being undertaken by the Korean Peninsula Energy Development Organization (KEDO) pursuant to the Agreed Framework, and the government wants to preserve the Agreed Framework, a second missile launch is likely to have a serious impact on domestic political support for the Agreed Framework and have wider ramifications within Japan about its security policy.

The policy review team made the following key findings, which have formed the basis for our recommendations:

1. DPRK acquisition of nuclear weapons and continued development, testing, deployment, and export of long-range missiles would undermine the relative stability of deterrence on the Korean Peninsula, a precondition for ending the Cold War and pursuing a lasting peace in the longer run. These activities by the DPRK also have serious regional and global consequences adverse to vital U.S. interests. The United States must, therefore, have as its objective ending these activities.

2. The United States and its allies would swiftly and surely win a second war on the Korean Peninsula, but the destruction of life and property would far surpass anything in recent American experience. The U.S. must pursue its objectives with respect to nuclear weapons and ballistic missiles in the DPRK without taking actions that would weaken deterrence or increase the probability of DPRK miscalculation.

3. If stability can be preserved through the cooperative ending of DPRK nuclear weapons- and long-range missile-related activities, the U.S. should be prepared to establish more normal diplomatic relations with the DPRK and join in the ROK's policy of engagement and peaceful coexistence.

4. Unfreezing Yongbyon is North Korea's quickest and surest path to acquisition of nuclear weapons. The Agreed Framework, therefore, should be preserved and implemented by the United States and its allies. With the Agreed Framework, the DPRK's ability to produce plutonium at Yongbyon is verifiably frozen. Without the Agreed Framework, however, it is estimated that the North could reprocess enough plutonium to produce a significant number of nuclear weapons per year. The Agreed Framework's limitations, such as the fact that it does not verifiably freeze all nuclear weapons-related activities and does not cover ballistic missiles, are best addressed by supplementing rather than replacing the Agreed Framework.

5. No U.S. policy toward the DPRK will succeed if the ROK and Japan do not actively support it and cooperate in its implementation. Securing such trilateral coordination should be possible, since the interests of the three parties, while not identical, overlap in significant and definable ways.

6. Considering the risks inherent in the situation and the isolation, suspicion, and negotiating style of the DPRK, a successful U.S. policy will require steadiness and persistence even in the face of provocations. The approach adopted now must be sustained into the future, beyond the term of this Administration. It is, therefore, essential that the policy and its ongoing implementation have the broadest possible support and the continuing involvement of the Congress. . . .

Source: Institute for Science and International Security. "Solving the North Korean Nuclear Puzzle. Appendix 6: Review of United States Policy Toward North Korea: Findings and Recommendations ("Perry Report")." Available online. URL: http://www.isisonline.org/publications/dprk/book/perryrpt.html. Accessed March 23, 2007.

Untitled Central Intelligence Paper Provided to Congress (November 19, 2002)

In October 2002, U.S. officials confronted North Korean officials about their clandestine uranium enrichment program, triggering an end to the eight-year freeze on its nuclear program by expelling inspectors and reopening its plutonium production facilities. The CIA estimated that North Korea could produce five to six nuclear weapons by the middle of 2003. The progress

North Korea had made in the production of ballistic missiles gave additional cause for concern.

Nuclear Weapons

The US has been concerned about North Korea's desire for nuclear weapons and has assessed since the early 1990s that the North has one or possibly two weapons using plutonium it produced prior to 1992.

In 1994, P'yongyang halted production of additional plutonium under the terms of the US-DPRK Agreed Framework.

- We have assessed, however, that despite the freeze at Yongbyon the North has continued its nuclear weapons program.

If the Framework Collapses

If North Korea abandoned the Agreed Framework P'yongyang could resume production of plutonium.

- Reprocessing the spent 5 MWe reactor fuel now in storage at Yongbyon site under IAEA safeguards would recover enough plutonium for several more weapons.
- Restarting the 5 MWe reactor would generate about 6 kg per year.
- The 50 MWe reactor at Yongbyon and the 200 MWe reactor at Taechon would generate about 275 kg per year, although it would take several years to complete construction of these reactors.

Uranium Enrichment

The United States has been suspicious that North Korea has been working on uranium enrichment for several years. However, we did not obtain clear evidence indicating the North had begun constructing a centrifuge facility until recently. We assess that North Korea embarked on the effort to develop a centrifuge-based uranium enrichment program about two years ago.

- Last year the North began seeking centrifuge-related materials in large quantities. It also obtained equipment suitable for use in uranium feed and withdrawal systems.
- We recently learned that the North is constructing a plant that could produce enough weapons-grade uranium for two or more nuclear

weapons per year when fully operational—which could be as soon as mid-decade.

- We continue to monitor and assess the North's nuclear weapons efforts, which given the North's closed society and the obvious covert nature of the program, remains a difficult intelligence collection target.

Source: Wampler, Robert A., ed. "Document 22: CIA, Untitled, November 2002." In *North Korea and Nuclear Weapons: The Declassified U.S. Record.* National Security Archive Electronic Briefing Book No. 87. Available online. URL: http://www.gwu.edu/~nsarchiv/NSAEEBB/NSAEBB87nk22.pdf

North Korea's Nuclear Weapons Program (March 17, 2003)

In late 2002, North Korea expelled the nuclear weapons inspectors of the IAEA, and in January 2003, it withdrew from the Nuclear Nonproliferation Treaty, as it had threatened to do in 1993, and from the Agreed Framework, the 1994 pact that had acted as a restraint on North Korea's nuclear ambitions. Though the actions of North Korea's secretive government can be mysterious, failures of other parties to live up to their obligations under the Agreed Framework and President Bush's decision to brand North Korea a member of the "axis of evil" may have contributed to North Korea's decision to resume its quest for the bomb. This paper, prepared by the Congressional Research Service, a nonpartisan research arm of the U.S. Congress, reviews the implementation of the Agreed Framework and other U.S. attempts to halt North Korea's nuclear weapons program since the early 1990s.

Summary

North Korea's decisions to restart nuclear installations at Yongbyon that were shut down under the U.S.-North Korean Agreed Framework of 1994 and withdraw from the Nuclear Non-Proliferation Treaty create an acute foreign policy problem for the United States. North Korea's major motive appears to be to escalate pressure on the Bush Administration to negotiate over Pyongyang's proposed nonaggression pact and/or a new nuclear agreement that would provide new U.S. benefits to North Korea. However, restarting the Yongbyon facilities opens up a possible North Korean intent to stage a "nuclear breakout" of its nuclear program and openly produce nuclear weapons within six months. North Korea's actions follow the disclosure in October 2002 that North Korea is operating a secret nuclear program based on uranium enrichment and the decision by the Korean Peninsula Energy Development Organization (KEDO) in November 2002 to suspend shipments of heavy oil to North Korea.

The main elements of Bush Administration policy are (1) terminating the Agreed Framework; (2) no bilateral negotiations with North Korea until it satisfies U.S. concerns over its unclear program; (3) assembling an international coalition to pressure North Korea; and (4) proposing multilateral talks involving North Korea and other countries, possibly under United Nations auspices; (5) warning and planning for future economic sanctions against North Korea; and (6) warning North Korea not to reprocess nuclear weapons-grade plutonium, including asserting that "all options are open," including military options. China, South Korea, and Russia have criticized the Bush Administration for not negotiating directly with North Korea, and they voice opposition to economic sanctions and to the use of force against Pyongyang. The Administration has placed emphasis on China as a source of pressure on North Korea.

The crisis is the culmination of eight years of implementation of the 1994 Agreed Framework, which provides for the shutdown of North Korea's nuclear facilities in return for the delivery to North Korea of 500,000 tons of heavy oil and the construction in North Korea of two light water nuclear reactors. The United States pledged to issue a nuclear security guarantee to North Korea as North Korea complied with its 1992 safeguards agreement with the International Atomic Energy Agency.

Most Recent Developments

In mid-January 2003, the Bush Administration attempted to develop a new strategy toward North Korea after North Korea withdrew from the Nuclear Non-Proliferation Treaty, reopened nuclear installations shut down under the 1994 U.S.-North Korean Agreed Framework, expelled monitors from the International Atomic Energy Agency (IAEA), re-started operation of a nuclear reactor (February 2003), and demanded new negotiations with the United States. The Administration also was influenced to adjust policy by increased criticisms from South Korea, China, and Russia, calling on the Bush Administration to negotiate with North Korea and opposing statements by Administration officials concerning future economic sanctions against North Korea. In February 2003, the Administration promoted a multilateral forum for talks on the North Korean nuclear issue, involving the five permanent members of the U.N. Security Council and five other countries, including Japan, South Korea, and North Korea. Secretary of State Powell gained qualified support of the proposal from Japan and South Korea during his February trip to East Asia. However, the Administration reportedly was unwilling to commit to U.S.-North Korean talks within a multilateral framework. As war with Iraq appeared closer, the Administration gave mixed signals on whether it would use military force to prevent North Korea from taking advantage of the war to reprocess weapons-grade plutonium and use the plutonium to produce several atomic bombs.

Background and Analysis Implications of North Korea's Actions Since October 2002

The Bush Administration disclosed on October 16, 2002, that North Korea had revealed to U.S. Assistant Secretary of State James Kelly in Pyongyang that it was conducting a secret nuclear weapons program based on the process of uranium enrichment. North Korea admitted the program in response to U.S. evidence presented by Kelly. The program is based on the process of uranium enrichment, in contrast to North Korea's pre-1995 nuclear program based on plutonium reprocessing. North Korea began a secret uranium enrichment program after 1995 reportedly with the assistance of Pakistan. North Korea provided Pakistan with intermediate range ballistic missiles in the late 1990s. The Central Intelligence Agency issued a statement in December 2002 that North Korea likely could produce an atomic bomb through uranium enrichment in 2004.

In admitting to the secret program, Vice Foreign Minister Kang Sok-ju (an important figure in the North Korean regime) declared to Kelly that North Korea also possesses "more powerful" weapons. North Korea proposed a new U.S.-North Korean negotiation of a bilateral non-aggression pact and an agreement for the United States to cease "stifling" North Korea's economy. The North Korean proposal asserts that these agreements would open the way for resolving the nuclear issue. Some U.S. experts, however, believe that the non-aggression pact proposal is a "smokescreen" for North Korea's long-standing proposal (since 1974) of a U.S.-North Korean bilateral peace treaty. As stated, both proposed pacts would replace the 1953 Korean armistice, and neither would include South Korea as a participant. North Korea has long stated that a negotiation of a bilateral peace treaty would include provisions for the withdrawal of U.S. military forces from South Korea. The United States and South Korea have rejected consistently the bilateral peace agreement proposal. However, reports in early January 2003 held that the South Korean government was exploring formulas under which the United States could offer North Korea a security guarantee as part of a nuclear settlement. Some experts also believe that North Korea's demand for the cessation of U.S. "stifling" of its economy is a subterfuge for Pyongyang's demand since 1999 that the United States remove North Korea from the U.S. list of terrorist countries, thus, in effect, making North Korea eligible for financial assistance from the World Bank, the International Monetary Fund, and the Asian Development Bank.

By their own admission, Bush Administration officials were surprised by the intensity of North Korea's moves in late December 2002 to re-start nuclear facilities at Yongbyon and expel officials of the International Atomic Energy Agency placed there under the U.S.-North Korean Agreed Framework of 1994 to monitor the shutdown. North Korea announced that it would re-start the small, five megawatt nuclear reactor shut down under the Agreed Framework and resume construction of two larger reactors that was frozen under the agreement. The reactor began operating in February 2003. It also announced that it would re-start the plutonium reprocessing plant that operated up to 1994. It withdrew from the Nuclear Non-Proliferation Treaty (NPT) in January 2003. It justified its action by citing the U.S.-initiated cut-off of heavy oil shipments in December 2002 and by charging that the Bush Administration planned a "pre-emptive nuclear attack" on North Korea.

North Korea's major motive appears to be to escalate pressure on the Bush Administration to negotiate over Pyongyang's proposed non-aggression pact and/or a new nuclear agreement that would provide new U.S. benefits to North Korea. Pyongyang long has emphasized "intimidation tactics" in its diplomacy; and since October 2002 it has issued other threats including a resumption of long-range missile tests and stepped-up proliferation of weapons to other countries. However, re-starting the Yongbyon facilities opens up a possible North Korean intent or option to stage a "breakout" of its nuclear program in 2003 by openly producing nuclear weapons. The most dangerous follow-up North Korean move would be to move 8,000 stored nuclear fuel rods at Yongbyon into the plutonium reprocessing plant for the production of nuclear weapons-grade plutonium. According to estimates by nuclear experts and reportedly by U.S. intelligence agencies, if North Korea began to reprocess the fuel rods, it would take about four months to produce weapons grade plutonium and another one or two months to produce four to six atomic bombs.

Bush Administration Policy

The Bush Administration's policy response to North Korean actions since October 2002 consists of:

(1) Continuing priority to Iraq: President Bush reportedly has said that he does not want two simultaneous crises. U.S. officials say they will rely on diplomacy and expect diplomacy to run well into 2003. They argue that North Korea's actions do not constitute a crisis.

(2) Progressive suspension of the Agreed Framework: Administration officials have stated that the Agreed Framework will be terminated. Statements indicate a debate with the Administration over the timing of ending it.

(3) Ambivalence toward negotiations with North Korea: Until January 7, 2003, the Administration rejected negotiation of any new agreement with North Korea over the secret nuclear program, insisting that North Korea first abide by its past nuclear agreements, which Pyongyang increasingly has violated. On January 7, 2003, the Administration proposed a dialogue with North Korea that would not be the negotitation of a new agreement. In a communique of January 7, 2003, with Japan and South Korea, the proposal stated that "the United States is willing to talk to North Korea about how it will meet its obligations to the international community" but that "the United States will not provide quid pro quos to North Korea to live up to its existing obligations."

(4) Forming an international coalition to pressure North Korea to end its nuclear program: The Administration's "five plus five proposal" is the latest tactical move in this strategy.

(5) Warning of the prospect of economic sanctions if North Korea does not end its nuclear program: The Administration reportedly is drafting plans for economic sanctions, including cutting off financial flows to North Korea from Japan and other sources and interdicting North Korean weapons shipments to the Middle East and South Asia. References to economic sanctions have produced an open dispute with South Korea; Roh Moo-hyun, the new President, strongly criticized the idea of economic sanctions. China and Russia also oppose economic sanctions.

(6) Ambivalence concerning U.S. military options if North Korea fully activates its nuclear program.

The Administration's strategy is to employ public accusations and warnings to pressure North Korea to make policy changes regarding its military assets in line with U.S. objectives. (For a discussion of overall Bush policy toward North Korea, see CRS Issue Brief IB98045, *Korea: U.S.-South Korean Relations–Issues for Congress.*) According to Administration officials, the policy insists that North Korea come into full compliance with its obligations to the International Atomic Energy Agency (IAEA) regarding its nuclear program. When President Bush waived certification in March 2002 that North Korea was in compliance with the Agreed Framework, Administration officials asserted that this was an added warning to North Korea to begin the process of compliance with its obligations to the IAEA.

North Korea's Nuclear Program

Most of North Korea's plutonium-based nuclear installations are located at Yongbyon, 60 miles of the North Korean capital of Pyongyang. The key installations are:

- **An atomic reactor, with a capacity of about 5 electrical megawatts, constructed between 1980 and 1987:** it reportedly is capable of expending enough uranium fuel to produce about 7 kilograms of plutonium annually—enough for the manufacture of a single atomic bomb annually. North Korea in 1989 shut down the reactor for about 70 days; U.S. intelligence agencies believe that North Korea removed fuel rods from the reactor at that time for reprocessing into plutonium suitable for nuclear weapons. In May 1994, North Korea shut down the reactor and removed about 8,000 fuel rods, which could be reprocessed into enough plutonium for 4–6 nuclear weapons. These fuel rods remain in storage.
- **Two larger (estimated 50 electrical megawatts and 200 electrical megawatts) atomic reactors under construction at Yongbyon and Taechon since 1984:** According to U.S. Ambassador Robert Gallucci, these plants, if completed, would be capable of producing enough spent fuel annually for 200 kilograms of plutonium, sufficient to manufacture nearly 30 atomic bombs per year.
- **A plutonium reprocessing plant about 600 feet long and several stories high:** The plant would separate weapons grade Plutonium-239 from spent nuclear fuel rods for insertion into the structure of atomic bombs or warheads.

Satellite photographs reportedly also show that the atomic reactors have no attached power lines, which they would have if used for electric power generation.

Source: CRS Issue Brief for Congress. Available online. URL: http://fpc.state.gov/documents/organization/9566.pdf. Accessed March 11, 2007.

North Korea Nuclear Deal a "Breakthrough," Rice Says (February 13, 2007)

Facing criticism from its allies for its policy toward North Korea, in 2003 the United States helped organize a series of multilateral discussions among the countries with a special interest in East Asia—North Korea, South Korea,

China, Japan, Russia, and the United States. Over a three-year period, several rounds of Six-Party Talks made little headway. On October 6, 2006, North Korea announced that it had successfully tested an atomic bomb. The UN Security Council voted to impose sanctions on North Korea, imposing restrictions on its weapons sales, banning travel to North Korea, and freezing the overseas assets of people associated with North Korea's weapons programs. Soon afterward, North Korea agreed to resume the Six-Party Talks. This last round of talks concluded in an agreement, which was hailed as a breakthrough in the U.S. State Department press release excerpted here.

Washington—Secretary of State Condoleezza Rice says North Korea's decision to dismantle its nuclear weapons in exchange for energy aid is a "breakthrough step."

Rice spoke to reporters February 13 following the latest round of Six-Party Talks, held in Beijing among North Korea, South Korea, China, Japan, Russia and the United States.

She said the agreement is part of a "broad and comprehensive effort" not only to achieve a nuclear-free Korean Peninsula but also "to advance the future of peace and prosperity in Northeast Asia."

President Bush praised the February 13 deal in a separate statement, saying, "These talks represent the best opportunity to use diplomacy to address North Korea's nuclear programs." Bush called the agreement a "first step" toward implementing the September 19, 2005, statement between the six countries in which they agreed on the goal of a nuclear-free Korean Peninsula.

Christopher Hill, the lead U.S. envoy for the Six-Party Talks, told reporters the breakthrough in the current round of talks came after North Korean diplomats insisted aid deliveries be defined clearly. Negotiators agreed, but demanded that North Korea discuss the disabling of its nuclear programs immediately rather than leaving the issue for future talks.

"We took what was essentially a sticking point and used it as a way to make further progress on the road to denuclearization," said Hill, the assistant secretary for East Asian and Pacific affairs.

The February 13 agreement is divided between an initial 60-day "action" phase and a future "disablement" phase. Rice described it as "a reasonable way to go about removing nuclear programs from the Korean Peninsula," as well as to "turn back" North Korea's 30-year nuclear program.

According to the initial action plan of the agreement, North Korea, during the first 60-day phase, will shut down and seal its main nuclear reactor at Yongbyon, allow international verification and provide a list of all of its nuclear programs to the other Six-Party Talks participants.

During the same period, the other members will provide North Korea an initial shipment of 50,000 tons of heavy fuel oil (HFO) as emergency energy assistance. If the provisions of the initial phase have been satisfied, an additional 950,000 tons of HFO will be provided.

The agreement also calls for the creation of five working groups that will meet within the next 30 days. Those groups are focused on achieving a nuclear-free Korean Peninsula, the normalization of U.S.-North Korean relations, the normalization of Japan-North Korean relations, economic and energy cooperation, and the creation of a Northeast Asia peace and security mechanism.

Under the U.S.-North Korean working group, the two countries will hold discussions aimed at resolving "pending bilateral issues" and moving toward the establishment of full diplomatic relations, according to the action plan.

The United States also will review North Korea's membership on its list of state sponsors of terrorism. "This is, I think, the right time to do that. We will see what the record shows on North Korea during this period of time, but we think it makes perfectly good sense to start that review, and we'll look at the record," Secretary Rice said.

The secretary said the agreement was multilateral, and all six parties are its guarantors. "All of the major players in the region now share a stake in its outcome, as well as a demand for results and accountability," she said.

Source: "North Korea Deal a 'Breakthrough,' Rice Says." Available online. URL: http://usinfo.state.gov/xarchives/display.html?p=washfile-english&y=2007&m=February&x=20070213150224esnamfuak0.8298456. Accessed March 27, 2007.

5

International Documents

The Baruch Plan (June 14, 1946)

It was less than a year since the world had learned of the existence of the atomic bomb, the rubble was only beginning to be cleared from the major cities of Germany and Japan, and the UN was a new, untested institution when U.S. delegate Bernard Baruch delivered this speech to the first meeting of the UN Atomic Energy Commission (a body established in the UN General Assembly's first resolution). "We are here to make a choice between the quick and the dead," Baruch told the other delegates on June 14, and proceeded to outline a plan for the international control of atomic energy. The proposal would have given enormous power to a proposed International Atomic Energy Authority.

Though it would be unfair to dismiss the Baruch Plan as propaganda, the administration of President Harry Truman failed to make a serious effort to negotiate an agreement based on it. The world was asked to take it or leave it, and the world decided to leave it. The Soviet Union in particular would not agree to the plan as originally presented because it required it to give up its atomic bomb program before the United States surrendered its monopoly on nuclear weapons. Meanwhile, many U.S. policy makers considered atomic weapons a legitimate tool of foreign policy and did not see the point of giving them up to the UN.

The Baruch Plan, presented to the United Nations Atomic Energy Commission, June 14, 1946

My Fellow Members of the United Nations Atomic Energy Commission, and My Fellow Citizens of the World:

We are here to make a choice between the quick and the dead.

That is our business.

Behind the black portent of the new atomic age lies a hope which, seized upon with faith, can work out salvation. If we fail, then we have damned every man to be the slave to Fear. Let us not deceive ourselves: We must elect World Peace or World Destruction.

Science has torn from nature a secret so vast in its potentialities that our minds cower from the terror it creates. Yet terror is not enough to inhibit the use of the atomic bomb. The terror created by weapons has never stopped man from employing them. For each new weapon a defense has been produced, in time. But now we face a condition in which adequate defense does not exist. . . .

The United States proposes the creation of an International Atomic Development Authority, to which should be entrusted all phases of the development and use of atomic energy, starting with the raw material and including—

1. Managerial control or ownership of all atomic-energy activities potentially dangerous to world security.
2. Power to control, inspect, and license all other atomic activities.
3. The duty of fostering the beneficial uses of atomic energy.
4. Research and development responsibilities of an affirmative character intended to put the Authority in the forefront of atomic knowledge and thus to enable it to comprehend, and therefore to detect, misuse of atomic energy. To be effective, the Authority must itself be the world's leader in the field of atomic knowledge and development and thus supplement its legal authority with the great power inherent in possession of leadership in knowledge. . . .

1. Manufacture of atomic bombs shall stop;
2. Existing bombs shall be disposed of pursuant to the terms of the treaty; and
3. The Authority shall be in possession of full information as to the know-how or the production of atomic energy.

Let me repeat, so as to avoid misunderstanding: My country is ready to make its full contribution toward the end we seek, subject of course to our constitutional processes and to an adequate system of control becoming fully effective, as we finally work it out.

Now as to violations: In the agreement, penalties of as serious a nature as the nations may wish and as immediate and certain in their execution as possible should be fixed for—

1. Illegal possession or use of an atomic bomb;
2. Illegal possession, or separation, of atomic material suitable for use in an atomic bomb;
3. Seizure of any plant or other property belonging to or licensed by the Authority;
4. Willful interference with the activities of the Authority;
5. Creation or operation of dangerous projects in a manner contrary to, or in the absence of, a license granted by the international control body.

It would be a deception, to which I am unwilling to lend myself, were I not to say to you and to our peoples that the matter of punishment lies at the very heart of our present security system. It might as well be admitted, here and now, that the subject goes straight to the veto power contained in the Charter of the United Nations so far as it related to the field of atomic energy. The Charter permits penalization only by concurrence of each of the five great powers—the Union of Soviet Socialist Republics, the United Kingdom, China, France, and the United States.

I want to make very plain that I am concerned here with the veto power only as it affects this particular problem. There must be no veto to protect those who violate their solemn agreements not to develop or use atomic energy for destructive purposes....

Source: Atomic Archive. Available online. URL: http://www.atomicarchive.com/Docs/Deterrence/BaruchPlan.shtml. Accessed December 10, 2007.

The Russell-Einstein Manifesto (July 9, 1955)

In 1955, Albert Einstein was the most famous scientist in the world, recognized everywhere for his wild hair and casual sweatshirts and closely associated in the public mind with the atomic bomb. Bertrand Russell, though far less well known to the general public, was celebrated in the academic community as one of the fathers of analytic philosophy and as an active proponent of left-leaning international causes. Both Einstein and Russell had responded to the use of the atomic bomb on Japan in 1945 with warnings of the danger of a nuclear arms race; 10 years later, the situation looked even worse. The United States and the Soviet Union each possessed thermonuclear bombs 1,000 times more powerful than the one that destroyed Hiroshima. On February 11, 1955, a few months before Einstein's death, Russell wrote to him, suggesting that "eminent men of science ought to do something dramatic to bring home to the public and governments the disasters that may occur." Einstein agreed, and Russell drafted a statement that he circulated among a distinguished group of scientists in the hope of their joining him in signing it. Scientists in the Soviet Union and China refused to sign the statement, and Einstein died before it was published. In part because it amounted to the great scientist's last words, the media in the West gave the Russell-Einstein Manifesto a great deal of attention, and it helped to launch the antinuclear movement.

[. . .]

> We are speaking on this occasion, not as members of this or that nation, continent, or creed, but as human beings, members of the species Man, whose continued existence is in doubt. The world is full of conflicts; and, overshadowing all minor conflicts, the titanic struggle between Communism and anti-Communism. . . .
>
> It is stated on very good authority that a bomb can now be manufactured which will be 2,500 times as powerful as that which destroyed Hiroshima. Such a bomb, if exploded near the ground or under water, sends radio-active particles into the upper air. They sink gradually and reach the surface of the earth in the form of a deadly dust or rain. It was this dust which infected the Japanese fishermen and their catch of fish. No one knows how widely such lethal radio-active particles might be diffused, but the best authorities are unanimous in saying that a war with H-bombs might possibly put an end to the human race. It is feared that if many H-bombs are used there will be universal death, sudden only for a minority but for the majority a slow torture of disease and disintegration.
>
> Many warnings have been uttered by eminent men of science and by authorities in military strategy. None of them will say that the worst results are certain. What they do say is that these results are possible, and no one can be sure that they will not be realized. We have not yet found that the views of experts on this question depend in any degree upon their politics or prejudices. They depend only, so far as our researches have revealed, upon the extent of the particular expert's knowledge. We have found that the men who know most are the most gloomy.

Here, then, is the problem which we present to you, stark and dreadful and inescapable: Shall we put an end to the human race; or shall mankind renounce war? People will not face this alternative because it is so difficult to abolish war.

The abolition of war will demand distasteful limitations of national sovereignty. But what perhaps impedes understanding of the situation more than anything else is that the term "mankind" feels vague and abstract. People scarcely realize in imagination that the danger is to themselves and their children and their grandchildren, and not only to a dimly apprehended humanity. They can scarcely bring themselves to grasp that they, individually, and those whom they love are in imminent danger of perishing agonizingly. And so they hope that perhaps war may be allowed to continue provided modern weapons are prohibited.

This hope is illusory. Whatever agreements not to use H-bombs had been reached in time of peace, they would no longer be considered binding in time of war, and both sides would set to work to manufacture H-bombs as soon as war broke out, for, if one side manufactured the bombs and the other did not, the side that manufactured them would inevitably be victorious.

Although an agreement to renounce nuclear weapons as part of a general reduction of armaments would not afford an ultimate solution, it would serve certain important purposes. First, any agreement between East and West is to the good in so far as it tends to diminish tension. Second, the abolition of thermonuclear weapons, if each side believed that the other had carried it out sincerely, would lessen the fear of a sudden attack in the style of Pearl Harbour, which at present keeps both sides in a state of nervous apprehension. We should, therefore, welcome such an agreement though only as a first step. . . .

Source: "Russell-Einstein Manifesto." Available online. URL: http://www.pugwash.org/about/manifesto.htm. Accessed March 25, 2007.

The Antarctic Treaty (1959)

A frozen continent at the "bottom" of the world, Antarctica was uninhabited and inhospitable to human life, but fishermen and explorers from various countries had been conducting expeditions to it since the 18th century. By the 1950s, seven nations—Argentina, Australia, Chile, France, New Zealand, Norway, and the United Kingdom—claimed sovereignty over areas of Antarctica. Eight other nations, including the Untied States and the Soviet Union, had engaged in exploration in Antacrtica but made no legal claims on it; the Soviets and the United States also disputed the claims of other nations.

Exploration of Antarctica had been conducted in an atmosphere of peace and amity—in fact, U.S. and Soviet scientists had assisted each other with the blessings of their governments—but that might change if valuable mineral resources were discovered beneath the ice. And since the continent was uninhabited, it could become a site of nuclear weapons testing unless an international agreement forbade it. A desire to head off trouble led to this treaty, which preserved the status quo in Antarctica, declaring it international property, preventing the militarization of the continent, and banning nuclear weapons there. The treaty was first presented by the United States as a proposal to the International Geophysical Year of 1957–58, a multination scientific conference; it was signed by the 12 nations participating in the conference and ratified by the U.S. Senate in 1960. The Antarctic Treaty was important in itself, saving a large landmass from radioactive contamination. Additionally, it set a valuable precedent as the first major nuclear arms limitation agreement and the first of several treaties that established nuclear-free zones in outer space, in the seabed, and in various regions of the world.

Signed at Washington December 1, 1959
Ratification advised by U.S. Senate August 10, 1960
Ratified by U.S. President August 18, 1960
U.S. ratification deposited at Washington August 18, 1960
Proclaimed by U.S. President June 23, 1961
Entered into force June 23, 1961

The Governments of Argentina, Australia, Belgium, Chile, the French Republic, Japan, New Zealand, Norway, the Union of South Africa, the Union of Soviet Socialist Republics, the United Kingdom of Great Britain and Northern Ireland, and the United States of America. . . .

Have agreed as follows:

Article I

1. Antarctica shall be used for peaceful purposed only. There shall be prohibited, *inter alia,* any measures of a military nature, such as the establish-

ment of military bases and fortifications, the carrying out of military maneuvers, as well as the testing of any type of weapons.

2. The present treaty shall not prevent the use of military personnel or equipment for scientific research or for any other peaceful purposes. . . .

Article V

1. Any nuclear explosions in Antarctica and the disposal there of radioactive waste material shall be prohibited. . . .

Source: "The Antarctic Treaty—British Antarctic Survey." Available online. URL: http://www.antarctica.ac.uk/About_Antarctica/Treaty/treaty.html. Accessed March 25, 2007.

Ambassador Adlai Stevenson Addresses the United Nations Security Council (October 25, 1962)

On October 14, 1962, a U-2 spy plane discovered missile sites under construction in western Cuba. The missiles were obviously being installed with Soviet assistance and would be equipped with nuclear warheads if they were not already. John F. Kennedy's Joint Chiefs of Staff advised him to respond with an invasion of Cuba. Kennedy instead decided on a naval blockade of Cuba. The United States's ambassador to the United Nations, Adlai Stevenson, gave a presentation at an emergency session of the Security Council. In a famous confrontation with the Soviet representative, Valerian Zorin, Stevenson asked him point blank if his country was installing missiles in Cuba, then, when Zorin refused to answer, showed photographs.

American newspapers and television reporters frequently retold the story of Adlai Stevenson's 1962 address as U.S. secretary of state Colin Powell prepared to address the UN on the subject of Saddam Hussein in early 2003.

We are here today and have been this week for one single reason—because the Soviet Union secretly introduced this menacing offensive military buildup into the island of Cuba while assuring the world that nothing was further from their thoughts. . . .

I noted that there is still at least some delegates in the Council, possibly—I suspect very few—who say that they don't know whether the Soviet Union has in fact built in Cuba installations capable of firing nuclear missiles over ranges from 1000 to 2000 miles. As I say, Chairman Khrushchev did not deny these facts in his letter to Earl Russell, nor did Ambassador Zorin on

Tuesday evening. And if further doubt remains on this score, we shall gladly exhibit photographic evidence to the doubtful.

One other point I'd like to make, Mr. President and gentlemen, is invite attention to the casual remark of the Soviet representative claiming that we have 35 bases in foreign countries. The facts are that there are missiles comparable to these being placed in Cuba with the forces of only three of our allies. They were only established there by a decision of the heads of government meeting in December 1957 which was compelled to authorize such arrangements by virtue of a prior Soviet decision to introduce its own missiles capable of destroying the countries of Western Europe.

In the next place, there are some troublesome questions in the minds of members that are entitled to serious answers. There are those who say that conceding the fact that the Soviet Union has installed these offensive missiles in Cuba, conceding the fact that this constitutes a grave threat to the peace of the world—Why was it necessary for the nations of the Western hemisphere to act with such speed? Why could not the quarantine against the shipment of offensive weapons have been delayed until the Security Council and the General Assembly had a full opportunity to consider this—the situation and make recommendations?

Let me remind the members that the United States was not looking for some pretext to raise the issue of the transformation of Cuba into a military base. On the contrary, the United States made no objection whatever to the shipment of defensive arms by the Soviet Union to Cuba, even though such shipments offended the traditions of this hemisphere. Even after the first hard evidence reached Washington concerning the change in the character of Soviet military assistance to Cuba, the President of the United States responded by directing an intensification of surveillance. And only after the facts and the magnitude of the buildup had been established beyond all doubt did we begin to take this limited action of barring only those nuclear—only these nuclear weapons, equipment, and aircraft.

To understand the reasons for this prompt action it is necessary to understand the nature and the purposes of this operation. It has been marked above all by two characteristics: speed and stealth. As the photographic evidence makes clear, the installation of these missiles, the erection of these missile sites, has taken place with extraordinary speed. One entire complex was put up in 24 hours. This speed need not only—not only demonstrates the methodical organization and the careful planning involved, but it also demonstrates a premeditated attempt to confront this hemisphere with a fait accompli. By quickly completing the whole process of nuclearization of Cuba, the Soviet Union would be in a position to demand that the status quo be maintained and left undisturbed. And if we were to have delayed our counteraction, the nuclearization of Cuba would have been quickly completed. This is not a risk which this hemisphere is prepared to take. . . .

Source: "Adlai Stevenson: United Nations Security Council Address on Soviet Missiles in Cuba." Available online. URL: http://www.americanrhetoric.com/speeches/adlaistevensonunitednationscuba.html. Accessed March 11, 2007.

Hot Line Agreement (June 20, 1963)

The existence of nuclear-tipped intercontinental ballistic missiles that can reach their targets in half an hour puts a new kind of pressure on heads of state. In a supposedly democratic age, it concentrates awesome power in the hands of a very few people, and it may force them to make momentous decisions quickly based on inadequate information. The mutual distrust and secretiveness of the United States and the Soviet Union during the cold war increased the danger of a fateful misunderstanding, and from time to time during the 1950s and early 1960s, proposals were made to reduce the possibility of accidental war without resulting in international agreements.

The need for better communication between the leaders of the Soviet Union and the United States was underlined during the Cuban missile crisis. During the tense negotiations between U.S. president John F. Kennedy and Soviet premier Nikita Khrushchev, messages sent between Washington and Moscow crossed, and the leaders found themselves planning their next move based on a proposal that had already been superseded by a later message. A few months later, on December 12, 1962, the United States proposed a number of measures to reduce the risk of war, including the establishment of communications links between the major capitals to ensure rapid and reliable communication in times of crisis. This suggestion led to the Hot Line agreement, a limited but practical step to bring the perils inherent in modern nuclear weapons systems under rational control. It was the first of a series of such agreements. The Hot Line was used in 1967 to prevent possible misunderstanding of U.S. fleet movements in the Mediterranean. It was used again during the 1973 Arab-Israeli war. It was improved and modernized by agreements in 1971, 1984, and 1988.

Memorandum of Understanding Between The United States of America and The Union of Soviet Socialist Republics Regarding the Establishment of a Direct Communications Link

Signed at Geneva June 20, 1963
Entered into force June 20, 1963

For use in time of emergency the Government of the United States of America and the Government of the Union of Soviet Socialist Republics have agreed to establish as soon as technically feasible a direct communications link between the two Governments.

Each Government shall be responsible for the arrangements for the link on its own territory. Each Government shall take the necessary steps to ensure continuous functioning of the link and prompt delivery to its head of government of any communications received by means of the link from the head of government of the other party.

Arrangements for establishing and operating the link are set forth in the Annex which is attached hereto and forms an integral part hereof.

DONE in duplicate in the English and Russian languages at Geneva, Switzerland, this 20th day of June, 1963. . . .

ANNEX

TO THE MEMORANDUM OF UNDERSTANDING BETWEEN THE UNITED STATES OF AMERICA AND THE UNION OF SOVIET SOCIALIST REPUBLICS REGARDING THE ESTABLISHMENT OF A DIRECT COMMUNICATION LINK

The direct communications link between Washington and Moscow established in accordance with the Memorandum, and the operation of such link, shall be governed by the following provisions:

1. The direct communications link shall consist of:

a. Two terminal points with telegraph-teleprinter equipment between which communications shall be directly exchanged;

b. One full-time duplex wire telegraph circuit, routed Washington-London-Copenhagen- Stockholm-Helsinki-Moscow, which shall be used for the transmission of messages;
c. One full-time duplex radiotelegraph circuit, routed Washington-Tangier-Moscow, which shall be used for service communications and for coordination of operations between the two terminal points.

Source: "Hot Line Agreement." Available online. URL: http://www.state.gov/t/ac/trt/4785.htm. Accessed March 25, 2007.

Limited Test Ban Treaty (August 5, 1963)

Since the invention of the atomic bomb, nuclear weapons states have caused nuclear explosions, all except two for the purpose of testing the weapons . These tests cause immense, permanent damage to the environment. Radioactive materials harmful to animal and plant life are spread far from the site of the initial explosion by wind and rain; they enter groundwater, and they enter the food chain and thus the human diet. Since wind, rain, birds, and fish do not respect international borders, the tests affect people in non-nuclear weapons states, leading in the 1950s to an international outcry against the testing by nuclear weapons states. A dozen resolutions of the UN General Assembly urged nuclear weapons states to reach an agreement to ban tests. Though all nuclear explosions are harmful to plant and animal life, atmospheric testing causes the most immediate devastation and therefore the greatest international anger. In the early 1960s, as the United States and the Soviet Union developed a means to test weapons underground, they responded to international pressure to cease testing of nuclear weapons in the atmosphere.

Treaty Banning Nuclear Weapon Tests in the Atmosphere, in Outer Space and Under Water

Moscow August 5, 1963
Entered into force October 10, 1963

The Governments of the United States of America, the United Kingdom of Great Britain and Northern Ireland, and the Union of Soviet Socialist Republics. . . .

Have agreed as follows:

Article I

1. Each of the Parties to this Treaty undertakes to prohibit, to prevent, and not to carry out any nuclear weapon test explosion, or any other nuclear explosion, at any place under its jurisdiction or control:

(a) in the atmosphere; beyond its limits, including outer space; or under water, including territorial waters or high seas; or

(b) in any other environment if such explosion causes radioactive debris to be present outside the territorial limits of the State under whose jurisdiction or control such explosion is conducted. It is understood in this connection that the provisions of this subparagraph are without prejudice to the conclusion of a Treaty resulting in the permanent banning of all nuclear test explosions, including all such explosions underground, the conclusion of which, as the Parties have stated in the Preamble to this Treaty, they seek to achieve.

2. Each of the Parties to this Treaty undertakes furthermore to refrain from causing, encouraging, or in any way participating in, the carrying out of any nuclear weapon test explosion, or any other nuclear explosion, anywhere which would take place in any of the environments described, or have the effect referred to, in paragraph 1 of this Article.

Source: "Limited Test Ban Treaty." Available online. URL: http://www.state.gov/t/ac/trt/4797.htm. Accessed March 25, 2007.

The Nuclear Non-proliferation Treaty (July 1, 1968)

The proposals that led to the Nuclear Non-proliferation Treaty (NPT) were first advanced by Irish foreign minister Frank Aiken in 1959. Calling on the UN to recognize that nuclear weapons states were unlikely to give up their weapons in the near future, Aiken pointed out that the international situation would be even worse if nuclear weapons continued to spread to new nations. He argued that it was possible as well as desirable to use international agreements to keep nuclear weapons from spreading still further. Since such a treaty was obviously in the interest of the existing nuclear weapons states, they were willing to make concessions to nonnuclear weapons states to get them to sign on. Under the Nuclear Non-proliferation Treaty, as finally signed in 1968, nuclear weapons states promised to provide assistance to nonnuclear weapons states that would forgo the development of nuclear weapons. Nuclear weapons states also promised, albeit in ambiguous, loophole-laden language, to work toward the ultimate abolition of nuclear weapons. Criticized over the years for its loopholes and patched and buttressed by many other side agreements, today the Nuclear Non-proliferation Treaty remains the core of international efforts to control the spread of nuclear weapons. Its 11 articles are provided here in full.

Treaty On The Non-Proliferation Of Nuclear Weapons

Signed at Washington, London, and Moscow July 1, 1968
Ratification by U.S. Senate March 13, 1969

Article I

Each nuclear-weapon State Party to the Treaty undertakes not to transfer to any recipient whatsoever nuclear weapons or other nuclear explosive devices or control over such weapons or explosive devices directly, or indirectly; and not in any way to assist, encourage, or induce any non-nuclear weapon State to manufacture or otherwise acquire nuclear weapons or other nuclear explosive devices, or control over such weapons or explosive devices.

Article II

Each non-nuclear-weapon State Party to the Treaty undertakes not to receive the transfer from any transferor whatsoever of nuclear weapons or other nuclear explosive devices or of control over such weapons or explosive devices directly, or indirectly; not to manufacture or otherwise acquire nuclear weapons or other nuclear explosive devices; and not to seek or receive any assistance in the manufacture of nuclear weapons or other nuclear explosive devices.

Article III

1. Each non-nuclear-weapon State Party to the Treaty undertakes to accept safeguards, as set forth in an agreement to be negotiated and concluded with the International Atomic Energy Agency in accordance with the Statute of the International Atomic Energy Agency and the Agencys safeguards system, for the exclusive purpose of verification of the fulfillment of its obligations assumed under this Treaty with a view to preventing diversion of nuclear energy from peaceful uses to nuclear weapons or other nuclear explosive devices. Procedures for the safeguards required by this article shall be followed with respect to source or special fissionable material whether it is being produced, processed or used in any principal nuclear

facility or is outside any such facility. The safeguards required by this article shall be applied to all source or special fissionable material in all peaceful nuclear activities within the territory of such State, under its jurisdiction, or carried out under its control anywhere.

2. Each State Party to the Treaty undertakes not to provide: (a) source or special fissionable material, or (b) equipment or material especially designed or prepared for the processing, use or production of special fissionable material, to any non-nuclear-weapon State for peaceful purposes, unless the source or special fissionable material shall be subject to the safeguards required by this article.

3. The safeguards required by this article shall be implemented in a manner designed to comply with article IV of this Treaty, and to avoid hampering the economic or technological development of the Parties or international cooperation in the field of peaceful nuclear activities, including the international exchange of nuclear material and equipment for the processing, use or production of nuclear material for peaceful purposes in accordance with the provisions of this article and the principle of safeguarding set forth in the Preamble of the Treaty.

4. Non-nuclear-weapon States Party to the Treaty shall conclude agreements with the International Atomic Energy Agency to meet the requirements of this article either individually or together with other States in accordance with the Statute of the International Atomic Energy Agency. Negotiation of such agreements shall commence within 180 days from the original entry into force of this Treaty. For States depositing their instruments of ratification or accession after the 180-day period, negotiation of such agreements shall commence not later than the date of such deposit. Such agreements shall enter into force not later than eighteen months after the date of initiation of negotiations.

Article IV

1. Nothing in this Treaty shall be interpreted as affecting the inalienable right of all the Parties to the Treaty to develop research, production and use of nuclear energy for peaceful purposes without discrimination and in conformity with articles I and II of this Treaty.

2. All the Parties to the Treaty undertake to facilitate, and have the right to participate in, the fullest possible exchange of equipment, materials and

scientific and technological information for the peaceful uses of nuclear energy. Parties to the Treaty in a position to do so shall also cooperate in contributing alone or together with other States or international organizations to the further development of the applications of nuclear energy for peaceful purposes, especially in the territories of non-nuclear-weapon States Party to the Treaty, with due consideration for the needs of the developing areas of the world.

Article V

Each party to the Treaty undertakes to take appropriate measures to ensure that, in accordance with this Treaty, under appropriate international observation and through appropriate international procedures, potential benefits from any peaceful applications of nuclear explosions will be made available to non-nuclear-weapon States Party to the Treaty on a nondiscriminatory basis and that the charge to such Parties for the explosive devices used will be as low as possible and exclude any charge for research and development. Non-nuclear-weapon States Party to the Treaty shall be able to obtain such benefits, pursuant to a special international agreement or agreements, through an appropriate international body with adequate representation of non-nuclear-weapon States. Negotiations on this subject shall commence as soon as possible after the Treaty enters into force. Non-nuclear-weapon States Party to the Treaty so desiring may also obtain such benefits pursuant to bilateral agreements.

Article VI

Each of the Parties to the Treaty undertakes to pursue negotiations in good faith on effective measures relating to cessation of the nuclear arms race at an early date and to nuclear disarmament, and on a Treaty on general and complete disarmament under strict and effective international control.

Article VII

Nothing in this Treaty affects the right of any group of States to conclude regional treaties in order to assure the total absence of nuclear weapons in their respective territories.

Article VIII

1. Any Party to the Treaty may propose amendments to this Treaty. The text of any proposed amendment shall be submitted to the Depositary Governments which shall circulate it to all Parties to the Treaty. Thereupon, if requested to do so by one-third or more of the Parties to the Treaty, the Depositary Governments shall convene a conference, to which

they shall invite all the Parties to the Treaty, to consider such an amendment.

2. Any amendment to this Treaty must be approved by a majority of the votes of all the Parties to the Treaty, including the votes of all nuclear-weapon States Party to the Treaty and all other Parties which, on the date the amendment is circulated, are members of the Board of Governors of the International Atomic Energy Agency. The amendment shall enter into force for each Party that deposits its instrument of ratification of the amendment upon the deposit of such instruments of ratification by a majority of all the Parties, including the instruments of ratification of all nuclear-weapon States Party to the Treaty and all other Parties which, on the date the amendment is circulated, are members of the Board of Governors of the International Atomic Energy Agency. Thereafter, it shall enter into force for any other Party upon the deposit of its instrument of ratification of the amendment.

3. Five years after the entry into force of this Treaty, a conference of Parties to the Treaty shall be held in Geneva, Switzerland, in order to review the operation of this Treaty with a view to assuring that the purposes of the Preamble and the provisions of the Treaty are being realized. At intervals of five years thereafter, a majority of the Parties to the Treaty may obtain, by submitting a proposal to this effect to the Depositary Governments, the convening of further conferences with the same objective of reviewing the operation of the Treaty.

Article IX

1. This Treaty shall be open to all States for signature. Any State which does not sign the Treaty before its entry into force in accordance with paragraph 3 of this article may accede to it at any time.

2. This Treaty shall be subject to ratification by signatory States. Instruments of ratification and instruments of accession shall be deposited with the Governments of the United States of America, the United Kingdom of Great Britain and Northern Ireland and the Union of Soviet Socialist Republics, which are hereby designated the Depositary Governments.

3. This Treaty shall enter into force after its ratification by the States, the Governments of which are designated Depositaries of the Treaty, and forty other States signatory to this Treaty and the deposit of their instruments of

ratification. For the purposes of this Treaty, a nuclear-weapon State is one which has manufactured and exploded a nuclear weapon or other nuclear explosive device prior to January 1, 1967.

4. For States whose instruments of ratification or accession are deposited subsequent to the entry into force of this Treaty, it shall enter into force on the date of the deposit of their instruments of ratification or accession.

5. The Depositary Governments shall promptly inform all signatory and acceding States of the date of each signature, the date of deposit of each instrument of ratification or of accession, the date of the entry into force of this Treaty, and the date of receipt of any requests for convening a conference or other notices.

6. This Treaty shall be registered by the Depositary Governments pursuant to article 102 of the Charter of the United Nations.

Article X

1. Each Party shall in exercising its national sovereignty have the right to withdraw from the Treaty if it decides that extraordinary events, related to the subject matter of this Treaty, have jeopardized the supreme interests of its country. It shall give notice of such withdrawal to all other Parties to the Treaty and to the United Nations Security Council three months in advance. Such notice shall include a statement of the extraordinary events it regards as having jeopardized its supreme interests.

2. Twenty-five years after the entry into force of the Treaty, a conference shall be convened to decide whether the Treaty shall continue in force indefinitely, or shall be extended for an additional fixed period or periods. This decision shall be taken by a majority of the Parties to the Treaty.

Article XI

This Treaty, the English, Russian, French, Spanish and Chinese texts of which are equally authentic, shall be deposited in the archives of the Depositary Governments. Duly certified copies of this Treaty shall be transmitted by the Depositary Governments to the Governments of the signatory and acceding States.

Source: "Nuclear Non-proliferation Treaty (NPT)." Available online. URL: http://www.fas.org/nuke/control/npt/. Accessed March 25, 2007.

Antiballistic Missile Treaty (ABM Treaty) (May 26, 1972)

By the end of the 1960s, top military planners in both the United States and the USSR believed in a philosophy of nuclear deterrence summed up in the phrase "mutually assured destruction" (its critics find the acronym MAD highly appropriate). According to this view, the prevention of nuclear war between the Soviet Union and the United States depended on the certainty that both sides had a "second strike capability" that would make a sneak nuclear attack suicidal. It was felt that confidence in this second strike ability might be undermined by systems then in development that were intended to destroy incoming long-range ballistic missiles. Thus, the ABM Treaty restricted missile defense systems due to the uncertainty they added to this balance of terror. It also saved the Soviet Union and the United States the expense of adding yet another enormous and elaborate arm to their already gigantic military establishments. Military and political leaders critical of the mutually assured destruction doctrine also disliked the ABM Treaty, and starting with U.S. president Ronald Reagan in the 1980s, they began efforts to evade it or withdraw from it. With the reduction in tensions between the United States and the Soviet Union in the 1990s, critics argued that the ABM Treaty was no longer needed. On December 13, 2001, U.S. president George W. Bush announced that the United States would withdraw from the treaty, claiming that it prevented U.S. development of defenses against possible terrorist or "rogue state" ballistic missile attacks.

The Limitations of the Anti-Ballistic Missile-Defense Systems

The United States of America and the Union of Soviet Socialist Republics, hereinafter referred to as the Parties.

Have agreed as follows:

Article I

1. Each Party undertakes to limit anti-ballistic missile (ABM) systems and to adopt other measures in accordance with the provisions of this Treaty.

2. Each Party undertakes not to deploy ABM systems for a defense of the territory of its country and not to provide a base for such a defense, and not to deploy ABM systems for defense of an individual region except as provided for in article III of this Treaty.

Article II

1. For the purposes of this Treaty an ABM system is a system to counter strategic ballistic missiles or their elements in flight trajectory, currently consisting of:

(a) ABM interceptor missiles, which are interceptor missiles constructed and deployed for an ABM role, or of a type tested in an ABM mode;

(b) ABM launchers, which are launchers constructed and deployed for launching ABM interceptor missiles; and

(c) ABM radars, which are radars constructed and deployed for an ABM role, or of a type tested in an ABM mode.

2. The ABM system components listed in paragraph 1 of this article include those which are:

(a) operational;

(b) under construction;

(c) undergoing testing;

(d) undergoing overhaul, repair or conversion; or

(e) mothballed.

Article III

Each Party undertakes not to deploy ABM systems or their components except that:

(a) within one ABM system deployment area having a radius of one hundred and fifty kilometers and centered on the Party's national capital, a Party may deploy: (1) no more than one hundred ABM launchers and no more than one hundred ABM interceptor missiles at launch sites, and (2) ABM radars within no more than six ABM radar complexes, the area of each complex being circular and having a diameter of no more than three kilometers; and

(b) within one ABM system deployment area having a radius of one hundred and fifty kilometers and containing ICBM silo launchers, a Party may deploy: (1) no more than one hundred ABM launchers and no more than one hundred ABM interceptor missiles at launch sites, (2) two large phased-array ABM radars comparable in potential to corresponding ABM radars operational or under construction on the date of signature of the Treaty in an ABM system deployment area containing ICBM silo launchers, and (3) no more than eighteen ABM radars each having a potential less than the potential of the smaller of the above-mentioned two large phased-array ABM radars.

Source: "Treaties and Agreements." Available online. URL: http://www.state.gov/www/global/arms/treaties/abm/abm2.html. Accessed March 24, 2007.

The Missile Technology Control Regime (April 16, 1987)

The Nuclear Non-proliferation Treaty (NPT) did nothing to restrict the sale of ballistic missile technology, which might be used together with nuclear warheads by states that had not signed the NPT or by nations that withdrew from it. Weapons sales are lucrative, so advanced technological states had a strong temptation to market ballistic missiles, even though the spread of this technology was against their citizens' interests. Suppliers could resist this temptation only if they acted together, all forgoing the profits and influence these sales might bring them. Thus, on April 16, 1987, the world's seven most industrialized nations (Canada, France, Italy, Japan, the United Kingdom, the United States, and West Germany) established the Missile Technology Control Regime (MTCR), an agreement to contain the spread of missiles capable of delivering nuclear weapons. Over time, the MTCR was amended and enlarged into a more general attempt to reduce sales of ballistic missile technology to nonmember states that could use the capability to deliver biological and chemical weapons and to restrict the spread of rockets, missiles, and unmanned aerial vehicles (UAVs), including some cruise missiles and drones. Russia and Ukraine were added to the MTCR in 1995, but some members feel they have made too many preconditions for MTCR action, weakening the regime rather than strengthening it. Possibly for this reason, China has not been invited to join. This excerpt from the January 1993 update explains the purpose of the regime.

Missile Technology Control Regime

January 7, 1993

The United States Government has, after careful consideration and subject to its international treaty obligations, decided that, when considering the transfer of equipment and technology related to missiles, it will act in accordance with the attached Guidelines beginning on January 7, 1993. These Guidelines replace those adopted on April 16, 1987.

Guidelines For Sensitive Missile-Relevant Transfers

1. The purpose of these Guidelines is to limit the risks of proliferation of weapons of mass destruction (i.e. nuclear, chemical and biological weapons), by controlling transfers that could make a contribution to delivery systems (other than manned aircraft) for such weapons. The Guidelines are not designed to impede national space programs or international cooperation in such programs as long as such programs could not contribute to delivery systems for weapons of mass destruction. These Guidelines, including the attached Annex, form the basis for controlling transfers to any destination beyond the Government's jurisdiction or control of all delivery systems (other than manned aircraft) capable of delivering weapons of mass destruction, and of equipment and technology relevant to missiles whose performance in terms of payload and range exceeds stated parameters. Restraint will be exercised in the consideration of all transfers of items contained within the Annex and all such transfers will be considered on a case-by-case basis. The Government will implement the Guidelines in accordance with national legislation.

2. The Annex consists of two categories of items, which term includes equipment and technology. Category I items, all of which are in Annex Items 1 and 2, are those items of greatest sensitivity. If a Category I item is included in a system, that system will also be considered as Category I, except when the incorporated item cannot be separated, removed or duplicated. Particular restraint will be exercised in the consideration of Category I transfers regardless of their purpose, and there will be a strong presumption to deny such transfers. Particular restraint will also be exercised in the consideration of transfers of any items in the Annex, or of any missiles (whether or not in the Annex), if the Government judges, on the basis of all available, persuasive information, evaluated according to factors including those in paragraph 3, that they are intended to be used for the delivery of weapons of mass destruction, and there will be a strong presumption to deny such transfers. Until further notice, the transfer of Category I production facilities will not be authorized. The transfer of other Category I items will be authorized only on rare occasions and where the Government (A) obtains binding government-to-government undertakings embodying the assurances from the recipient government called for in paragraph 5 of these Guidelines and (B) assumes responsibility for taking all steps necessary to ensure that the item is put only to its stated end-use. It is understood that the decision to transfer remains the sole and sovereign judgment of the United States Government.

3. In the evaluation of transfer applications for Annex items, the following factors will be taken into account:

A. Concerns about the proliferation of weapons of mass destruction;

B. The capabilities and objectives of the missile and space programs of the recipient state;

C. The significance of the transfer in terms of the potential development of delivery systems (other than manned aircraft) for weapons of mass destruction;

D. The assessment of the end-use of the transfers, including the relevant assurances of the recipient states referred to in sub-paragraphs 5.A and 5.B below;

E. The applicability of relevant multilateral agreements.

4. The transfer of design and production technology directly associated with any items in the Annex will be subject to as great a degree of scrutiny and control as will the equipment itself, to the extent permitted by national legislation.

5. Where the transfer could contribute to a delivery system for weapons of mass destruction, the Government will authorize transfers of items in the Annex only on receipt of appropriate assurances from the government of the recipient state that:

A. The items will be used only for the purpose stated and that such use will not be modified nor the items modified or replicated without the prior consent of the United States Government;

B. Neither the items nor replicas nor derivatives thereof will be retransferred without the consent of the United States Government.

6. In furtherance of the effective operation of the Guidelines, the United States Government will, as necessary and appropriate, exchange relevant information with other governments applying the same Guidelines.

7. The adherence of all States to these Guidelines in the interest of international peace and security would be welcome.

Source: "Missile Technology Control Regime January 7, 1993." Available online. URL: http://www.state.gov/t/ac/trt/5073.htm. Accessed March 25, 2007.

START 1 (July 31, 1991)

In 1991, shortly before the collapse of the Soviet Union, U.S. president George H. W. Bush and Soviet leader Mikhail Gorbachev signed the Strategic Arms Reductions Treaty (later known as START I), the fruit of negotiations between Reagan and Gorbachev in the late 1980s. After the Soviet Union was dissolved, its successor states, including the Russian Federation, assumed its obligations. This excerpt, from a U.S. State Department Web site, summarizes the arms reductions ultimately enacted by each side in compliance with the treaty.

START 1 was due to expire in 2009. In 2002, shortly after the United States officially withdrew from the ABM Treaty, the Russian Federation withdrew from START 1. The current treaty limiting the number of weapons deployed by the United States and the Russian Federation is the Strategic Offensive Reduction Treaty (SORT), signed in 2002 by U.S. president George W. Bush and Russian president Vladimir Putin. This treaty expires as soon as it comes into full force in 2012. At that time, the United States and the Russians may begin redeploying nuclear weapons unless some other agreement is reached first.

December 5, 2001, marks the successful completion of the third and final phase of reductions in strategic offensive arms required by the Strategic Arms Reduction Treaty (START Treaty). The United States and Russia each now maintain fewer than the Treaty's mandated limits of 1,600 deployed strategic delivery vehicles and 6,000 accountable warheads, a reduction of some 30 to 40 percent of aggregate levels since 1994, when the Treaty entered into force. In addition, all nuclear warheads and strategic offensive arms have been removed from Belarus, Kazakhstan, and Ukraine.

The START Treaty reductions, inspection regime, notifications and telemetry exchanges have produced stabilizing changes that have contributed to international security and strategic stability.

The START Treaty was signed in Moscow on July 31, 1991, by President George H. W. Bush, for the United States, and President Mikhail Gorbachev, for the Soviet Union. The instruments of ratification of the START Treaty were exchanged in Budapest, Hungary, in December 1994, after several years of sustained effort to adapt the Treaty's original bilateral implementation regime to a new multilateral context that established

Belarus, Kazakhstan, Russia, and Ukraine as the legal successors to the Soviet Union for the purposes of the START Treaty.

Although the START Treaty's required reductions have been met within the required seven years, the Treaty, including its inspection and verification provisions, remains in force. The Treaty's fifteen-year duration may be extended by agreement among the Parties for successive five-year periods.

A significant aspect of the START Treaty's regime lies in its use of rigorous, equitable and verifiable methods to monitor its implementation. The right to perform on-site inspections and other verification measures will continue for the duration of the Treaty, in order to verify compliance. In addition, data exchanges and notifications on each side's strategic systems and facilities as well as exchanges of telemetry data from missile flight tests will help to maintain confidence in the status and level of the Parties' strategic forces. The Parties will also continue to meet as necessary within the framework of the Treaty's implementing body, the Joint Compliance and Inspection Commission, which the Treaty established to ensure continued effective implementation of the Treaty and to seek resolution of compliance and implementation issues.

START has achieved significant reductions from Cold War nuclear force levels. President George W. Bush is committed to achieve significant additional cuts in offensive nuclear forces to the lowest possible number of nuclear weapons consistent with our national security needs and our obligations to friends and allies. The United States seeks to create a new strategic framework with Russia based on a broad array of cooperation on political, economic, and security issues, including substantial reductions in the number of operationally deployed nuclear forces and measures to promote confidence and transparency. Thus, during the November 2001 Washington/Crawford Summit, President Bush announced that the United States will further reduce the number of operationally deployed warheads to between 1,700 and 2,200 over the next ten years, a level consistent with American security.

Source: "Strategic Arms Reduction Treaty (START)." Available online. URL: http://www.state.gov/t/ac/trt/18535.htm. Accessed March 27, 2007.

The Soviet Nuclear Threat Reduction Act of 1991

As the Soviet Union collapsed in 1991, the U.S. Congress acted to assist the former Soviet republics in securing the safety of their nuclear arsenal as well as to prevent the theft or illicit transfer of biological, chemical, and nuclear weapons over which the crumbling Soviet system had insufficient control. Not long after the program's founding, it grew to include a comprehensive array of goals addressing all aspects of the former Soviet Union's weapons of mass destruction. These programs are known collectively under the heading Cooperative Threat Reduction (CTR). From the beginning, the Department of Defense administered the CTR program to handle dismantlement and destruction of the weapons. Later the Energy and State Departments launched related nonproliferation initiatives such as scientific "brain drain," (the problem of jobless former Soviet scientists tempted to lend their talents to rogue states) and the safe shutdown of production facilities for the weapons.

H.R.3807 (P.L. 102-228)

Agreed to November 27, 1991
One Hundred Second Congress of the United States of America

AT THE FIRST SESSION

Begun and held at the City of Washington on Thursday, the third day of January, one thousand nine hundred and ninety-one

TITLE II—SOVIET WEAPONS DESTRUCTION

PART A—SHORT TITLE
SEC. 201. SHORT TITLE.

This title may be cited as the "Soviet Nuclear Threat Reduction Act of 1991".

PART B—FINDINGS AND PROGRAM AUTHORITY
SEC. 211. NATIONAL DEFENSE AND SOVIET WEAPONS DESTRUCTION.

(a) Findings.—The Congress finds—

(1) that Soviet President Gorbachev has requested Western help in dismantling nuclear weapons, and President Bush has proposed United States cooperation on the storage, transportation, dismantling, and destruction of Soviet nuclear weapons;

(2) that the profound changes underway in the Soviet Union pose three types of danger to nuclear safety and stability, as follows: (A)

ultimate disposition of nuclear weapons among the Soviet Union, its republics, and any successor entities that is not conducive to weapons safety or to international stability; (B) seizure, theft, sale, or use of nuclear weapons or components; and (C) transfers of weapons, weapons components, or weapons know-how outside of the territory of the Soviet Union, its republics, and any successor entities, that contribute to worldwide proliferation; and

(3) that it is in the national security interests of the United States (A) to facilitate on a priority basis the transportation, storage, safeguarding, and destruction of nuclear and other weapons in the Soviet Union, its republics, and any successor entities, and (B) to assist in the prevention of weapons proliferation.

(b) Exclusions.—United States assistance in destroying nuclear and other weapons under this title may not be provided to the Soviet Union, any of its republics, or any successor entity unless the President certifies to the Congress that the proposed recipient is committed to—

(1) making a substantial investment of its resources for dismantling or destroying such weapons;

(2) forgoing any military modernization program that exceeds legitimate defense requirements and forgoing the replacement of destroyed weapons of mass destruction;

(3) forgoing any use of fissionable and other components of destroyed nuclear weapons in new nuclear weapons;

(4) facilitating United States verification of weapons destruction carried out under section 212;

(5) complying with all relevant arms control agreements; and

(6) observing internationally recognized human rights, including the protection of minorities.

SEC. 212. AUTHORITY FOR PROGRAM TO FACILITATE SOVIET WEAPONS DESTRUCTION.

(a) In General.—Notwithstanding any other provision of law, the President, consistent with the findings stated in section 211, may establish a program as authorized in subsection (b) to assist Soviet weapons destruction. Funds for carrying out this program shall be provided as specified in part C.

(b) Type of Program.—The program under this section shall be limited to cooperation among the United States, the Soviet Union, its republics, and any successor entities to (1) destroy nuclear weapons, chemical weapons, and other weapons, (2) transport, store, disable, and safeguard weapons in connection with their destruction, and (3) establish verifiable safeguards against the proliferation of such weapons. Such cooperation may involve assistance in planning and in resolving technical problems associated with weapons destruction and proliferation. Such cooperation may also involve the funding of critical short-term requirements related to weapons destruction and should, to the extent feasible, draw upon United States technology and United States technicians.

Source: "Soviet Nuclear Threat Reduction Act of 1991." Available online. URL: http://www.fas.org/nuke/control/ctr/docs/hr3807.html. Accessed March 27, 2007.

The Comprehensive Test Ban Treaty (September 24, 1996)

All testing of nuclear weapons is damaging to the environment. Nonaligned nations (countries aligned neither with the Soviet Union nor the United States) began calling for an international ban on nuclear weapons testing in the 1950s, but there was little chance that such an agreement would be reached while the cold war continued. The easing of U.S.-Soviet tensions in the late 1980s, followed by the collapse of the Soviet Union in 1991, made a complete ban on nuclear weapons testing possible for the first time since their invention. In 1991, parties to the Partial or Limited Test Ban Treaty held a conference to discuss a proposal to convert the treaty into an instrument banning all nuclear weapons tests. With support from the UN General Assembly, negotiations for a comprehensive test-ban treaty began in 1993. The Comprehensive Nuclear Test Ban Treaty (CTBT) was adopted by the UN General Assembly on September 10, 1996, and signed by the United States on September 24, 1996. On October 13, 1999, the U.S. Senate refused to ratify the treaty.

Affirming the purpose of attracting the adherence of all States to this Treaty and its objective to contribute effectively to the prevention of the proliferation of nuclear weapons in all its aspects, to the process of nuclear disarmament and therefore to the enhancement of international peace and security.

Have agreed as follows:

Article 1

Basic Obligations

1. Each State Party undertakes not to carry out any nuclear weapon test explosion or any other nuclear explosion, and to prohibit and prevent any such nuclear explosion at any place under its jurisdiction or control.

2. Each State Party undertakes, furthermore, to refrain from causing, encouraging, or in any way participating in the carrying out of any nuclear weapon test explosion or any other nuclear explosion.

Source: "Comprehensive Test Ban Treaty, September 24, 1996." Available online. URL: http://www.fas.org/nuke/control/ctbt/text/ctbt1.htm. Accessed March 24, 2007.

India's Prime Minister Announces Nuclear Test (May 27, 1998)

After India's "peaceful" nuclear explosion in 1974, nearly two and a half decades went by during which both India and Pakistan steadily built up their nuclear capability. India began work on thermonuclear weapons in the 1980s. In 1989, William H. Webster, director of the U.S. CIA, testified before the Senate Governmental Affairs Committee that "indicators tell us India is interested in thermonuclear weapons capability." Still, neither India nor Pakistan conducted tests of their nuclear weapons. In March 1998, a new coalition government was sworn in led by the Hindu-nationalist Baharatiya Janata Party (BJP); BJP politicians had campaigned for office on a proposal to add nuclear weapons to India's arsenal, and they moved quickly to fulfill their campaign promise. On May 11, 1998, India tested three devices at the Pokhran underground testing site, followed by two more tests on May 13, 1998. In the excerpt reprinted here, India's prime minister, Shri Atal Bihari Vajpayee, announces India's official entry into the "nuclear club" while insisting that "disarmament was and continues to be a major plank in our foreign policy."

Suo Motu Statement by Prime Minister Shri Atal Bihari Vajpayee in Parliament on 27th May, 1998

Sir,

I rise to inform the House of momentous developments that have taken place while we were in recess. On 11 May, India successfully carried out three underground nuclear tests. Two more underground tests on 13 May completed the planned series of tests. I would like this House to join me in paying fulsome tribute to our scientists, engineers and defence personnel whose singular achievements have given us a renewed sense of national pride and self-confidence. Sir, in addition to the statement I make, I have also taken the opportunity to submit to the House a paper entitled "Evolution of India's Nuclear Policy."

2. In 1947, when India emerged as a free country to take its rightful place in the comity of nations, the nuclear age had already dawned. Our leaders then took the crucial decision to opt for self-reliance, and freedom of thought and action. We rejected the Cold War paradigm and chose the more difficult path of non-alignment. Our leaders also realised that a nuclear-weapon-free-world would enhance not only India's security but also the security of all nations. That is why disarmament was and continues to be a major plank in our foreign policy.

3. During the 50's India took the lead in calling for an end to all nuclear weapon testing. Addressing the Lok Sabha on 2 April, 1954, Pt. Jawaharlal, to whose memory we pay homage today, stated "nuclear, chemical and biological energy and power should not be used to forge weapons of mass destruction". He called for negotiations for prohibition and elimination of nuclear weapons and in the interim, a standstill agreement to halt nuclear testing. This call was not heeded.

4. In 1965, along with a small group of non-aligned countries, India put forward the idea of an international non-proliferation agreement under which the nuclear weapon states would agree to give up their arsenals provided other countries refrained from developing or acquiring such weapons. This balance of rights and obligations was not accepted. In the 60's our security concerns deepened. The country sought security guarantees but the countries we turned to were unable to extend to us the expected assurances. As a result, we made it clear that we would not be able to sign the NPT....

6. Our decision not to sign the NPT was in keeping with our basic objectives. In 1974, we demonstrated our nuclear capability. Successive Governments thereafter have taken all necessary steps in keeping with that resolve and national will, to safeguard India's nuclear option. This was the primary reason behind the 1996 decision for not signing the CTBT, a decision that also enjoyed consensus of this House.

7. The decades of the 80's and 90's had meanwhile witnessed the gradual deterioration of our security environment as a result of nuclear and missile proliferation. In our neighbourhood, nuclear weapons had increased and more sophisticated delivery systems inducted. In addition, India has also been the victim of externally aided and abetted terrorism, militancy and clandestine war.

8. At a global level, we see no evidence on the part of the nuclear weapon states to take decisive and irreversible steps in moving towards a nuclear-weapon-free-world. Instead, we have seen that the NPT has been extended indefinitely and unconditionally, perpetuating the existence of nuclear weapons in the hands of the five countries.

9. Under such circumstances, the Government was faced with a difficult decision. The touchstone that has guided us in making the correct choice clear was national security. These tests are a continuation of the policies set into motion that put this country on the path of self-reliance and independence of thought and action.

10. India is now a nuclear weapon state. This is a reality that cannot be denied. It is not a conferment that we seek; nor is it a status for others to grant. It is an endowment to the nation by our scientists and engineers. It is India's due, the right of one-sixth of humankind. Our strengthened capability adds to our sense of responsibility. We do not intend to use these weapons for aggression or for mounting threats against any country; these are weapons of self-defence, to ensure that India is not subjected to nuclear threats or coercion. We do not intend to engage in an arms race. . . .

Source: "Prime Minister Vajpayee's Statement in the Parliament on May 27, 1998." Available online. URL: http://www.indianembassy.org/pic/pm-parliament.htm. Accessed March 11, 2007.

CNN Reports Pakistan's Second Nuclear Test (May 30, 1998)

Pakistan's and India's nuclear weapons programs had been continuing in tandem for decades by 1998. From time to time, leaders on each side would make a statement of nuclear capability intended to intimidate the other side. In September, Prime Minister Benazir Bhutto said that Pakistan could rapidly produce a nuclear weapon in the event of a serious threat. On May 12, 1998, a day after India broke its 24-year moratorium on testing, Pakistani president Muhammad Rafiq Tarar said that Pakistan had the capability to counter India's threats. On May 28, a Pakistani foreign ministry statement said that it had received information that India was planning a preemptive strike against Pakistan's nuclear sites. The strike did not occur, and that same day the Pakistani prime minister announced that Pakistan had conducted five nuclear tests. The underground tests were relatively small fission, or "atomic," explosions. Prime Minister Sharif said that Pakistan would arm its intermediate-range ballistic missiles with nuclear warheads.

Pakistan conducts additional nuclear test

Will there be more?

May 30, 1998
Web posted at: 12:46 p.m. EDT (1646 GMT)

ISLAMABAD, Pakistan (CNN)—Pakistan conducted one more nuclear test Saturday, completing a series of tests, Pakistan's Foreign Secretary said. But the Pakistani government did not say whether it plans another series of tests.

The explosion in Pakistan's remote southwest came two days after the government said it detonated five other devices in the same area.

"Pakistan completed the current series by another nuclear test today. Let me clarify that there was only one test conducted," Foreign Secretary Shamshad Ahmed Khan said during a televised news conference.

Earlier reports said Pakistan detonated two nuclear devices.

Khan told the nation that the tests were fully contained, and that no radioactivity had been released.

Pakistani defense experts told CNN the government had now gathered all the data it needed from the six nuclear tests.

"The devices tested corresponded to weapons configuration compatible with delivery system," Khan said Saturday.

"The fact of our existence as the neighbor of an expansionist and a hegemonistic power taught us the inevitable lesson that we must search for security. Contemporary history held only one lesson for us. The answer lay in credible deterrence," he said.

Source: "Pakistan Conducts Additional Nuclear Test: Will There Be More?" Available online. URL: http://www.cnn.com/WORLD/asiapcf/9805/30/pakistan.nuclear/index.html. Accessed March 24, 2007.

George W. Bush's Remarks at the United Nations General Assembly (September 12, 2002)

On September 12, 2002, as the United States prepared for war with Iraq, U.S. President George W. Bush attempted to gather international support for the operation with this address to the UN General Assembly. In making the case that Saddam Hussein's Iraq posed an unacceptable threat to world peace, Bush reviewed Saddam Hussein's crimes, his deceptions, and the sanctions imposed on Iraq after the first Gulf War. As Bush noted, Saddam Hussein had expelled UN weapons inspectors from his country in 1998, making it very difficult to know the current state of his weapons programs.

President's Remarks at the United Nations General Assembly September 12, 2002

THE PRESIDENT: Mr. Secretary General, Mr. President, distinguished delegates, and ladies and gentlemen: We meet one year and one day after a terrorist attack brought grief to my country, and brought grief to many citizens of our world. Yesterday, we remembered the innocent lives taken that terrible morning. Today, we turn to the urgent duty of protecting other lives, without illusion and without fear.

We've accomplished much in the last year—in Afghanistan and beyond. We have much yet to do—in Afghanistan and beyond. Many nations represented here have joined in the fight against global terror, and the people of the United States are grateful.

The United Nations was born in the hope that survived a world war—the hope of a world moving toward justice, escaping old patterns of conflict and fear. The founding members resolved that the peace of the world must never again be destroyed by the will and wickedness of any man. We created the United Nations Security Council, so that, unlike the League of Nations, our deliberations would be more than talk, our resolutions would be more than wishes. After generations of deceitful dictators and broken treaties and squandered lives, we dedicated ourselves to standards of human dignity shared by all, and to a system of security defended by all.

Today, these standards, and this security, are challenged. Our commitment to human dignity is challenged by persistent poverty and raging disease. The suffering is great, and our responsibilities are clear. The United States is joining with the world to supply aid where it reaches people and lifts up lives, to extend trade and the prosperity it brings, and to bring medical care where it is desperately needed.

As a symbol of our commitment to human dignity, the United States will return to UNESCO. (Applause.) This organization has been reformed and America will participate fully in its mission to advance human rights and tolerance and learning.

Our common security is challenged by regional conflicts—ethnic and religious strife that is ancient, but not inevitable. In the Middle East, there can be no peace for either side without freedom for both sides. America stands committed to an independent and democratic Palestine, living side by side with Israel in peace and security. Like all other people, Palestinians deserve a government that serves their interests and listens to their voices. My nation will continue to encourage all parties to step up to their responsibilities as we seek a just and comprehensive settlement to the conflict.

Above all, our principles and our security are challenged today by outlaw groups and regimes that accept no law of morality and have no limit to their violent ambitions. In the attacks on America a year ago, we saw the destructive intentions of our enemies. This threat hides within many nations, including my own. In cells and camps, terrorists are plotting further destruction, and building new bases for their war against civilization. And our greatest fear is that terrorists will find a shortcut to their mad ambitions when an outlaw regime supplies them with the technologies to kill on a massive scale.

In one place—in one regime—we find all these dangers, in their most lethal and aggressive forms, exactly the kind of aggressive threat the United Nations was born to confront.

Twelve years ago, Iraq invaded Kuwait without provocation. And the regime's forces were poised to continue their march to seize other countries and their resources. Had Saddam Hussein been appeased instead of stopped, he would have endangered the peace and stability of the world. Yet this aggression was stopped—by the might of coalition forces and the will of the United Nations.

To suspend hostilities, to spare himself, Iraq's dictator accepted a series of commitments. The terms were clear, to him and to all. And he agreed to prove he is complying with every one of those obligations.

He has proven instead only his contempt for the United Nations, and for all his pledges. By breaking every pledge—by his deceptions, and by his cruelties—Saddam Hussein has made the case against himself.

In 1991, Security Council Resolution 688 demanded that the Iraqi regime cease at once the repression of its own people, including the systematic repression of minorities—which the Council said, threatened international peace and security in the region. This demand goes ignored.

Last year, the U.N. Commission on Human Rights found that Iraq continues to commit extremely grave violations of human rights, and that the regime's repression is all pervasive. Tens of thousands of political opponents and ordinary citizens have been subjected to arbitrary arrest and imprisonment, summary execution, and torture by beating and burning, electric shock, starvation, mutilation, and rape. Wives are tortured in front of their husbands, children in the presence of their parents—and all of these horrors concealed from the world by the apparatus of a totalitarian state.

In 1991, the U.N. Security Council, through Resolutions 686 and 687, demanded that Iraq return all prisoners from Kuwait and other lands. Iraq's regime agreed. It broke its promise. Last year the Secretary General's high-level coordinator for this issue reported that Kuwait, Saudi, Indian, Syrian, Lebanese, Iranian, Egyptian, Bahraini, and Omani nationals remain unaccounted for—more than 600 people. One American pilot is among them.

In 1991, the U.N. Security Council, through Resolution 687, demanded that Iraq renounce all involvement with terrorism, and permit no terrorist organizations to operate in Iraq. Iraq's regime agreed. It broke this promise. In violation of Security Council Resolution 1373, Iraq continues to shelter and support terrorist organizations that direct violence against Iran, Israel, and Western governments. Iraqi dissidents abroad are targeted for murder. In 1993, Iraq attempted to assassinate the Emir of Kuwait and a former American President. Iraq's government openly praised the attacks of September the 11th. And al Qaeda terrorists escaped from Afghanistan and are known to be in Iraq.

In 1991, the Iraqi regime agreed to destroy and stop developing all weapons of mass destruction and long-range missiles, and to prove to the world it has done so by complying with rigorous inspections. Iraq has broken every aspect of this fundamental pledge.

From 1991 to 1995, the Iraqi regime said it had no biological weapons. After a senior official in its weapons program defected and exposed this lie, the regime admitted to producing tens of thousands of liters of anthrax and other deadly biological agents for use with Scud warheads, aerial bombs, and aircraft spray tanks. U.N. inspectors believe Iraq has produced two to four times the amount of biological agents it declared, and has failed to account for more than three metric tons of material that could be used to produce biological weapons. Right now, Iraq is expanding and improving facilities that were used for the production of biological weapons.

United Nations' inspections also revealed that Iraq likely maintains stockpiles of VX, mustard and other chemical agents, and that the regime is rebuilding and expanding facilities capable of producing chemical weapons.

And in 1995, after four years of deception, Iraq finally admitted it had a crash nuclear weapons program prior to the Gulf War. We know now, were it not for that war, the regime in Iraq would likely have possessed a nuclear weapon no later than 1993.

Today, Iraq continues to withhold important information about its nuclear program—weapons design, procurement logs, experiment data, an accounting of nuclear materials and documentation of foreign assistance.

Iraq employs capable nuclear scientists and technicians. It retains physical infrastructure needed to build a nuclear weapon. Iraq has made several attempts to buy high-strength aluminum tubes used to enrich uranium for a nuclear weapon. Should Iraq acquire fissile material, it would be able to build a nuclear weapon within a year. And Iraq's state-controlled media has reported numerous meetings between Saddam Hussein and his nuclear scientists, leaving little doubt about his continued appetite for these weapons.

Iraq also possesses a force of Scud-type missiles with ranges beyond the 150 kilometers permitted by the U.N. Work at testing and production facilities shows that Iraq is building more long-range missiles that it can inflict mass death throughout the region.

In 1990, after Iraq's invasion of Kuwait, the world imposed economic sanctions on Iraq. Those sanctions were maintained after the war to compel the regime's compliance with Security Council resolutions. In time, Iraq was allowed to use oil revenues to buy food. Saddam Hussein has subverted this program, working around the sanctions to buy missile technology and military materials. He blames the suffering of Iraq's people on the United Nations, even as he uses his oil wealth to build lavish palaces for himself, and to buy arms for his country. By refusing to comply with his own agreements, he bears full guilt for the hunger and misery of innocent Iraqi citizens.

In 1991, Iraq promised U.N. inspectors immediate and unrestricted access to verify Iraq's commitment to rid itself of weapons of mass destruction and long-range missiles. Iraq broke this promise, spending seven years deceiving, evading, and harassing U.N. inspectors before ceasing cooperation entirely. Just months after the 1991 cease-fire, the Security Council twice renewed its demand that the Iraqi regime cooperate fully with inspectors, condemning Iraq's serious violations of its obligations. The Security Council again renewed that demand in 1994, and twice more in 1996, deploring Iraq's clear violations of its obligations. The Security Council renewed its demand three more times in 1997, citing flagrant violations; and three more times in 1998, calling Iraq's behavior totally unacceptable. And in 1999, the demand was renewed yet again.

As we meet today, it's been almost four years since the last U.N. inspectors set foot in Iraq, four years for the Iraqi regime to plan, and to build, and to test behind the cloak of secrecy.

We know that Saddam Hussein pursued weapons of mass murder even when inspectors were in his country. Are we to assume that he stopped when they left? The history, the logic, and the facts lead to one conclusion: Saddam Hussein's regime is a grave and gathering danger. To suggest otherwise is to hope against the evidence. To assume this regime's good faith is to bet the lives of millions and the peace of the world in a reckless gamble. And this is a risk we must not take.

Delegates to the General Assembly, we have been more than patient. We've tried sanctions. We've tried the carrot of oil for food, and the stick of coalition military strikes. But Saddam Hussein has defied all these efforts and continues to develop weapons of mass destruction. The first time we may be completely certain he has a—nuclear weapons is when, God forbid, he uses one. We owe it to all our citizens to do everything in our power to prevent that day from coming.

The conduct of the Iraqi regime is a threat to the authority of the United Nations, and a threat to peace. Iraq has answered a decade of U.N. demands with a decade of defiance. All the world now faces a test, and the United Nations a difficult and defining moment. Are Security Council resolutions to be honored and enforced, or cast aside without consequence? Will the United Nations serve the purpose of its founding, or will it be irrelevant?

The United States helped found the United Nations. We want the United Nations to be effective, and respectful, and successful. We want the resolutions of the world's most important multilateral body to be enforced. And right now those resolutions are being unilaterally subverted by the Iraqi regime. Our partnership of nations can meet the test before us, by making clear what we now expect of the Iraqi regime.

If the Iraqi regime wishes peace, it will immediately and unconditionally forswear, disclose, and remove or destroy all weapons of mass destruction, long-range missiles, and all related material.

If the Iraqi regime wishes peace, it will immediately end all support for terrorism and act to suppress it, as all states are required to do by U.N. Security Council resolutions.

If the Iraqi regime wishes peace, it will cease persecution of its civilian population, including Shi'a, Sunnis, Kurds, Turkomans, and others, again as required by Security Council resolutions.

If the Iraqi regime wishes peace, it will release or account for all Gulf War personnel whose fate is still unknown. It will return the remains of any who are deceased, return stolen property, accept liability for losses resulting from the invasion of Kuwait, and fully cooperate with international efforts to resolve these issues, as required by Security Council resolutions.

If the Iraqi regime wishes peace, it will immediately end all illicit trade outside the oil-for-food program. It will accept U.N. administration of funds from that program, to ensure that the money is used fairly and promptly for the benefit of the Iraqi people.

If all these steps are taken, it will signal a new openness and accountability in Iraq. And it could open the prospect of the United Nations helping to build a government that represents all Iraqis—a government based on respect for human rights, economic liberty, and internationally supervised elections.

The United States has no quarrel with the Iraqi people; they've suffered too long in silent captivity. Liberty for the Iraqi people is a great moral cause, and a great strategic goal. The people of Iraq deserve it; the security of all nations requires it. Free societies do not intimidate through cruelty and conquest, and open societies do not threaten the world with mass murder. The United States supports political and economic liberty in a unified Iraq.

We can harbor no illusions—and that's important today to remember. Saddam Hussein attacked Iran in 1980 and Kuwait in 1990. He's fired ballistic missiles at Iran and Saudi Arabia, Bahrain, and Israel. His regime once ordered the killing of every person between the ages of 15 and 70 in certain Kurdish villages in northern Iraq. He has gassed many Iranians, and 40 Iraqi villages.

My nation will work with the U.N. Security Council to meet our common challenge. If Iraq's regime defies us again, the world must move deliberately, decisively to hold Iraq to account. We will work with the U.N. Security Council for the necessary resolutions. But the purposes of the United States should not be doubted. The Security Council resolutions will be enforced—the just demands of peace and security will be met—or action will be unavoidable. And a regime that has lost its legitimacy will also lose its power.

Events can turn in one of two ways: If we fail to act in the face of danger, the people of Iraq will continue to live in brutal submission. The regime will have new power to bully and dominate and conquer its neighbors, condemning the Middle East to more years of bloodshed and fear. The regime will remain unstable—the region will remain unstable, with little hope of freedom, and isolated from the progress of our times. With every step the Iraqi regime takes toward gaining and deploying the most terrible weapons, our own options to confront that regime will narrow. And if an emboldened regime were to supply these weapons to terrorist allies, then the attacks of September the 11th would be a prelude to far greater horrors.

If we meet our responsibilities, if we overcome this danger, we can arrive at a very different future. The people of Iraq can shake off their captivity. They can one day join a democratic Afghanistan and a democratic Palestine, inspiring reforms throughout the Muslim world. These nations can show by their example that honest government, and respect for women, and the great Islamic tradition of learning can triumph in the Middle East and beyond. And we will show that the promise of the United Nations can be fulfilled in our time.

Neither of these outcomes is certain. Both have been set before us. We must choose between a world of fear and a world of progress. We cannot stand by and do nothing while dangers gather. We must stand up for our security, and for the permanent rights and the hopes of mankind. By heritage and by choice, the United States of America will make that stand. And, delegates to the United Nations, you have the power to make that stand, as well.

Thank you very much.

Source: "President's Remarks at the United Nations General Assembly." Available online. URL: http://www.whitehouse.gov/news/releases/2002/09/20020912-1.html. Accessed March 26, 2007.

United Nations Security Council Resolution 1441 (November 8, 2002)

Responding to Saddam Hussein's continuing defiance of previous UN resolutions and to the evident intention of the United States to go to war with Iraq with or without UN cooperation, the UN Security Council passed the latest of a series of resolutions it had issued over the years calling on Saddam Hussein to live up to his obligations. In this resolution, reproduced here almost in its entirety, the Security Council reviewed Saddam Hussein's previous history of defiance and called on him to cooperate with UN weapons inspectors (the UN Special Commission and the International Atomic Energy Agency). On November 13, 2002, Saddam Hussein accepted the resolution and agreed to open his country to a UN inspection team. Despite earlier calls by the inspection team to be permitted to do its work, on March 19, the U.S.-led coalition began its military action against Iraq.

Resolution 1441 (2002)

Adopted by the Security Council at its 4644th meeting, on 8 November 2002

The Security Council,

Recalling all its previous relevant resolutions, in particular its resolutions 661 (1990) of 6 August 1990, 678 (1990) of 29 November 1990, 686 (1991) of 2 March 1991, 687 (1991) of 3 April 1991, 688 (1991) of 5 April 1991, 707 (1991) of 15 August 1991, 715 (1991) of 11 October 1991, 986 (1995) of 14 April 1995, and 1284 (1999) of 17 December 1999, and all the relevant statements of its President,

Recalling also its resolution 1382 (2001) of 29 November 2001 and its intention to implement it fully,

Recognizing the threat Iraq's non-compliance with Council resolutions and proliferation of weapons of mass destruction and long-range missiles poses to international peace and security,

Recalling that its resolution 678 (1990) authorized Member States to use all necessary means to uphold and implement its resolution 660 (1990) of 2 August 1990 and all relevant resolutions subsequent to resolution 660 (1990) and to restore international peace and security in the area,

Further recalling that its resolution 687 (1991) imposed obligations on Iraq as a necessary step for achievement of its stated objective of restoring international peace and security in the area,

Deploring the fact that Iraq has not provided an accurate, full, final, and complete disclosure, as required by resolution 687 (1991), of all aspects of its programmes to develop weapons of mass destruction and ballistic missiles with a range greater than one hundred and fifty kilometres, and of all holdings of such weapons, their components and production facilities and locations, as well as all other nuclear programmes, including any which it claims are for purposes not related to nuclear-weapons-usable material,

Deploring further that Iraq repeatedly obstructed immediate, unconditional, and unrestricted access to sites designated by the United Nations Special Commission (UNSCOM) and the International Atomic Energy Agency (IAEA), failed to cooperate fully and unconditionally with UNSCOM and IAEA weapons inspectors, as required by resolution 687 (1991), and ultimately ceased all cooperation with UNSCOM and the IAEA in 1998,

Deploring the absence, since December 1998, in Iraq of international monitoring, inspection, and verification, as required by relevant resolutions, of weapons of mass destruction and ballistic missiles, in spite of the Council's repeated demands that Iraq provide immediate, unconditional, and unrestricted access to the United Nations Monitoring, Verification and Inspection Commission (UNMOVIC), established in resolution 1284 (1999) as the successor organization to UNSCOM, and the IAEA, and regretting the consequent prolonging of the crisis in the region and the suffering of the Iraqi people,

Deploring also that the Government of Iraq has failed to comply with its commitments pursuant to resolution 687 (1991) with regard to terrorism, pursuant to resolution 688 (1991) to end repression of its civilian population and to provide access by international humanitarian organizations to all those in need of assistance in Iraq, and pursuant to resolutions 686 (1991), 687 (1991), and 1284 (1999) to return or cooperate in accounting for Kuwaiti and third country nationals wrongfully detained by Iraq, or to return Kuwaiti property wrongfully seized by Iraq,

Recalling that in its resolution 687 (1991) the Council declared that a ceasefire would be based on acceptance by Iraq of the provisions of that resolution, including the obligations on Iraq contained therein,

Determined to ensure full and immediate compliance by Iraq without conditions or restrictions with its obligations under resolution 687 (1991) and other relevant resolutions and recalling that the resolutions of the Council constitute the governing standard of Iraqi compliance,

Recalling that the effective operation of UNMOVIC, as the successor organization to the Special Commission, and the IAEA is essential for the implementation of resolution 687 (1991) and other relevant resolutions,

Noting that the letter dated 16 September 2002 from the Minister for Foreign Affairs of Iraq addressed to the Secretary-General is a necessary first step toward rectifying Iraq's continued failure to comply with relevant Council resolutions,

Noting further the letter dated 8 October 2002 from the Executive Chairman of UNMOVIC and the Director-General of the IAEA to General Al-Saadi of the Government of Iraq laying out the practical arrangements, as a follow-up to their meeting in Vienna, that are prerequisites for the resumption of inspections in Iraq by UNMOVIC and the IAEA, and expressing the gravest concern at the continued failure by the Government of Iraq to provide confirmation of the arrangements as laid out in that letter,

Reaffirming the commitment of all Member States to the sovereignty and territorial integrity of Iraq, Kuwait, and the neighbouring States,

Commending the Secretary-General and members of the League of Arab States and its Secretary-General for their efforts in this regard,

Determined to secure full compliance with its decisions,

Acting under Chapter VII of the Charter of the United Nations,

1. *Decides* that Iraq has been and remains in material breach of its obligations under relevant resolutions, including resolution 687 (1991), in particular through Iraq's failure to cooperate with United Nations inspectors and the IAEA, and to complete the actions required under paragraphs 8 to 13 of resolution 687 (1991);

2. *Decides*, while acknowledging paragraph 1 above, to afford Iraq, by this resolution, a final opportunity to comply with its disarmament obligations under relevant resolutions of the Council; and accordingly decides to set up an enhanced inspection regime with the aim of bringing to full and verified completion the disarmament process established by resolution 687 (1991) and subsequent resolutions of the Council;

3. *Decides* that, in order to begin to comply with its disarmament obligations, in addition to submitting the required biannual declarations, the Government of Iraq shall provide to UNMOVIC, the IAEA, and the Council, not later than 30 days from the date of this resolution, a currently accurate, full, and complete declaration of all aspects of its programmes to develop chemical, biological, and nuclear weapons, ballistic missiles, and other delivery systems such as unmanned aerial vehicles and dispersal systems designed for use on aircraft, including any holdings and precise locations of such weapons, components, subcomponents, stocks of agents, and related material and equipment, the locations and work of its research, development and production facilities, as well as all other chemical, biological, and nuclear programmes, including any which it claims are for purposes not related to weapon production or material;

4. *Decides* that false statements or omissions in the declarations submitted by Iraq pursuant to this resolution and failure by Iraq at any time to comply with, and cooperate fully in the implementation of, this resolution shall constitute a further material breach of Iraq's obligations and will be reported to the Council for assessment in accordance with paragraphs 11 and 12 below;

5. *Decides* that Iraq shall provide UNMOVIC and the IAEA immediate, unimpeded, unconditional, and unrestricted access to any and all, including underground, areas, facilities, buildings, equipment, records, and means of transport which they wish to inspect, as well as immediate, unimpeded, unrestricted, and private access to all officials and other persons whom UNMOVIC or the IAEA wish to interview in the mode or location of UNMOVIC's or the IAEA's choice pursuant to any aspect of their mandates; further decides that UNMOVIC and the IAEA may at their discretion conduct interviews inside or outside of Iraq, may facilitate the travel of those interviewed and family members outside of Iraq, and that, at the sole discretion of UNMOVIC and the IAEA, such interviews may occur without the presence of observers from the Iraqi Government; and instructs UNMOVIC and requests the IAEA to resume inspections no later than 45 days following adoption of this resolution and to update the Council 60 days thereafter;

6. *Endorses* the 8 October 2002 letter from the Executive Chairman of UNMOVIC and the Director-General of the IAEA to General Al-Saadi of the Government of Iraq, which is annexed hereto, and decides that the contents of the letter shall be binding upon Iraq;

7. *Decides* further that, in view of the prolonged interruption, by Iraq of the presence of UNMOVIC and the IAEA and in order for them to accomplish the tasks set forth in this resolution and all previous relevant resolutions and notwithstanding prior understandings, the Council hereby establishes the following revised or additional authorities, which shall be binding upon Iraq, to facilitate their work in Iraq:

- UNMOVIC and the IAEA shall determine the composition of their inspection teams and ensure that these teams are composed of the most qualified and experienced experts available;
- ALL UNMOVIC and IAEA personnel shall enjoy the privileges and immunities, corresponding to those of experts on mission, provided in the Convention on Privileges and Immunities of the United Nations and the Agreement on the Privileges and Immunities of the IAEA;

– UNMOVIC and the IAEA shall have unrestricted rights of entry into and out of Iraq, the right to free, unrestricted, and immediate movement to and from inspection sites, and the right to inspect any sites and buildings, including immediate, unimpeded, unconditional, and unrestricted access to Presidential Sites equal to that at other sites, notwithstanding the provisions of resolution 1154 (1998) of 2 March 1998;

– UNMOVIC and the IAEA shall have the right to be provided by Iraq the names of all personnel currently and formerly associated with Iraq's chemical, biological, nuclear, and ballistic missile programmes and the associated research, development, and production facilities;

– Security of UNMOVIC and IAEA facilities shall be ensured by sufficient United Nations security guards;

– UNMOVIC and the IAEA shall have the right to declare, for the purposes of freezing a site to be inspected, exclusion zones, including surrounding areas and transit corridors, in which Iraq will suspend ground and aerial movement so that nothing is changed in or taken out of a site being inspected;

– UNMOVIC and the IAEA shall have the free and unrestricted use and landing of fixed- and rotary-winged aircraft, including manned and unmanned reconnaissance vehicles;

– UNMOVIC and the IAEA shall have the right at their sole discretion verifiably to remove, destroy, or render harmless all prohibited weapons, subsystems, components, records, materials, and other related items, and the right to impound or close any facilities or equipment for the production thereof; and

– UNMOVIC and the IAEA shall have the right to free import and use of equipment or materials for inspections and to seize and export any equipment, materials, or documents taken during inspections, without search of UNMOVIC or IAEA personnel or official or personal baggage;

8. *Decides* further that Iraq shall not take or threaten hostile acts directed against any representative or personnel of the United Nations or the IAEA or of any Member State taking action to uphold any Council resolution;

9. *Requests* the Secretary General immediately to notify Iraq of this resolution, which is binding on Iraq. . . .

Source: "Text of UN Security Council Resolution on Iraq: November 8, 2002." Available online. URL: http://www.state.gov/p/nea/rls/15016.htm. Accessed March 24, 2007.

United Nations Security Council Resolution 1718 (October 14, 2006)

North Korea, a very poor country with a totalitarian government that poured a vastly disproportionate amount of the country's resources into its military establishment, announced in 1993 that it would withdraw from the Nuclear Non-proliferation Treaty (NPT). In an effort to prevent North Korea from becoming a nuclear weapons state, the United States and a few key allies negotiated a deal with North Korea called the Agreed Framework, under which North Korea would receive aid in exchange for remaining in the NPT. On January 9, 2003, as relations between the United States and North Korea deteriorated, North Korea again announced its intention to withdraw from the NPT. A series of talks were held over a three-year period, the "Six-Party Talks," in an effort to reach an agreement to contain North Korea's nuclear ambitions. The talks failed to achieve significant progress toward an agreement. On October 9, 2006, after threatening to do so for 13 years, North Korea conducted a test of a nuclear weapon. The UN Security Council responded with a resolution condemning the test and imposing sanctions on North Korea.

Resolution 1718 (2006)

Adopted by the Security Council at its 5551st meeting, on 14 October 2006

The Security Council,

1. *Condemns* the nuclear test proclaimed by the DPRK on 9 October 2006 a flagrant disregard of its relevant resolutions, in particular resolution 1695 (2006), as well as of the statement of its President of 6 October 2006 (S/PRST/2006/41), including that such a test would bring universal condemnation of the international community and would represent a clear threat to international peace and security;

2. *Demands* that the DPRK not conduct any further nuclear test or launch of ballistic missile;

3. *Demands* that the DPRK immediately retract its announcement of withdrawal from the Treaty on the Non-Proliferation of Nuclear Weapons;

4. *Demands* further that the DPRK return to the Treaty on the Non-Proliferation of Nuclear Weapons and International Atomic Energy Agency (IAEA) safeguards, and *underlines* the need for all States Parties to the Treaty on the Non-Proliferation of Nuclear Weapons to continue to comply with their Treaty obligations;

5. *Decides* that the DPRK shall suspend all activities related to its ballistic missile programme and in this context re-establish its pre-existing commitments to a moratorium on missile launching;

6. *Decides* that the DPRK shall abandon all nuclear weapons and existing nuclear programmes in a complete, verifiable and irreversible manner, shall act strictly in accordance with the obligations applicable to parties under the Treaty on the Non-Proliferation of Nuclear Weapons and the terms and conditions of its International Atomic Energy Agency (IAEA) Safeguards Agreement (IAEA INFCIRC/403) and shall provide the IAEA transparency measures extending beyond these requirements, including such access to individuals, documentation, equipments and facilities as may be required and deemed necessary by the IAEA;

7. *Decides* also that the DPRK shall abandon all other existing weapons of mass destruction and ballistic missile programme in a complete, verifiable and irreversible manner;

8. *Decides* that:

(c) All Member States shall prevent any transfers to the DPRK by their nationals or from their territories, or from the DPRK by its nationals or from its territory, of technical training, advice, services or assistance related to the provision, manufacture, maintenance or use of the items in subparagraphs (a) (i) and (a) (ii) above;

(d) All Member States shall, in accordance with their respective legal processes, freeze immediately the funds, other financial assets and economic resources which are on their territories at the date of the adoption of this resolution or at any time thereafter, that are owned or controlled, directly or indirectly, by the persons or entities designated by the Committee or by the Security Council as being engaged in or providing support for, including through other illicit means, DPRK's nuclear-related, other weapons of mass destruction-related and ballistic missile-related programmes, or by persons or entities acting on their behalf or at their direction, and ensure that any funds, financial assets or economic resources are prevented from being made available by their nationals or by any persons or entities within their territories, to or for the benefit of such persons or entities;

Source: "Security Council Condemns Nuclear Test by Democratic People's Republic of Korea, Unanimously Adopting Resolution 1718 (2006)." Available online. URL: http://www.un.org/News/Press/docs/2006/sc8853.doc.htm. Accessed March 27, 2007.

UN Press Release: Security Council Demands Iran Suspend Uranium Enrichment by 31 August or Face Possible Economic, Diplomatic Sanctions (July 31, 2006)

In late 2002, photographs from commercial satellites provided evidence that Iran was building new nuclear facilities it had not reported to the International Atomic Energy Agency (IAEA). If these new facilities are uranium enrichments sites, as the United States maintains, then to build them in secret is a violation of the Nuclear Non-proliferation Treaty, which Iran has signed. In the years since this discovery, Iran has played a tough game with the IAEA, sometimes offering cooperation, sometimes withdrawing it. Iran insists that it forswears nuclear weapons but that it has the right to master the entire nuclear fuel cycle, which is really necessary to Iran only if Iran wants to have the material needed to make nuclear weapons. On July 31, 2006, the UN Security Council adopted a resolution demanding that Iran suspend uranium enrichment.

This excerpt from a UN press release describes the resolution and summarizes the protest of the Iranian representative to the council's action.

Security Council
5500th Meeting (AM)

Security Council Demands Iran Suspend Uranium Enrichment By 31 August, or Face Possible Economic, Diplomatic Sanctions Resolution 1696 (2006) Adopted by Vote of 14–1 (Qatar), Iran Says Peaceful Programme No Threat, Council's Consideration Unwarranted

The Security Council, seriously concerned that the International Atomic Energy Agency (IAEA) was still unable to provide assurances about Iran's undeclared nuclear material and activities after more than three years, today demanded that Iran suspend all enrichment-related and reprocessing activities, including research and development, and gave it one month to do so or face the possibility of economic and diplomatic sanctions to give effect to its decision.

Adopting resolution 1696 (2006), under Chapter VII, by a vote of 14 in favour to 1 against (Qatar), the Council expressed its conviction that such suspension, as well as full, verified Iranian compliance with the IAEA Board of Governor's requirements, would contribute to a diplomatic, negotiated solution that guaranteed Iran's nuclear programme was for exclusively peaceful purposes.

The 15-member body called on Iran to without further delay take the steps required by the IAEA Board of Governors in its resolution GOV/2006/14, which it said were essential to build confidence in the exclusively peaceful purpose of the nuclear programme and resolve outstanding questions. It, meanwhile, underlined the international community's willingness to work positively for such a solution and encouraged Iran to reengage with the international community and IAEA.

The Council endorsed the proposals of China, France, Germany, the Russian Federation, the United Kingdom and the United States, with the support of the European Union's High Representative, for a long-term comprehensive arrangement, which would allow for the development of relations with Iran based on mutual respect and the establishment of international confidence in the exclusively peaceful nature of Iran's nuclear programme.

JAVAD ZARIF (*Iran*) said his delegation had requested to be given an opportunity to speak before the Council took action, so that it would be appraised of the views of the concerned party before it adopted a decision. His previous request to speak before the Council when it adopted a presidential statement on 29 March had also been denied. It was indicative of the degree of transparency and fairness that the Security Council had adopted a presidential statement and a draft resolution, without allowing the views of the concerned party to be heard. For the record, he would make the statement intended for presentation before action. He expressed profound appreciation to Qatar for the negative vote based on their principles, as well as their legitimate concern for the regime.

He said it was not the first time that Iran's endeavours to stand on its own feet and make technological advances had faced the stiff resistance and concerted pressure of some powers permanently represented in the Council. Iran's struggle to nationalize its oil industry had been touted in a draft resolution submitted in October 1951 by the United Kingdom and supported by the United States and France as a threat to international peace and security. That draft had preceded a coup d'état, organized by the United States and United Kingdom, in a less veiled attempt to restore their short-sighted interests. More recently, Saddam Hussein's massive invasion of Iran in 1980 had not troubled the same permanent members to consider it a threat to international peace and security.

Over the past several weeks, the Council had been prevented from moving to stop the massive aggression against the Palestinian and Lebanese people and the resulting terrible humanitarian crises, he said. The Council would not have the slightest chance of addressing the oppressor's nuclear arsenal. Likewise, the Council had been prevented from reacting to the daily threats of resort to force against Iran uttered at the highest levels by the United States, the United Kingdom and the lawless Israeli regime, in violation of the Charter. On the other hand, in the past few years, a few big Powers had spared no efforts in turning the Security Council into a tool for attempting to prevent Iran from exercising its inalienable right to nuclear technology for peaceful purposes, recognized explicitly under the NPT.

The people and Government of Iran were determined to exercise their inalienable right to nuclear technology for peaceful purposes and build on their own scientific advances in developing various peaceful aspects of that technology, he continued. At the same time, as the only victims of the use of weapons of mass destruction in recent history, they rejected the development and use of all those inhumane weapons on ideological, as well as strategic, grounds. Iran's leader had issued a public and categorical religious decree against the development, production, stockpiling and use of nuclear weapons. Iran had also clearly stressed that nuclear weapons had no place in its military doctrine.

He noted that, in order to dispel any doubt about its peaceful nuclear programme, Iran had enabled IAEA to carry out a series of inspections, which had amounted to the most robust inspection of any IAEA Member State, including more than 2,000 inspector days of scrutiny in the past three years; the signing of the Additional Protocol on 18 December 2003 and implementing it immediately, until 6 February 2006; the submission of more than 1,000 pages of declarations in accordance with the Additional Protocol; and permitting inspectors to investigate baseless allegations, by taking the unprecedented step of providing repeated access to military sites.

Consequently, he said, all IAEA reports since November 2003 had been indicative of the peaceful nature of the Iranian nuclear programme. In November of that year and in the wake of sensational media reports on the so-called 18 years of concealment by war, IAEA had confirmed that "to date, there is no evidence that the previously undeclared nuclear material and activities . . . were related to a nuclear weapons programme". The same can be found in other IAEA reports, as recent as February 2006.

Much had been made, included in today's resolution, of a statement by IAEA that it was not yet in a position to conclude that there were no undeclared nuclear materials or activities in Iran, he said. The sponsors had ignored, however, the repeated acknowledgement by the IAEA Director

General that the process of drawing such a conclusion was a time-consuming process. They had also ignored the addendum to the 2005 IAEA Safeguards Implementation Report, released in June 2006, which indicated that 45 other countries were in the same category as Iran, including 14 European and several members of the Council.

Iran's peaceful nuclear programme posed no threat to international peace and security, he said. Dealing with the issue in the Council was, therefore, unwarranted and void of any legal basis or practical utility. Far from reflecting the international community's concerns, the approach of the sponsors flouted the stated position of the overwhelming majority of the international community, clearly reflected in the most recent statements by foreign ministers of the Non-Aligned Movement and the Organization of the Islamic Conference, and partly reflected in the June 2006 IAEA Board Chairman's Conclusion.

Claiming to represent the international community, the EU-3, in their so-called package of incentives of last August, had asked Iran to "make a binding commitment not to pursue fuel cycle activities". A cursory look at the chronology of events since last August indicated that Iran's rejection of that illegal and unwarranted demand had, and continued to be, the sole reason for the imposition of resolutions and statements on the IAEA Board and the Council.

Today's action by the Council—which was the culmination of those efforts aimed at making the suspension of uranium enrichment mandatory—violated the fundamental principles of international law, the NPT and IAEA resolutions. It also ran counter to the views of the majority of United Nations Member States, which the Council was obliged to represent. The sole reason for pushing the Council to take action was that Iran had decided, after over two years of negotiations, to resume the exercise of its inalienable right to nuclear technology for peaceful purposes, by partially reopening its fully safeguarded facilities and ending a voluntary suspension. Iran's right to enrich uranium was recognized under the NPT. And, upholding the right of States parties to international regimes was as essential as ensuring respect for their obligations. Those regimes, including the NPT, were sustained by a balance between rights and obligations. Threats would not sustain the NPT or other international regimes. Ensuring that members could draw rightful benefits from membership, and non-members were not rewarded for their intransigence, did.

"Yet, exactly the opposite is the trend today", he said. Today, the world was witness to a dangerous trend. While members of the NPT were denied their rights and punished, those who defied the NPT, particularly the perpetrators of current carnage in Lebanon and Palestine, were rewarded by generous nuclear cooperation agreements. "This is one awkward way to safeguard the NPT or ensure its universality", he said.

The trend, he added, had reached a horrendous, and indeed ridiculous, state with the Israeli regime. That regime, a non-member of the NPT, whose nuclear arsenal was coupled with its expansionist, repressive and state-terror policies, was repeatedly recognized as the most serious threat to regional and international peace and security. Yet, it had the audacity to cry wolf about Iran's peaceful nuclear programme and lead a global campaign of threats, lies, deception, pressure, blackmail and outright extortion. In spite of the massive political and propaganda machine, no one in today's world could accept the convoluted logic that it was okay for some to have nuclear weapons, while others were prevented from developing nuclear energy.

Another destructive trend was the imposition of arbitrary thresholds, which were often a function of bilateral considerations, rather than objective or technical criteria, he said. The new threshold regarding enrichment was as arbitrary as the previous ones, and was simply another excuse to begin a trend to prevent the realization of the rights of the NPT members to peaceful use, while, according to the United States Ambassador, non-members could "legitimately" continue producing nuclear bombs.

He said it had been argued that the Council's intervention was needed to ensure cooperation by Iran with IAEA, and to bring Iran back to the negotiating table. He suggested that, in order to achieve that goal, Security Council involvement was not needed. In fact, the Council's involvement hindered, rather than helped the ongoing process, because it was designed as an instrument of pressure. Iran's cooperation with the Agency was far more extensive and comprehensive before action was imposed on the Board to engage the Council. As for coming back to the negotiating table,

Iran had always been ready for negotiations. For almost three years, Iran had tried to sustain or even resuscitate negotiations with the EU-3. Iran had offered far-reaching proposals to usher in a new era of cooperation, in August 2004, in January, March, April, July and September 2005, and in January, February and March 2006.

Throughout that period, Iran had adopted extensive and extremely costly confidence-building measures, including suspension of its rightful enrichment activities for two years, to ensure the success of negotiations, he said.

All along, it had been the persistence of some to draw arbitrary red lines and deadlines that had closed the door to any compromise. That tendency had single-handedly blocked success and, in most cases, killed proposals in their infancy. That had been Washington's persistent strategy ever since Iran and the EU-3 had started their negotiations in October 2003. "Only the tactics have changed", he said.

"All along, the threats by some to bring this issue before the Council and take it out of its proper technical and negotiated structure has loomed large over the negotiations and has impeded progress, derailed discussions and prevented focus on a mutually acceptable resolution," he said. The manner in which negotiations over the recently proposed package had been conducted was a further indication of the same propensity to resort to threats and the lack of a genuine will to reach a mutually acceptable resolution. Iran had publicly, and in a show of good faith, reacted positively to that initiative and had indicated its readiness to engage in fair, non-discriminatory and result-oriented negotiations about the package, within a mutually agreed time frame and without preconditions. Yet, an arbitrary deadline had been set, ex post facto, without any justification, and only to serve the totally ulterior objective of "maximizing pressure".

Indeed, it had taken the EU-3 nearly five months, from March to August 2005, to consider a very serious proposal by Iran last year and, even then, the EU-3 had come up with a response that did not address any elements of that proposal, he noted. And yet, while Iran had clearly stated that it required three more weeks to conclude its evaluation of the proposed package and come up with a substantive reaction, it was astonishing to see that the EU-3 and the United States were in such a rush to prematurely hamper the path of negotiations by imposing a destructive and totally unwarranted Council resolution. Compare that rush to the fact that some of the very same Powers had for the last three weeks prevented any action, not even a 72-hour truce, by the Council on the urgent situation in Lebanon. "You be the judge of how much credibility this leaves for the Security Council. Millions of people around the world have already passed their judgement."

Concluding, he said it was pertinent to ask what the motive was behind the long-standing urge of some permanent members to bring Iran before the Council. Was it anything but pressure and coercion? That approach would not lead to any productive outcome and, in fact, it could only exacerbate the situation. The people and Government of Iran were not seeking any confrontation and had always shown their readiness to engage in serious and result-oriented negotiation, based on mutual respect and equal footing. They had also showed, time and again, their resilience in the face of pressure, threat, injustice and imposition.

Source: "Security Council Demands Iran Suspend Uranium Enrichment by 31 August or Face Possible Economic, Diplomatic Sanctions." Available online. URL: http://www.un.org/News/Press/docs/2006/sc8792.doc.htm. Accessed March 24, 2007.

United Nations Security Council Resolution 1747 (March 24, 2007)

On December 23, 2006, the UN Security Council passed another resolution on Iran's nuclear program, this one calling upon UN member states to restrict their sales of materials that might be used in Iran's nuclear program. A third UN resolution, passed on March 24, 2007, restricted sales to and from Iran of conventional weapons as well as nuclear materials.

The Security Council,

Recalling the Statement of its President, S/PRST/2006/15, of 29 March 2006, and its resolution 1696 (2006) of 31 July 2006, and its resolution 1737 (2006) of 23 December 2006, and reaffirming their provisions,

Reaffirming its commitment to the Treaty on the Non-Proliferation of Nuclear Weapons, the need for all States party to that Treaty to comply fully with all their obligations, and recalling the right of States parties, in conformity with articles I and II of that Treaty, to develop research, production and use of nuclear energy for peaceful purposes without discrimination,

Recalling its serious concern over the reports of the IAEA Director General as set out in its resolutions 1696 (2006) and 1737 (2006),

Recalling the latest report by the IAEA Director General (GOV/2007/8) of 22 February 2007 and deploring that, as indicated therein, Iran has failed to comply with resolution 1696 (2006) and resolution 1737 (2006),

Emphasizing the importance of political and diplomatic efforts to find a negotiated solution guaranteeing that Iran's nuclear programme is exclusively for peaceful purposes, and noting that such a solution would benefit nuclear non-proliferation elsewhere, and welcoming the continuing commitment of China, France, Germany, the Russian Federation, the United

Kingdom and the United States, with the support of the European Union's High Representative, to seek a negotiated solution,

Recalling the resolution of the IAEA Board of Governors (GOV/2006/14), which states that a solution to the Iranian nuclear issue would contribute to global non-proliferation efforts and to realizing the objective of a Middle East free of weapons of mass destruction, including their means of delivery,

Determined to give effect to its decisions by adopting appropriate measures to persuade Iran to comply with resolution 1696 (2006) and resolution 1737 (2006) and with the requirements of the IAEA, and also to constrain Iran's development of sensitive technologies in support of its nuclear and missile programmes, until such time as the Security Council determines that the objectives of these resolutions have been met,

Recalling the requirement on States to join in affording mutual assistance in carrying out the measures decided upon by the Security Council,

Concerned by the proliferation risks presented by the Iranian nuclear programme and, in this context, by Iran's continuing failure to meet the requirements of the IAEA Board of Governors and to comply with the provisions of Security Council resolutions 1696 (2006) and 1737 (2006), mindful of its primary responsibility under the Charter of the United Nations for the maintenance of international peace and security,

Acting under Article 41 of Chapter VII of the Charter of the United Nations,

1. Reaffirms that Iran shall without further delay take the steps required by the IAEA Board of Governors in its resolution GOV/2006/14, which are essential to build confidence in the exclusively peaceful purpose of its nuclear programme and to resolve outstanding questions and, in this context, affirms its decision that Iran shall without further delay take the steps required in paragraph 2 of resolution 1737 (2006);

2. Calls upon all States also to exercise vigilance and restraint regarding the entry into or transit through their territories of individuals who are engaged in, directly associated with or providing support for Iran's proliferation sensitive nuclear activities or for the development of nuclear weapon delivery systems, and decides in this regard that all States shall

notify the Committee established pursuant to paragraph 18 of resolution 1737 (2006) (herein "the Committee") of the entry into or transit through their territories of the persons designated in the Annex to resolution 1737 (2006) or Annex I to this resolution, as well as of additional persons designated by the Security Council or the Committee as being engaged in, directly associated with or providing support for Iran's proliferation sensitive nuclear activities or for the development of nuclear weapon delivery systems, including through the involvement in procurement of the prohibited items, goods, equipment, materials and technology specified by and under the measures in paragraphs 3 and 4 of resolution 1737 (2006), except where such travel is for activities directly related to the items in subparagraphs 3 (b) (i) and (ii) of that resolution;

3. Underlines that nothing in the above paragraph requires a State to refuse its own nationals entry into its territory, and that all States shall, in the implementation of the above paragraph, take into account humanitarian considerations, including religious obligations, as well as the necessity to meet the objectives of this resolution and resolution 1737 (2006), including where article XV of the IAEA Statute is engaged;

4. Decides that the measures specified in paragraphs 12, 13, 14 and 15 of resolution 1737 (2006) shall apply also to the persons and entities listed in Annex I to this resolution;

5. Decides that Iran shall not supply, sell or transfer directly or indirectly from its territory or by its nationals or using its flag vessels or aircraft any arms or related materiel, and that all States shall prohibit the procurement of such items from Iran by their nationals, or using their flag vessels or aircraft, and whether or not originating in the territory of Iran;

6. Calls upon all States to exercise vigilance and restraint in the supply, sale or transfer directly or indirectly from their territories or by their nationals or using their flag vessels or aircraft of any battle tanks, armoured combat vehicles, large calibre artillery systems, combat aircraft, attack helicopters, warships, missiles or missile systems as defined for the purpose of the United Nations Register on Conventional Arms to Iran, and in the provision to Iran of any technical assistance or training, financial assistance, investment, brokering or other services, and the transfer of financial resources or services, related to the supply, sale, transfer, manufacture or use of such items in order to prevent a destabilising accumulation of arms;

7. Calls upon all States and international financial institutions not to enter into new commitments for grants, financial assistance, and concessional loans, to the government of the Islamic Republic of Iran, except for humanitarian and developmental purposes;

Source: "United Nations Security Council Resolution 1747." Available online. URL: http://www.iaea.org/NewsCenter/Focus/IaeaIran/unsc_res1747-2007.pdf. Accessed March 27, 2007.

PART III

Research Tools

6

How to Research Nuclear Nonproliferation Issues

For anyone beginning to research the subject of nuclear nonproliferation, the good news is that information will not be hard to find. Indeed, it will be virtually unavoidable in the form of newspaper and magazine headlines and radio and talking heads on TV discussing the nuclear programs of Iran and North Korea. Literally hundreds of books have been published in English on the subject since the beginning of this decade; each year several new books appear in the form of general introductions to nuclear nonproliferation, or the spread of WMD. On the Internet, to search for nuclear nonproliferation, or WMD, or even some subtopic such as "Iran highly enriched uranium" or "United Nations Security Council Resolution 1747" is to be presented instantly with access to all a general student of the subject needs to know and much more—for many, indeed, it will be far too much more.

GETTING STARTED

One way of beginning research is simply to go to a search engine, type in the keywords, and surf. For some researchers, this will work as a starting point. Others may find themselves overwhelmed or quickly misled, unable to sort out reliable information from dubious conspiracy sites, political advocacy sites, or highly opinionated blogs. This research guide is designed for those interested in a systematic approach that focuses attention first on authoritative sources of information. After that, the bloggers, who often have interesting things to say, can be listened to and their arguments placed in the context of a general understanding of the subject.

A short review of the different forms this information takes will be useful as a starting point. The most useful quick portals to the subject are books, government and international Web sites, research institute ("think tank") Web sites, and mass market magazines and newspapers.

Books

It pays to read more than one general book on nuclear nonproliferation to get a rounded view of the issue. No matter how objective the authors attempt to be, each book frames the subject a bit differently, embodies a different set of assumptions, and asks and answers different questions. The best way to grasp the hidden assumptions is to read more than one would-be "objective" book. The special virtues of books as opposed to the many quicker sources available on the Internet are depth and context. Books give background as well as analysis. They provide the historical context in which to understand the nuclear arms race or special subjects of missile defense, nuclear deterrence, and the specific histories and security problems of individual countries and regions.

Web Sites of Governments and International Institutions

Web sites of the U.S. president, the Department of State, the Department of Defense, the Central Intelligence Agency (CIA), The Department of Energy (which is in charge of bomb-making as well as energy policy), and many other government Web sites provide search fields in which the words *nuclear proliferation* or other key words can be typed to generate a list of articles or documents. Government Web sites typically give the latest press releases of the institution, provide links to treaties and other important primary source documents, and also provide summaries and analyses. Some U.S. government agencies, such as the Congressional Research Service and the General Office of Accountability, are specifically devoted to producing research papers that analyze special problems, including foreign policy problems, that the U.S. government faces; these papers give a history of the problem, evaluate the effects of U.S. policies that address the problem, and suggest new policies. Written to help lawmakers reach decisions, these articles are often clear, easy to read, surprisingly frank and objective, and highly informative to the rest of us.

Web Sites of Research Institutes ("Think Tanks")

The spread of nuclear weapons and the international efforts to contain them are subjects of intense and constant study by research institutes such as the Brookings Institution, the Arms Control Association, the RAND Corporation, the Geneva Center for Security Policy, and many others. Though many think tanks in the United States are accused, with good reason, of being overly partisan, the Web sites of some think tanks can be a good source both of quick information on specific subjects and deep background and analysis on a host of nuclear proliferation and national security issues. They respond quickly to breaking news with opinion articles written by people who have made their careers as political scientists, defense analysts, or public servants. Comparing analysis of one think tank with another gives a sense of the controversies that beset the field.

Web Sites of Academic Institutions

Similar to think tanks but affiliated with a university, academic Web sites are also a useful source of key documents, histories, and analysis.

Magazines and Newspapers

Magazines aimed at the general reader, such as *Time, Newsweek,* and the *Economist,* and national newspapers such as the *New York Times,* the *Wall Street Journal,* and the *Washington Post* are useful both as sources of breaking news on issues such as a recent UN Security Council resolution on Iran's nuclear weapons program and also for the occasional background piece that gives an overview. The articles in the back issues of these magazines qualify as history, though of a special kind—they may contain errors, since they do not benefit from what was learned later. On the other hand, they serve as a reminder of how things looked at the time. If, through a school or library, a student has access to an online catalog such as *Proquest Direct,* these magazines can by easily searched using keywords and are available online.

Scholarly Journals

Scholarly journals, whether affiliated with think tanks or universities or independent, produce "peer-reviewed" articles, articles that to be published must pass the scrutiny of experts in the field. Peer review is no guarantee of truth, especially in subjects such as political science and international relations, but it does help to catch factual errors and exerts a steady pressure for high quality. The *Bulletin of the Atomic Scientists, Nonproliferation Review,* and *Foreign Policy* are some of the many peer-reviewed journals that frequently treat the subject of nuclear nonproliferation.

LOOK FOR BIAS AND TAKE IT INTO ACCOUNT

The spread of nuclear weapons is a highly contentious issue. It has a long history that has given rise to countless historical debates—all the way from why did President Truman drop the atomic bomb on Japan in 1945 to whether Secretary of State Condoleezza Rice was right to make a deal with North

Korea in 2007. Opinions expressed today about nuclear nonproliferation attempt to affect the spending of tax dollars, the outcome of congressional and presidential elections, the rise and fall of foreign governments, the decision to go to war, the long-term victory of various ideologies, and the fate of the Earth. To be absolutely unemotional about these subjects is not quite sane. No one who is the least interesting to read on this subject is without a point of view.

This is not to say that the truth does not exist. It is rather that the truth is seen from various perspectives. To shun sources that display some sort of bias—liberal or conservative, for security through nuclear deterrence or for security through disarmament, for missile defense or against it—would mean not listening to what the best and most passionate minds have to say about these matters. Bias should not be avoided, it should be noted and considered as an element in the discussion. It must be realized that one is listening to a debate between individuals who care deeply about their subject.

Different sorts of bias, together with different kinds of benefits, are associated with different sources.

Academic Sources

People in the universities who study policy and people who write books and articles in scholarly journals have two forms of bias. Like everyone else, they have their politics, and they will usually represent some political point of view. Since they are people of ideas, they have another form of bias that may be more important for them, an intellectual bias toward a particular theory. The good thing about academic writing is that the standards of evidence it employs are usually high. Book-writing professors are trained to show their hand. Not invariably, but usually, they tell you what their bias is, they tell you what their theory is, and they explain the arguments for the other side. They also explain why they tell you what the arguments of the other side are and why they disagree. Academic writers are well informed and take the long view, and they think deeply about the principles of history and policy. An occasional drawback of academic sources is that sometimes they are overly technical and narrow in scope.

Magazines, Newspapers, and Broadcast Media

All news outlets fit somewhere or other on the political spectrum; traditionally, magazines and newspapers have been open in their adherence to party or ideology. For example, the *Washington Post* is generally regarded as liberal; the *Washington Times* is generally regarded as conservative. Neither bias is a reason to dismiss reporting by these newspapers, but it should be considered when reading them. Broadcast media, especially television, have a history of being relatively timid in their expression of a political point of view. Conservatives often accuse broadcast media of having a liberal bias; liberals think the broadcast media have become conservative and point to the right-wing bias of talk radio and to the Fox Network as an organ of the right, which has no equivalent on the left. Generally, the great weakness of television news is its superficiality and its reluctance to criticize those in power. It becomes more conservative during a conservative administration and more liberal during a liberal administration.

Governments and International Institutions

The Web sites of entities such as the U.S. government, the International Atomic Energy Agency (IAEA), and the UN should be read with the understanding that they express the perspectives of the institutions that produced them. The degree of bias varies with the institution. For example, the Web sites and publications of the executive branch of the U.S. government are seldom critical of U.S. policy or U.S. officials, and they tend to be updated to favor the policies of the administration in power. The publications of the Congressional Research Service (an agency within the Library of Congress) are remarkably independent and may be critical of U.S. policy. As one might expect, international organizations such as the IAEA and the UN have an institutional bias in favor of multilateral diplomacy. Some UN institutions have been accused of other biases, and the institution as a whole has a point of view quite different than the point of view of the U.S. government.

Research Institutes and Their Journals ("Think Tanks")

Think tanks, organizations such as the Brookings Institution, the Arms Control Association, and the Nonproliferation Policy Education Center (NPEC), can be staffed by very well-informed people. Their analysis is usually on a high level, and it is usually readable, since the think tanks are not merely places where a quest for truth is pursued, they are centers of advocacy. Whether or not they say so in their mission statements, most think tanks want to influence public opinion. They, too, usually have a consistent ideological perspective that varies greatly from one think tank to another.

Think tanks vary greatly in quality. Some think tanks are little more than propaganda organs; their research consists of the latest scandal about the opposing party; and their response to policy initiatives is to boo or cheer rather than to seriously engage with the complexities of each issue. Others, though they may have a consistent political philosophy, nevertheless maintain high standards of accuracy, argue for their positions in a nuanced way, and, most importantly, engage in serious discussions with their ideological opponents.

Think tanks may be genuinely nonpartisan, openly partisan, or covertly partisan. Some think tanks, such as the Cato Institute, a libertarian organization that devotes most of its "About Us" page to a discussion of its precise place on the political spectrum, or the American Enterprise Institute, which describes itself as "conservative" in its mission statement, were specifically designed to advance a particular set of political ideas conservatives felt were underrepresented in the think tanks that existed prior to the 1970s. Others, such as the Carnegie Endowment for International Peace, which is one of the oldest, do not define themselves as putting forward a particular political agenda but would be classed by conservatives as liberal. The Nonproliferation Policy Education Center has often but not invariably favored the policies of the George W. Bush administration; the Brookings Institution has often but not always criticized those policies. Both at least give a hearing to the policy positions with which they ultimately may disagree and do not attempt to conceal facts that may refute their own conclusions.

CREDENTIALS MATTER

As research branches out from the relatively staid sources provided in this guide, the challenge for new students of nuclear nonproliferation will be to find a way to tell the good information from the bad information. Researching this topic is like coming to a very large room in which an argument has been going on for so long that nobody is shouting anymore and the debaters have learned a great deal of subtlety. These people have all taken sides. They have formed temporary alliances with each other, and they all have complicated plans. They all want to recruit you. The first person who speaks to you is the crackpot, who tells you that the World Trade Center was actually brought down by small nuclear devices; those two planes flying into the towers could never have done that damage (search for "9/11" and you are only a link away from this theory and many others of its ilk).

Because there is so much information and it is of such varying quality, it is absolutely necessary to discriminate between sources. So even though experts are often wrong and crackpots are occasionally correct, students must learn to recognize crackpots and not waste too much time on them. Not every theory deserves a hearing. Credentials matter and authority matters; they are useful as minimum guarantees of expertise. As a rule of thumb, the *Nation* and the *National Review* (two reputable political magazines, one liberal, one conservative) are better sources on political matters than *People.* Books on nuclear proliferation put out by Oxford University Press and found mostly in college libraries are usually better, though not always better, than those by Time/Warner Books and found mostly in drugstores and supermarkets. An author with academic credentials from Harvard who has served as an assistant to the undersecretary of state in some U.S. presidential administration probably deserves more attention than the author of a popular blog who has no credentials (unless you are in search of the latest political scandal, in which case, the blog may be a better source). In the end, the Harvard professor may be wrong and the blogger may be right, but it is a mistake to take the word of the blogger without having heard from the Harvard professor.

In our personal relations, we are told not to judge a book by its cover; in debate, it is best to address the evidence and not the pedigree of the other debater. But in research the rules are different. We do judge a book by its cover. To listen to everyone is impossible; to leave it to chance is inadvisable. The best course is to use credentials to distinguish between different levels of expertise and to give more attention to usually reliable sources than to sources with no credentials at all.

With that said, let it be remembered that in the run-up to the 2003 war in Iraq, the *New York Times,* the *Wall Street Journal,* the Brookings Institution, and virtually the entire reasonable, respectable mainstream media establishment all agreed that Saddam Hussein's Iraq possessed weapons of mass destruction. They were all proven wrong a year later. Excellent credentials are no guarantee of accuracy, but they are usually a reliable sign of basic competence and professionalism. And of course, never rely on one source alone, no matter how good its credentials or how persuasive its reasoning.

BOOKS AND ARTICLES TO BEGIN RESEARCHING THE SUBJECT

Part II of this book contains a large annotated bibliography. Extensive as it is, it represents a tiny portion of the material that exists on this subject in libraries and on the Web. It should be of use to students interested in particular aspects of nuclear nonproliferation. A handful of these books and articles will be highlighted here because they offer good general introductions to nuclear nonproliferation or to special aspects of the subject, such as the U.S.-Soviet arms race, the theory of nuclear deterrence, and the history of the Nuclear Non-proliferation Treaty.

The Pulitzer prize–winning author Richard Rhodes has written books both on the development of the atomic bomb and the hydrogen bomb: *The Making of the Atomic Bomb* and *Dark Sun: The Making of the Hydrogen Bomb.* Both are quite long, but both are also very readable. Rhodes is an excellent science writer, a diligent researcher, and a compelling narrator. He conducted interviews with many of the people involved in the bomb projects. In the course of telling the story of the bombs, Rhodes does about as much as can be done to make their principles clear to a nonscientist. Also as a part of the story, he explains the military and political circumstances and consequences of the bombs. A reader comes away from these books knowing not only a great deal about the history of the bombs but also about the impact of nuclear weapons on the cold war and the early debates concerning the ethics of nuclear weapons and the means of controlling their spread. For a student who wants to understand the historical context of nuclear nonproliferation, the Richard Rhodes books may be a better introduction than many that have the words *nuclear nonproliferation* or *weapons of mass destruction* in their titles.

Another recommended early stop for readers new to the subject of nuclear nonproliferation is *The Spread of Nuclear Weapons: A Debate Renewed,* by Stanford University political science professor Scott D. Sagan and Columbia professor Kenneth N. Waltz. This book consists of essays in which Waltz, a proponent of the realist school of international relations, argues that the spread of nuclear weapons is inevitable and will make for a more peaceful world, and others in which Sagan, basing his stance on a study of the flaws in organizational thinking, argues that the spread of nuclear weapons can and should be stopped. The debate is lively, and the positions are well argued and clear. The book provides an excellent introduction to the thinking about deterrence and international security that is at the heart of decisions about arms control and nuclear nonproliferation. Readers will have some of their easy assumptions questioned; they will come away with a better understanding of the theoretical framework political scientists bring to the subject, and they will also have had a glimpse of the complicated arrangements that are made to safeguard nuclear weapons, to keep them from being used by rogue generals or from being stolen by terrorists, and to keep them from being fired by mistake as the result of a computer error.

The security and safety of nuclear arsenals (for example, their safety from accidental or unauthorized launches that might start a nuclear war) is a key element in the dispute between Sagan and Waltz. Readers especially interested in this question may want to obtain a copy of *No End in Sight: The Continuing Menace of Nuclear Proliferation,* by Nathan E. Busch. *No End in Sight* is a somewhat academic but very clear and methodical examination of what is known about nuclear safety in all the countries that had nuclear weapons as of 2004.

A useful short introduction to the history of nuclear nonproliferation, seen from the U.S. perspective, is Henry D. Sokolski's *Best of Intentions:*

America's Campaign Against Strategic Weapons Proliferation. Sokolski explains the reasoning and special historical circumstances that led to nonproliferation initiatives such as the Baruch Plan, Atoms for Peace, the Nuclear Non-proliferation Treaty, and the Nuclear and Missile Control Regimes.

Most Americans manage not to think very much about the depth of the United States's own commitment to nuclear weapons and the enormous size of our nuclear arsenal—it is a huge chunk of the economy that remains hidden. Americans push it to the margins of consciousness because it is frightening, and most of the public does not feel they can do much about it. However, it is hard to understand others if one does not understand oneself; examining the U.S. nuclear arsenal and studying the decisions that have led the United States to build and maintain it are essential to an understanding of the decisions that have led India, Pakistan, Iran, North Korea—or any other country—to pursue nuclear weapons in the face of the world's disapproval. Two books by Cleveland State University history professor Ronald E. Powaski are devoted to this subject. The first, published in 1987 and telling the story to that date, is called *March to Armageddon: The United States and the Nuclear Arms Race, 1939 to the Present,* and the second, published in 2000 and updating the story to that date, is called *Return to Armageddon.* Despite the use of the word *Armageddon* in the titles, both books are balanced and unsensational studies of the subject. Though their subject is the U.S.-Soviet arms race, Powaski's books dwell a great deal on arms negotiations and treaties, including those associated with the broader nonproliferation efforts that extend beyond the world's two great proliferators.

For a fresh angle on the sheer size of the expenditure that has gone into this submerged part of the U.S. economy, no volume is better than *Atomic Audit: The Costs and Consequences of U.S. Nuclear Weapons Since 1940,* edited by Stephen I. Schwartz, a guest scholar with the Brookings Institution. A sample of facts and figures from *Atomic Audit* is available at the Web site "50 Facts About Nuclear Weapons," a page maintained by the Brookings Institution, which published the book, at www1.hamiltonproject.org/fp/projects/nucwcost/50.htm.

For a "glass-half-full" view of the Nuclear Non-proliferation Treaty, readers can turn to *Common Sense on Weapons of Mass Destruction,* by Thomas Graham, Jr., who was ambassador to the UN during the Clinton administration. In this short book, he criticizes the nonproliferation policies of the George W. Bush administration and urges a multilateral approach to nonproliferation that makes better use of the UN. The book also briefly examines other problems, such as the proliferation of biological and chemical weapons and land mines, which are often considered together with the spread of nuclear weapons.

Those researching the nuclear programs of particular countries should seek out sources that examine their nuclear programs in the context of the political history of the countries and the pressures of the regions in which they exist. On the subject of South Asia, Salem State College professor Kanishkan Sathasivam's *Uneasy Neighbors: India, Pakistan and US Foreign Policy* gives an intelligent, easy to read account of the modern history of India and Pakistan and the motivations of both countries' nuclear bomb programs. George Perkovich's *India's Nuclear Bomb: The Impact on Global Proliferation* (1999) is a massive tome doing for India's bomb what Richard Rhodes did for the U.S. bomb. Perkovich is a vice president for Studies—Global Security and Economic Development—at the Carnegie Endowment for International Peace.

As of 2008, no country's nuclear program was subject to greater international scrutiny and speculation than Iran's. *Iran's Nuclear Ambitions* (2006) by Shahram Chubin, director of studies at the Geneva Centre for Security Policy, is particularly valuable for subtlety, nonpartisanship, and insight into the internal functioning of Iranian society. A quick overview of what is known and suspected about Iran's nuclear program is available on the Web as a Congressional Research Service report by Sharon Squassoni, "Iran's Nuclear Program: Recent Developments," at http://fpc.state.gov/documents/organization/81930.pdf. A specialist in WMD proliferation, Squassoni is currently a senior associate at the Carnegie Endowment for International Peace. A *New York Times Magazine* article from a few years back, James Traub's "The Netherworld of Nuclear Nonproliferation," would also be helpful to those wanting to know the basic story and its implications for nuclear proliferation and U.S. policy.

The 2003 U.S. invasion of Iraq, its causes, and its consequences are a study in the pitfalls of nuclear nonproliferation at gunpoint. Two U.S. government publications provide the best introduction to this debacle: the "Senate Select Committee on Intelligence Report on the U.S. Intelligence Community's Prewar Intelligence Assessments on Iraq, July 9, 2004," available online at http://www.gpoaccess.gov/serialset/creports/iraq.html, and the report of the Iraq Study Group, available online at http://bakerinstitute. org/Pubs/iraqstudygroup_findings.pdf.

North Korea is a secretive country and a strange one by any standards except its own. A highly recommended first stop on the path to understanding this fossil of the cold war is *North Korea: The Paranoid Peninsula—A Modern History* (2005) by Paul French, a journalist who writes regularly on North Korean and Chinese economics and politics for a wide variety of publications. Two reports excerpted in part II of the present book specifically examine U.S. attempts to contain North Korea's nuclear program.

They are both available online and are worth reading in full: "Review of United States Policy Toward North Korea: Findings and Recommendations," by William Perry and Wendy Sherman, can be accessed at http://www.gwu.edu/~nsarchiv/NSAEBB/NSAEBB87/nk20.pdf, and "North Korea's Nuclear Weapons Program," by Larry A. Niksch, can be accessed at http://fpc.state.gov/documents/organization/74904.pdf.

Of course, many of these stories are unfolding and will continue to make headlines and history for the foreseeable future. The best way to bring them up to date is an intelligent and selective use of the Internet; a list of helpful Web sites to begin collecting facts and analysis on nuclear nonproliferation and related subjects can be found in chapter 9, Organizations and Agencies.

7

Facts and Figures

INTERNATIONAL WEAPONS STOCKPILE

1.1 U.S.—Soviet Nuclear Weapons Stockpiles, 1945–2006

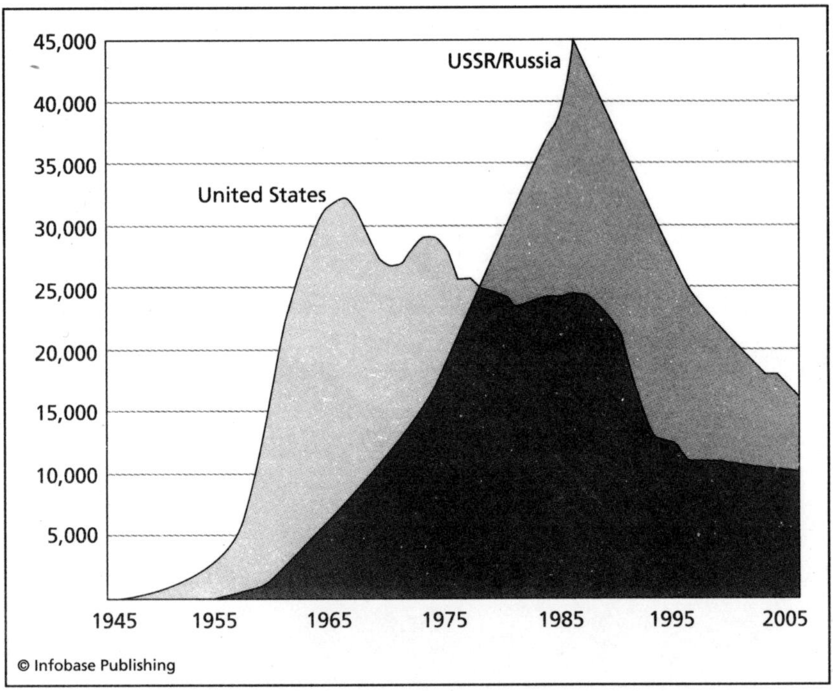

Source: Natural Resources Defense Council and *Bulletin of the Atomic Scientists*

1.2 Nuclear Weapons States and Their Weapons

COUNTRY	WARHEADS ACTIVE	WARHEADS TOTAL (INCLUDING STOCKPILED WARHEADS)	YEAR OF FIRST TEST
United States	3,735	9,960	1945
Russia (formerly Soviet Union)	5,830	16,000	1949
United Kingdom	200	200	1952
France	350	350	1960
China	130	130	1964
India	70–120	70–120	1974
Pakistan	30–52	30–52	1998
Israel[1]	75–200	75–200	Unknown
North Korea	1–10	1–10	2006

[1] Israel has not declared itself a nuclear weapons state but is believed to possess nuclear weapons.

Source: Facts On File based on estimates of the Natural Resources Defense Council, published in the *Bulletin of the Atomic Scientists*

1.3 Proliferation Status Map 2005

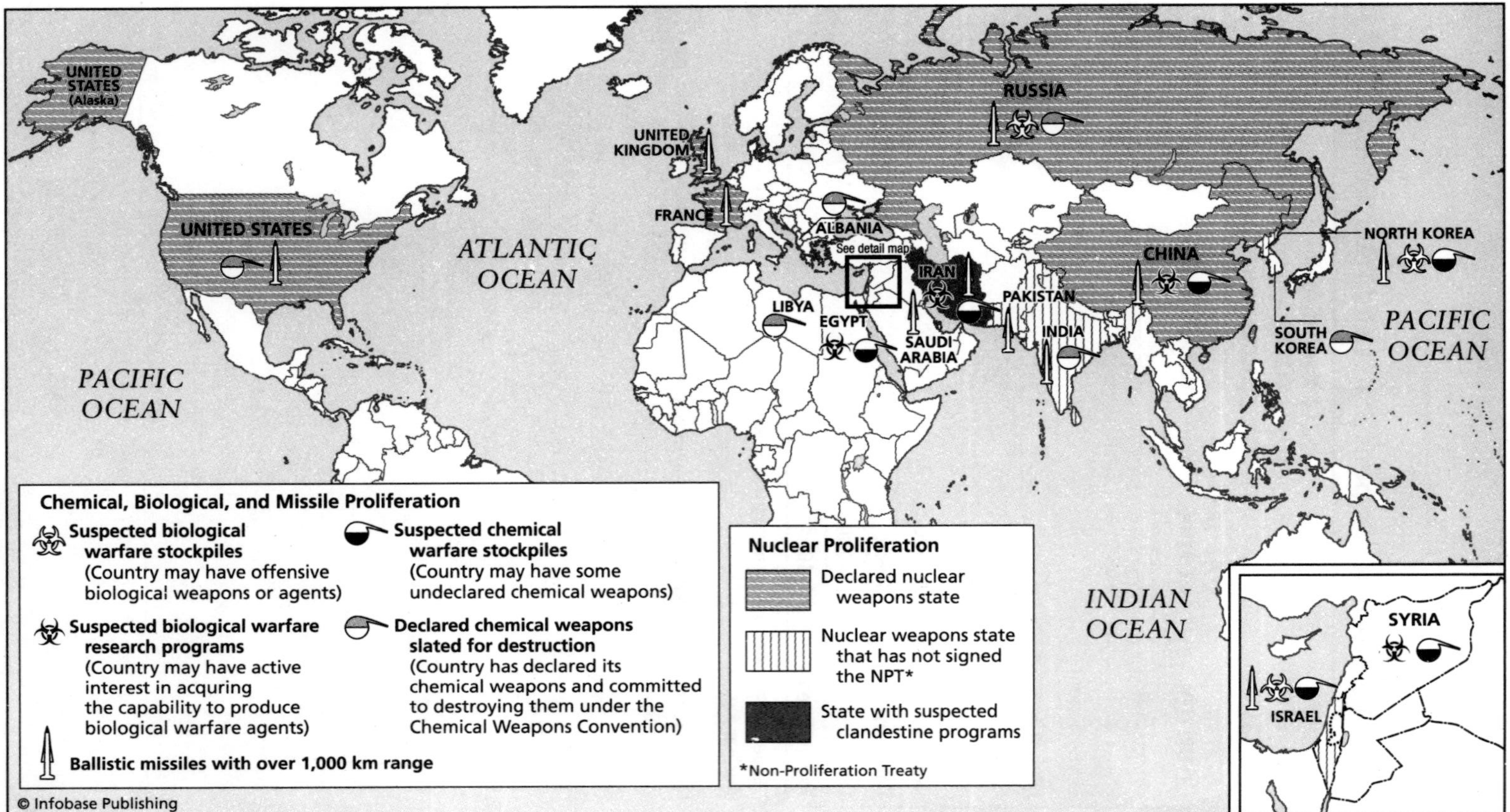

Source: Carnegie Endowment for International Peace

1.4 U.S. Strategic Nuclear Forces (Under START I, START II, and Treaty of Moscow)

U.S. Strategic Nuclear Forces

	START I		START II		TREATY OF MOSCOW	
	LAUNCHERS	WARHEADS	LAUNCHERS	WARHEADS	LAUNCHERS	WARHEADS
ICBMs	550	1,700	500	500	450	500–600
SLBMs	432	3,168	336	1,680	264	1,056–1,152
Bombers	206	1,098	97	1,276	77	500–850
Total	1,188	5,966	933	3,456	791	2,200

Source: Congressional Research Service—Amy F. Woolf "Nuclear Arms Control: The Strategic Offensive Reductions Treaty" updated January 3, 2007—Order Code RL31448

1.5 Russian Strategic Nuclear Forces (Under START I, START II, and Treaty of Moscow)

Russian Strategic Nuclear Forces						
	START I		**START II**		**TREATY OF MOSCOW**	
	LAUNCHERS	**WARHEADS**	**LAUNCHERS**	**WARHEADS**	**LAUNCHERS**	**WARHEADS**
ICBMs	542	2,168	805	805	300	900
SLBMs	292	1,592	228	1,512	96	384
Bombers	78	624	78	936	65	780
Total	912	4,384	1,111	3,253	461	2,064

Source: Congressional Research Service—Amy F. Woolf "Nuclear Arms Control: The Strategic Offensive Reductions Treaty" updated January 3, 2007—Order Code RL31448

1.6 U.S. Nuclear Tests by Calendar Year					
1945–1949	6	1960–1964	202	1980–1984	92
1950–1954	43	1965–1969	231	1985–1989	75
1955–1959	145	1970–1974	137	1990–1992	23
		1975–1979	100	Total	1,054

Note: These figures include all U.S. nuclear tests, of which 24 were joint U.S.-U.K. tests conducted at the Nevada Test Site between 1962 and 1991. They reflect data on unannounced tests that DOE declassified on December 7, 1993. They exclude the two atomic bombs that the United States dropped on Japan in 1945. On June 27, 1994, Secretary O'Leary announced that DOE had redefined three nuclear detonations (one each in 1968, 1970, and 1972) as separate nuclear tests. This table reflects these figures. She also declassified the fact that 63 tests, conducted from 1963 through 1992, involved more than one nuclear explosive device.

Source: U.S. Department of Energy.

NONPROLIFERATION

2.1 List of States That Have Ratified or Acceded to the NPT as of March 1, 2005

1. Afghanistan
2. Albania
3. Algeria
4. Andorra
5. Angola
6. Antigua and Barbuda
7. Argentina
8. Armenia
9. Australia
10. Austria
11. Azerbaijan
12. Bahamas
13. Bahrain
14. Bangladesh
15. Barbados
16. Belarus
17. Belgium
18. Belize
19. Benin
20. Bhutan
21. Bolivia
22. Bosnia and Herzegovina
23. Botswana
24. Brazil
25. Brunei Darussalam
26. Bulgaria
27. Burkina Faso
28. Burundi
29. Cambodia
30. Cameroon

31. Canada
32. Cape Verde
33. Central African Republic
34. Chad
35. Chile
36. China
37. Colombia
38. Comoros
39. Congo
40. Costa Rica
41. Côte d'Ivoire
42. Croatia
43. Cuba
44. Cyprus
45. Czech Republic
46. Democratic People's Republic of Korea*
47. Democratic Republic of the Congo
48. Denmark
49. Djibouti
50. Dominica
51. Dominican Republic
52. Ecuador
53. Egypt
54. El Salvador
55. Equatorial Guinea
56. Eritrea
57. Estonia
58. Ethiopia
59. Fiji
60. Finland
61. France
62. Gabon
63. Gambia
64. Georgia
65. Germany
66. Ghana
67. Greece
68. Grenada
69. Guatemala
70. Guinea
71. Guinea-Bissau
72. Guyana
73. Haiti
74. Holy See
75. Honduras
76. Hungary
77. Iceland
78. Indonesia
79. Iran (Islamic Republic of)
80. Iraq
81. Ireland
82. Italy
83. Jamaica
84. Japan
85. Jordan
86. Kazakhstan
87. Kenya
88. Kiribati
89. Kuwait
90. Kyrgyzstan
91. Lao People's Democratic Republic

*Announced its withdrawal on 10 January 2003.

92. Latvia
93. Lebanon
94. Lesotho
95. Liberia
96. Libyan Arab Jamahiriya
97. Liechtenstein
98. Lithuania
99. Luxembourg
100. Madagascar
101. Malawi
102. Malaysia
103. Maldives
104. Mali
105. Malta
106. Marshall Islands
107. Mauritania
108. Mauritius
109. Mexico
110. Micronesia (Federated States of)
111. Monaco
112. Mongolia
113. Morocco
114. Mozambique
115. Myanmar
116. Namibia
117. Nauru
118. Nepal
119. Netherlands
120. New Zealand
121. Nicaragua
122. Niger
123. Nigeria
124. Norway
125. Oman
126. Palau
127. Panama
128. Papua New Guinea
129. Paraguay
130. Peru
131. Philippines
132. Poland
133. Portugal
134. Qatar
135. Republic of Korea
136. Republic of Moldova
137. Romania
138. Russian Federation
139. Rwanda
140. Saint Kitts and Nevis
141. Saint Lucia
142. Saint Vincent and the Grenadines
143. Samoa
144. San Marino
145. Sao Tome and Principe
146. Saudi Arabia
147. Senegal
148. Serbia and Montenegro
149. Seychelles
150. Sierra Leone
151. Singapore
152. Slovakia
153. Slovenia
154. Solomon Islands
155. Somalia

156. South Africa
157. Spain
158. Sri Lanka
159. Sudan
160. Suriname
161. Swaziland
162. Sweden
163. Switzerland
164. Syrian Arab Republic
165. Tajikistan
166. Thailand
167. The former Yugoslav Republic of Macedonia
168. Timor-Leste
169. Togo
170. Tonga
171. Trinidad and Tobago
172. Tunisia
173. Turkey
174. Turkmenistan
175. Tuvalu
176. Uganda
177. Ukraine
178. United Arab Emirates
179. United Kingdom of Great Britain and Northern Ireland
180. United Republic of Tanzania
181. United States of America
182. Uruguay
183. Uzbekistan
184. Vanuatu
185. Venezuela
186. Viet Nam
187. Yemen
188. Zambia
189. Zimbabwe

Source: UN Department for Disarmament Affairs

2.2 Funding for U.S. State Department Nonproliferation, Anti-Terrorism, Demining, and Related Programs

($ million)

	FY2005	FY2006 REQUEST	FY2006 P.L. 109-102
Nonproliferation and Disarmament Fund	31.7	37.5	37.5
Export Control Assistance	37.7	44.4	43.4
Nonproliferation of WMD Expertise	50.1	52.6	52.6
IAEA Voluntary Contribution	52.6	50.0	50.0
International Monitoring System (CTBT)	18.8	14.4	14.4
Antiterrorism Assistance	117.8	133.5	123.5
Terrorist Interdiction Program	5.0	7.5	5.5
Counterterrorism Engagement	2.0	2.0	1.0
Counterterrorism Financing	7.2	7.5	7.5
Other	75.9	90.7	74.7
Total, NADR Program	**398.8**	**440.1**	**410.1**

Source: Congressional Research Service—Carl E. Behrens, Nuclear Nonproliferation Issues, updated January 20, 2006—Order Code IB10091

2.3. Illicit Trafficking (2005)

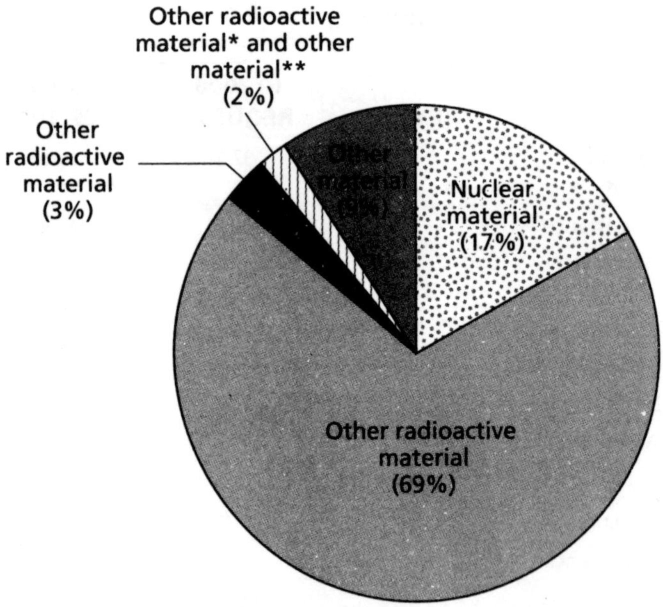

Confirmed incidents of illicit trafficking and other related unauthorized activities involving nuclear and other radioactive material, as reported to the Illicit Trafficking Database in 2005.

*Includes mainly radioactively contaminated materials

**Includes radioactive sources

Source: IAEA Annual Report 2005

2.4 Defense Department Former Soviet Union Threat Reduction Programs

($ million)

	FY2005	FY2006 REQUEST	FY2006 P.L. 109-148
Strategic Offensive Arms Elimination—Russia	58.5	78.9	78.9
Weapons Storage Security—Russia	48.7	74.1	74.1
Weapons Transportation Security—Russia	26.3	30.0	30.0
WMD Proliferation Prevention—Former Soviet Union	40.0	40.6	40.6
Other (Including Biological & Chemical Weapons programs)	235.7	223.6	223.6
Total, FSU Threat Reduction	**409.2**	**415.5**	**415.5**

Source: Congressional Research Service—Carl E. Behrens, Nuclear Nonproliferation Issues, updated January 20, 2006—Order Code IB10091

2.5 Department of Energy Nuclear Nonproliferation Programs

PROGRAM	FY2005	FY2006 REQUEST	FY2006 P.L. 109-103
Nonproliferation and Verification R&D	224.0	272.2	322.0
Nonproliferation and International Security	91.3	80.2	75.0
International Materials Protection, Control, and Accounting (MPC&A)	294.7	343.4	427.0
Global Initiatives for Proliferation Prevention	40.7	37.9	40.0
Elimination of Weapons-Grade Plutonium Production	44.0	132.0	176.2
HEU Transparency Implementation	20.8	20.5	19.5
Fissile Materials Disposition	613.1	653.1	473.5
Global Threat Reduction Initiative	93.8	98.0	98.0
Total, Defense Nuclear Nonproliferation	**1,422.1**	**1,637.2**	**1,631.2**

Source: Congressional Research Service—Carl E. Behrens, Nuclear Nonproliferation Issues, updated January 20, 2006—Order Code IB10091

2.6 Number of Facilities under Safeguards or Containing Safeguarded Material

	NUMBER OF FACILITIES (NUMBER OF INSTALLATIONS)			
FACILITY TYPE	**COMPREHENSIVE SAFEGUARDS AGREEMENTS[a]**	**INFCIRC/66[b]**	**NUCLEAR WEAPON STATES**	**TOTAL**
Power reactors	186 (223)	11 (14)	1 (1)	198 (238)
Research reactors and critical assemblies	141 (152)	7 (7)	1 (1)	149 (160)
Conversion plants	13 (13)	1 (1)	—(—)	14 (14)
Fuel fabrication plants	38 (39)	3 (3)	—(—)	6 (6)
Reprocessing plants	5 (5)	1 (1)	—(—)	6 (6)
Enrichment plants	8 (8)	—(—)	2 (4)	10 (12)
Separate storage facilities	67 (68)	3 (3)	7 (8)	77 (79)
Other facilities	82 (92)	1 (1)	1 (1)	84 (94)
Subtotals	540 (600)	27 (30)	12 (15)	579 (645)
Other locations	325 (423)	3 (30)	—(—)	328 (453)
Non-nuclear Installations	—(—)	1 (1)	—(—)	1 (1)
Totals	**865 (1023)**	**32 (61)**	**12 (15)**	**908 (1099)**

[a]Covering safeguards agreements pursuant to NPT and/or Treaty of Tlatelolco and other comprehensive safeguards agreements.

[b]Excluding installation in nuclear weapon states; including installations in Taiwan, China.

Source: "IAEA Safeguards: Stemming the Spread of Nuclear Weapons" International Atomic Energy Agency Information Series

IRAQ

3.1 Iraq: Declared Nuclear Facilities

Source: U.S. Central Intelligence Agency, "Iraq's Weapons of Mass Destruction," 2002

3.2 UN Security Council Resolutions and Provisions for Inspections and Monitoring: Theory and Practice

RESOLUTION REQUIREMENT	REALITY
Res. 687 (3 April 1991) Requires Iraq to declare, destroy, remove, or render harmless under UN or IAEA supervision and not to use, develop, construct, or acquire all chemical and biological weapons, all ballistic missiles with ranges greater than 150 km, and all nuclear weapons-usable material, including related material, equipment, and facilities. The resolution also formed the Special Commission and authorized the IAEA to carry out immediate on-site inspections of WMD-related facilities based on Iraq's declarations and UNSCOM's designation of any additional locations.	Baghdad refused to declare all parts of each WMD program, submitted several declarations as part of its aggressive efforts to deny and deceive inspectors, and ensured that certain elements of the program would remain concealed. The prohibition against developing delivery platforms with ranges greater than 150 km allowed Baghdad to research and develop shorter-range systems with applications for longer-range systems and did not affect Iraqi efforts to convert full-size aircraft into unmanned aerial vehicles as potential WMD delivery systems with ranges far beyond 150 km.
Res. 707 (15 August 1991) Requires Iraq to allow UN and IAEA inspectors immediate and unrestricted access to any site they wish to inspect. Demands Iraq provide full, final, and complete disclosure of all aspects of its WMD programs; cease immediately any attempt to conceal, move, or destroy WMD-related material or equipment; allow UNSCOM and IAEA teams to use fixed-wing and helicopter flights throughout Iraq; and respond fully, completely, and promptly to any Special Commission questions or requests.	Baghdad in 1996 negotiated with UNSCOM Executive Chairman Ekeus modalities that it used to delay inspections, to restrict to four the number of inspectors allowed into any site Baghdad declared as "sensitive," and to prohibit them altogether from sites regarded as sovereign. These modalities gave Iraq leverage over individual inspections. Iraq eventually allowed larger numbers of inspectors into such sites but only after lengthy negotiations at each site.
Res. 715 (11 October 1991) Requires Iraq to submit to UNSCOM and IAEA long-term monitoring of Iraqi WMD programs; approved detailed plans called for in UNSCRs 687 and 707 for long-term monitoring.	Iraq generally accommodated UN monitors at declared sites but occasionally obstructed access and manipulated monitoring cameras. UNSCOM and IAEA monitoring of Iraq's WMD programs does not have aspecified end date under current UN resolutions.

(continues)

3.2 (*Continued*)

RESOLUTION REQUIREMENT	REALITY
Res. 1051 (27 March 1996) Established the Iraqi export/import monitoring system, requiring UN members to provide IAEA and UNSCOM with information on materials exported to Iraq that may be applicable to WMD production, and requiring Iraq to report imports of all dual-use items.	Iraq is negotiating contracts for procuring—outside of UN controls—dual-use items with WMD applications. The UN lacks the staff needed to conduct thorough inspections of goods at Iraq's borders and to monitor imports inside Iraq.
Res. 1060 (12 June 1996) and Resolutions 1115, 1134, 1137, 1154, 1194, and 1205. Demands that Iraq cooperate with UNSCOM and allow inspection teams immediate, unconditional, and unrestricted access to facilities for inspection and access to Iraqi officials for interviews. UNSCR 1137 condemns Baghdad's refusal to allow entry to Iraq to UNSCOM officials on the grounds of their nationality and its threats to the safety of UN reconnaissance aircraft.	Baghdad consistently sought to impede and limit UNSCOM's mission in Iraq by blocking access to numerous facilities throughout the inspection process, often sanitizing sites before the arrival of inspectors and routinely attempting to deny inspectors access to requested sites and individuals. At times, Baghdad would promise compliance to avoid consequences, only to renege later.
Res. 1154 (2 March 1998) Demands that Iraq comply with UNSCOM and IAEA inspections and endorses the Secretary General's memorandum of understanding with Iraq, providing for "severest consequences" if Iraq fails to comply.	UNSCOM could not exercise its mandate without Iraqi compliance. Baghdad refused to work with UNSCOM and instead negotiated with the Secretary General, whom it believed would be more sympathetic to Iraq's needs.
Res. 1194 (9 September 1998) Condemns Iraq's decision to suspend cooperation with UNSCOM and the IAEA.	
Res. 1205 (5 November 1998) Condemns Iraq's decision to cease cooperation with UNSCOM.	
Res. 1284 (17 December 1999) Established the United Nations Monitoring, Verification, and Inspection Commission (UNMOVIC), replacing UNSCOM; and demanded that Iraq allow UNMOVIC teams immediate, unconditional, and unrestricted access to any and all aspects of Iraq's WMD program.	Iraq repeatedly has rejected the return of UN arms inspectors and claims that it has satisfied all UN resolutions relevant to disarmament. Compared with UNSCOM, 1284 gives the UNMOVIC chairman less authority, gives the Security Council a greater role in defining key disarmament tasks, and requires that Inspectors be full-time UN employees.

Source: U.S. Central Intelligence Agency, "Iraq's Weapons of Mass Destruction," 2002

NORTH KOREA

4.1 Ranges North Korean Missiles Would Need to Reach American Targets

TARGET	WASHINGTON, DC	CHICAGO	SAN FRANCISCO	SEATTLE	ANCHORAGE	HONO-LULU
Range (km)	10,700	10,000	8,600	7,900	5,600	7,100

Source: Congressional Research Service—Steven A. Hildreth, "North Korean Ballistic Missile Threat to the United States" updated September 20, 2006—Order Code RS21473

4.2 U.S. Assistance to North Korea (1995–2005)

	FOOD AID (PER FY)				
CALENDAR OR FISCAL YEAR (FY)	METRIC TONS	COMMODITY VALUE ($ MILLION)	KEDO ASSISTANCE (PER CALENDAR YR; $ MILLION)	MEDICAL SUPPLIES & OTHER (PER FY; $ MILLION)	TOTAL ($ MILLION)
1995	0	$0.0	$9.5	$0.2	$9.7
1996	19,500	$8.3	$22.0	$0.0	$30.3
1997	177,000	$52.4	$25.0	$5.0	$82.4
1998	200,000	$72.9	$50.0	$0.0	$122.9
1999	695,194	$222.1	$65.1	$0.0	$287.2
2000	265,000	$74.3	$64.4	$0.0	$138.7
2001	350,000	$102.8	$74.9	$0.0	$177.6
2002	207,000	$82.4	$90.5	$0.0	$172.9
2003	40,200	$25.5	$2.3	$0.0	$27.8
2004	110,000	$52.8	$0.0	$0.1	$52.9
2005	22,800	$7.5	—	—	—
Total	**2,086,694**	**$701.0**	**$403.7**	**$5.3**	**$1,102.4**

Source: Congressional Research Service—Mark E. Manyin - "U.S. Assistance to North Korea: Fact Sheet" updated January 31, 2006—Order Code RS21834

8

Key Players A to Z

MAHMOUD AHMADINEJAD (1956–) President of Iran. Elected in August 2005, he holds the highest elected office in Iran but under Iran's constitution is subordinate to Supreme Leader Ali KHAMANEI. A combative politician whose indifference to world opinion recalls the early days of the Iranian revolution, Ahmadinejad is highly critical of the United States and supports closer relations between Iran and Russia. He calls the Holocaust a "myth," says that the state of Israel should be "wiped off the map," and is a vocal and defiant supporter of Iran's nuclear program. Though he says that Iran will never produce nuclear weapons, soon after coming to office he replaced Hasan ROWHANI with Ali LARIJANI as head of Iran's Supreme National Security Council, and Larijani's statements suggest that he does seek nuclear weapons for Iran.

FRANK AIKEN (1898–1983) Served two terms as Ireland's minister for external affairs, from 1951 to 1954, and again from 1957 to 1969. Starting in 1959, he offered to the UN General Assembly a series of proposals aimed at limiting the spread of nuclear weapons. His proposals eventually became the basis for the Nuclear Non-proliferation Treaty.

BERNARD BARUCH (1870–1965) American financier who was an adviser to U.S. presidents. In 1946, President Harry TRUMAN appointed Baruch the U.S. representative to the UN Atomic Energy Commission. On June 14, 1946, Baruch presented the UNAEC with the Baruch Plan, proposing international control of atomic energy.

ZULFIKAR ALI BHUTTO (1928–1979) Founder of the Pakistan People's Party (PPP), president of Pakistan from 1971 to 1973, and prime minister from 1973 to 1977. As head of Pakistan's government, he reshaped Pakistan's constitution, introducing a parliamentary system. But his government was charged with corruption, and he was accused of unlawfully suppressing the opposition. As head of the government, Bhutto encouraged the development of Pakistan's nuclear weapons program. His government came to an end on July 5, 1977, when he was deposed by Chief of Army Staff General Muhammad Zia-ul-Haq; he was arrested shortly afterward, and in 1979, he was executed for the murder of a political opponent.

GEORGE H. W. BUSH (1924–) President of the United States from 1989 to 1993. As president, he participated in the START I arms reduction agreement with the Soviet Union, which entered into force after he was out of office, continuing the trend toward nuclear arsenal cutbacks that began in the last years of the REAGAN administration. In 1991, after SADDAM HUSSEIN invaded and annexed Kuwait, Bush led the coalition that invaded Iraq and drove its forces out of Kuwait. The Bush administration chose to leave Saddam Hussein in power. Explaining this decision later, Bush said that he did not give the order to overthrow the Iraqi government because it would have "incurred incalculable human and political costs. . . . We would have been forced to occupy Baghdad and, in effect, rule Iraq." His son George W. BUSH as president in 2003 did choose to topple Saddam Hussein, with the predicted results.

GEORGE W. BUSH (1946–) President of the United States from 2001 to 2009. The election in 2000 was a close race, which Bush was judged to have won only after the Supreme Court ordered a halt to a recount of the ballots in Florida. Political pundits wondered if Bush would have enough of a mandate to accomplish his goals. Then, as a result of the September 11, 2001, attacks, which empowered conservatives and made the American people rally behind their leaders, Bush achieved a freedom of action not enjoyed by any president since Franklin ROOSEVELT. His administration changed the nation's security doctrine to include the option of preventive war to meet "gathering threats." In 2003, under Bush's direction, the United States invaded Iraq and deposed its dictator, SADDAM HUSSEIN. The pretext for the invasion was proliferation: Saddam Hussein might soon possess weapons of mass destruction, including nuclear weapons, and he might give them to terrorists.

HANS BLIX (1928–) Swedish diplomat and politician. Blix was the head of the UN Monitoring, Verification and Inspection Commission from January 2000 to June 2003. In 2003, the commission began searching Iraq for weapons of mass destruction, ultimately finding none. He was succeeded by MOHAMED ELBARADEI.

JAMES EARL CARTER (1924–) President of the United States from 1977 to 1981 and winner of the Nobel Peace Prize in 2002. One of his first acts on assuming office was to order the removal of all U.S. nuclear weapons from South Korea. In 1978, he helped negotiate the Camp David Accords, a peace agreement between Israel and Egypt. Carter, who said in his inaugural address that his main goal was to banish nuclear weaponry from the face of the Earth, worked hard on the second round of Strategic Arms Limitations Talks (SALT II, successor to SALT I negotiated by Nixon and Ford) with the Soviet Union; the SALT II treaty was signed in 1979 but never entered into force. Believing that support for human rights and not simply cold war politics should be the basis for America's foreign policy, Carter withdrew support from staunchly anticommunist but repressive regimes in Latin America. In the 1980 election, voter dissatisfaction with a stagnant U.S. economy and Carter's inability to defuse the Iran hostage crisis led to his defeat by Ronald REAGAN. Carter has had a remarkably active postpresidency, earning praise for his support for human rights and free elections around the world. In 1994, Carter went on a mission to persuade North Korea to desist from uranium enrichment. Carter's visit resulted in the signing of the Agreed Framework, under which North Korea agreed to stop processing nuclear fuel in exchange for various concessions from the United States.

WILLIAM JOSEPH CASEY (1913–1987) Director of the Central Intelligence Agency (CIA) from 1981 to 1987. A corporate lawyer for much of his career, between 1971 and 1973 Casey served as a chairman of the Security and Exchange Commission (SEC). As head of the CIA during the Reagan administration, Casey was known for extremely aggressive policies when it came to pursuing communists. He allegedly supported illegal aid to the Nicaraguan contras but died before giving formal testimony. In 1983, he told Reagan that a recent NATO maneuver had nearly been mistaken by the Soviets as preparation for a U.S.-initiated nuclear war.

DICK CHENEY (1941–) Secretary of defense from March 1989 to January 1993 in the presidential administration of GEORGE H. W. BUSH and vice president in the administration of GEORGE W. BUSH. Cheney is widely viewed as the most powerful vice president in the history of the United States. His influence was especially important in decisions concerning the 2003 invasion of Iraq and in promoting the necessity of the war to the American public.

WILLIAM JEFFERSON CLINTON (1946–) President of the United States from 1993 to 2001. As president, Clinton cut back spending on missile defense programs, in which he seems to have had little faith, though he sometimes said this technology might help defend against missiles launched by a rogue state. Officials in Clinton's administration negotiated the Agreed Framework, a deal offering assistance to North Korea in exchange for its agreement not to withdraw from the Nuclear Non-proliferation Treaty. Clinton's critics in the U.S. Congress accused his administration of rewarding North Korea for bad behavior and of supporting a government that would otherwise have collapsed.

DWIGHT D. EISENHOWER (1890–1969) Commander of U.S. armed forces in World War II, U.S. president from 1953 to 1959. As part of an out-of-control arms race with the Soviet Union, Eisenhower presided over a massive U.S. program to build and deploy atom bombs, thermonuclear bombs, and systems that would deliver them to enemy targets. Concerned about the further spread of nuclear weapons, in December 1953, he introduced the Atoms for Peace program to the UN, a program for the diffusion of nuclear energy technology and the restriction of nuclear weapons.

ALBERT EINSTEIN (1879–1955) The most influential theoretical physicist of the 20th century, and the best-known scientist of modern times. Einstein's most enduring scientific accomplishments are the special theory of relativity and the general theory of relativity, two theories that changed the modern understanding of space, time, energy, and matter. Einstein used his celebrity to promote causes he believed in such as cultural Zionism, world peace, and, in one fateful instance, the nuclear arms race. In 1939, his fellow-scientist LEO SZILARD persuaded Einstein, who had immigrated to the United States in 1932, to send a letter to U.S. president Franklin Delano ROOSEVELT advising the president that Nazi Germany might be developing nuclear weapons. Szilard and Einstein's letter to Roosevelt suggested that it would be better if the United States developed them first. According to the biochemist Linus Pauling, Einstein later wished he had not sent the letter. Shortly before his death in 1955, Einstein joined with the philosopher Bertrand Russell in circulating a petition calling for the abolition of nuclear weapons. The petition became known as the Einstein-Russell Manifesto and is a founding document of the antinuclear movement.

MOHAMED ELBARADEI (1942–) Director of the UN International Atomic Energy Agency, succeeding Hans BLIX in 1997. In October 2005, Dr. ElBaradei and the IAEA were jointly awarded the Nobel Peace Prize "for their efforts to prevent nuclear energy from being used for military purposes and to ensure that nuclear energy for peaceful purposes is used in the safest possible way." In its citation, the Norwegian Nobel Committee praised

Dr. ElBaradei for his advocacy of new measures to strengthen the nuclear nonproliferation regime.

LEVI ESHKOL (1895–1969) Israeli prime minister from 1963 to his death in 1969. Though the secrecy that surrounds the Israeli nuclear program makes it difficult to be certain, many analysts believe that Israel already had nuclear weapons by the time of Eskhol's term as prime minister. It has been reported that in 1967 during Israel's Six-Day War, Eshkol ordered the deployment of two atomic bombs that Israel supposedly possessed at that time.

INDIRA GANDHI (1917–1984) Prime minister of India from January 19, 1966, to March 24, 1977, and again from January 15, 1980, to her death on October 31, 1984. During her first period as prime minister, India intervened on the Bangladesh side in the fight between Bangladesh (formerly East Pakistan) and Pakistan. She encouraged the acceleration of India's nuclear program and India's 1974 underground test of a "peaceful" nuclear explosion. In 1975, faced with an accusation of election fraud and calls for her resignation, she persuaded India's president to declare a state of emergency and ruled India as an autocrat, suppressing dissent and launching a campaign in which thousands of political activists were arrested and tortured. In 1977, she dared to hold elections, was voted out of office, and did India's democracy the great favor of agreeing to step down. In an amazing political comeback, she became prime minister again with the return of the Congress Party to power in 1980. She was assassinated in 1984 by two of her own bodyguards.

MOHANDAS KARAMCHAND GANDHI (1869–1948) Major leader of India's struggle to achieve independence from Great Britain. Believing that all violence was unjustified, Gandhi convinced the Indian independence movement to work toward its goals by means of civil disobedience and peaceful resistance to unjust authority.

MIKHAIL SERGEYEVICH GORBACHEV (1931–) General secretary of the Communist Party, and thus the Soviet Union's head of state, from 1985 to 1990, and president of the USSR from 1990 to 1991. As head of the Soviet Union, Gorbachev inherited a stagnant system and tried to save it through a program of sweeping reform. He promoted greater freedom of expression, democratic political institutions, and economic liberalization in the hope of improving Soviet living standards. Believing the huge Soviet military establishment was a drag on economic progress, in January 1986, Gorbachev proposed the elimination of intermediate-range nuclear weapons in Europe and the ultimate elimination of all nuclear weapons by the year 2000. To the surprise of many observers, his proposal received an enthusiastic response from U.S. president RONALD REAGAN, leading to the

Intermediate-Range Nuclear Forces (INF) Treaty and to other arms-reduction treaties such as START 1 and SORT, signed by their successors. It proved impossible to keep the Soviet Union together without the use of force, however. Gorbachev's ability to influence events came to an end with the breakup of the Soviet Union in 1991.

HIROHITO (1901–1989) Emperor of Japan from 1926 until his death in 1989; grandson of the first Meiji emperor of Japan. On August 14, 1945, soon after the United States dropped atomic bombs on Hiroshima and Nagasaki, Hirohito addressed his subjects for the first time in a radio speech. Acknowledging that "the war situation has developed not necessarily to Japan's advantage," the emperor added, "The enemy has begun to employ a new and most cruel bomb, the power of which to do damage is, indeed, incalculable, taking the toll of many innocent lives," and Japan must therefore "suffer what is unsufferable," that is, surrender.

SADDAM HUSSEIN (1937–2006) Officially the president and really the absolute ruler of Iraq from 1979 to 2003. After playing a key role in the 1968 coup that brought the revolutionary Baath Party to power in Iraq, Saddam became vice president of Iraq. Throughout the 1970s, he built a repressive security apparatus that would help him gain and retain power until his overthrow by the U.S. invasion in 2003. As president, Saddam presided over programs to develop chemical, biological, and nuclear weapons in Iraq, and he ordered the use of chemical weapons against Iranian forces and Kurdish separatists during the Iraq-Iran war (1980–88). In 1990 at his order, Iraq invaded and annexed Kuwait, an action that led to a U.S.-led invasion of Iraq in 1991. After the war, Iraq's secret nuclear, chemical, and biological weapons program was eliminated as part of the peace settlement imposed on Iraq. However, some countries, particularly the United States, suspected Iraq of reviving the program, which provided grounds for a second U.S. invasion of Iraq in 2003 and became the world's first war conducted in the name of nuclear nonproliferation. A search conducted following the U.S. invasion of the country turned up no signs of a viable nuclear weapons program. Saddam Hussein, who had gone into hiding, was captured by U.S. forces in December 2003. On December 30, 2006, having been convicted of crimes against humanity, he was executed by hanging.

DAVID A. KAY (1940–) UN chief weapons inspector from 1991 to 1992 and head of the Iraqi Survey Group charged with finding the weapons of mass destruction (WMD) in Iraq following the 2003 U.S.-led invasion of that country. Prior to the war, Kay had strongly believed that SADDAM HUSSEIN was in possession of WMD. In September 2002, Kay told *U.S. News and*

World Report, "Iraq stands in clear violation of international orders to rid itself of these weapons." On January 28, 2004, after his survey group combed the country for evidence of WMD, Kay told the U.S. Congress, "We were almost all wrong."

JOHN F. KENNEDY (1917–1963) President of the United States from 1961 to his assassination on November 22, 1963. During his 1960 presidential campaign against Richard Nixon, Kennedy spoke of a "missile gap," the perception that, under the administration of his predecessor, Dwight D. Eisenhower, the United States had been allowed to lag behind the Soviet Union in the construction and deployment of ballistic missiles. In October 1962, he faced down Russian leader Nikita Khrushchev in a tense episode of nuclear brinksmanship known as the Cuban missile crisis. Chastened by this brush with Armageddon, Kennedy later pursued arms control agreements with the Soviet Union and signed the Limited Test Ban Treaty (LTBT), the first treaty controlling nuclear testing. The United States, the United Kingdom, and the Soviet Union were the first parties to the LTBT, which Kennedy signed into law in August 1963.

ALI KHAMENEI (GRAND AYATOLLAH SAYYED ALI HOSSYNI KHAMENEI) (1939–) President of Iran from 1981 to 1989 and supreme leader (ayatollah) since 1989, succeeding Ayatollah Ruhalla Khomeini. Khamenei was a key figure in Iran's 1979 Islamic revolution and a close associate of Khomeini. He issued a fatwa (Islamic religious ruling) saying the production, stockpiling, and use of nuclear weapons is forbidden under Islam. The Iranian government cited this fatwa in an official statement at an August 2005 meeting of the International Atomic Energy Agency (IAEA) in Vienna; it was cited to prove that Iran would not make nuclear weapons (even though it was determined to master the entire uranium fuel cycle, unnecessary for nuclear energy production but very useful for bomb making).

ABDUL QADEER KHAN (1935–) Pakistani scientist widely regarded as the founder of Pakistan's nuclear program. In January 2004, he confessed to his involvement in a secret international network of nuclear weapons technology sales to Libya, Iran, and North Korea. This international black market in nuclear technology, whose existence the Pakistani government denied until the moment of Khan's confession, is generally referred to as the "A. Q. Khan" network. On February 5, 2004, Pakistan's president, General Pervez Musharraf, announced that he had pardoned Dr. Khan, who is under house arrest but continues to be regarded as a national hero in Pakistan.

Key Players A to Z

AYATOLLAH RUHALLA KHOMEINI (1902–1989) Iranian cleric and politician, the chief leader of Iran's 1979 Islamic revolution. Forced by Shah Mohammed Reza PAHLAVI to leave the country, Khomeini proved to be a more effective critic in exile than he had been at home: The illegal circulation of cassette tapes of his speeches from abroad turned him into an inspiration to opponents of the shah and a mystical, occult figure among religious Iranians. Later, as Iran's supreme leader and de facto ruler of Iran throughout the 1980s, Khomeini led an effort to remove all Western influence from Iran and to export his brand of Islamic fundamentalism.

NIKITA SERGEYEVICH KHRUSHCHEV (1894–1971) Premier of the Soviet Union from 1958 to 1964; as the strongest leader of the Soviet Union since the death of STALIN in 1953, Khrushchev attempted to loosen and reform the Soviet system from within while practicing nuclear brinksmanship against the West. His decision to place nuclear-armed missiles in Cuba led to the famous 13-day confrontation between the Soviet Union and the United States, an episode that is believed to have brought the two countries close to nuclear war. Khrushchev was not an absolute ruler in the mold of Stalin, and his missteps on the world stage led to his overthrow by Soviet Communist Party bureaucrats.

KIM DAE-JUNG (1926–) President of South Korea from 1998 to 2003 and winner of the Nobel Peace Prize in 2000. Prior to being elected president, he survived five attempts on his life and spent five years in jail and one under house arrest for his determined opposition to South Korea's ruling party. He became a symbol of resistance to dictatorial government and lived to see South Korea become a genuine democracy.

KIM JONG IL (1941–) Leader of North Korea since 1997. He is the son of KIM Il Sung, the founder of North Korea. Officially referred as "Dear Leader," in contrast to his father, who was called "Great Leader" during his life and promoted after his death to "Eternal Leader," he is also chairman of the National Defense Commission, supreme commander of the Korean People's Army, and general secretary of the Workers' Party of Korea, which has been the ruling party of North Korea's one-party state since 1948. For virtually the entirety of Kim's rule, North Korea has been in a state of severe economic crisis. While unable to feed its people, the government of Korea has poured money into its military, which is the nation's chief employer as well as an indispensable prop to Kim's hold on power.

KIM IL SUNG (1912–1994) Leader of North Korea from the year of its founding, 1948, until his death in 1994. Under his rule, North Korea became a totalitarian state combining features of Stalinism with a religiously tinged, homegrown ideology called Juche (literally, "self-reliance"). The cult of personality that surrounded Kim Il Sung during his lifetime, and which continues, amounted to deification; his death in 1994 was followed by three years of mourning during which North Koreans could be punished for not expressing sufficient grief. He is referred to even now in North Korea's constitution as the country's "Eternal Leader."

HENRY KISSINGER (1923–) Richard Nixon's National Security Advisor and U.S. secretary of state during the Nixon and Ford administrations, from 1973 to 1977. Prior to his career in government, Kissinger acquired a reputation as an expert in the theory of nuclear deterrence. In his 1957 book *Nuclear Weapons and Foreign Policy,* he argued that the existence of nuclear weapons should not prevent countries from fighting "limited wars." As Nixon's key foreign policy adviser, he advocated a policy of détente, a relaxation of tensions, between the United States and the Soviet Union. In pursuit of this policy, he helped negotiate the Strategic Arms Limitation Treaty and the Anti-Ballistic Missile Treaty with Soviet general secretary Leonid Brezhnev.

OSAMA BIN LADEN (1957–) Cofounder and head of al-Qaeda, the terrorist network whose agents conducted the September 11, 2001, attacks on the United States. In a December 24, 1998, interview with *Time* magazine, bin Laden was asked whether he was seeking to obtain chemical or nuclear weapons, and he replied, "aquiring weapons for the defense of Muslims is a religious duty. If I have indeed acquired these weapons, then I thank God for enabling me to do so." Asked the same question in an *ABC News* interview two days later, bin Laden stated, "If I seek to acquire such weapons, this is a religious duty. How we use them is up to us."

ALI LARIJANI (1958–) Head of Iran's Supreme National Security Council with authority over Iran's nuclear program; he was appointed to the position on August 15, 2005, by Iran's president, Mahmoud Ahmadinejad, soon after Ahmadinejad took office. "If Iran becomes atomic Iran," Larijani told a group of Iranian Revolutionary Guard Corps commanders in 2005, "no longer will anyone dare challenge it, because they would have to pay too high a price."

RICHARD GREEN LUGAR (1932–) Elected U.S. senator from Indiana in 1976, 1982, 1988, 1994, and 2000. In 1992 with Georgia Senator Sam Nunn, he drafted the Nunn-Lugar bill, providing assistance to Russia and the former Soviet republics to help them secure and destroy their excess nuclear, biological, and chemical weapons. This effort, which continues today, is called the Cooperative Threat Reduction Program.

ALFRED THAYER MAHAN (1840–1914) U.S. Navy officer and military theorist whose ideas on the importance of sea power influenced navies around the world. In 1902, Mahan invented the term *Middle East,* which he used in an article entitled "The Persian Gulf and International Relations."

MOHAMMED MOSSADEGH (1882–1967) Prime minister of Iran from 1951 to 1953. In 1953, after Mossadegh nationalized Iran's oil industries, he was overthrown in a coup supported by Great Britain and engineered with the help of the U.S. Central Intelligence Agency (CIA). Shah MOHAMMED REZA PAHLAVI, who had fled the country in 1953, returned to Iran after Mossadegh's ouster. Iran became a close ally of the United States until its 1979 Islamic revolution led by Ruhalla KHOMEINI. The overthrow of Mossadegh was a rallying cry during the revolution and is still a cause of Iranian hostility to the United States.

LORD LOUIS MOUNTBATTEN (1990–1979) Last viceroy of British India, from March 24, 1947, to August 15, 1947. Unable to negotiate a compromise between India's Hindu-dominated Congress Party and the Muslim League, he encouraged India's partition into India and Pakistan.

SYED PERVEZ MUSHARRAF (1943–) Head of Pakistan's government since 1999, when he overthrew its prime minister, Nawaz SHARIF, in a military coup. On June 20, 2001, he declared himself president. Prior to the attacks of September 11, 2001, Pakistan was a major supporter and defender of the extreme Islamic fundamentalist government of the Taliban in Afghanistan, which shares a border with Pakistan. The attacks originated from the leadership of the al-Qaeda terrorist network, which operated out of Afghanistan under the Taliban's protection. Following the attacks, Musharraf agreed to assist the United States in its assault on the Taliban and its efforts to disrupt al-Qaeda. In 2004, the Pakistani scientist Abdul Qadeer KHAN, known as the father of Pakistan's atomic bomb, admitted on Pakistani television that for years he had been supplying information about nuclear technology to Libya, North Korea, and Iran. Musharraf denied that the government of Pakistan had any knowledge of Dr. Khan's illegal activities, but shortly afterward he pardoned Dr. Khan, who is a national hero in Pakistan.

JAWAHARLAL NEHRU (1889–1964) A leader of India's independence movement and India's first prime minister, holding office from the beginning of the country's independence in 1947 to the time of his death in 1964. As prime minister, he worked to shape India into a modern, secular, socialist, yet democratic state. He aroused Western anxieties by leading an international movement of "nonalignment" in the cold war between the Soviet Union and the United States. While criticizing the nuclear arms race, he encouraged the development of nuclear energy in India and believed that India should have the option of developing nuclear weapons. "Of course, if we are compelled as a nation to use [nuclear energy] for other purposes, possibly no pious sentiments of any of us will stop the nation from using it that way."

SAM NUNN (1938–) U.S. senator from Georgia from 1972 to 1997. In 1992, when he was chairman of the Senate Armed Services Committee, he joined with Indiana senator Richard LUGAR to draft the legislation that provided the basis for the Cooperative Threat Reduction Program (CTR). The CTR provides assistance to Russia and the former Soviet republics to help them secure and destroy their excess nuclear, biological, and chemical weapons.

J. ROBERT OPPENHEIMER (1904–1967) American theoretical physicist. He directed the Manhattan Project, the secret U.S. effort that successfully developed the atomic bomb during World War II. Like many of the other scientists who worked on the bomb, Oppenheimer regretted its use on the Japanese cities of Hiroshima and Nagasaki. After the war, as an adviser to the U.S. Atomic Energy Commission, he attempted to promote the peaceful uses of atomic energy and to avert the nuclear arms race with the Soviet Union. His opposition to the development of the hydrogen bomb led to the revocation of his security clearance after a much-publicized hearing in 1954 that left him smeared as a communist sympathizer and effectively ended his ability to influence U.S. policy.

MOHAMMAD REZA PAHLAVI (1919–1980) Shah of Iran from 1941 to his overthrow by an Islamic revolution in 1980; son of the founder of modern Iran, Reza Shah Pahlavi. In 1953, after he fled the country in a dispute with the nationalist leader MOHAMMED MOSSADEGH, the shah was restored to power with the help of a coup organized by the U.S. Central Intelligence Agency. During the 1970s, a time of close relations between Iran and the United States, the United States encouraged the shah to invest in nuclear technology and to send bright Iranian students to the United States to train as nuclear engineers.

SHIMON PERES (1923–) President of Israel since 2007 and prime minister from 1984 to1986 and 1995 to 1996. In 1994, Shimon Peres won the Nobel Peace Prize together with Yitzhak Rabin and Yasser Arafat for the peace talks that produced the Oslo Accords. Defending Israel's policy of letting it be known that it possesses nuclear weapons while officially claiming not to have them, he has said: "The suspicion and fog surrounding this question are constructive, because they strengthen our deterrent."

GENERAL COLIN LUTHER POWELL (1937–) U.S. secretary of state during the George W. Bush administration from January 20, 2001, to January 23, 2005. As a general in the U.S. Army, Powell also served as National Security Advisor (1987–89) and chairman of the Joint Chiefs of Staff (1989–93). Powell was perceived as one of the moderates within the Bush administration. Though he personally had doubts about the wisdom of the 2003 invasion of Iraq, he helped to justify the invasion to the international community. Speaking to the UN Security Council on February 5, 2003, Powell cited evidence that Saddam Hussein was working to obtain key components to produce nuclear weapons. Much of the evidence cited in Powell's speech was based on faulty intelligence, and he later described it as a "blot on my record."

VLADIMIR PUTIN (1952–) Acting president of the Russian Federation from 1999 to 2004, president from 2004 to 2008, and prime minister since 2008. Under the Russian constitution, he cannot be reelected president. Putin, who began his career as an agent of the KGB, the Soviet Union's secret police, has consistently taken steps to strengthen the power of the central government and of his office and to reshape the relatively young democratic Russia into an authoritarian mold. All three of Russia's major television stations are now in the hands of individuals loyal to Putin and his policies, and critical journalism, very freewheeling in Gorbachev and Yeltsin's time, has gradually become restricted to print media that reach a relatively small percentage of the population. Under Putin's leadership, the Russian Federation has begun to modernize its nuclear force. Putin has let it be known that he regards the antiballistic missile systems the United States plans to install in Europe as a threat to Russia and has warned that it would prompt Russia to point its nuclear weapons at European targets.

MUAMMAR EL-QADDAFI (1942–) De facto dictator of Libya since he led a small group of military officers in a coup d'état in 1969, abolishing the Libyan monarchy and proclaiming the new Libyan Arab Republic. Though Qaddafi portrays his regime as a utopian society "ruled by the people," in practice it is a dictatorship in which opposition leaders are crushed at home and targeted for assassination in exile. Over the years, Qaddafi is believed to have provided support for a wide variety of terrorist activities, including the Palestinian "Black September Movement," which was responsible for a massacre of Israeli athletes at the 1972 summer Olympics and the 1986 Berlin discotheque bombing. For most of the 1990s, Libya endured economic sanctions and diplomatic isolation as a result of Qaddafi's refusal to allow the extradition to the United States or United Kingdom of two Libyans accused of planting a bomb on Pan Am Flight 103, which exploded over Lockerbie, Scotland, on December 21, 1988. In the late 1990s, Qaddafi began a sustained effort to improve his country's image and relations with outsiders. Two years before the September 11, 2001, attacks, Libya pledged its commitment to fighting al-Qaeda and offered to open up its weapons program to international inspection. On May 15, 2006, the U.S. State Department announced that it would restore full diplomatic relations with Libya once Qaddafi declared he was abandoning Libya's weapons of mass destruction program.

RONALD REAGAN (1911–2004) President of the United States from 1981 to 1989. He was deeply distrustful of the Soviet Union, which he called an "evil empire," whose leaders, he said, could not be trusted to comply with treaties. He presided over a massive nuclear arms buildup and spoke rather lightly of the possibility of waging and winning a nuclear war. Later in his presidency, he called for research into an elaborate, high-tech missile defense program, the Strategic Defense Initiative. He had so much faith in this technology that he offered to share it with the Soviets, believing that it would offer both sides so perfect a defense that it would make nuclear weapons obsolete. During his second term of office, Reagan and the last Soviet leader, Mikhail GORBACHEV, negotiated the first of a series of agreements that would lead to sharp reductions in the nuclear arsenals of the United States and the Soviet Union.

CONDOLEEZZA RICE (1954–) U.S. secretary of state since 2005 and National Security Advisor during the first term of George W. BUSH. As National Security Advisor, she used her authority to make the administration's case for the invasion of Iraq on the grounds that SADDAM HUSSEIN might soon have nuclear weapons. In a January 10, 2003, interview on CNN, before the invasion of Iraq, Rice said, "The problem here is that there will always be some uncertainty about how quickly [Saddam Hussein] can acquire nuclear weapons. But we don't want the smoking gun to be a mushroom cloud." In the private councils of the administration, however, she is believed to have favored diplomacy over force. As secretary of state in the second term, she favored negotiations with North Korea.

HASAN ROWHANI (DATES UNKNOWN) Secretary of Iran's Supreme National Security Council from 1997 to 2005. Considered to be a moderate conservative among Iran's leaders, his responsibilities as leader of the Supreme National Security Council included conducting negotiations regarding Iran's nuclear programs. In 2005, he was replaced in this position by Ali LARIJANI, who has a reputation as a hard-liner.

DONALD HENRY RUMSFELD (1932–) Secretary of defense from November 1975 to January 1977 in the administration of U.S. president Gerald Ford, special envoy to the Middle East from November 1983 to May 1984, and secretary of defense from January 2001 to December 2006 in the administration of U.S. president George W. BUSH. As special envoy to the Middle East, he helped supply Iraqi dictator SADDAM HUSSEIN with military intelligence, military hardware, and strategic advice, in keeping with the REAGAN administration's desire to prevent Iran from winning a decisive victory in the Iran-Iraq war. As secretary of defense, he was in charge of the 2002 U.S. invasion of Afghanistan, the 2003 invasion of Iraq, and the long, chaotic occupations that followed.

NAWAZ SHARIF (1949–) Prime minister of Pakistan from November 1, 1990, to July 18, 1993, and from February 17, 1997, to October 12, 1999. During his second term, on May 26, 1998, Pakistan detonated five nuclear devices in reply to a similar series of nuclear tests by India earlier that same month. "Today, we have settled a score," Sharif declared in a televised speech. In 1999, he was overthrown in a military coup by army chief PERVEZ MUSHARRAF.

JOSEPH STALIN (1879–1953) Absolute ruler of the USSR from 1928 to 1953. A participant, but not a major one, in the October Revolution, which brought the communists to power in Russia in 1917, Stalin used bureaucratic skills and ruthlessness to gain control of the Communist Party hierarchy and thereby control of the Soviet Union. In 1945, soon after the United States dropped atom bombs on Hiroshima and Nagasaki, Stalin ordered a crash program to develop a Soviet bomb.

LEO SZILARD (1898–1964) Nuclear physicist and molecular biologist. Born in Austro-Hungary, he fled Germany in 1933 and later emigrated to the United States in 1938. In 1933, Szilard conceived of the nuclear chain reaction that is the basis for the atomic bomb and filed the first British patent application for nuclear energy. In 1939, with the physicists EUGENE WIGNER and EDWARD TELLER, he persuaded ALBERT EINSTEIN to write his August 2, 1939, letter to President ROOSEVELT; the letter advised the president of the possibility of the atomic bomb and of Germany's interest in it: "I understand that Germany has actually stopped the sale of uranium from the Czechoslovakian mines which she has taken over." In 1945, with other atomic scientists, he coauthored the Franck Report, which predicted that the United States would not long retain its monopoly on atomic weapons and proposed international control of atomic energy.

EDWARD TELLER (1908–2003) Theoretical physicist, considered the "father of the hydrogen bomb." Born in Austro-Hungary and educated in Germany, he emigrated to the United States in the 1930s. While participating in the Manhattan Project to develop the atomic bomb during World War II, Teller exhibited greater interest in the "super," or hydrogen, bomb, in which an atomic fission explosion would be used to set off a potentially more powerful fusion reaction. In the late 1940s and early 1950s, he was active in research on the "super." Partly from his theoretical work and partly because of his passionate belief that the United States ought to develop such a weapon, he became known as the "father of the hydrogen bomb." With a profound distrust of attempts at arms control and complete faith in technological answers to international problems, Teller became an advocate for missile defense research in the 1980s.

HARRY TRUMAN (1884–1972) U.S. president from 1945 to 1950. Truman gave the order that resulted in the dropping of an atom bomb on the Japanese city of Hiroshima on August 6, 1945, and another on Nagasaki on August 9, 1945, the only nuclear weapons yet used in warfare.

ATAL BEHARI VAJPAYEE (1924–) Prime minister of India from May 16 to May 31, 1996, and from March 19, 1998, to May 13, 2004. Leader of India's conservative, nationalist Bharatiya Janata Party (BJP), Vajpayee promised that in power the BJP would allow India to announce itself as the nuclear weapons state it already was in reality. As prime minister, he moved swiftly to fulfill this campaign promise—it was relatively easy, since India had spent decades refining its nuclear arms capability while refraining from testing and deploying the weapons. In May 1998, India conducted five underground nuclear weapons tests. Two weeks later, Pakistan responded with its own nuclear weapons tests, making it the newest nation with nuclear weapons. The government's critics charged that the BJP had involved India in a nuclear arms race with Pakistan.

MORDECHAI VANUNU (1954–) Former Israeli nuclear worker who in 1986 revealed details about the Israeli nuclear weapons program to a British newspaper. He was kidnapped in Rome on September 30, 1986, by an agent of the Israeli spy agency, Mossad, and smuggled to Israel, where he was tried in secret and convicted of treason. After serving 18 years in prison, he was released in 2004 subject to a range of restrictions on his speech and movement.

EUGENE WIGNER (1902–1995) Theoretical physicist and nuclear engineer. He was born in Austro-Hungary, educated in Germany, and immigrated to the United States in 1930. In 1939, with LEO SZILARD, EDWARD TELLER, and ALBERT EINSTEIN, he worked to persuade the United States of the importance of nuclear energy. From 1942 to 1945 at the University of Chicago, he worked with Enrico Fermi on the nuclear chain reaction important to the development of the atomic bomb.

9

Organization and Agencies

A wide range of organizations and agencies provide information on nuclear nonproliferation. Some of the most thorough research is conducted by various arms of the U.S. government and the UN. In addition, many nongovernmental agencies, research institutes (think tanks), and advocacy groups are devoted entirely or partly to the study of nuclear nonproliferation, to promoting the abolishment of nuclear weapons, or to the promotion of specific policies in relation to emerging nuclear weapons states such as India, Pakistan, Iran, and North Korea. Many such groups study problems of nuclear proliferation and international security in an effort to influence public opinion and government policy. The following is a compilation of these organizations and agencies useful for the study of nuclear nonproliferation.

Alliance for Nuclear Accountability
Seattle Office
1914 N. 34th Street, Suite 407
Seattle, WA 98103
Phone: (206) 547-3175

Washington, DC, Office
322 4th Street NE
Washington, DC 20002
Phone: (202) 544-0217
Web: http://www.ananuclear.org/

The Alliance for Nuclear Accountability is a national network of organizations working to address issues of nuclear weapons production and waste cleanup.

The American Enterprise Institute (AEI)
1150 Seventeenth Street NW
Washington, DC 20036

Phone: (202) 862-5800
Web: http://www.aei.org/

The American Enterprise Institute is a private, not-for-profit institution that conducts research and education on issues of government, politics, economics, and social welfare. Though the AEI describes itself as nonpartisan, its mission statement includes a forthright assertion of conservative principles, stating that its purpose is to "defend the principles and improve the institutions of American freedom and democratic capitalism—limited government, private enterprise, individual liberty and responsibility, vigilant and effective defense and foreign policies, political accountability, and open debate."

Arms Control Association (ACA)
1313 L St NW, Suite 130
Washington, DC 20005
Phone: (202) 463-8270
Web: http://www.armscontrol.org/

The Arms Control Association, founded in 1971, is a national organization dedicated to promoting public understanding of and support for effective arms control policies. Through its public education and media programs and its magazine, *Arms Control Today (ACT),* ACA provides policy makers, the press, and the interested public with authoritative information, analysis, and commentary on arms control proposals, negotiations and agreements, and related national security issues.

The Asian Institute at the University of Toronto
1 Devonshire Place
Toronto, Ontario M5S 3K7
Canada
Phone: (416) 946-8996
Web: http://webapp.mcis.utoronto.ca/ai/

The mission of the Asian Institute is to provide the intellectual core for interdisciplinary research and teaching on Asia. The institute is organized along subregional lines, with centers for South Asian Studies, Korean Studies, and related groups focusing on Southeast Asia and Central and Inner Asia.

Belfer Center for Science and International Affairs
John F. Kennedy School of Government
Harvard University
Box 53

79 John F. Kennedy Street
Cambridge, MA 02138 USA
Phone: (617) 495-1400
Web: http://bcsia.ksg.harvard.edu/

The Belfer Center for Science and International Affairs is a research institute devoted to international security and other critical issues where science, technology, environmental policy, and international affairs intersect.

The Brookings Institution
1775 Massachusetts Ave. NW
Washington, DC 20036
Phone: (202) 797-6000
Web: http://www.brook.edu/

The Brookings Institution, a think tank whose origins go back as far as 1916, describes itself as a "nonprofit organization devoted to independent research and innovative policy solutions." Its studies are frequently cited by members of Congress. A keyword search using "nuclear" on the Brookings Web site turns up around 7,000 articles.

Bulletin of the Atomic Scientists
6042 South Kimbark Ave.
Chicago, IL 60637
Phone: (773) 702-2555
Web: http://www.thebulletin.org/

The *Bulletin of the Atomic Scientists is* both a magazine devoted to the study of nuclear proliferation and a nonprofit organization "dedicated to security, science & survival since 1945." The bulletin was founded specifically to study the problems created by the advent of nuclear weapons. It has since expanded its focus to include other planet-threatening trends such as the degradation of the environment and global warming, but it remains an excellent source of information and opinion on the effort to contain the spread of nuclear weapons.

Bureau of International Security and Nonproliferation (ISN)
U.S. Department of State
2201 C Street NW
Washington, DC 20520
Phone: (202) 647-4000
Web: http://www.state.gov/t/isn/

The Bureau of International Security and Nonproliferation (ISN), a bureau within the State Department, is responsible for managing a broad range of nonproliferation, counterproliferation, and arms control functions. The ISN Bureau's Web page contains links to information concerning nonproliferation regimes and export controls. All the major nonproliferation and arms control treaties that are in force and that the United States has signed can be accessed through this site.

Carnegie Endowment for International Peace
1779 Massachusetts Ave. NW
Washington, DC 20036-2103
Phone: (202) 483-7600
Web: http://www.carnegieendowment.org/

The Carnegie Endowment for International Peace is a private, nonprofit organization dedicated to advancing cooperation between nations and promoting active international engagement by the United States. Founded in 1910, its work is nonpartisan and dedicated to achieving practical results.

The Cato Institute
1000 Massachusetts Avenue NW
Washington, DC 20001-5403
Phone (202) 842-0200
Web: http://www.cato.org/index.html

The Cato Institute was founded in 1977 by Edward H. Crane. It is a nonprofit public policy research foundation headquartered in Washington, D.C. The institute is named for Cato's Letters, a series of libertarian pamphlets that helped lay the philosophical foundation for the American Revolution.

The Center for Arms Control, Energy and Environmental Studies
9 Institutski
Dolgoprudny, Moscow reg.
141700 Russia
Phone: (7-495) 408-6381
Web: http://www.armscontrol.ru/

The Center for Arms Control, Energy and Environmental Studies, which is affiliated with the Moscow Institute of Physics and Technology (MPTI), was founded in 1990 and initially funded by the International Foundation for the Survival and Development of Humanity, the John Merck Fund, and the Ploughshares Fund. Its purpose is to conduct research and educate a community of independent and politically sophisticated technical experts who can formulate the technical basis for new policies in a changing international and domestic environment. In particular, the center aims to provide independent technology and policy assessments for the Russian government.

Center for Strategic and International Studies (CSIS)
1800 K. Street NW
Washington, DC 20006
Phone: (202) 887-0200
Web: http://www.csis.org/

The Center for Strategic and International Studies (CSIS) seeks to advance global security and prosperity in an era of economic and political transformation by providing strategic insights and practical policy solutions to decision makers. CSIS serves as a strategic planning partner for the government by conducting research and analysis and developing policy initiatives that look into the future and anticipate change.

Central Intelligence Agency (CIA)
Office of Public Affairs
Washington, DC 20505
Phone: (703) 482-0623
Web: https://www.cia.gov/

The Central Intelligence Agency is the best known of several U.S. agencies devoted to the collection of foreign intelligence. It was created in 1947 with the signing of the National Security Act, which also created a director of central intelligence (DCI) to serve as head of the U.S. intelligence community and act as the principal adviser to the president for intelligence matters related to national security. The Intelligence Reform and Terrorism Prevention Act of 2004 amended the National Security Act to provide for a director of national intelligence who would assume some of the roles formerly fulfilled by the DCI, with a separate director of the Central Intelligence Agency.

Chatham House
Royal Institute of International Affairs
London SW1Y 4LE
United Kingdom
Phone: +44 (44-20)20 7957 5700
Web: http://www.chathamhouse.org.uk/contact/

Founded in 1920 and based in London, Chatham House is one of Europe's leading foreign policy think tanks. It is an independent membership-based organization that brings together people from government, politics, business, NGOs, the academic world, and the media.

Congressional Research Service (CRS)
The Library of Congress
101 Independence Avenue SE
Washington, DC 20540-7500
Phone: (202) 707-5627
Web: http://www.loc.gov/crsinfo/whatscrs.html

The Congressional Research Service is the public policy research arm of the U.S. Congress. Created by Congress as a source of nonpartisan, objective analysis and research on all legislative issues, the CRS produces reports many of which are subsequently made available to the public. Currently, the easiest way to access CRS reports is through the following U.S. State Department Web page: Congressional Research Service (CRS) Reports and Issue Briefs http://fpc.state.gov/c4763.htm.

Council on Foreign Relations
New York Office
The Harold Pratt House
58 East 68th Street
New York, NY 10065
Phone: (212) 434-9400
Web: http://www.cfr.org/

Washington Office
1779 Massachusetts Avenue NW
Washington, DC 20036
Phone: (202) 518-3400

Founded in 1921, the Council on Foreign Relations is an independent, national membership organization and a nonpartisan center for scholars dedicated to producing and disseminating ideas so that individual and corporate members as well as policy makers, journalists, students, and interested citizens in the United States and other countries can better understand the world and the foreign policy choices facing the United States and other governments.

Department of Defense (DOD)
Secretary of Defense
1000 Defense Pentagon
Washington, DC 20301-1000
Phone: (703) 428-0711
Web: http://www.defenselink.mil/
Web: http://www.usa.gov/Agencies/Federal/Executive/Defense.shtml

The mission of the Department of Defense is to provide the military forces needed to deter war and to protect the security of the United States. The Department of Defense Web site directs browsers to many separate addresses and phone numbers for specific requests. The Defense Department's home page, DefenseLINK, dispenses information about defense policies, organizations, functions, and operations. Through this page researchers can link to press releases promoting the department's views, transcripts of news briefings, and the home pages of other organizations within the Defense Department, including those of all the armed services.

Department of Homeland Security
U.S. Department of Homeland Security
Washington, DC 20528
Phone: (202) 282-8000
Web: http://www.dhs.gov/index.shtm

The Department of Homeland Security, established as a response to the terrorist attacks of September 11, 2001, is a U.S. government federal agency whose primary mission is to help prevent, protect against, and respond to acts of terrorism in the United States. The protection of the nation against acts of nuclear terrorism falls within its area of responsibility.

Department of State
U.S. Department of State
2201 C Street NW
Washington, DC 20520
Phone: (202) 647-4000
Web: http://www.state.gov/

The U.S. Department of State is the foreign policy arm of the executive branch of the U.S. government. It currently defines its mission as being to "Create a more secure, democratic, and prosperous world for the benefit of the American people and the international community." Its Web sites are a source of information about past and present U.S. diplomatic efforts, including the major arms control treaties to which the Untied States is a party, and the specific sanctions currently being used to deter nuclear proliferation.

Federation of American Scientists (FAS)
1717 K St. NW, Suite 209
Washington, DC 20036
Phone: (202) 546-3300
Web: http://www.fas.org/main/home.jsp

The Federation of American Scientists (FAS) was formed in 1945 by atomic scientists from the Manhattan Project who felt that scientists, engineers, and other innovators had an ethical obligation to bring their knowledge and experience to bear on critical national decisions, especially pertaining to nuclear technology and nuclear weapons. FAS addresses a broad spectrum of issues in carrying out its mission to promote humanitarian uses of science and technology.

Geneva Centre for Security Policy
7 bis, Avenue de la Paix
P.O. Box 1295
1211 Geneva 1
Switzerland
Phone: (41-22) 41 22 906 1600
Web: http://www.gcsp.ch/e/index.htm

The Geneva Centre for Security Policy (GCSP) is an international foundation that was established in 1995 under Swiss law to promote the building and maintenance of peace, security, and stability.

Gewaltfreie Aktion Atomwaffen Abschaffen (GAAA)
(Nonviolent Action to Abolish Nuclear Weapons)
Haubmannstr. 6
70188 Stuttgart
Germany
Phone: (0711) 2155112
Web: http://www.gaaa.org/

The Gewaltfreie Aktion Atomwaffen Abschaffen (GAAA) is a German organization dedicated to the total abolition of nuclear weapons. The GAAA monitors and pressures nuclear weapons states to fulfill their obligations under international law and treaties to start to abolish their nuclear weapons.

The Henry L. Stimson Center
1111 19th Street, Twelfth Floor
Washington, DC 20036
Phone: (202) 223-5956
Email: info@stimson.org
Web: http://www.stimson.org/home.cfm

Founded in 1989, the Henry L. Stimson Center is a nonprofit, nonpartisan institution devoted to enhancing international peace and security through a unique combination of rigorous analysis and outreach.

Institute for Science and International Security (ISIS)
236 Massachusetts Avenue NE
Suite 500
Washington, DC 20002
Phone: (202) 547-3633
Web: http://www.isis-online.org/

ISIS is a nonprofit, nonpartisan institution dedicated to informing the public about science and policy issues affecting international security. Its efforts focus on stopping the spread of nuclear weapons, bringing about greater transparency of nuclear activities worldwide, and achieving deep reductions in nuclear arsenals.

International Atomic Energy Agency (IAEA)
P.O. Box 100, Wagramer Strasse 5, A-1400
Vienna, Austria
Phone: (+431) 2600-0
Fax: (+431) 2600-7
Email: Official.Mail@iaea.org
Web: http://www.iaea.org/

The IAEA was set up as the world's "Atoms for Peace" organization in 1957 within the UN family; its missions is to promote the peaceful uses of nuclear energy and to stop or slow the spread of nuclear energy for military purposes. One of its functions is to inspect existing nuclear facilities to ensure peaceful use. The IAEA Web page links to books and articles on many nuclear issues, including controversies such as the IAEA's effort to inspect Iran's nuclear facilities.

James Martin Center for Nonproliferation Studies (CNS)
460 Pierce Street
Monterey, CA 93940, USA
Phone: (831) 647-4154
Web: http://cns.miis.edu

The James Martin Center for Nonproliferation Studies (CNS) strives to combat the spread of weapons of mass destruction (WMD) by training the next generation of nonproliferation specialists and disseminating timely information and analysis. CNS, at the Monterey Institute of International Studies, is the largest nongovernmental organization in the United States devoted exclusively to research and training on nonproliferation issues.

Lawyers' Committee on Nuclear Policy (LCNP)
675 Third Avenue, Suite 315
New York, NY 10017
Phone: (212) 818 1861
E-Mail: lcnp@lcnp.org
Web:

The Lawyers' Committee on Nuclear Policy (LCNP) is the U.S. arm of the International Association of Lawyers Against Nuclear Arms (IALANA), an organization of lawyers devoted to the abolition of nuclear weapons.

Library of Congress
The Library of Congress
101 Independence Ave. SE
Washington, DC 20540
Phone; (202) 707-5000
Web: http://www.loc.gov/index.html

The Library of Congress serves as a research arm of Congress and is also the largest library in the world, with more than 130 million items on approximately 530 miles of bookshelves. There are many ways to search through the Library of Congress collections. For a quick start, enter keywords into the search field on the home page.

Library of Congress
Country Studies
http://lcweb2.loc.gov/frd/cs/cshome.html

Library of Congress
Federal Research Division (FRD)
101 Independence Ave. SE
John Adams Building, LA 5281
Washington, DC 20540-4840
Phone: (202) 707-3900
Web: http://lcweb2.loc.gov/pow/powhome.html

The Federal Research Program of the Library of Congress performs research on domestic and international subjects for agencies of the U.S. government, the District of Columbia, and authorized federal contractors. Some of these studies are available to the public and can be accessed through FRD's Web pages. A link can be found on the FRD Web site to the Library of Congress's Country Studies, which can be very useful in the early stages of research and as a source of statistics. Each country study presents a description and analysis of the historical setting and the social, economic, political, and national security systems and institutions of countries throughout the world.

Library of Congress Thomas Congressional Service
101 Independence Avenue SE
Washington, DC 20540
Phone: (202) 707-5000
Web: http://thomas.loc.gov/home/abt_thom.html

Thomas was launched in January of 1995, at the inception of the 104th Congress. The leadership of the 104th Congress directed the Library of Congress to make federal legislative information freely available to the public. Since that time Thomas has expanded the scope of its offerings to include bills, resolutions, activity in congress, the *Congressional Record,* schedules, calendars, committee information, presidential nominations, treaties, and government resources. On the Thomas Web site researchers can search by keyword or type for treaties or bills.

The Markland Group for the Integrity of Disarmament Treaties
203-150 Wilson Street West
Ancaster, Ontario L9G 4E7
Canada
Phone: (905) 648-3306
Web: http://www.hwcn.org/link/mkg/

The Markland Group was formed in 1987 to address the problem of ensuring compliance with disarmament treaties. It monitors the behavior of treaty parties in relation to compliance and looks for ways to improve treatyprovisions dealing with verification and compliance.

Missile Defense Agency (MDA)
7100 Defense Pentagon
Washington, DC, 20301-7100
Phone: (703) 882-6144
Web: http://www.mda.mil/mdalink/html/mdalink.html

The Missile Defense Agency is an agency of the U.S. Department of Defense. Its mission is to "develop and field an integrated BMDS capable of providing a layered defense for the homeland, deployed forces, friends, and allies against ballistic missiles of all ranges in all phases of flight."

Missile Defense Data Center (MDDC)
DCP Registrar:
Phone: (256) 313-8642
DSN: 897-8642
FAX: (256) 895-5800
E-mail: DCPRegistrar@mda.mil
Web: http://www.smdc.army.mil/mddc/

The MDDC is one of three MDA data centers under the Data Center Program. The MDDC serves as a data repository for missile defense data and information resulting from tests, experiments, models and simulations (M&S), analyses, and assessments for ballistic missile defense systems (BMDS) development. The data center has archived more than 75 terabytes of BMD related data collected over the past 50 years from air, ground, sea, and space-based tests and experiments.

The National Security Archive
George Washington University
Gelman Library, Suite 701
21030 H Street NW
Washington, DC 20037
Phone: (202) 994-7000
Web: http://www.gwu.edu/~nsarchiv/index.html

An independent nongovernmental research institute and library located at George Washington University, the archive collects and publishes declassified documents obtained through the Freedom of Information Act. The archive also serves as a repository of government records on a wide range of topics pertaining to national security, foreign, intelligence, and economic policies of the United States. The archive won the 1999 George Polk Award, one of U.S. journalism's most prestigious prizes, for—in the words of the citation—"piercing the self-serving veils of government secrecy, guiding journalists in the search for the truth and informing us all."

Nonproliferation Policy Education Center (NPEC)
1718 M Street NW, Suite 244
Washington, DC 20036
Phone: (202) 466-4406
Web: http://www.npec-web.org/

The Nonproliferation Policy Education Center (NPEC), a project of the Institute for International Studies (IIS), is a nonpartisan, nonprofit educational organization founded in 1994 to promote a better understanding of strategic weapons proliferation issues. NPEC educates policy makers, journalists, and university professors about proliferation threats and possible new policies and measures to meet them.

The Nuclear Control Institute (NCI)
1000 Connecticut Avenue NW, Suite 400
Washington, DC 20036
Phone: (202) 822-8444
Web: www.NCI.org

The Nuclear Control Institute, founded in 1981, is a research and advocacy center for preventing nuclear proliferation and nuclear terrorism. Nonprofit and nonpartisan, NCI is a tax-exempt 501(c)(3) organization supported by philanthropic foundations and individuals.

Nuclear Threat Initiative (NTI)
1747 Pennsylvania Avenue NW, 7th Floor
Washington, DC 20006
Phone: (202) 296-4810
Web: http://www.nti.org/

A nongovernmental organization founded by former U.S. senator Sam Nunn and CNN founder Ted Turner, NTI's mission is to strengthen global security by reducing the risk of use and preventing the spread of nuclear, biological, and chemical weapons. NTI seeks to raise public awareness, serve as a catalyst for new thinking, and take direct action to reduce these threats.

Oxford Research Group (ORG)
Development House
56-64 Leonard Street
London EC2A 4LT
United Kingdom
Phone: (44-20) 7549 0298 (London)
Phone: +44 (0)1865 242 819 (Oxford)
Web: http://www.oxfordresearchgroup.org.uk/

Oxford Research Group (ORG) is an independent nongovernmental organization and registered charity that works with others to promote a more sustainable approach to security for the U.K. and the world. The ORG works to promote disarmament and nonviolent methods for resolving conflict. In April 2005, it was named one of the top 20 think tanks in the U.K. by the *Independent* newspaper.

Partnership for Global Security (PGS)
1025 Connecticut Avenue NW
Suite 1106
Washington, DC 20036
Phone: (202) 332-1412
Web: http://www.partnershipforglobalsecurity.org/

The Partnership for Global Security (PGS) mounts a global effort to decrease the dangers posed by weapons of mass destruction (WMD) by working for a world in which all WMD are secured and the threat of their use is eliminated. PGS makes a critical difference in the world's ability to address the greatest international security issue of the 21st century and is leading the world to a safer future.

Physicians for Social Responsibility
1875 Connecticut Avenue NW, Suite 1012
Washington, DC 20009
Phone: (202) 667-4260
Email: psrnatl@psr.org

Physicians for Social Responsibility is a nonprofit advocacy organization that is the medical and public health voice for policies to stop nuclear war and proliferation and to slow, stop, and reverse global warming and toxic degradation of the environment.

RAND Corporation
National Defense Research Institute

1776 Main Street
Santa Monica, CA 90401-3208
Phone: (310) 393-0411
Web: http://www.rand.org/nsrd/ndri.html

Originally a think tank serving the U.S. Defense Department, RAND has branched out to study a variety of matters, from obesity to international terrorism, for a variety of private and government clients. One RAND division, the federally funded National Defense Research Institute (NDRI), continues to do national security research for the Defense Department, the Marine Corp, and other U.S. agencies.

United Nations
UN Headquarters
First Avenue at 46th Street
New York, NY 10017
Phone: (212) 963-5012
Web: http://www.un.org/ and
http://www.un.org/english/

The United Nations (UN), which has its headquarters in New York City, is an international organization whose mission is to facilitate cooperation in international law, international security, economic development, social progress, and human rights. Many of the major diplomatic initiatives intended to slow the spread of nuclear weapons, including Atoms for Peace and the Nuclear Non-prolfieration Treaty, were negotiated through the UN, and it is an arena of diplomacy and negotiation for the United States, its allies, and such would-be nuclear weapons states as Iraq, Iran, and North Korea. The UN is a prolific creator of reports, analysis, and statistics useful to researchers. Much of this information is available through its extensive Web pages.

United Nations Weapons of Mass Destruction Branch, Department for Disarmament Affairs
First Avenue at 46th Street
New York, NY 10017
Phone: (212) 963-5012
Web: http://disarmament.un.org/wmd/

The Weapons of Mass Destruction Branch of the UN's Department for Disarmament supports the activities of the UN in the area of weapons of mass destruction (WMD) by tracking developments and trends affecting the spread of WMD. The WMD Branch Web page links to information on many disarmament issues, including nuclear weapons and ballistic missiles proliferation and the international agreements governing them.

The UN Security Council
First Avenue at 46th Street
New York, NY 10017
Phone: (212) 963-5012
Web: http://www.un.org/Docs/sc/

The UN Security Council is the UN's most powerful organ. It makes decisions that member governments must carry out under the UN Charter. The decisions of the council are known as United Nations Security Council Resolutions. Of the Security Council's 15 member states, five have permanent seats, and five have temporary seats. The five permanent members (China, France, Russia, the United Kingdom, and the United States) have a veto power over Security Council votes. The five states that have permanent seats on the Security Council states are also the five official nuclear weapons states, that is, the five nuclear weapons states that are signatories to the Nuclear Nonproliferation Treaty. The Security Council's Web pages can be used for quick access to information regarding Security Council debates and resolutions, UN peacekeeping operations, reports of the UN's Secretary General, and the progress of other operations directed by the UN Security Council.

United Nations Monitoring, Verification and Inspection Commission
First Avenue at 46th Street
New York, NY 10017
Phone: (212) 963-5012
Web: http://www.unmovic.org/

The United Nations Monitoring, Verification and Inspection Commission (UNMOVIC) was created through the adoption of Security Council Resolution 1284 of December 17, 1999. UNMOVIC replaced the former UN Special Commission (UNSCOM). Its job was was to verify Iraq's compliance with its obligation to be rid of its WMD. UNMOVIC's Web site is of use to those researching the background of the 2003 U.S.-led invasion of Iraq.

U.S. Government Web Portal
Web: http://www.usa.gov/

The U.S. Government Web Portal provides access to the public web pages of all U.S. government departments and agencies—those described here as well as many more. The page contains a search field. Entering a phrase or word such as "nuclear nonproliferation" or "Iraq" will produce articles from various U.S. government Web sites, departments, and agencies. Most other U.S. government Web pages also provide search fields and can be searched by keyword.

U.S. Army Space & Missile Defense Command/U.S. Army Forces Strategic Command
(SMDC/ARSTRAT)
Public Affairs
P.O. Box 1500
Huntsville, AL 35807-3801
Phone: (256) 955-3887
Web: http://www.msl.army.mil

The U.S. Army Space & Missile Defense Command/U.S. Army Forces Strategic Command conducts space and missile defense operations and provides planning, integration, control, and coordination of army forces and capabilities in support of USSTRATCOM (U.S. Strategic Command) missions; serves as a proponent for space and ground-based midcourse defense; is the army operational integrator for global missile defense; conducts mission-related research, development, and acquisition in support of Army Title 10 responsibilities; and serves as the focal point for desired characteristics and capabilities in support of USSTRATCOM missions. Fact sheets that can be linked from the Web site provide a great deal of information on military hardware, including ballistic missile defense systems.

United States Strategic Command
Public Affairs Office
901 SAC Blvd, Ste 1A1
Offutt AFB, NE 68113-6020
Phone: (402) 294-4130 (DSN prefix 271)
Web: http://www.stratcom.mil/

The mission of the United States Strategic Command is: "Provide the nation with global deterrence capabilities and synchronized DoD effects to combat adversary weapons of mass destruction worldwide." The Strategic Command's fact sheets supply information about U.S. ballistic missile and strategic forces (that is, nuclear weapons).

The Washington Institute for Near East Policy
1828 L Street NW, Suite 1050
Washington, DC 20036

Phone: (202) 452-0650
Web: http://www.washingtoninstitute.org/templateI01.php

Founded in 1985, the Washington Institute for Near East Policy was established to advance a balanced and realistic understanding of American interests in the Middle East.

The White House
1600 Pennsylvania Avenue NW
Washington, DC 20500
Phone: (202) 456-1111 (comments); (202) 456-1414 (switchboard)
Web: http://www.whitehouse.gov/

The White House is the headquarters of the president of the United States. Its Web pages track the activities of the president and advocate the policies of the president's administration.

10

Annotated Bibliography

To make it easier to use, this bibliography is divided into topical sections, each of which contains books, articles, and Web sites on the following subjects:

The Race to Develop the Bomb: U.S. and Soviet efforts to develop a nuclear weapons capability

Nuclear War: the experience of Hiroshima and Nagasaki; military strategists' plans for fighting a nuclear war; and the probable effects of nuclear war

Theories of Nuclear Proliferation: including the "Is Proliferation Good" debate. Why do some countries develop nuclear weapons, while other countries forgo them? How can we apply lessons learned from their experience to the goal of nonproliferation? Have nuclear weapons been a force for peace and stability?

The U.S.-Russian Nuclear Arms Race in the Cold War: the nuclear arms race and its consequences

U.S. Nuclear Policy Since the Cold War: changes in U.S. nuclear policy and strategy

Nonproliferation History: efforts to combat nuclear proliferation from the earliest proposals for international control in 1945; includes histories and discussions of successful nuclear rollbacks and countries that have dismantled their nuclear weapons programs

Nuclear Proliferation and Nonproliferation Efforts Today: the spread of nuclear weapons, current efforts to combat them, and policy recommendations for the future

Nuclear Terrorism: the threat, its causes, current policies, and recommendations

The Missile Defense Debate: the history of ballistic missile defense, ballistic missile defense today, arguments favoring it and criticizing it

Nuclear Proliferation in South Asia: South Asian history and politics, the nuclear programs of India and Pakistan, and efforts to cope with the fact of these two new nuclear weapons states

Nuclear Proliferation in the Middle East: past Middle Eastern history and current politics; the nuclear programs of Israel, Iran, Iraq and Libya; nonproliferation and counterproliferation

Nuclear Proliferation in Northeast Asia: recent history and politics of the region, North Korea's nuclear weapons program, the U.S. and regional response, recommendations for the future

THE RACE TO DEVELOP THE BOMB

Bernstein, Jeremy. *Oppenheimer: Portrait of an Enigma.* Chicago: Ivan R. Dee, 2004. A biography of the director of the Manhattan project.

Fermi, Rachel and Esther Samra. *Picturing the Bomb: Photographs from the Secret World of the Manhattan Project.* New York: Harry N. Abrams, 1995. A collection of private and official photos depicts the Manhattan Project scientists who built the first atomic bombs, the military men who delivered them to the target, and various sites connected with that effort; included are pictures of the components of the atomic devices, the first explosion at the Trinity test site, and photos of blast damage of the bombs dropped on Hiroshima and Nagasaki.

Gowing, Margaret. *Britain and Atomic Energy, 1939–1945.* London: Macmillan, 1964. A history of Great Britain's involvement in the development of the atomic bomb.

Groves, General Leslie R. *Now It Can Be Told: The Story of the Manhattan Project.* New York: Da Capo Press, 1962. Groves, an engineer who was the primary military leader in charge of the Manhattan Project, presents the story of the making of the atomic bomb from the outset of the project through the bombing of Japan.

Holloway, David. *Stalin and the Bomb: The Soviet Union and Atomic Energy, 1939–1956.* New Haven, Conn: Yale University Press, 1994. A history of the Soviet Union's quest for the bomb.

———. "Entering the Nuclear Arms Race: The Soviet Decision to Build the Atomic Bomb, 1939–45." *Social Studies of Science II* (1981): 159–197. This paper traces the path from the discovery of nuclear fission in Berlin in December 1938 to the Soviet decision of August 1945 to launch an all-out effort to develop the atomic bomb.

Powers, Thomas. *Heisenberg's War: The Secret History of the German Bomb.* New York: Knopf, 1993. Powers looks at the failure of the Germans to develop an atomic bomb and puts forward the controversial theory that the German physicist Werner Heisenberg deliberately deceived the Nazi authorities, convincing them that the project was unfeasible.

Rhodes, Richard. *The Making of the Atomic Bomb.* New York: Simon & Schuster, 1986. Richard Rhodes won a Pulitzer prize for this thorough, vivid account of the Manhattan Project, with a clear exposition of the science involved, biographical sketches of the key participants, and an analysis of the consequences.

———. *Dark Sun: The Making of the Hydrogen Bomb.* New York: Simon & Schuster, 1995. An engrossing history of the scientific discoveries, political maneuverings, and cold war espionage leading to the creation of mankind's most destructive weapon.

Richelson, Jeffrey T. *Spying on the Bomb: American Nuclear Intelligence from Nazi Germany to Iran and North Korea.* New York: W.W. Norton, 2006. Account of U.S. nuclear espionage from the earliest days of atomic research to the present.

Smyth, Henry DeWolf. *Atomic Energy for Military Purposes: The Official Report on the Development of the Atomic Bomb under the Auspices of the United States Government, 1940–1945.* Princeton, N.J.: Princeton University Press, 1945. This book, released the year of the Hiroshima bomb, attempted to strike a balance between public education and the keeping of military secrets.

Teller, Edward. *The Legacy of Hiroshima.* New York: Doubleday, 1962. A memoir of the atomic age by the "father of the hydrogen bomb."

Weart, Spencer R., and Gertrude Weiss Szilard, eds. *Leo Szilard: His Version of the Facts.* Cambridge, Mass.: MIT Press, 1978.

NUCLEAR WAR

Alperovitz, Gar. *The Decision to Use the Atomic Bomb.* New York: Vintage Books, 1996. Alperovitz argues that America's use of the atomic bomb on Japan was motivated by politics rather than by military necessity.

Carter, Ashton B., John D. Steinbruner, and Charles A. Zraket, eds. *Managing Nuclear Operations.* Washington, D.C.: Brookings Institution, 1989. Analysis of nuclear strategy.

Freedman, Lawrence. *The Evolution of Nuclear Strategy.* New York: St. Martin's Press, 1981. History of nuclear decision making in United States.

Goldstein, Donald M., et al. *Rain of Ruin: A Photographic History of Hiroshima and Nagasaki.* Washington, D.C.: Brassey's, 1995. This photographic history of Hiroshima and Nagasaki provides a photographic record of the bombings and their aftermath, presenting a history of the two cities before and after the bombs and including photos of American and Japanese politicians and military men involved in the bombing.

Kaplan, Fred. *The Wizards of Armageddon.* New York: Simon & Schuster, 1983. Analysis of nuclear decision making in the United States.

Hersey, John. *Hiroshima.* New York: Knopf, 1946. A Pulitzer prize–winning book presenting the stories of Hiroshima residents Hersey interviewed shortly after the explosion.

Paul, Richard. "How Is Hiroshima Remembered in America?" *Morning Edition.* National Public Radio, August 5, 2005. Available online. URL: http://www.npr.org/templates/story/story.php?storyId=4786615. Accessed March 23, 2007. Radio piece looks at changes in the way Americans have felt about the bombing of Hiroshima over the years.

Sagan, Carl. "The Nuclear Winter." *Science,* December 1983: 1283. Available online. URL: www.cooperativeindividualism.org/sagan_nuclear_winter.html. Accessed March 23, 2007. An article about the devastating effects of nuclear war on the Earth's ecosystem.

Schell, Jonathan. *The Fate of the Earth.* New York: Knopf, 1982. Written near the height of the U.S.-Soviet nuclear arms race, Schell's book describes the likely consequences of a nuclear war.

Toon, Owen B, Alan Robock, Richard P Turco, Charles Bardeen, et al., "Consequences of Regional-Scale Nuclear Conflicts." *Science* 315, no. 5816 (March 2, 2007): 1224–1225. Estimates the potential for casualties and effects on the environment of a regional scale nuclear conflict or a terrorist attack.

THEORIES OF NUCLEAR PROLIFERATION

Blair, Bruce. *The Logic of Accidental Nuclear War.* Washington, D.C.: Brookings Institution, 1993. Argues that the nuclear realists' assumptions about the rational behavior of nuclear weapons states are not supported by what is known of the actions of the nuclear superpowers.

———. *Global Zero Alert for Nuclear Forces.* Washington, D.C.: Brookings Institution, 1993; Washington, D.C.: Brookings Institution, 1995. Bruce Blair examines the command and control procedures in place for nuclear forces deployed in Russia, the United States, and elsewhere, finds deficiencies that might lead to accidental, unauthorized or inadvertent use of nuclear weapons, and suggests changes that would reduce these risks.

Blight, James G. and David A. Welch, "Risking the Destruction of Nations: Lessons of the Cuban Missile Crisis for New and Aspiring Nuclear States." *Security Studies* 4, no. 4 (summer 1995): 815. A critical discussion of the perils of "rational deterrence."

Brito, Dagobert L., Michael D. Intriligator, and Adele E. Wick, eds., *Strategies for Managing Nuclear Proliferation.* Lexington, Mass: Lexington Books, 1983. A series of articles examining approaches to nonproliferation from a theoretical perspective.

Busch, Nathan E. *No End in Sight: The Continuing Menace of Nuclear Proliferation.* Lexington, Ky.: University Press of Kentucky, 2004. A careful examination of nuclear safety, especially of the effectiveness of the systems in place in nuclear weapons states to prevent theft or accidental or unauthorized use of nuclear weapons.

de Mesquita, Bruce Bueno, and William H. Riker. "An Assessment of the Merits of Selective Nuclear Proliferation." *Journal of Conflict Resolution* 26, no. 2 (June

1982). A theoretical discussion of nuclear deterrence and the problem of proliferation from the point of view of the structural realist school, setting forth the likely nuclear war scenarios "when nuclear weapons are held by both sides, by one side, and by neither side."

Carpenter, Ted Galen. "Not All Forms of Nuclear Proliferation Are Equally Bad." Cato Institute, November 21, 2004. Available online.URL: http://www.cato.org/pub_display.php?pub_id=2886. Accessed March 23, 2007. Online opinion piece argues that "Washington's nonproliferation efforts should focus on delaying rogue states in their quest for nuclear weapons, not beating up on peaceful states who might want to become nuclear powers for their own protection."

Carpenter, Ted Galen, and Charles V. Pena. "Nuclear Proliferation and the Terrorist Threat." In the *Cato Handbook of Policy,* December 8, 2004. Available online. URL: http://www.cato.org/pubs/handbook/hb109/hb_109–54.pdf. Accessed March 23, 2007. Analyzes the threat of nuclear proliferation from a libertarian and realist perspective; suggests that a rush to acquire nuclear weapons may be an unintended result of the United States's aggressive foreign policy.

Feaver, Peter D. *Guarding the Guardians: Civilian Control of Nuclear Weapons in the United States.* Ithaca, N.Y.: Cornell University Press, 1992. A study of the problems of assuring civilian control of nuclear weapons.

———. "Command and Control in Emerging Nuclear Nations," *International Security* 21, no. 3 (winter 1996/97). Argues that the emerging small nuclear states, due to their limited resources, are more likely to have nuclear accidents.

———. "Neooptimists and the Enduring Problem of Nuclear Proliferaiton." *Security Studies* 6, no. 4 (summer 1997). A "nuclear pessimist" replies to "nuclear optimists" on degree of threat of emerging nuclear weapons.

Forden, Geoffrey, Pavel Podvig, and Theodore A. Postol. "False Alarm, Nuclear Danger." *IEEE Spectrum* 37, no. 3 (March 2000). An article about the dangers of accidental nuclear war using lessons from the United States.

Jo, Dong-Joon, and Erik Gartzke. "Determinants of Nuclear Weapons Proliferation." *Journal of Conflict Resolution* 51, no. 1 (February 2007): 167–194. Analyzes causes of nuclear proliferation.

Kang, Jungmin, Frank N von Hippel, Hui Zhang, and Harold Smith. "The North Korean Test and the Limits of Nuclear Forensics/Harold Smith Responds." *Arms Control Today* 37, no. 1: 42–43. Letters discussing the methods and accuracy of the means by which the United States detected North Korea's 2006 nuclear test.

Kaufmann, Chaim. "Why Nuclear Proliferation is Getting Easier." *Peace Review* 18, no. 3: 315–324. Asserts that nuclear proliferation is becoming easier, not harder. As reasons for this alarming trend, the author cites advances in technology and the ease with which uranium enrichment facilities may be hidden.

Lavoy, Peter R. "The Strategic Consequences of Nuclear Proliferation." *Security Studies* 4, no. 4 (summer 1995): 699–711. A summary of the history of the proliferation debate from the 1940s to 1995.

Mearsheimer, John J. "Back to the Future: Instability in Europe after the Cold War." *International Security* 15, no. 1 (summer 1990). Argues that the post–cold war world, with one superpower and several small nuclear weapons states, may be less stable than a world balanced between two superpowers.

Meyer, Stephen M. *The Dynamics of Nuclear Proliferation.* Chicago: University of Chicago Press, 1984. Analyzes the causes of nuclear proliferation.

Nolan, Janne E. *Guardians of the Arsenal.* New York: New Republic, 1989. A book about military control of nuclear weapons in the United States, arguing that the military's nuclear war planning is often at odds with stated U.S. government policy.

Panofsky, Wolfgang K. H. "A Nuclear-Weapons-Free World: Prohibition Versus Elimination." *The Bulletin Online,* March 5, 2007. Available online. URL: http://www.thebulletin.org/columns/wolfgangpanofsky/20070305.html. Accessed March 27, 2007. Discusses the practical differences between nuclear abolition, disarmament, and prohibition and makes the case that prohibition—making nuclear weapons illegal in the sense that chemical and biological weapons are now prohibited—is a desirable and attainable goal.

Quester, George H. *Nuclear First Strike: The Consequences of a Broken Taboo.* Baltimore: Johns Hopkins University Press, 2005. Examines various scenarios in which the deployment of nuclear weapons could occur and the probable consequences of such an escalation.

———. *The Politics of Nuclear Proliferation.* Baltimore: Johns Hopkins University Press, 1973. A theoretical analysis of the causes of nuclear proliferation from a realist perspective.

Rosen, Stephen Peter. "After Proliferation: What To Do If More States Go Nuclear." *Foreign Affairs* 85, no. 5: 9–14. Maintains that in a "multipolor nuclear world" international politics will continue but in an environment dominated by fear and uncertainty, with new dangers and new possibilities for miscommunication adding to and complicating familiar ones.

Sagan, Scott D., and Kenneth N. Waltz. *The Spread of Nuclear Weapons: A Debate Renewed.* New York: W. W. Norton, 2003. Two political scientists debate the proposition: Has the spread of nuclear weapons made the world less safe or more safe?

Sagan, Scott D. "Why Do States Build Nuclear Weapons? Three Models in Search of a Bomb." *International Security* 21, no. 3 (winter 1996/1997). Sagan challenges the traditional realist assumption that states seek to acquire or develop nuclear weapons primarily for military and strategic reasons.

———. *The Limits of Safety: Organizations, Accidents, and Nuclear Weapons.* Princeton, N.J.: Princeton University Press, 1993. Analyzes flaws in U.S. nuclear safety and details a disturbing series of near-catastrophes in the handling of nuclear weapons and bombers.

Schelling, Thomas C. *Arms and Influence.* New Haven, Conn.: Yale University Press, 1996. Influential game theorist outlines the theory of nuclear deterrence.

Seng, Jorden. "Less Is More: Command and Control Advantages of Minor Nuclear States." *Security Studies* 6, no. 4 (summer 1997). A nuclear proliferation "optimist" argues that budgetary constraints will force small nuclear states to rely on smaller arsenals that will not require the complex command and control structures of the U.S. and Russian arsenals.

Theyer, Bradley. "The Causes of Nuclear Proliferation and the Utility of the Nuclear Nonproliferation Regime." *Security Studies* 4, no. 3 (spring 1995). Analysis of the effectiveness of the nuclear nonproliferation control regimes in which nuclear suppliers agree to control exports of nuclear technology.

Waltz, Kenneth N. "Thoughts about the Virtual Nuclear Arsenals." *Washington Quarterly* 20, no. 3 (summer 1977). Waltz discusses the military needs of nuclear weapons states from the point of view of the structural realist school of international relations.

THE U.S.–RUSSIAN NUCLEAR ARMS RACE IN THE COLD WAR

"50 Facts About U.S. Nuclear Weapons" *The U.S. Nuclear Weapons Cost Study Project.* Available online. URL: http://www.brook.edu/fp/projects/nucwcost/50.htm.

Boyer, Paul. *By the Bomb's Early Light: American Thought and Culture at the Dawn of the Atomic Age.* Chapel Hill: University of North Carolina Press, 1994. Boyer examines America's changing attitudes toward the bomb in the years 1945 to 1950.

Bundy, McGeorge. *Danger and Survival.* New York: Vintage Books, 1988. Bundy's book explains top-level decision making at key turning points of the U.S.-Soviet nuclear arms race.

Cantelon, Philip L., Robert C. Williams, and Richard G. Hewlett, eds. *The American Atom: A Documentary History of Nuclear Policies from the Discovery of Fission to the Present.* Philadelphia: University of Philadelphia Press, 2002. A book of primary sources documenting the development of American nuclear policy.

Cochran, Thomas B., William M. Arkin, Robert S. Norris, and Milton M. Hoeing. *Nuclear Weapons Databook, Vol. 1, U.S. Forces and Capabilities.* Cambridge, Mass.: Ballinger, 1987. A description of the U.S. nuclear arsenal at the peak of the nuclear buildup.

Coleman, David. "Camelot's Nuclear Conscience." *Bulletin of the Atomic Scientists.* 62, no. 3: 40–45. Coleman presents never before published transcripts of tapes recorded during a top-secret 1962 meeting between President John F. Kennedy and his advisers. The topic was not an uncommon one: How much nuclear deterrence is too much?

D'Antonio, Michael. *Atomic Harvest: Hanford and the Lethal Toll of America's Nuclear Arsenal.* New York: Crown Publishers, 1993. A look at the environmental impact of nuclear weapons production.

Ford, Daniel. *The Cult of the Atom: The Secret Papers of the Atomic Energy Commission.* New York: Simon & Schuster, 1982. A documentary history of the inner workings of the Atomic Energy Commission and its successor, the Department of Energy.

Annotated Bibliography

Gerstell, Richard. *How To Survive an Atomic Bomb.* Washington, D.C.: Combat Forces Press, 1950. A civil defense manual to inform people on what they could do to survive an atomic bomb, this book was meant to reassure people about the possibility of an atomic attack; some of its recommendations seem almost comical today. The appendix contains a simple explanation of how an atomic bomb works. It is available on line at http://alsos.wlu.edu/information.aspx?id=2056&search=Civil+Defense+.

Gibson, James N. *Nuclear Weapons of the United States: An Illustrated History.* Atglen, Penn.: Schiffer Publishing, 1996. This book covers every nuclear delivery system the United States ever deployed before 1996. With few exceptions, each weapon and system is illustrated by either color or black-and-white photographs.

Herken, Gregg. *Brotherhood of the Bomb: The Tangled Lives and Loyalties of Robert Oppenheimer, Ernest Lawrence, and Edward Teller.* New York: Henry Holt, 2002. Explores the relationships between three nuclear physicists who had an impact on American nuclear policy during the cold war.

———. *The Winning Weapon: The Atomic Bomb in the Cold War, 1945–1950.* Princeton, N.J.: Princeton University Press, 1988. Describes the influence of the atomic bomb in international relations between the end of World War II and the Korean War. It discusses the debate over the internationalization of the atom.

Miller, David. *The Cold War: A Military History.* New York: St. Martin's Press, 1998. British military historian David Miller documents the military aspects of the decades-long struggle between East and West, explaining the complex disagreements among the Allied powers over how the post–World War II world was to be ruled and how those disagreements led in time to the iron curtain, the arms race, and the specter of nuclear holocaust.

Powaski, Ronald E. *March to Armageddon: The United States and the Nuclear Arms Race, 1939 to the Present.* New York: Oxford University Press, 1987. An examination of the policy decisions that fueled the nuclear arms race. The "present," of course, means 1987.

———. *Return to Armageddon.* New York: Oxford University Press, 2000. Powaski continues his history of U.S. nuclear policy from 1987 to 2000.

Schwartz, Stephen I., ed. *Atomic Audit: The Costs and Consequences of U.S. Nuclear Weapons Since 1940.* Washington, D.C.: Brookings Institution Press, 1998. Stephen Schwartz and his colleagues have calculated for the first time the cost of all aspects of the U.S. nuclear weapons program, from its inception in 1940 to the end of 1996. In constant 1996 dollars, the authors estimate total U.S. spending on its nuclear weapons program at a stunning $5.48 trillion dollars, almost 11 percent of all government expenditure.

Titus, Costandina A. *Bombs in the Backyard: Atomic Testing and American Politics.* Reno: University of Nevada Press, 1986. A study of atomic testing in the United States, with special attention to the legislative history of laws leading to compensation for victims of radioactivity from atmospheric testing.

United States Atomic Energy Commission. *Nuclear Milestones: A Collection of Speeches by Glenn T. Seaborg. Volume 1, Builders and Discoverers.* Washington, D.C.: U.S. Atomic Energy Commission, 1971.

United States Department of Energy. *Closing the Circle on the Splitting of the Atom: The Environmental Legacy of Nuclear Weapons Production in the United States and What the Department of Energy Is Doing About It.* Washington, D.C.: U.S. Department of Energy, 1995.

———. *Linking Legacies: Connecting the Cold War Nuclear Weapons Production Processes to Their Environmental Consequences.* Washington, D.C.: U.S. Department of Energy, 1997.

Walker, Martin. *The Cold War: A History.* New York: Henry Holt, 1993. A concise introduction to the history of the cold war between the United States and the Soviet Union.

Wittner, Lawrence S. "The Success of the Nuclear Freeze Campaign." *Peace Review* 18, no. 3: 353–356. Discusses the successes of the nuclear freeze campaign during the presidencies of Ronald Reagan and George H. W. Bush.

U.S. NUCLEAR POLICY SINCE THE COLD WAR

Brumfiel, Geoff. "Nuclear Weapons: The Next Nuke." *Nature.* 442, no. 7098: 18–21. U.S. nuclear weapons scientists are designing a warhead that is meant to be "reliable" without ever having been tested. Some are wondering whether such weapons could renew the U.S. aging stockpile.

———. "US Backs Revamp of Nuclear Warheads." *Nature* 444, no. 7120: 660. Reports that the U.S. government is pushing ahead with a plan to overhaul its nuclear stockpile despite a scientific review showing that existing warheads will last at least another half century.

Cimbala, Stephen J. "Nuclear Force Reductions, Missile Defenses, and U.S.-Russian Relations: Managing Contextual Complexity." *Journal of Slavic Military Studies.* 19, no. 3: 469. Examines the way changing technologies and geopolitical alignments, together with the spread of nuclear weapons outside of Europe, have complicated the pursuit of U.S.-Russian nuclear arms control.

Drell, Sidney D. "The Shadow of the Bomb, 2006" *Policy Review* no. 136: 55–68. Discusses U.S. security in the face of emerging nuclear weapon threats.

"Enough Warheads, Already." *Nature* 444, no. 7120: 653. Discusses the quiet debate within the United States on whether to replace nuclear warheads and create new types of nuclear weapons.

Flory, Peter C. W., Keith Payne, Pavel Podvig, et al. "Nuclear Exchange: Does Washington Really Have (or Want) Nuclear Primacy?" *Foreign Affairs* 85, no. 5: 149–157. A series of essays on the question of the United States's need for superior nuclear weapons force.

Kokoshin, Andrei. "A Nuclear Response to Nuclear Terror: Reflections of Nuclear Preemption." *Annals of the American Academy of Political and Social Science* 607 (September 2006): 59–63. Argues that the threat of nuclear terrorism in the

United States has led its leadership to contemplate an extreme military response, namely, nuclear preemption. The nuclear "taboo" has once again ceased to exist.

Kunsman, David M., and Douglas B. Lawson. *A Primer on U.S. Strategic Nuclear Policy.* Livermore, Calif.: Sandia National Labs, 2001. Summarizes the evolution of U.S. nuclear deterrence policy using unclassified government documents and writings of noted nuclear strategists and historians.

The National Security Strategy, March 2006. Available online. URL: http://www.whitehouse.gov/nsc/nss/2006/. Accessed March 23, 2007. Home page, with link to printer-friendly version, of the National Security Strategy of the United States.

Norris, Robert S. "Where the Bombs Are, 2006. *Bulletin of the Atomic Scientists* 62, no. 6: 57–58. Although it is the smallest it has been since 1958, the U.S. nuclear arsenal continues to sprawl across the country. Norris presents a report on where in the United States nuclear bombs are located.

Norris, Robert S., Hans M. Kristensen, and Christopher E. Paine. *Nuclear Insecurity: A Critique of the Bush Administration's Nuclear Weapons Policies.* New York: Natural Resources Defense Counsel, 2004. Charges U.S. policies after 2001 with making the world less safe and recommends a renewed commitment to the Nuclear Non-proliferation Treaty.

"Nuclear Stalemates." *Nature* 442, no. 7098: 2. Editorial notes that the nuclear powers are maintaining their aging stockpiles without much thought or explanation and says it is past time for the nuclear weapons states to fulfill their obligations under disarmament treaties.

Nunn, Sam. "The Race Between Cooperation and Catastrophe: Reducing the Global Nuclear Threat." *Annals of the American Academy of Political and Social Science* 607 (September 2006): 43–50. This article presents four hypothetical nuclear crises and suggests a series of steps that, if taken, could help prevent each crisis.

O'Hanlon, Michael E., Susan E. Rice, and James B. Steinberg. "Policy Brief #113, the New National Security Strategy and Preemption." Washington, D.C.: The Brookings Institution, 2002. Available online. URL: www.brook.edu/comm/policybriefs/pb113.pdf. Retrieved January 4, 2007. A critique of the 2002 U.S. strategy that expanded the concept of "preemptive war" to include what had previously been defined as "preventive war."

Pincus, Walter. "Pentagon Revises Nuclear Strike Plan," *Washington Post,* September 11, 2005: A1. Discusses the controversial "Doctrine for Joint Nuclear Operations," which the Bush administration had planned for release in 2006 and which proposed an expanded war fighting role for nuclear weapons.

Tannenwald, Nina. "A Taboo Subject." *Bulletin of the Atomic Scientists* 62, no. 3: 64. Comments on the growing erosion of nuclear self-restraint among nations and the sense that the thought of nuclear weapons of mass destruction is no longer as abhorrent as it once was.

Tauscher, Ellen O. "Rep. Tauscher Cautions Against Aggressive Nuclear Policy." Available online. URL: www.nukestrat.com/us/jcs/JP_Congress120205.pdf. Retrieved January 4, 2007. Open letter by Tauscher and 15 other congressional representatives objecting to the draft of the "Doctrine for Joint Nuclear Operations" leaked in late 2005.

Vaughn, Bruce. "U.S. Strategic and Defense Relationships in the Asia-Pacific Region." Available online. URL: http://www.fas.org/sgp/crs/row/RL33821.pdf. Accessed January 22, 2007. Discusses what changes in U.S. policy are needed to respond to developments such as the nuclear tests of India, Pakistan, and North Korea and China's emergence as a major world power.

Woolf, Amy F. "Conventional Warheads for Long-Range Ballistic Missiles: Background and Issues for Congress." Available online. Updated February 9, 2007. URL: http://fpc.state.gov/documents/organization/81935.pdf. Accessed March 27, 2007. For 40 years, long-range ballistic missiles have been considered a delivery vehicle for nuclear weapons. It was recently proposed that these missiles be tipped with conventional weapons, enabling the U.S. military to attack overseas targets instantly. But would such a conventional attack increase the risk of an error leading to nuclear war?

———. "Nonstrategic Nuclear Weapons." CRS Report for Congress, Order Code RL32572. Updated January 9, 2007. Nonstrategic weapons are the "tactical" "battlefield" nuclear weapons that were intended to be used in support of troops during a conflict; in 1991 the United States and the Soviet Union agreed to eliminate most of their nonstrategic nuclear weapons, but both the United States and Russia continue to deploy many of them. Some think that Russia plans to increase its deployment. This report examines the debate that now surrounds these weapons.

———. "Nuclear Arms Control: The Strategic Offensive Reductions Treaty." Available online. Updated January 3, 2007. URL: http://www.fas.org/sgp/crs/nuke/RL31448.pdf. Discusses the current status of the Strategic Offensive Reductions Treaty (known as the Treaty of Moscow) that will reduce strategic nuclear weapons to between 1,700 and 2,200 warheads by December 31, 2012.

NONPROLIFERATION HISTORY

Albright, David. "South Africa's Secret Nuclear Weapons. *ISIS Report* 1, no. 4, 1994. Available online. URL: http://www.isis-online.org/publications/southafrica/ir0594.html. Brief history of South Africa's nuclear weapons program, along with South Africa's efforts to evade detection.

Allison, Graham T., Herve De Carmoy, and Therese Delpech. *Nuclear Proliferation: Risk and Responsibility.* Washington, D.C.: Trilateral Commission, 2007. Authors from North America, Europe, and Pacific Asia examine the risks posed by nuclear proliferation with particular attention to Iran and North Korea and offer recommendations to prevent nuclear catastrophe.

Altmann, Jurgen, and Joseph Rotblat, eds. *Verifying Treaty Compliance: Limiting Weapons of Mass Destruction and Monitoring Kyoto Protocol Provisions.* Berlin: Springer-Verlag, 2006. Expert analyses of international systems that test countries' compliance with nonproliferation agreements.

Annotated Bibliography

Eisenhower, Dwight D. "United States 'Atoms for Peace' Proposal: Address by President Eisenhower to the General Assembly, December 8, 1953." In U.S. Department of State, *Documents on Disarmament, 1945–59*, vol. 2, 399. A complete transcript of the speech in which Eisenhower introduced the proposal that eventually became the Atoms For Peace program.

FAS Weapons of Mass Destruction. Nuclear Nonproliferation Treaty (NPT) Chronology. Available online. URL: www.fas.org/nuke/control/npt/chron.htm. Accessed March 23, 2007.

Fischer, David. *History of the International Atomic Energy Agency: The First Forty Years.* Vienna: International Atomic Energy Agency, 1997. Official History of the IAEA.

Goldemberg, José. "Looking Back: Lessons from the Denuclearization of Brazil and Argentina." *Arms Control Today* 36, no. 3: 41–43. Examines the case of Brazil and Argentina, both of which (like Iran today) claimed to have produced fissile material for purely civilian purposes in an effort to gain access to the full nuclear fuel cycle from uranium enrichment to plutonium reprocessing.

Goodby, James E. "Looking Back: The 1986 Reykjavik Summit." *Arms Control Today* 36, no. 7: 49–51. Discusses the historic U.S.-Soviet meeting in which Mikhail Gorbachev proposed dramatic reductions in both countries' nuclear arms and Reagan responded with unexpected enthusiasm.

Hymans, Jacques E. C. *The Psychology of Nuclear Proliferation: Identity, Emotions, and Foreign Policy.* Cambridge: Cambridge University Press, 2006. Examination of the emotional motives behind countries' choices to acquire nuclear weapons, reasons that go beyond strictly "realistic" security concerns.

Joyner, Daniel, ed. *Non-Proliferation Export Controls: Origins, Challenges, and Proposals for Strengthening.* Aldershot, England: Ashgate Publishing, 2006. In a variety of articles, several authors analyze the global export control system.

Kay, Alan F. "Public Opinion on Nonproliferation and Disarmament." *Peace Review* 18, no. 3: 357–360. Notes that in the 1980s, surveys showed that public opinion was 70 to 80 percent in favor of freezing development, production, and deployment of nuclear weapons and examines the reasons why the strong public sentiment of those days is mostlv forgotten today.

McNamee, Terence, and Greg Mills. "Denuclearizing a Regime: What South Africa's Nuclear Rollback Might Tell Us About Iran." *Defense & Security Analysis* 22, no. 3: 329–335. McNamee and Mills discuss the most unique chapter in the history of nuclear proliferation, South Africa's nuclear rollback. They speculate on what international strategies might be applied to persuade Iran to take similar action today.

Office of the Secretary of Defense. *Proliferation: Threat and Response.* Washington, D.C.,: U.S. Government Printing Office, 1996. The official view of the threat, its causes, and U.S. options as seen by Clinton administration soon after the 1995 NPT review.

Pilat, Joseph, ed. *Atoms for Peace: A Future After Fifty Years?* Baltimore: Johns Hopkins University Press, 2007. A total of 25 contributors, including official's and scientists, discuss the outcome of the bargain to spread nuclear energy technology in exchange for the promise not to develop nuclear weapons.

Reiss, Mitchell. *Bridled Ambition: Why Countries Constrain Their Nuclear Capabilities.* Washington, D.C.: Woodrow Wilson Center Press, 1995. Draws on interviews with senior officials around the world to present information on how politics and international relationships have led them to avoid or reverse the course on the road to nuclear weapons capability. Discusses South Africa, Argentina, Brazil, Belarus, Kazakhstan, Ukraine, India, Pakistan, and North Korea.

Schneider, Barry R., and Jim A. Davis, eds. *Avoiding the Abyss: Progress, Shortfalls, and the Way Ahead in Combating the WMD Threat.* Westport, Conn.: Praeger Security International, 2006. The editors and other contributors assess the challenges of nuclear proliferation from a military perspective.

Schrafsetter, Susanna, and Stephen Twigge. *Avoiding Armageddon: Europe, the United States, and the Struggle for Nuclear Non-Proliferation, 1945–1970.* New York: Praeger Publishers, 2004. An examination of European nuclear policy decisions during the first half of the cold war.

Sidhu, Waheguru Pal Singh, ed. *Arms Control After Iraq: Normative and Operational Challenges.* Tokyo: United Nations University, 2006. Many contributors address problems of nonproliferation in the aftermath of the Iraq war.

Sokolski, Henry D. *Best of Intentions: America's Campaign Against Strategic Weapons Proliferation.* Westport, Conn.: Praeger, 2001. Sokolski examines the history of international efforts at nuclear nonproliferation.

Spector, Leonard S. *The Undeclared Bomb.* Cambridge, Mass.: Ballinger, 1988. Assesses the extent of undeclared nuclear arsenals, discusses the risk of nuclear warfare in the Middle East, and evaluates South Africa's current interest in nonproliferation.

Stumpf, Waldo. "South Africa's Nuclear Weapons Program: From Deterrence to Dismantlement." *Arms Control Today* 25, no. 10 (December 1995/January 1996). Brief article examines South Africa's current nuclear policies.

Teller, Edward. "Comments on the 'Draft of a World Constitution.'" *Bulletin of the Atomic Scientists,* July 1948: 204. An article arguing that only world government can solve the dilemma created by the existence of nuclear weapons. Teller would later change his mind, putting his faith in technology such as the H-bomb and missile defense systems.

Vaughn, Bruce. "U.S. Strategic and Defense Relationships in the Asia-Pacific Region." Available online. URL: http://www.fas.org/sgp/crs/row/RL33821.pdf. Accessed March 23, 2007. Discusses what changes in U.S. policy are needed to respond to developments such as the nuclear tests of India, Pakistan, and North Korea and China's emergence as a major world power.

Wigner, Eugene. "Are We Making the Transition Wisely?" *Saturday Review of Literature* 28, (November 17, 1945). A few months after the atomic bomb was used on Hiroshima and Nagasaki, an atomic scientist wrote this article concerning its implications for the future of war and government.

NUCLEAR PROLIFERATION AND NONPROLIFERATION EFFORTS TODAY

Allison, Graham T. "Flight of Fancy." *Annals of the American Academy of Political and Social Science* 507 (September 2006): 162–166. An adaptation of a speech delivered to the International Atomic Energy Agency in January 2005. Allison makes predictions regarding nuclear proliferation for the next four years.

Allison, Graham T., Ashton Carter, Steven Miller, and Philip Zelikow. *Cooperative Denuclearization: From Pledges to Deeds.* Cambridge, Mass.: Center for Science and International Affairs, Harvard University, 1993. Discusses the proliferation challenges created by the breakup of the Soviet Union.

Andemicael, Berhanykun, and John Mathiason. *Eliminating Weapons of Mass Destruction.* New York: Palgrave, 2005. Examines the management of the International Atomic Energy Agency, the Comprehensive Test Ban Treaty Organization, and the Organization for the Prohibition of Chemical Weapons.

Avenhaus, Rudolf, Victor A Kremenvuk, and Gunnar Sjostedt, eds. *Containing the Atom: International Negotiations on Nuclear Security and Safety.* Lexington, Mass.: Lexington Books, 2002. A comprehensive study of the theory and practice of international nuclear negotiations.

Blackwill, Robert D., and Alrbert Carnesale, eds. *New Nuclear Nations: Consequences for U.S. Policy.* New York: Council on Foreign Relations Press, 1993. Foreign policy experts analyze the threats posed by nuclear weapons states.

Blix, Hans, et. al. "Weapons of Terror: Freeing the World of Nuclear, Biological and Chemical Weapons." Weapons of Mass Destruction Commission, 2006. Available online. URL: http://www.wmdcommission.org/files/Weapons_of_Terror.pdf. A program for outlawing weapons of mass destruction.

Boese, Wade, Paul Kerr, and Daryl G Kimball. "Reviving Disarmament: An Interview With Hans Blix." *Arms Control Today* 36, no. 6: 12–18. Interview with Blix, who has been chairman of the WMD Commission, head of the International Atomic Energy Agency (IAEA), and was head of the UN Monitoring, Verification, and Inspection Commission (UNMOVIC) in Iraq.

Boese, Wade. "U.S. Reports on Nuclear Treaty Implementation." *Arms Control Today.* Available online. URL: http://www.armscontrol.org/act/2006_12/NuclearTreaty.asp. Retrieved January 4, 2007.

Bowen, Wyn O. *The Politics of Ballistic Missile Nonproliferation.* New York: Palgrave, 2000. Describes the efforts to implement the Missile Technology Control Regime during the presidency of George H. W. Bush (1989–93).

Brumfiel, Geoff. "Sceptics Detect Flaws in US Nuclear Monitor Plan." *Nature* 443, no. 7114: 890–891. The United States is intent on preventing North Korea from selling its nuclear know-how and materials abroad. But proliferation experts disagree about whether such a screening regime is practical or even possible. Spotting radioactive material aboard ships, trucks, and aircraft is technically difficult and would require unprecedented regional cooperation.

Bunn, Matthew. *The Next Wave: Urgently Needed New Steps to Control Warheads and Fissile Materials.* Washington, D.C.: Carnegie Endowment for International Peace and Harvard University, 2000. Available online. URL: http://bcsia.ksg.harvard.edu/publication.cfm?ctype=book&item_id=28. A former Clinton administration adviser addresses the problem of safely destroying nuclear weapons, storing nuclear waste, and preventing theft of nuclear materials.

Butler, Kenley, Sammy Salam, and Leonard S. Spector. "Where Is the Justice?" *Bulletin of the Atomic Scientists* 62, no. 6, 25–34. Article on the A. Q. Khan nuclear smuggling network.

Campbell, Kurt M. *The Nuclear Tipping Point: Why States Reconsider Their Nuclear Choices.* Washington, D.C.: Brookings Institution Press, 2004. Discussion of the conditions under which some states have reversed course on the path to nuclear weapons.

Cirincione, Joseph. *Bomb Scare: The History and Future of Nuclear Weapons.* New York: Columbia University Press, 2007. A brief examination of the history and challenges of the nuclear arms race.

Cirincione, Joseph, ed. *Repairing the Regime: Preventing the Spread of Weapons of Mass Destruction.* New York: Routledge, 2000. Presents a range of recommendations for hindering the spread of weapons of mass destruction.

Clark, William Jr., ed. *Next Steps in Arms Control and Nonproliferation.* Washington, D.C.: Carnegie Endowment for International Peace, 1996. Japanese and American experts view 13 key arms control and nonproliferation issues facing East Asia and the world.

Committee on International Security and Arms Control, National Research Council. *Monitoring Nuclear Weapons and Nuclear Explosive Materials: An Assessment of Methods and Capabilities.* On-line book published by National Academies Press, 2005. Available online. URL: http://www.nap.edu/catalog.php?record_id=11265#toc. Accessed March 23, 2007. Verification is a key ingredient of efforts to control the spread of nuclear weapons. This report argues that the technical means exist for sensitive and accurate verification and detection of nuclear weapons, materials, and components.

Corera, Gordon. *Shopping for Bombs: Nuclear Proliferation, Global Insecurity, and the Rise and Fall of the A. Q. Khan Network.* New York: Oxford University Press, 2006. Offers a measured account of how a young Pakistani metallurgist named A. Q. Khan became the world's leading dealer in nuclear technology.

"The Fewer the Better: Nuclear Disarmament." *The Economist* 379, no. 8481: 11. Editorial arguing that the original five nuclear weapons states, the United States, Russia, Britain, France and China, should do more to fulfill their disarmament obligations under the Nuclear Non-proliferation Treaty. "The belief . . . that the five are not holding up their end of the bargain . . . makes it harder to encourage the three treaty outsiders—India, Pakistan, and Israel—to curb their nuclear arsenals."

Forsberg, Randall, William Driscoll, Gregory Webb, and Jonathan Dean. *Nonproliferation Primer: Preventing the Spread of Nuclear, Chemical and Biological Weap-*

ons. Cambridge, Mass.: MIT Press, 1995. Brief introduction to the subject written the year of an NPT review.

"A Global Folly." *Nature* 443, no. 7112: 605. Editorial calling for a return to arms control and nonproliferation treaties. "Scientists working at the nuclear-weapons laboratories, with think-tanks or in government have looked on aghast as disarmament skeptics around the world have scorned the value of international treaties."

Godson, Roy, and James J. Wirtz, ed. *Strategic Denial and Deception: The Twenty-First Century Challenge*. New Brunswick, N.J.: Transaction Publishers, 2002. Essays on the problems posed by states' evasion of nuclear inspections.

Goldschmidt, Pierre. "Priority Steps to Strengthen the Nonproliferation Regime," *Carnegie Endowment for International Peace Policy Outlook No. 33*, January 2007. A Web-only publication. Available online. URL: http://www.carnegieendowment.org/files/goldschmidt_priority_steps_final.pdf. Accessed March 27, 2007. Suggests steps to dissuade and deter nonnuclear weapons states from seeking nuclear weapons.

Graham, Thomas Jr., *Common Sense on Weapons of Mass Destruction*. Seattle & London: University of Washington Press, 2004. A former Clinton administration official urges a multilateral approach to nonproliferation, one making better use of the UN.

Haeckel, Erwin. *Tightening the Reins: Towards a Strengthened International Nuclear Safeguards System*. New York: Springer-Verlag, 2000. Discusses the merits and problems of the Strengthened Safeguards System of the International Atomic Energy Agency.

Harrison, Selig S. "The Forgotten Bargain: Nonproliferation and Nuclear Disarmament." *World Policy Journal* 23, no. 3: 1–13. Countering the growing international belief that further proliferation is inevitable, this article proposes a new nuclear bargain in which realistic negotiations with Pyongyang and Tehran are linked with a parallel process of global nuclear weapons reductions.

Huntington, William. "France, Libya Agree to Nuclear Cooperation." *Arms Control Today* 36, no. 3: 31. Report that France and Libya have signed a civil nuclear cooperation agreement, the first of its kind for Libya since its 2003 pledge to comprehensively dismantle its nuclear and chemical weapons programs.

Jenkins, Tony. "Disarming the System, Disarming the Mind." *Peace Review* 18, no. 3: 361–368. Jenkins discusses the policy concept of general and complete disarmament (GCD). Dismissed by many as utopian and idealistic, GCD is in danger of extinction.

Langewiesche, William. *The Atomic Bazaar: The Rise of the Nuclear Poor*. New York: Farrar, Straus & Giroux, 2007. Investigates the spread of nuclear weapons technology to relatively underdeveloped nations, with special attention to the A. Q. Khan network.

Lewis, Jeffrey. "Nuclear Non-Proliferation Treaty (NPT)." *Arms Control Wonk*, August 29, 2005. Available online. URL: http://www.armscontrolwonk.com/749/nuclear non-proliferation-treaty-npt. Online article taking a "glass half-full" view of the NPT.

Lewis, John W., and Litai Xue. *China Builds the Bomb.* Stanford, Calif.: Stanford University Press, 1988. History of China's nuclear weapons program.

Lewis, Julian. "Nuclear Disarmament versus Peace in the Twenty-first Century." *International Affairs* 82, no. 4: 667–674. Maintains that Britain still needs its nuclear deterrent.

Marsh, Gerald E., and George S. Standford. "Batteries Included: How to Spread Nuclear Power with Sharing Nuclear Know-How." *Bulletin of the Atomic Scientists* 62, no. 6: 19–20. Discusses flaws in the Nuclear Non-proliferation Treaty and proposes corrections.

Nolan, Janne E., Bernard I. Finel, and Brian D. Finlay, eds. *Ultimate Security: Combatting Weapons of Mass Destruction.* New York: Century Foundation Press, 2003. Eight scholars, academics, and policy practitioners address the major issues underlying the changes in the global security environment and evaluate the effectiveness of recent U.S. policy innovations.

Norris, Robert S. "Global Nuclear Stockpiles, 1945–2006." *Bulletin of the Atomic Scientists* 62, no. 4: 64–67. Norris reports on current estimates of nuclear weapons stockpiles country by country. Nine countries possess approximately 27,000 nuclear warheads, of which 97 percent are in U.S. and Russian stockpiles.

Norris, Robert S., Andrew S. Burrows, and Richard W. Fieldhouse. *Nuclear Weapons Databook, Vol. 5, British, French, and Chinese Nuclear Weapons.* Boulder, Colo.: Westview Press, 1994. History and description of the British, French, and Chinese nuclear weapons programs.

Nuclear Threat Initiative (NTI). Available online. URL: http://www.nti.org/b_aboutnti/b_index.html. Accessed March 27, 2007. Web site of NTI, a nonprofit organization devoted to reducing the risk of use and preventing the spread of nuclear, biological, and chemical weapons. Useful resource for data and analysis on nuclear proliferation.

O'Hanlon, Michael. "What If a Nuclear-Armed State Collapses?" *Current History* 105, no. 694: 379–384. Discusses the problem of dealing with nuclear weapons in the chaos of a failed state, with lessons from the civil war in Iraq.

Overcoming Impediments to U.S.-Russian Cooperation on Nuclear Non-Proliferation: Report of a Joint Workshop. Online book of National Academies Press, 2004. Available online. URL: http://books.nap.edu/openbook.php?record_id=10928&page=13. Accessed March 23, 2007. Advocates better U.S.-Russian cooperation.

Paul, T. V. *Power Versus Prudence: Why Nations Forgo Nuclear Weapons.* Montreal and Kingston: McGill-Queen's University Press, 2003. Discusses states that have decided not to pursue nuclear weapons capability and the possibility of applying lessons from their experience to nuclear disarmament efforts.

Perkovich, George. "The End of the Nonproliferation Regime?" *Current History* 105, no. 694: 355–362. Suggests government experts, the IAEA, and others produce detailed road maps of the technical and institutional steps that would have to be taken to verifiably eliminate nuclear arsenals.

———. "Bush's Nuclear Revolution: A Regime Change in Nonproliferation." *Foreign Affairs.* Available online. URL: http://www.foreignaffairs.org/20030301facomment10334/georgeperkovich/bush-s<->nuclear-revolution-a-regime-change-in-nonproliferation.html. Accessed March 24, 2007. Criticizes the Bush administration's nonproliferation policy.

Perkovich, George, Jessica Tuchman Mathews, Joseph Cirincione, et al. *Universal Compliance: A Strategy for Nuclear Security.* Washington, D.C.: Carnegie Endowment for International Peace, 2005. Available online. URL: http://www.carnegieendowment.org/files/UC2.FINAL3.pdf. Accessed March 24, 2007. Lays out the details of a nuclear nonproliferation strategy designed to win international support. Includes a new solution to the "three state problem" posed by the three nuclear weapons states that have not signed the NPT (India, Israel, and Pakistan).

Potter William, and Harlan Jencks. *The International Missile Bazaar: The New Suppliers' Network,* Boulder, Colo.: Westview Press, 1994. Examines the international trade in missile technology in the early 1990s.

Price, Richard. "Nuclear Weapons Don't Kill People, Rogues Do." *International Politics* 44, no. 2/3: 232–249. This article examines weaknesses in the nuclear nonproliferation regime, the "chronic legitimacy deficit of the NPT."

Sauer, Tom. "The Nuclear Nonproliferation Regime in Crisis." *Peace Review* 18, no. 3: 333–340. Sauer examines the current treaties, international organizations, and other initiatives that make up the nuclear nonproliferation advocacy movement.

Scheinman, Lawrence. *Atomic Energy Policy in France under the Fourth Republic.* Princeton, N.J.: Princeton University Press, 1965. A history of the French nuclear program.

Schell, Jonathan. "Proliferation and Possession, Nonproliferation and Disarmament." *Peace Review* 18, no. 3: 349–352. Schell argues that the desire to become a nuclear power would not exist if those countries that already have such power insist on maintaining it.

Schram, Martin. *Avoiding Armageddon: Our Future, Our Choice.* Toronto: HarperCollins Canada, 2003. Companion book to a PBS series that details the threats facing the United States from nuclear, chemical, and biological attack and from terrorism and outlines possible solutions.

Sokolski, Henry D. "Nuclear 1914: The Next Big Worry." In Henry Sokolsi, ed., *Taming the Next Set of Strategic Weapons Threats.* Carlisle, Penn.: Strategic Studies Institute, 2006. Sokolski suggests that networks of alliances among nuclear states could lead to a "1914 scenario" in which nations are drawn into a nuclear world war.

Traub, James. "Why Not Build a Bomb?" *New York Times Magazine,* January 29, 2006. Discusses proposals to improve the Nuclear Nonproliferation Treaty.

United States Congress, Office of Technology Assessment. *Export Controls and Nonproliferaiton Policy.* Washington, D.C.: U.S. Government Printing Office, 1994. Looks at ways to strengthen export controls "while reducing the burdens of export regulations on U.S. exporters."

United States Congress, Office of Technology Assessment. *Proliferation of Weapons of Mass Destruction: Assessing the Risks.* Washington D.C.:U.S. Government

Printing Office, 1993. An overview of nuclear nonproliferation issues prepared for the U.S. Congress.

United States Congress, Office of Technology Assessment. *Technologies Underlying Weapons of Mass Destruction.* Washington, D.C.: U.S. Government Printing Office, 1993. Discusses nonproliferation issues from a technical point of view.

Wier, Anthony. "Traffick Jamming." *Bulletin of the Atomic Scientists* 62, no. 5: 72. Argues that Congress should require the executive branch to assess annually how well countries are meeting their legal obligations to prevent the proliferation of WMD and withhold aid to those governments that refuse to meet those obligations.

NUCLEAR TERRORISM

Allison, Graham. "The Will to Prevent." *Harvard International Review* 28, no. 3: 50–55. Nuclear terrorism is preventable by a feasible, affordable checklist of actions that can be summed up in a "Doctrine of Three No's": no loose nukes, no new nascent nukes, and no new nuclear weapons states. The crucial challenge to this principle today is Iran.

Billingslea, Marshall. "Moscow's Missile Defense Bluster." *Wall Street Journal* (Eastern edition). March 7, 2007. Editorial praising the proposed missile defense deployments in Poland and the Czech Republic, which "would further preserve and strengthen Alliance solidarity in the face of real and growing threats. It is a good thing that some allies, such as the U.S., already have a missile shield. But should not all NATO partners be afforded such protection?"

Blanchard, Christopher M. "Al Qaeda: Statements and Evolving Ideology," Updated January 24, 2007. Available online. URL: http://fpc.state.gov/documents/organization/80743.pdf. Accessed March 24, 2007. Interprets the ideology of the al-Qaeda terror network based on the public statements of Osama bin Laden and other al-Qaeda leaders.

Bukharin, Oleg, and William Potter. "Potatoes Were Guarded Better." *Bulletin of the Atomic Scientists* 51, no. 13 (1995). Report on the poor control of nuclear materials in the former Soviet republics after the breakup of the Soviet Union.

Cameron, Gavin. *Nuclear Terrorism: A Threat Assessment for the 21st Century.* New York: Palgrave, 1999. Argues that nuclear terrorism is the greatest nontraditional threat to international security in the world today.

Committee on Indigenization of Programs to Prevent Leakage of Plutonium and Highly Enriched Uranium from Russian Facilities, Office for Central Europe and Eurasia, National Research Council. *Strengthening Long-Term Nuclear Security.* Online book of National Academies Press, 2005. Available online. URL: http://books.nap.edu/catalog.php?record_id=11377#toc. Accessed March 23, 2007. Examines the problems and obstacles that may arise during the transition from U.S.-run, U.S.-funded programs to secure Russia's nuclear materials to a Russian-run, Russian-funded program.

Annotated Bibliography

Eldridge, Christopher, ed. *Protection, Control, and Accounting of Nuclear Materials: International Challenges and National Programs—Workshop Summary.* Online monograph published by National Academies Press, 2005. Available online. URL: http://books.nap.edu/catalog.php?record_id=11343#toc. Accessed March 23, 2007. Summary of a 2003 workshop on the best methods of securing nuclear materials.

"Europe's Space Wars—Missile Defense." *The Economist* 382, no. 8517: 17. Editorial arguing that Russian complaints about new missile defense deployments planned for Poland and the Czech Republic are propaganda, since these defenses are meant to counter potential threats from Iran and North Korea, not from Russia.

Ferguson, Charles D. "Preventing Catastrophic Nuclear Terrorism." Washington, D.C.: Council on Foreign Relations Press, 2006. Available online. URL: http://www.cfr.org/content/publications/attachments/NucTerrCSR.pdf. Accessed March 24, 2007. Argues that more must be done to secure the safety of nuclear materials.

Ferguson, Charles D., William C. Potter, Amy Sands, et al. *The Four Faces of Nuclear Terrorism.* New York: Routledge, 2005. Warns that substandard security at nuclear facilities in Europe, Central Asia, Russia, and Pakistan increases the risk of terrorists seizing highly enriched uranium to make crude but devastating nuclear explosives.

Government Accountability Office. "Security of U.S. Nuclear Materials: DOE Needs to Take Action to Safely Consolidate Plutonium. United States Government Accountability Office Report to Congressional Committees, July 2005." Available online. URL: http://www.gao.gov/new.items/d05665.pdf. Accessed March 23, 2007. Evaluates the U.S. Department of Energy's progress in consolidating America's plutonium to safeguard it from theft and to prevent it from damaging the environment.

Hecker, Siegfried S. "Toward a Comprehensive Safeguards System: Keeping Fissile Materials out of Terrorists' Hands." *Annals of the American Academy of Political and Social Science* 607 (September 2006): 121–132. Lack of attention to the technical difficulties is hampering our ability to build a comprehensive safeguards system and prevent nuclear terrorism.

Hynes, Michael V., John E Peters, and Joel Kvitky. "Denying Armageddon: Preventing Terrorist Use of Nuclear Weapons." *Annals of the American Academy of Political and Social Science* 607 (September 2006): 150–161. Outlines a strategy to reduce the likelihood of a nuclear terrorist attack.

Krepon, Michael. *Cooperative Threat Reduction, Missile Defense, and the Nuclear Future.* New York: Palgrave Macmillan, 2005. Discusses new nuclear security threats, particularly the possibility of nuclear weapons in the hands of terrorists.

Lee, Rennselaer W. *Smuggling Armageddon: The Nuclear Black Market in the Former Soviet Union and Europe.* New York: Palgrave, 1999. A report on the surge in the black market of nuclear material in the Soviet Union in the 1990s.

Leventhal, Paul, and Yonah Alexander, eds., *Preventing Nuclear Terrorism.* Lexington, Mass.: Lexington Books, 1987. Collection of articles on the threat of nuclear terrorism.

Levi, Michael A. "Prepared Testimony Before the Senate Subcommittee on Terrorism, Technology, and Homeland Security." Council on Foreign Relations, July 27, 2006. Available online. URL: http://www.cfr.org/publication/11160/prepared_testimony_before_the_senate_subcommittee_on_terrorism_technology_and_homeland_security.html. Accessed March 23, 2007. Discusses programs to detect nuclear materials that terrorists may attempt to smuggle into the United States.

Luongo, Kenneth N., and William E. Hoehn III. "Reform and Expansion of Cooperative Threat Reduction." *Arms Control Today* June 2003. Available online. URL: http://www.armscontrol.org/act/2003_06/luongohoehn_june03.asp. Retrieved January 4, 2007. Accessed March 27, 2007. Describes new responsibilities for the Nunn-Lugar CTR program.

May, Michael, and Jay Davis. "Preparing for the Worst." *Nature* 443, no. 7114: 907–908. Article suggests preparing an international data bank of nuclear explosives so that the source of nuclear materials after a terrorist nuclear attack can be determined.

Moltz, James Clay, Vladimir A. Orlov, and Adam N. Stulberg. *Preventing Nuclear Meltdown: Managing Decentralization of Russia's Nuclear Complex.* Burlington, Vt: Ashgate, 2004. Leading U.S. and Russian policy experts explore the intersecting problems of Russian nuclear insecurity and decentralization.

Ogilvie-White, Tanya. "Non-proliferation and Counter-terrorism Cooperation in Southeast Asia: Meeting Global Obligations through Regional Security Architectures?" *Contemporary Southeast Asia* 28, no. 1: 1–26. Discusses nuclear black market networks and reports that Osama bin Laden considers it a "duty" for al-Qaeda to acquire nuclear weapons and Asian governments' responses.

Perl, Raphael F. "International Terrorism: Threat, Policy and Response." Updated January 3, 2007. Available online URL: http://www.fas.org/sgp/crs/terror/RL33600.pdf. Accessed March 23, 2007. An overview of terrorist threats today, with special attention to the threat posed by state sponsors of terrorism that also possess or will soon possess nuclear weapons.

Smith, Derek D. *Deterring America: Rogue States and the Proliferation of Weapons of Mass Destruction.* Cambridge: Cambridge University Press, 2006. Analysis of the new security challenges posed by the combination of terrorism and rogue states with weapons of mass destruction.

Sokolski, Henry D., ed. *Twenty-First Century Weapons Proliferation: Are We Ready?* London: Frank Cass Publishers, 2001. Evaluates the U.S. response to the threats from the nuclear weapons programs of India, Iraq, North Korea, China, and Pakistan and from the possibility of nuclear terrorism.

Sokova, Elena, William C. Potter, and Cristina Chuen. "Recent Weapons Grade Uranium Smuggling Case: Nuclear Materials are Still on the Loose." Center for Nonproliferation Studies, January 26, 2007. Available online. URL: http://cns.miis.edu/pubs/week/070126.htm. Accessed March 24, 2007. Says that reports of the seizure of weapons grade uranium traffickers in Georgia raise concerns about poor cooperation against nuclear terrorism.

Tanter, Raymond. *Rogue Regimes: Terrorism and Proliferation.* New York: Palgrave, 1999. Explores U.S. foreign policy with regard to so-called rogue states such as Iran, Iraq, Syria, and Libya.

U.S. Congress, Office of Technology Assessment. *Technology Against Terrorism: Structuring Security.* Washington, D.C.: U.S. Government Printing Office, 1992. Overview of international terrorism in the early 1990s, suggesting tactics and strategies to meet the threat.

Wright, Lawrence. *The Looming Tower: Al-Qaeda and the Road to 9/11.* New York: Knopf, 2006. Well-written narrative tracing the rise of Osama bin Laden's terrorist organization.

THE MISSILE DEFENSE DEBATE

American Foreign Policy Council. *Missile Defense and American Security 2003: Proceedings from the 2003 Conference on Missile Defenses and American Security.* Lanham, Md.: University Press of America, 2006. Leading defense and foreign policy experts take stock of the emerging American missile defense system in a volume based on proceedings from the 2003 Conference on Missile Defenses and American Security.

"Ballistic Missile Defense System Overview." Available online. URL: http://www.mda.mil/mdalink/pdf/bmdsbook.pdf. Accessed March 24, 2007. Description of the U.S. Missile Defense System by the U.S. Missile Defense Agency.

BBC News. "America Withdraws from ABM Treaty." Available online. URL: news.bbc.co.uk/2/hi/americas/1707812.stm. Retrieved March 8, 2007. Article reports the relatively quiet announcement that the Unites States was withdrawing from the decades-old Anti-Ballistic Missile Treaty in order to expand its missile defense research and deployment.

Boese, Wade. "Missile Defense Spending Soars to New Heights." *Arms Control Today.* Available online. URL: www.armscontrol.org/act/2007_01-02/index.asp. Retrieved March 8, 2007. Reports on the record request for missile defense appropriations in the Bush administration's 2007 budget.

Broad, William J. *Teller's War: The Top-Secret Story Behind the Star Wars Deception.* New York: Simon & Schuster, 1992. A look at the career of nuclear physicist Edward Teller, the "father of the H-bomb," and his impact on Ronald Reagan's missile defense proposal in the 1980s.

Brookes, Peter, and Baker Spring. "A Successful Test Shows the Way Forward on Missile Defense." Available online. URL: http://www.heritage.org/Research/NationalSecurity/wm1335.cfm. Retrieved February 1, 2007. Commentary giving a thumbs-up to missile defense.

NUCLEAR NONPROLIFERATION

Butler, Richard. *Fatal Choice: Nuclear Weapons and the Illusion of Missile Defense.* Amazon Remainders Account, 2001. An advocate of nuclear disarmament recommends Senate confirmation of the Comprehensive Nuclear Test Ban Treaty, a bilateral agreement between the United States and Russia to reduce their nuclear stockpiles and to create an international Council on Weapons of Mass Destruction.

Cimbala, Stephen J. *Shield of Dreams: Missile Defenses and Nuclear Strategy.* Westport, Conn.: Preager, 2000. A guide to the debate on missile defense.

Ferguson, Charles. "Sparking a Buildup: U.S. Missile Defense and China's Nuclear Arsenal." *Arms Control Today* 30, no. 2: Article examines China's likely reaction to the installation of missile defense systems by the United States on the territory of China's Asian neighbors.

Garwin, Richard L. "The Wrong Plan (A Better Ballistic Missile Defense Strategy)." *Bulletin of the Atomic Scientists,* 2005. Critics missile defense plans on technical grounds, arguing that a system based on "hit-to-kill interceptors" is unlikely to be effective in its stated mission.

Handberg, Roger. *Ballistic Missile Defense and the Future of American Security: Agendas, Perceptions, Technology and Policy.* Westport, Conn.: Praeger, 2001. Explains the missile defense debate and shows how decision makers' political philosophies affect their evaluation of the technology.

Hey, Nigel. *The Star Wars Enigma: Behind the Scenes of the Cold War Race for Missile Defense.* Washington, D.C.: Potomac Books, 2006. Explores the mysteries of Reagan's Strategic Defense Initiative, including the possibility that it was the greatest bluff in history.

Missilethreat.com. Available online. URL: http://www.missilethreat.com/. Accessed March 24, 2007. Pro–missile defense Web site created by the Claremont Institute, a conservative think tank. Contains information on missiles and advocacy of missile defense systems.

"National Missile Defense Independent Review Team Executive Summary." Available online. URL: http://www.mda.mil/mdalink/pdf/welchsum.pdf. Accessed March 24, 2007. Review of the U.S. missile defense program as of 2000.

Tellis, Ashley J. *India and Missile Defense.* Washington, D.C.: Carnegie Endowment for International Peace, 2007. Describes the evolution of Indian attitudes toward missile defense.

U.S. Congress, Office of Technology Assessment. *Ballistic Missile Defense Technologies.* Honolulu: University Press of the Pacific, 2002. This report examines both the "why" and the "what" of ballistic missile defenses.

United States Department of Defense. *2006 Essential Guide to Ballistic Missile Defense (BMD) and Missile Defense Agency (MDA), "Star Wars" SDI Program, Threats, Sensors, History, Boost, Midcourse, and Terminal Defense Segments (DVD-ROM, CD-ROM).* Progressive Management, 2006. Privately compiled collections of official public domain U.S. government files and documents concerning ballistic missile defense.

Warner, John. *Rockets Red Glare: Missile Defense and the Future of World Politics.* Toronto: HarperCollins Canada, 2001. Taking it as a given that some form of missile defense will become a reality, this book goes on to discuss the relative merits of different systems that have been proposed.

Yanarella, Ernest J. *The Missile Defense Controversy: Technology in Search of a Mission.* Lexington, Ky. University Press of Kentucky, 2002. Traces the story of missile defense, "the strategic idea that simply will not die," from its beginnings to the outset of the George W. Bush administration.

NUCLEAR PROLIFERATION IN SOUTH ASIA

General: History and Politics of South Asia, India, and Pakistan

Bidwai, Praful, and Achin Vanaik. *New Nukes.* New York: Olive Branch Press, 2000. Two antinuclear activists examine the causes and consequences of India's and Pakistan's nuclear tests and map out an approach to nuclear abolition.

"Kashmir Dreaming." *The Economist* 380, no. 8485: 10. Describes Pakistan's tentative moves toward lessening tensions with India over the disputed territory of Kashmir after years of provocative actions.

Lavoy, Peter R., and Stephen A. Smith. "The Risk of Inadvertent Nuclear Use between India and Pakistan." *Strategic Insight.* Available online. URL: www.ccc.nps.navy.mil/rsepResources/si/feb03/southAsia2.pdf. Accessed March 23, 2007.

McLeod, John. *The History of India.* Westport, Conn.: Greenwood Press, 2002. A brief and dry introduction to its subject.

Musharraf, Pervez. *In the Line of Fire: A Memoir.* New York: Free Press, 2006. Pakistan's military dictator, who seized power in a bloodless coup in 1999, attempts to explain himself and his country to the Western world.

Raman, J. Sri. *Flashpoint: How the U.S., India and Pakistan Brought Us to the Brink of Nuclear War,* Monroe, Maine: Common Courage Press, 2004. A vivid account useful for exciting details, but very partisan and prone to use the most extreme number in any range of estimates.

Sathasivam, Kanishkan. *Uneasy Neighbors: India, Pakistan and US Foreign Policy.* Hampshire, England: Ashgate Publishing, 2005. An analysis of the shifting relationships among these three countries; contains a clear, succinct explanation of the Kashmir conflict and of Pakistan's fear of India.

Talbot, Ian. *Pakistan: A Modern History.* New York: Palgrave MacMillan, 2005. Thorough history with special attention to the social and demographic tensions of Pakistan.

Yourish, Karen. "India, Pakistan, Trade Barbs Over Nukes." *Arms Control Today.* Available online. URL: www.armscontrol.org/act/2003_10/IndiaPakistan.asp. Retrieved March 8, 2007. Article reports Pakistani president Musharraf's reply to India's accusations that Pakistan had shared its nuclear technology with other countries.

Nuclear Weapons in India

Abraham, Itty. *The Making of the Indian Atomic Bomb.* London: Zed Books, 1998. A succinct analysis of India's nuclear policy since independence.

"Asia: The Home Front: India's Nuclear Options." *The Economist* 381, no. 8508: 70. Discusses the 2006 U.S.-India nuclear deal in the light of India's domestic politics.

Bhatia, Shyam. *India's Nuclear Bomb.* Ghaziabad: Vikas, 1979. The story of India's quest for the bomb.

"Blast from the Past: America's Nuclear Deal with India." *The Economist* 381, no. 8506: 16. Editorial argues that the 2006 U.S. agreement with India will damage nuclear nonproliferation efforts.

Boyd, Kerry. "India Establishes Formal Nuclear Command Structure." *Arms Control Today* 33, no. 1. Brief report on Indian government's announcement regarding its official nuclear command structure.

Chellaney, Brahma. *Nuclear Proliferation: The US-Indian Conflict.* New Delhi: Orient Longman, 1993. An account of the evolution of U.S. export controls on nuclear technology to India.

Chengappa, Raj. "The Bomb Makers." *India Today,* June 1998. Describes the circumstances of India's 1998 series of nuclear tests.

———. *Weapons of Peace: The Story of India's Quest to Be a Nuclear Power.* New Delhi: HarperCollins Publishers India, 2000. Account of India's nuclear weapons program.

Crook, John R. "U.S.-India Civil Nuclear Cooperation Faces Congressional Scrutiny." *American Journal of International Law* 100, no. 3: 717–719. In order for the 2006 U.S.-India nuclear deal to go forward, Congress must amend provisions of the U.S. Atomic Energy Act that bar such cooperation with countries that, like India, are not a party to the Non-proliferation Treaty.

"Dr. Strangedeal: Nuclear Proliferation." *The Economist* 378, no. 8468: 9. Editorial arguing that the U.S. nuclear deal with India will weaken efforts at nuclear nonproliferation.

"From Bad to Worse: America's Nuclear Deal With India." *The Economist* 380, no. 8487: 12. An editorial highly critical of the 2006 U.S. agreement with India, which, the article says, will make it easier for India to add more bombs to its nuclear arsenal.

Graham, Thomas Jr., Leonor Tomero, and Leonard Weiss. "Think Again: U.S.-India Nuclear Deal." *Foreign Policy.* Available online. URL: www.cfr.org/publication/10731/usindia_nuclear_deal.html. Retrieved March 8, 2007. Article maintains that the U.S. 2006 deal with India sets a dangerous precedent, allows too many nuclear reactors to remain off limits to inspections, and will help enlarge India's small nuclear weapons program.

Kapur, Ashok. *India's Nuclear Option.* New York: Praegar; 1976. Tells the story of India's nuclear program until 1974.

Annotated Bibliography

Kimball, Daryl G. "Another Chance for the Fissile Production Ban." *Arms Control Today* 36, no. 3: 3. Article critical of the 2006 U.S.-India nuclear deal, noting that foreign nuclear reactor fuel supplies could free up India's limited uranium reserves for the sole purpose of adding to its arsenal of 50 to 100 nuclear bombs.

Kronstadt, K. Alan. "India-U.S. Relations." Updated January 3, 2007. Available online. URL: http://fpc.state.gov/documents/organization/78553.pdf. Examines a variety of India-U.S. issues, including India's nuclear capability and tensions with Pakistan.

Malik, Aahid. *Dr. A. Q. Khan and the Islamic Bomb.* Islamabad: Hurmat, 1992. Story of the "father of Pakistan's atomic bomb" before the revelations of the A. Q. Khan network.

Perkovich, George. *India's Nuclear Bomb: The Impact on Global Proliferation.* Berkeley: University of California Press, 1999. A very thorough and exhaustively researched account of the making of India's bomb. Perkovich advances the view that security concerns alone cannot explain India's decision to acquire nuclear weapons capability.

Saksena, Jyotika. "Regime Design Matters: The CTBT and India's Nuclear Dilemma." *Comparative Strategy* 25, no. 3: 209–229. Argues that the flawed design of the Comprehensive Test Ban Treaty (CTBT) provided an incentive for India to conduct nuclear tests in 1998.

Sokolski, Henry D., ed. *Gauging U.S.-Indian Strategic Cooperation.* Washington, D.C.: Strategic Studies Institute Publication Office, 2007. Available online. URL: http://www.npecweb.org/Books/20070300-NPEC-GaugingUS-IndiaStratCoop.pdf. Accessed March 23, 2007. A collection of essays that assesses the likely effects of U.S.-Indian cooperation on nuclear energy. Some essays favor the U.S.-India deal, others deplore it.

Sokolski, Henry, and Teresita Schaffer. "The U.S.-India Deal: The Right Approach?" Available online. URL: www.cfr.org/publication/10731/usindia_nuclear_deal.html. Accessed March 23, 2007. A pro and con debate concerning the 2006 nuclear deal between India and the United States.

Squassoni, Sharon. "India's Nuclear Separation Plan: Issues and Views." Updated December 22, 2006. Available online. URL: http://fpc.state.gov/documents/organization/78421.pdf. Accessed March 23, 2007. Noting that the Bush administration's decision to engage in "full" civil nuclear cooperation between the U.S. and India is "at odds with nearly three decades of US nonproliferation policy and practice,' this report discusses the practicality of India's promise to separate its civilian nuclear facilities from its military nuclear facilities.

Woods, Scott. "Analysis of the US-India Nuclear Deal." *Defense & Security Analysis* 22, no. 3: 325–328. Presents an analysis of the controversial agreement signed between the United States and India in March 2006. The deal involves the sale of U.S. nuclear fuel and technology to India in return for certain concessions.

Nuclear Weapons in Pakistan

Ahmed, Samina. "Security Dilemmas of Nuclear-Armed Pakistan." *Third World Quarterly* 21, no. 5 (October 2000). Examines military strategic problems raised for Pakistan and its neighbors as a consequence of Pakistan's nuclear capability.

Ahmed, Samina, and David Cortright. *Pakistan and the Bomb: Public Opinion and the Nuclear Options.* New York: Oxford University Press, 1998. Collection of articles examining the issues raised by Pakistan's nuclear weapons program.

Ali, Akhtar. *Pakistan's Nuclear Dilemma.* Karachi: Pakistan Economist Research Unit, 1984. Pakistan's nuclear program before 1984.

Hinderstein, Corey. "The First Casualty of the War on Terrorism Must Not Be Pakistan: Pakistan's Nuclear Weapons Must Not Fall into Terrorists' Hands." *ISIS Issue Brief.* Article published as the United States mobilized for war in Afghanistan, highlighting a special danger of destabilizing a nuclear weapons state.

Kronstadt, K. Alan. "Pakistan-U.S. Relations." CRS Report for Congress, Order Code RL33496. Updated October 26, 2006. Noting that "a stable, democratic, economically thriving Pakistan is considered vital to U.S. interests," this report reviews the challenges to that goal posed by several issues including regional terrorism, weapons proliferation, the ongoing Kashmir problem, and Pakistan-India tensions.

Musharraf, Pervez. "On Iran's Nukes, A. Q. Khan and Hamas." *New Perspectives Quarterly* 23, no. 2: 49–51. Interview with Pakistan's ruler. He discusses among other issues the reasons Pakistan but not Iran should be allowed to have nuclear weapons.

NUCLEAR PROLIFERATION IN THE MIDDLE EAST

General: History and Politics of the Middle East, Iran, Israel, and Iraq

Adelson, Roger. *London and the Invention of the Middle East: Money, Power, and War, 1902–1922.* New Haven, Conn.: Yale University Press, 1995. A history of the decision making by the British government, banks, and other leaders that determined the name, shape, nature, and future of the Middle East.

Ajami, Fouad. *The Arab Predicament.* Cambridge: Cambridge University Press, 1981. Fouad's subject is the intellectual ferment caused in the Arab Middle East by Israel's victory in the 1967 Six-Day War.

Cleveland, William L. *A History of the Modern Middle East.* Boulder, Colo.: Westview Press, 1999. An introduction to the history of the region, useful as a guide to the Israeli-Palestinian conflict, Iran's Islamic state, and the evolution of Saddam Hussein's Iraq.

Gelvin, James L. *The Modern Middle East: A History.* New York: Oxford University Press, 2004. A guide to 500 years of history in the Middle East, from the heyday of the Ottoman Empire to the present.

Mansfield, Peter, and Nicolas Pelham. *A History of the Middle East.* 2d ed. New York: Penguin, 2003. Short introduction to its subject.

Nasr, Vali. *The Shia Revival: How Conflicts Within Islam Will Shape the Future.* New York: W. W. Norton, 2006. This book provides an introduction to the history and theology of Shia Islam and argues that the recent Iraq war has shaken the balance of power between the Sunni and Shia branches of Islam in the Middle East, with far-reaching consequences for the region.

Oren, Michael B. *Power, Faith, and Fantasy: America in the Middle East: 1776 to the Present.* New York: W. W. Norton, 2007. A useful introduction to the history of U.S. involvement in the Middle East.

Russell, James. *Proliferation of Weapons of Mass Destruction in the Middle East.* New York: Palgrave, 2006. A collection of essays on the challenges posed by the spread of weapons of mass destruction in the Middle East.

Smith, Dan. *The State of the Middle East: An Atlas of Conflict and Resolution.* Berkeley: University of California Press, 2006. Uses historical and contemporary maps to explain and illustrate the politics of the Middle East.

Williams, Daniel. "Nuclear Program in Libya Detailed." *Washington Post,* December 30, 2003.

Iran

"Ahmadinejad: Wipe Israel Off Map." Al Jazeera.net. Available online. URL: english.aljazeera.net/English/archive/archive?ArchiveId=15816. Accessed March 27, 2007. A report of Ahmadinejad's incendiary speech regarding Israel.

Albright, David. "When Could Iran Get the Bomb: What We Know and What We Don't Know About Iran's Nuclear Program." *Bulletin of the Atomic Scientists* 62, no. 4: 26–33. Available online. URL: http://thebulletin.metapress.com/content/d427773518542nn1/fulltext.pdf. Accessed March 24, 2007. Discusses the state of Iran's nuclear weapons program; the article says that U.S. intelligence estimates regarding Iran seem to be based on much firmer evidence than its previous estimates of Iraq's weapons programs.

Albright, David, and Corey Hinderstein. "The Clock Is Ticking, But How Fast?" Institute for Science and International Security (ISIS). Available online. URL: http://www.isisonline.org/publications/iran/clockticking.pdf. Accessed March 27, 2007. Educated guesses on the question of how long it will be before Iran has a nuclear weapon.

———. "Iran, Player or Rogue?" *Bulletin of the Atomic Scientists 59,* no. 5 (September/October 2003). Article analyzes Iranian motives and attempts to determine whether the Iranian government will reveal its true intentions regarding nuclear weapons.

Ansari, Ali M. *Confronting Iran: The Failure of American Foreign Policy and the Next Great Crisis in the Middle East.* New York: Basic Books, 2006. An expert on U.S.-Iranian relations explains the past, present, and possible future of a nuclear standoff between the United States and Iran.

NUCLEAR NONPROLIFERATION

Beeman, William O. *The "Great Satan," vs. the "Mad Mullahs": How the United States and Iran Demonize Each other.* New York: Preager, 2005. A study of the mutual perceptions and misconceptions of the United States and Iran.

Blix, Hans. "US Should Give Iran a Security Guarantee." *New Perspectives Quarterly* 23, no. 2: 43–46. The former chief UN arms inspector for Iraq discusses the 2006 nuclear deal between the United States and India, Iran's case for developing nuclear weapons, the need to induce Iran to forgo weapons with a guarantee of its security, and related topics.

Boureston, Jack, and Charles D. Ferguson. "Keep Your Enemy Closer." *Bulletin of the Atomic Scientists* 61, no. 6: 25, 76. An opinion piece suggests that "the best way to know the full extent of Iran's nuclear doings is to offer it help."

Chubin, Shahram. *Iran's Nuclear Ambitions.* Washington, D.C.: Carnegie Endowment for International Peace, 2006. Clear, even-handed analysis of pressures leading Iran to seek nuclear weapons and of the choices open to the United States and other countries in confronting Iran's nuclear program.

Cirincione, Joseph. "Controlling Iran's Nuclear Program." *Issues in Science and Technology* 22, no. 3: 75–82. Cirincione explains the fuel cycle of taking uranium and producing low-enriched uranium for nuclear weapons, coupled with estimates of Iran's plans and capabilities. He also offers steps to solve the Iranian nuclear problem.

Cordesman, Anthony H., and Khalid R. Al-Rodhan. *Iran's Weapons of Mass Destruction: The Real and Potential Threat.* Washington, D.C.: Center for Strategic and International Studies, 2006. Covers all facets of Iran's weapons of mass destruction, analyzing Iran's motivation for acquiring WMD capabilities; the history of its WMD program; its chemical, biological, and nuclear capabilities; and its delivery options, including its missile program, air force, and Revolutionary Guards.

"A Countdown to Confrontation—Dealing With Iran: To Come." *The Economist* 382, no. 8515: 23–25. Discusses the growing signs of a confrontation between the United States and Iran on the issues both of Iran's nuclear program and U.S. charges of Iran's interference in Iraq.

Crook, John R. "Ongoing U.S. Efforts to Curb Iran's Nuclear Program." *American Journal of International Law* 100, no. 2: 480–485. A blow-by-blow account of U.S. efforts to put pressure on Iran's nuclear program through work with the European Union, the IAEA, and the UN Security Council.

Dorraj, Manochehr. "Behind Iran's Nuclear Pursuit?" *Peace Review* 18, no. 3: 325–332. Argues that the primary factors informing Iranian nuclear ambitions are political. Increasingly, the Iranian government sees its survival linked to the possession of a credible deterrent.

Ebadi, Shirin, and Muhammad Sahimi. "Link Human Rights to Iran's Nuclear Ambitions." *New Perspectives Quarterly* 23, no. 2: 39–42. Says the West has leverage with Iran and should use it to provide it with incentives to move toward a democratic political system.

Annotated Bibliography

Encyclopedia Britannica. *Iran: The Essential Guide to a Country on the Brink.* New York: Wiley, 2006. An examination of Iran's social, cultural, and political landscape past and present.

Esposito, John L., and R. K. Remazani, eds. *Iran at the Crossroads.* New York, Palgrave, 2001. Articles on revolutionary Iran's past and future prospects.

Farley, Maggie. "U.N. Weights Ban on Iranian Arms Exports; the Security Council is Looking at Several New Penalties to Persuade Teheran to Rein in Its Nuclear Program." *Los Angeles Times,* March 16, 2007: A9. Discusses proposed UN Security Council resolution imposing stricter sanctions on Iran if it does not suspend uranium enrichment and return to negotiations about its nuclear program.

Feldman, Noah. "Islam, Terror, and the Second Nuclear Age." *New York Times Magazine,* October 29, 2006. An article discussing the potential consequences if Iran becomes a nuclear power in the Middle East. A nuclear Iran might cause a historic shift in the balance of power in the Persian Gulf.

Hassan, Hussein D. "Iran: Profile and Statements of President Mahmoud Ahmadinejad." Available online. URL: http://www.fas.org/sgp/crs/mideast/RS22569.pdf. Accessed March 23, 2007. A report summarizing the background of Iran's confrontational president and his recent acts and speeches.

———. "Iranian Nuclear Sites." Updated December 12, 2006. Available online. URL: http://fpc.state.gov/documents/organization/79310.pdf. Accessed March 23, 2007. This report describes Iran's known nuclear sites listed in official International Atomic Energy Agency reports and includes a map with the location of nuclear facilities.

Hersh, Seymour M. "The Iran Plans." *New Yorker* 82, no. 9: 30–37. In spring 2006, while publicly favoring diplomacy to stop Iran from pursuing nuclear weapons, the Bush administration prepared for a possible major air attack on Iran.

———. "Last Stand." *New Yorker* 82, no. 21: 42–49. U.S. generals and admirals have told the Bush administration that a bombing campaign will probably not succeed in destroying Iran's nuclear program.

Hoge, Warren. "U.N. Council Gets New Draft Decree on Iran Nuclear Sanctions." *New York Times.* March 16, 2007: 13. Article discussing the moves toward a UN Security Council resolution that would impose sanctions on Iran if it did not suspend its nuclear enrichment activities and return to negotiations regarding its nuclear program.

IAEA. "Implementation of the NPT Safeguards Agreement in the Islamic Republic of Iran." Available online. URL: http://www.isisonline.org/publications/iran/IAEAreport8June06.pdf. Accessed March 24, 2007. Official progress report on the International Atomic Energy Agency's dealings with Iran.

Kay, David A. "Denial and Deception Practices of WMD Proliferators: Iraq and Beyond." *Washington Quarterly* 18, no. 1 (winter 1995): The leader of the 2003 to 2005 Iraq Survey Group discusses the efforts of governments to evade weapons inspections in an article written before Operation Iraqi Freedom.

Keddie, Nikki R. *Modern Iran: Roots and Results of Revolution.* New Haven, Conn.: Yale University Press, 2003. The story of modern Iran to the present day, exploring the political, cultural, and social changes of the past quarter century.

Kerr, Paul "Divided from Within." *Bulletin of the Atomic Scientists* 62, no. 6: 17–19. Suggests that Iran's refusal to cooperate with the IAEA might at least in part be the result of bureaucratic and ideological infighting within Iran, which is divided over the nuclear issue.

———. "Russia, Iran Sign Deal to Fuel Nuclear Reactor." *Arms Control Today.* Available online. URL: www.armscontrol.org/act/2006_11/RussiaIran.asp. Accessed March 24, 2007. Discusses negotiations between Russia and Iran over technology for Iran's nuclear program.

Kile, Shannon N., ed. *Europe and Iran: Perspectives on Non-Proliferation.* New York: Oxford University Press, 2005. A collection of essays in which several authors examine Iran's quest for nuclear weapons from a European perspective.

Knowlton, Brian. "Iran: Nuclear Program Has No 'Reverse Gear'/Comment Comes as Six Nations Prepare to Meet Consider Sanctions." *Houston Chronicle,* February 26, 2007: 12. While six leading world powers prepared for a meeting to respond to Iran's nuclear enrichment activities, the Iranian president remained defiant.

Lynch, Colum. "6 Powers Agree on Sanctions For Iran; Ahmadinejad Says Pact Is No Deterrent." *Washington Post,* March 16, 2007: A14. The United States, Russia, China, Britain, France, and Germany agreed on a list of sanctions to compel Iran to suspend its most sensitive nuclear activities, which the United States maintains and Iran denies are intended to give Iran the capacity to build nuclear weapons.

McFaul, Michael, Abbas Milani, and Larry Diamond. "A Win-Win U.S. Strategy for Dealing with Iran." *Washington Quarterly* 30, no. 1: 121–138. Suggests ways the United States could engage Iran, allowing U.S. diplomats to pursue arms control and democratization at the same time.

"Next Stop Iran?; America and Iran." *The Economist* 382, no. 8515: 11. Editorial discussing the possibility that the United States will launch a military strike on Iran despite U.S. defense secretary Robert Gates's denial that such a strike is planned. The author says such an action would be a "reckless gamble."

Reese, Charley, and Jonathan Steele. "The U.S. and Iran: War or Dialogue?" *Washington Report on Middle East Affairs* 25, no. 6: 24–25. Commentaries by Reese and Steele about relations between the United States and Iran.

RIA Novosti Russian News and Information Agency. "Russian Exporter Denies Tor Air Defense System Supplies to Iran." Available online. URL: http://en.rian.ru/russia/20061124/55969586.html. Accessed March 24, 2007. Reports a routine denial, which was followed a few months later by a confirmation of the sale.

RIA Novosti Russian News and Information Agency. "Russia Completes Air Defense System Deliveries to Iran." Available online. URL: http://en.rian.ru/russia/20070116/59156706.html. Accessed March 24, 2007. Russian news report of Russia's controversial delivery of an air defense system to Iran a few months after the Russian government had denied the delivery.

Sanger, David E., and William J. Broad. "Iran Expanding Nuclear Effort, Agency Reports." *New York Times*. February 23, 2007: A1. Reports UN International Atomic Energy Agency estimate of Iran's nuclear program and the U.S. response.

Shen, Dingli. "Iran's Nuclear Ambitions Test China's Wisdom." *Washington Quarterly* 29, no. 2: 55–66. This article discusses the implications of Iran's nuclear program for China's foreign policy.

Sokolski, Henry, and Patrick Clawson, eds. *Getting Ready for a Nuclear Ready Iran*. Washington, D.C.: Strategic Studies Institute Publication Office, 2005. Available online. URL: http://www.npecweb.org/Books/Book051109GettingReadyIran.pdf. Accessed March 24, 2007. A series of essays exploring possible outcomes and responses to a nuclear Iran, including the likelihood that other states in the region may seek nuclear weapons.

Squassoni, Sharon. "Iran's Nuclear Program: Recent Developments." Updated March 8, 2007. Available online. URL: http://fpc.state.gov/documents/organization/81930.pdf. Accessed March 24, 2007. Report on the history of Iran's nuclear program and its response to outside attempts to stop the country's march toward nuclear weapons capability.

Stockman, Farah. "Iran's Nuclear Vision First Glimpsed at MIT: With the Shah's Fall, Students Sent to Cambridge Were Left to Choose between US and Theocracy." *Boston Globe*, March 12, 2007: A1. Tells the ironic story of how the United States helped train young Iranian students in nuclear science in the last years of the reign of the shah of Iran and how some of these students went on to work on Iran's nuclear program after the 1979 revolution.

Strauss, Mark. "A Matter of Timing." *Bulletin of the Atomic Scientists* 62, no. 4: 4. Editorial comments that it would take Tehran three years to acquire enough highly enriched uranium to build a nuclear bomb, time enough to pursue diplomatic means of resolving the crisis.

Traub, James. "The Netherworld of Nuclear Proliferation." *New York Times Magazine*, June 13, 2004. Discusses Iran's nuclear weapons program and its implications.

U.S. Government. *2006 Iranian Nuclear Showdown: Iran, Nuclear Technology and Weapons, and the Regime of Iranian President Ahmadinejad*. Progressive Management, 2006 (CD-ROM). A collection of U.S. federal documents and resources about Iran's nuclear program.

Iraq

Blanchard, Christopher M., Kenneth Katzman, Carol Migdalovitz, et al. "Iraq: Regional Persepectives and U.S. Policy." Available online. URL: http://www.fas.org/sgp/crs/mideast/RL33793.pdf. Speculates on the probable responses by Iraq's neighbors to various possible future outcomes of the war in Iraq.

Iraq Study Group. *The Iraq Study Group Report: The Way Forward: A New Approach*. New York: Vintage, 2006. A team of seasoned foreign policy experts offers a sobering assessment of the consequences of the 2003 U.S. invasion of Iraq, together with some hard-to-swallow remedies.

Kerr, Paul. "Three Years Later, Iraq Investigations Continue." *Arms Control Today* 36, no. 3: 38–39. Discusses the errors made by the intelligence community in assessing the state of Iraq's weapons programs.

Mearsheimer, John J., and Stephen M. Walt. "An Unnecessary War." *Foreign Policy* 134 (January/February 2003). Mearsheimer and Walt argue that the U.S. invasion of Iraq was unnecessary even if Saddam Hussein possessed weapons of mass destruction, since Saddam Hussein was not a "serial aggressor" (like Hitler) but had reacted in the past only to perceived threats to his regime.

Milhollin, Gary. "The Iraqi Bomb." *New Yorker,* February 1, 1993. Available online. URL: http://www.iraqwatch.org/wmd/iraqibomb.html. Accessed March 24, 2007. An account of the work of international weapons inspectors in Iraq following the first Gulf War.

Obeidi, Mahdi, and Kurth Pitzer. *The Bomb in My Garden: The Secrets of Saddam's Nuclear Mastermind.* Toronto: John Wiley & Sons Canada, 2004. Insider's account of Iraq's nuclear weapons program.

Whitney, Craig R., ed. *The WMD Mirage: Iraq's Decade of Deception and America's False Premise for War.* New York: Public Affairs, 2005. A history in documents.

Israel

BBC News Middle East. "'Scrap nuclear arms' Israel urged." December 12, 2003. Available online. URL: news.bbc.co.uk/2/hi/middle_east/3312865.stm. Accessed March 24, 2007. Reports the statements of the head of the UN International Atomic Energy Agency, Mohamed ElBaradei, urging Israel to disarm.

Carter, Jimmy. *Palestine: Peace Not Apartheid.* New York: Simon & Schuster, 2006. Former U.S. president Jimmy Carter offers an assessment of the Palestinian-Israeli conflict highly critical of the Israeli occupation and suggests steps toward a two-state resolution.

Cohen, Avner. *Israel and the Bomb.* New York: Columbia University Press, 1999. Detailed account of Israel's nuclear record drawing on interviews and recently declassified American and Israeli government documents.

Cohen, Yoel. *The Whistleblower of Dimona: Israel, Vanunu, and the Bomb.* New York: Holmes & Meier, 2003. An examination of the events surrounding the *London Times* article that revealed the inside secrets of Israel's nuclear arsenal and its aftermath for Israel and for Mordechai Vanunu.

Evron, Yair. *Israel's Nuclear Dilemma.* Ithaca, N.Y.: Cornell University Press, 1994. An assessment of the impact of Israel's nuclear weapons program on the Middle East, especially as a potential cause of nuclear proliferation.

Hersh, Seymour M. *The Sampson Option: Israel Nuclear Arsenal and American Foreign Policy.* New York: Random House, 1991. History of Israel's nuclear arsenal with a special focus on espionage.

Katz, Yaakov, and Herb Keinon. "Israel Warns Russia on Iran Arms Sale." *Jerusalem Post,* January 17, 2007. Available online. URL: www.jpost.com/servlet/Satellite?pagename=JPost/JPArticle/ShowFull&cid=116746774535. Accessed March 24, 2007. Reports official Israeli reaction to Russia's sales of air defense system to Iran.

Shalom, Zakai. *Israel's Nuclear Option: Behind the Scenes Diplomacy Between Dimona and Washington*. Brighton, England: Sussex Academic Press, 2005. A blow-by-blow account of the U.S.-Israeli dialogue on Israel's nuclear project.

NUCLEAR PROLIFERATION IN NORTHEAST ASIA

Background

Difilippo, Anthony. *Japan's Nuclear Disarmament and the U.S. Security Umbrella*. New York: Palgrave, 2006. This book explores the tensions between Japan's stated goal of nuclear disarmament and its tacit acceptance of being protected by the U.S. nuclear umbrella.

French, Paul. *North Korea: The Paranoid Peninsula—A Modern History*. New York: Zed Books, 2005. A smoothly written, vivid, well-researched account of history and daily life in the secretive state of North Korea, with a cool and reasonable analysis of the regime.

Harrison, Selig S. *Japan's Nuclear Future: The Plutonium Debate and East Asian Security*. Washington, D.C.: Carnegie Endowment for International Peace, 1996. Investigates the pressures that may lead Japan to produce nuclear weapons.

Larkin, John. "Mysterious Reform." *Far Eastern Economic Review* 165, no. 31 (August 8, 2002). Article discussing the North Korean government's tentative attempts to reform North Korea's economy.

———. "North Korea: Why Refugees Flee." *Far Eastern Economic Review* 166, no. 9 (March 6, 2003). Reports on the continued problems of North Korea's economy.

Olsen, Edward A. *Korea, The Divided Nation*. Westport, Conn.: Preager Security International, 2005. A history of North and South Korea.

China

Cheng, Ta-Chen. "The Evolution of China's Strategic Nuclear Weapons." *Defense & Security Analysis* 22, no. 3: 241–260. Traces the history of China's strategic nuclear weapons program.

Frieman, Wendy. *China, Arms Control, and Nonproliferation*. London and New York: Routledge, 2004. Examination of China's participation in international arms control efforts.

Kan, Shirley A. "China and Proliferation of Weapons of Mass Destruction and Missiles: Policy Issues." Available online. URL: http://fpc.state.gov/documents/organization/81947.pdf. Accessed March 24, 2007. Discusses China's role in nuclear proliferation.

Kan, Shirley and Mark Holt. "U.S.-China Nuclear Cooperation Agreement." Updated January 31, 2007. Available online. URL: http://fpc.state.gov/documents/organization/81949.pdf. Accessed March 23, 2007. Report on civilian nuclear cooperation between China and the United States and concerns about its relationship to nuclear proliferation by China.

Lewis, Jeffrey. *The Minimum Means of Reprisal: China's Search for Security in the Nuclear Age.* Cambridge, Mass.: MIT Press, 2007. Examines patterns in China's defense investments, strategic force deployments, and arms control behavior.

North Korea

Chang, Gordon G. *Nuclear Showdown: North Korea Takes on the World.* New York: Random House, 2006. Sensationalistic and rather pessimistic account of the challenge posed by North Korea's quest for nuclear weapons.

Choe, Julia. "Problems of Enforcement: Iran, North Korea, and the NPT." *Harvard International Review* 28, no. 2: 38–41. Discusses weaknesses in the enforcement of NPT policies, as highlighted by the defiance of North Korea and Iran, and suggests the failures of the NPT in addressing noncompliance and withdrawal make it apparent that the treaty warrants revision

Cooper, Helene, and David E. Sanger. "U.S. Signals New Incentives for North Korea." *New York Times,* November 19, 2006: 1.8. In closed-door meetings, Bush and his negotiating team hint at rewards for North Korea if it agrees to give up nuclear weapons and technology.

Duffy, Michael. "What Does North Korea Want?" *Time* 165. no. 8: 22–25. After North Korea announced that it had nuclear weapons, the United States sought China's help in bringing North Korea back to the negotiating table.

Gallucci, Robert L. "Let's Make a Deal," *Time,* October 23, 2006. Discusses the political consequences of the North Korean nuclear test and suggests a negotiated solution. "We must persuade Seoul, Tokyo and Beijing to support even more painful sanctions if necessary in the future so that the North is properly motivated."

Hildreth, Steven A. "North Korean Ballistic Missile Threat to the United States." Updated October 18, 2006. Available online. URL: http://fpc.state.gov/documents/organization/76930.pdf. Accessed March 24, 2007. Report on the state of North Korea's ballistic missile program.

Hoge, Warren, and David E. Sanger. "Security Council Supports Sanctions on North Korea" *New York Times,* October 15, 2006: 1.1 Reports Security Council vote of sanctions against North Korea.

"In Dangerous Waters—The Cold War in Asia." *The Economist* 381, no. 8498: 30. North Korea's decision to test a nuclear weapon occurred at a time when relations between the great powers of northern Asia (China and Japan) are bad.

Kamiya, Matake. "A Disillusioned Japan Confronts North Korea." *Arms Control Today* 33, no. 3 (May 2003). Examines the Japanese government's increasing suspicion of North Korea.

Maas, Peter. "Radioactive Nationalism." *New York Times Magazine,* October 22, 2006. Discusses North Korea's nuclear ambitions in the light of North Korea's isolation and intensely nationalistic political culture.

Maxwell, David S. "Catastrophic Collapse of North Korea: Implications for the United States Military, a Monograph." Fort Leavenworth, Kans.: United States Army Command and General Staff College, 1996. Available online. URL: www.kimsoft.

com/korea/Maxwell.htm#II. Accessed March 27, 2007. Ever since the early 1990s, the severe economic problems of North Korea have made a collapse of its government seem possible. This paper examines the consequences of such a collapse for North Korea and the United States from a humanitarian perspective, from a military perspective, and from the perspectives of other nations in the region.

O'Hanlon, Michael, and Mike Mochizuki. *Crisis on the Korean Peninsula: How to Deal with a Nuclear North Korea.* New York: McGraw-Hill, 2003. A short book urging specific solutions to the problem posed by North Korea's nuclear program.

Perl, Raphael F. "Drug Trafficking and North Korea: Issues for U.S. Policy." Available online. URL: http://fpc.state.gov/documents/organization/82013.pdf. Updated January 25, 2007. Discusses North Korea's drug trafficking activities and ways of limiting it without hindering other U.S. foreign policy objectives such as limiting WMD and ballistic missile production and export.

Perry, William J. "Proliferation on the Peninsula: Five North Korean Nuclear Crises." *Annals of the American Academy of Political and Social Science* 607, no. 78–86. This article reviews the efforts the United States has undertaken through the years to keep North Korea from building a nuclear arsenal, arguing that the history of proliferation on the Korean peninsula is marked by five nuclear crises.

Powell, Bill. "North Korea Has Agreed to Shut Down Its Nuclear Program. Is He Really Ready to Disarm?" *Time* 169, no. 9: 32. Describes the negotiations that led to the February 2007 nuclear agreement with North Korea and its implications for the future.

———. "When Outlaws Get the Bomb." *Time* 168, no. 17: 32. Commentary on the implications of North Korea's first nuclear test.

Pritchard, Charles L. *Failed Diplomacy: The Tragic Story of How North Korea Got the Bomb.* Washington, D.C.: Brookings Institution Press, 2007. Offers an analysis of developments on the Korean peninsula that is highly critical of the Bush administration.

Smith, Chadwick I. "North Korea: The Case for Strategic Entanglement." *Orbis* 50, no. 2: 343–353. Suggests ways to move beyond the 2006 "stalemate" with North Korea.

Sokolski Henry D., and Andrew J. Grotto. "Is the North Korea Deal Worth Celebrating?" Available online. URL: http://www.npec-web.org/Frameset.asp?PageType=Single&PDFFile=20070316-CFR-DprkDebate&PDFFolder=Presentations. Online panel discussion sponsored by the Council on Foreign Relations. Two panelists discuss the merits and drawbacks of the 2007 deal whereby North Korea would freeze its nuclear weapons programs in exchange for various kinds of assistance from the United States.

Stout, David, and John O'Neil. "U.N. Council Presses North Korea to Drop Plans for Nuclear Test." *New York Times*, October 7, 2006: A.3. Reports UN reaction to North Korea's announcement that it had tested a nuclear weapon.

"Trust Me? Dealing with North Korea." *The Economist* 382, no. 8516: 14. Opinion article critical of the 2007 U.S. nuclear agreement with North Korea, which "rewards an appalling dicator's serial nuclear effrontery in ways that will only encourage Iran's nuclear charged mullahs and other bomb-seekers in their ambitions."

U.S. Department of State. "North Korea—Denuclearization Action Plan: Statement by President Bush on Six Party Talks." Available online. URL: www.state.gov/r/pa/prs/ps/2007/february/80479.htm. Accessed March 23, 2007. The official statement released by the Bush administration at the conclusion of the Six-Party Talks on North Korea's nuclear program.

Chronology

1941

- ***December 6:*** The Manhattan Project to build the atomic bomb begins.
- ***December 7:*** The Japanese bomb Pearl Harbor, beginning U.S. entry as combatant in World War II.

1945

- ***July 16:*** The United States explodes the first atomic bomb in Trinity, New Mexico.
- ***March 25:*** In a letter to Franklin Roosevelt, physicist Leo Szilard warns that dropping the atom bomb on Japan would "precipitate a race in the production of these devices between the United States and Russia and . . . our initial advantage may be lost very quickly in such a race."
- ***August 6:*** Bomb dropped on Hiroshima.
- ***August 9:*** Bomb dropped on Nagasaki.
- ***August 15:*** Japanese emperor Hirohito announces Japan's surrender in a radio broadcast, giving among other reasons the fact that "the enemy has begun to employ a new and most cruel bomb, the power of which to damage is indeed incalculable, taking the toll of many innocent lives."
- ***November 23:*** In a secret agreement, the Soviet Union secures exclusive rights to all uranium mined in Czechoslovakia.

1946

- ***January 24:*** The UN General Assembly establishes an Atomic Energy Commission and calls for the "elimination" of "atomic weapons and all other major weapons for the purpose of mass destruction."
- ***June 14:*** Bernard Baruch presents Baruch Plan to the UN Atomic Energy Commission. The Soviets and the United States will not be able to agree on the details of this plan.

- ***July 1:*** The United States begins nuclear weapons testing in the Pacific.
- ***August 1:*** Congress establishes the U.S. Atomic Energy Commission (AEC).

1947

- ***August:*** The British leave India, which becomes two large countries, India and Pakistan.
- ***October:*** The U.S. Joint Chiefs of Staff decides that 150 "Nagasaki type" atomic bombs would be sufficient to defeat the USSR.
- India and Pakistan go to war over Kashmir.

1948

- ***March 13:*** Klaus Fuchs, a British physicist, gives the design for the construction of the hydrogen bomb to his Soviet contact.
- ***June 14:*** On the date of the expiration of the British mandate in Palestine, the state of Israel is declared. The new state is recognized that night by the United States and three days later by the Soviet Union.

1949

- ***January 1:*** India and Pakistan agree to a cease-fire arranged by the UN.
- ***April 4:*** Establishment of North Atlantic Treaty Organization (NATO), an alliance of the United States with Western European nations intended to protect against invasion from the Soviet bloc.
- ***August 29:*** The Soviet Union detonates its first atomic bomb.

1950

- ***June 25:*** North Korea invades South Korea. With authorization from the UN, the United States will intervene to push back the North Koreans.
- ***December 9:*** General Douglas MacArthur requests authority to use atomic bombs during the Korean War.

1951

- ***November 1:*** The United States detonates the first hydrogen bomb at Enewetak Atoll in the Marshall Islands.

1953

- ***April 19:*** The government of Iranian prime minister Mohammed Mossadegh is overthrown in a coup managed by agents of the United States.
- ***August 12:*** The Soviet Union tests its first hydrogen bomb.
- ***December 8:*** President Dwight D. Eisenhower, in a UN address, proposes the Atoms for Peace program.

Chronology

1954

- ***September 12:*** The U.S. Joint Chiefs of Staff recommend using atomic bombs on communist China to assist Taiwan in dispute over Quemoy and Matsu Islands.

1955

- ***May 14:*** Warsaw Pact established, a military alliance of the USSR and its Eastern European satellite states; a counter to NATO.

1956

- ***March:*** At the UN, the United States opposes nuclear disarmament on the grounds that nuclear weapons are a "powerful deterrent to war."

1957

- ***July 29:*** The UN establishes the International Atomic Energy Agency (IAEA).

1959

- ***October 31:*** The United States deploys the first operational intercontinental ballistic missile (ICBM).
- ***November 13:*** Irish foreign minister Frank Aiken offers to the UN General Assembly a proposal to limit the spread of nuclear weapons. Subsequent proposals by Aiken will eventually be refashioned into the Nuclear Non-proliferation Treaty (NPT).
- ***December 1:*** The first nuclear-free zone is established with the Antarctic Treaty, prohibiting "any nuclear explosion in Antarctica."

1960

- ***February 13:*** France explodes its first atomic bomb in the Sahara.
- ***October 5:*** Due to a radar malfunction, the central war room of NORAD receives a warning that a massive missile attack has been launched against North America.
- ***December:*** A war plan by the U.S. Joint Strategic Target Planning staff calls for the launch of 3,000 nuclear weapons to attack 1,000 separate targets in the first few hours of a war with the communist bloc.

1961

- ***January 17:*** In his farewell address, President Dwight D. Eisenhower tells the nation to beware of the "military industrial complex."

NUCLEAR NONPROLIFERATION

1962

- ***October 16–29:*** The Cuban missile crisis, begun when U.S. planes discover Soviet missiles in Cuba, brings the United States and the Soviet Union to the brink of nuclear war.

1963

- ***April 11:*** Pope John XXIII calls for an end to the nuclear arms race.
- ***August 5:*** The United States and the Soviets sign the Partial Test Ban Treaty, banning atmospheric testing of nuclear weapons.

1964

- ***October 16:*** China explodes its first atomic bomb.

1965

- ***August:*** War breaks out between India and Pakistan over Kashmir.

1966

- ***January:*** The governments of India and Pakistan agree to a cease-fire.
- ***October 27:*** China fires its first guided missile capable of carrying a nuclear warhead.

1967

- ***January 27:*** A treaty banning nuclear weapons in outer space is signed in Washington, Moscow, and London.
- ***February 14:*** The Treaty of Tlateloco establishes Latin America as a nuclear free zone.
- ***June 5–10:*** Six-Day War fought mainly between Israel and Egypt, Syria, and Jordan.
- ***June 17:*** China conducts its first thermonuclear weapon test.

1968

- Israel begins producing nuclear weapons.
- ***July 1:*** The Nuclear Non-proliferation Treaty (NPT) is signed in Washington, Moscow, and London.
- ***August 24:*** France tests its first hydrogen bomb.

1969

- ***November 17:*** The first Strategic Arms Limitations Talks (SALT I) between the United States and the Soviet Union begin in Helsinki, Finland.

Chronology

1970

- ***August 19:*** The United States deploys the first missile with multiple independently targetable reentry vehicles (MIRVs).

1971

- ***February 11:*** The United States, USSR, and United Kingdom sign the Seabed Treaty, prohibiting testing of nuclear weapons in the oceans and the soil under the oceans.
- ***December:*** India invades East Pakistan in support of an East Pakistani independence movement. The Pakistani army surrenders at Dhaka, and its army of more than 90,000 become Indian prisoners of war.
- ***December 6:*** East Pakistan becomes the independent country of Bangladesh.

1972

- ***May 26:*** President Richard Nixon and Soviet General Secretary Leonid Brezhnev sign the Anti-ballistic Missile (ABM) Treaty, the SALT Accord, and the Interim Agreement on Offensive Arms.

1973

- ***June 22:*** Responding to requests by Australia and New Zealand, the International Court of Justice calls on France to avoid nuclear tests that cause fallout in the South Pacific.
- ***October 6:*** Israel goes on nuclear alert during the Yom Kippur War. Brezhnev threatens to airlift Soviet forces in to aid the Egyptian army. President Richard Nixon brings the United States to a worldwide nuclear alert. A cease-fire ends the crisis.

1974

- ***May 18:*** India conducts what it calls a "peaceful nuclear explosion."

1975

- First meeting of the Nuclear Suppliers Group, an association of nuclear supplier nations who agree to restrict sales of nuclear technology to nations that might use it to make nuclear weapons.
- ***June 27:*** Brazil signs agreement with West Germany to obtain nuclear technology.

1977

- South Africa tests a nuclear explosive device.

- ***September 17:*** Israeli prime minister Menachem Begin and Egyptian president Anwar el-Sadat sign the Camp David accords, a peace agreement between Israel and Egypt.

1978

- ***July 7:*** The United States announces that it has tested a "neutron bomb." With only one-tenth of the blast of a normal hydrogen bomb, the neutron bomb is intended to kill troops with radiation while limiting damage to property and civilians far from the blast.

1979

- ***January 16:*** The shah of Iran leaves the country, an act that precipitates the Iranian revolution.
- ***February 1:*** Ayatollah Khomeini returns to Iran. Processes begin that will lead to the execution of hundreds of supporters of the shah.
- ***April 1:*** After a landslide victory in a national referendum in which only one choice was offered (Islamic republic: yes or no), Ayatollah Khomeini declares an Islamic republic whose new constitution reflects his idea of Islamic government.
- ***June 18:*** U.S. president Jimmy Carter and Soviet general secetary Leonid Brezhnev sign the Second Arms Limitation Treaty (SALT II) in Vienna, Austria. The treaty establishes a ceiling of 2,400 strategic offensive weapons and limits multiple independently targeted reentry vehicles (MIRV) to 1,320 launchers.
- ***November 4:*** Iranian Islamic students storm the U.S. embassy, taking 66 people, the majority Americans, as hostages; 14 will be released before the end of November.
- ***December 25:*** The Soviet Union deploys troops to Afghanistan to prop up a pro-Soviet government. This begins a long, unpopular war in which Soviet troops are pitted against Afghan insurgents; it will last until 1987.

1980

- ***September 22:*** Iraq invades Iran, beginning a war that will continue for eight years.
- ***December 27:*** President Jimmy Carter withdraws the SALT II Treaty from consideration by the U.S. Senate as a result of the Soviet invasion of Afghanistan.

1981

- ***January 20:*** Iran releases the hostages in the U.S. embassy after long negotiations as part of an agreement in which the United States concedes to transfer money as well as export military equipment to Iran.

- ***June 7:*** An Israeli F-16 fighter destroys Iraq's Osirak nuclear reactor to prevent Iraq from developing nuclear weapons.

1982

- A 1982 secret national security directive outlines a new U.S. military plan—to win a "protracted nuclear war."
- ***June 20:*** U.S. president Ronald Reagan removes the United States from the ongoing Comprehensive Test Ban Treaty talks in Geneva.

1983

- ***March 23:*** President Reagan calls on the scientific community to devise a space-based defense system to protect the United States from intercontinental ballistic missiles. Critics dub his proposal "Star Wars."
- ***November:*** NATO conducts a military exercise during which it simulates the procedures for the release of nuclear weapons. The Soviets, informed by their agents of the approaching exercise, take it for the real thing and consider striking first. They decide to wait to see if the missiles are actually launched.

1984

- ***March 24:*** Iraqi warplanes attack Iran's Bushehr nuclear power complex.

1986

- ***January 15:*** Soviet president Mikhail Gorbachev calls for the abolition of nuclear weapons by the year 2000.
- ***April 16:*** The Missile Technology Control Regime.
- ***October 11–12:*** President Ronald Reagan and President Mikhail Gorbachev meet at Reykjavik, Iceland, and discuss the possibility of abolishing nuclear weapons. The talks break down when Reagan refuses to abandon plans to develop the Strategic Defense Initiative.

1987

- ***July 20:*** The Soviet Union announces the withdrawal of its troops from Afghanistan.
- ***December 8:*** The Soviet Union and the United States sign the Intermediate Range Nuclear Forces (INF) Treaty in Washington. The treaty eliminates all land-based missiles held by the two states with ranges between 300 and 3,400 miles.

1988

- ***December 31:*** Pakistan's prime minister Benazir Bhutto and Indian prime minister Rajiv Gandhi sign an agreement not to attack each other's nuclear installations.

1989

- ***November 9:*** The Berlin Wall falls; East Germany opens its borders with West Germany.

1990

- ***August 2:*** Iraq invades Kuwait and is condemned by UN Security Council Resolution 660, calling for Iraq's full withdrawal from Kuwait.
- ***November 29:*** UN Security Council Resolution 678 authorizes the states cooperating with Kuwait to use "all necessary means" to uphold UNSC Resolution 660.

1991

- ***January 16–17:*** "Operation Desert Storm," the invasion of Iraq by U.S.-led coalition forces, begins with the aerial bombing of Iraq.
- ***January 18:*** The first Gulf war, code-named "Operation Desert Storm," begins.
- ***April 3:*** Soon after Iraq is pushed out of Kuwait, the UN Security Council passes Resolution 687, which states that Iraq must destroy its stockpile of weapons of mass destruction and its ability to produce them and undertake not to produce WMD in the future. International inspection teams from the UN and the International Atomic Energy Agency are assigned to document and destroy Iraq's WMD.
- ***April 6:*** Iraq agrees to comply with UN Security Council Resolution 687.
- ***June 3:*** France announces that it will sign the Nuclear Non-prolfieration Treaty as a nuclear weapons state.
- ***July 10:*** South Africa agrees to sign the Nuclear Non-proliferation Treaty as a nonnuclear weapons state. The South African government says it has made six nuclear weapons and has dismantled them all.
- ***October 11:*** Due to Iraqi efforts to thwart the actions of international inspection teams, the UN Security Council passes Resolution 715, stating that Iraq must "accept unconditionally the inspectors and all other personnel designated by the Special Commission."
- ***November 27:*** As the Soviet Union breaks up, the U.S. Congress passes the Soviet Nuclear Threat Reduction Act of 1991 (also called Nunn-Lugar after

the two senators who sponsored the bill). The act will fund a program to secure the nuclear materials of the former Soviet republics.

- ***December 25:*** Mikhail Gorbachev resigns as president of the USSR, declaring the office extinct and ceding all powers still vested in it to the president of Russia, Boris Yeltsin.
- ***December 26:*** The Supreme Soviet recognizes the extinction of the Soviet Union and dissolves itself. Over the course of the next several days, all official Soviet institutions cease operations as individual republics assume the roles of the central government.

1992

- ***March 9:*** China joins the Nuclear Non-proliferation Treaty as a nuclear weapons state.
- ***April 3:*** The 27 members of the Nuclear Suppliers Group agree on controls for dual-use nuclear-related equipment and technology.

1993

- ***January 3:*** U.S. president George Bush and Russian president Boris Yeltsin sign the Strategic Arms Reduction Treaty (START II), which reduces their nations' arsenals of long-range nuclear weapons to 3,000 to 35,000 and eliminates all MIRVed land-based missiles over the next 10 years.
- ***February 1–8:*** North Korea bars IAEA inspectors access to several facilities that are suspected to be part of the North Korean nuclear program.
- ***March 12:*** North Korea announces that it is withdrawing from the Nuclear Non-proliferation Treaty (NPT).

1994

- ***January 14:*** U.S. president Bill Clinton and Russian president Boris Yeltsin announce that by the end of May no country will be targeted by the missiles of the United States or Russia.
- ***August 8:*** Hussein Kamel, the former director of Iraq's WMD programs, defects to Jordan. As a result, Saddam Hussein's government admits to a more advanced biological weapons program than it had previously disclosed. Iraq also hands over documents related to its nuclear weapons program. The belated admission shows that Iraq has continued its attempts to deceive the international inspectors.
- ***October 21:*** North Korea and the United States sign the "Agreed Framework," whereby North Korea pledges to freeze and eventually dismantle its nuclear weapons program in exchange for international aid to build two power-producing nuclear reactors.

1996

- ***April 11:*** Representatives of 43 African nations sign the Treaty of Pelindaba in Cairo, Egypt, establishing an African Nuclear Weapons Free Zone and pledging not to build, test, or stockpile nuclear weapons.
- ***September 24:*** China, France, the United Kingdom, Russia, and the United States all sign the Comprehensive Test Ban Treaty. India says it will not sign the treaty until the five declared nuclear weapons states commit themselves to the elimination of their nuclear weapons.

1997

- ***May 15:*** The International Atomic Energy Agency approves a suggested "additional protocol" to the Nuclear Non-proliferation Treaty, giving IAEA inspectors more authority to investigate nuclear programs in member states. The program was developed in response to the realization that Iraq was able to move covertly toward the construction of a nuclear weapon in the 1980s despite the NPT's safeguards. By July 14, 2006, 103 NPT parties had signed additional protocols, and 76 of them were in force.
- ***November:*** President Clinton signs Presidential Decision Directive 60 (PDD 60) on U.S. nuclear warfare policy. Under this directive, the military will no longer prepare to win a protracted nuclear war. However, options for nuclear strikes against Russia are retained.

1998

- UNSCOM (United Nations Special Commission) and IAEA (International Atomic Energy Agency) weapons inspectors leave Iraq due to a lack of cooperation by Saddam Hussein's government.
- ***April 6:*** Pakistan announces that it has successfully test fired a medium-range, 1,000-mile surface-to-surface missile, which is believed to be capable of carrying a nuclear warhead.
- ***May 11:*** India conducts three underground nuclear tests. One of the tests is a thermonuclear weapon.
- ***May 13:*** India conducts two more nuclear tests.
- ***May 28:*** Pakistan conducts five nuclear tests. Pakistan's prime minister, Nawaz Sharif, says, "Today we have settled the score with India."
- ***August 31:*** North Korea fires a multistage missile over Japan and into the Pacific Ocean, proving it can strike into any part of Japan's territory.
- ***December 16–19:*** Desert Fox: The United States and Britain conduct four days of intense bombing raids on 100 industrial and military factories thought to be involved in Iraq's weapons programs.

Chronology

1999

- ***April 11:*** India successfully test fires an intermediate-range ballistic missile (IRBM), the *Agni II* ("fire"), from a rail platform on Wheeler Island in the Bay of Bengal. The *Agni II* is believed to be the mainstay of India's nuclear delivery system.
- ***April 14:*** Pakistan launches its *Ghauri II* medium-range ballistic missile (MRBM). The name *Ghauri* refers to a Muslim historical figure who defeated a Hindu ruler in the 12th century.
- ***April 23:*** The North Atlantic Treaty Organization (NATO) releases the Strategic Concept, which outlines its nuclear weapons policy. Despite the end of the cold war, NATO announces its continued reliance on nuclear weapons. Nuclear weapons will be deployed in Europe indefinitely.
- ***April 29:*** Russia signs a decree providing for future development and deployment of tactical nuclear weapons.
- ***May 25–28:*** Former defense secretary William Perry visits North Korea and delivers a U.S. disarmament proposal.
- ***August 2:*** China test fires its *Dongfeng-31* (DF-31) intercontinental ballistic missile (ICBM) within Chinese territory.
- ***September 13:*** North Korea pledges to freeze long-range missile tests.
- ***September 17:*** President Bill Clinton eases economic sanctions against North Korea.
- ***October 18:*** The U.S. Senate rejects the Comprehensive Test Ban Treaty (CTBT).

2000

- ***January 17:*** Acting Russian president Vladimir Putin signs into law a new national security strategy that lowers the threshold on first use of nuclear weapons.
- ***April 21:*** The Duma, Russia's parliament, ratifies the Comprehensive Test Ban Treaty (CTBT).
- ***July:*** North Korea threatens to restart its nuclear program if Washington does not compensate for the loss of electricity caused by delays in building nuclear power plants.

2001

- ***June:*** North Korea warns it will reconsider its moratorium on missile tests if the Bush administration does not resume contacts aimed at normalizing relations.

- ***June:*** The U.S. State Department reports North Korea is going ahead with development of its long-range missile. A Bush administration official says North Korea conducts an engine test of the *Taepodong-1* missile.
- ***December:*** President Bush warns Iraq and North Korea that they will be "held accountable" if they develop weapons of mass destruction "that will be used to terrorize nations."

2002

- ***January 29:*** Bush labels North Korea, Iran, and Iraq an "axis of evil" in his State of the Union address. "By seeking weapons of mass destruction, these regimes pose a grave and growing danger," he says.
- ***September:*** Photographs taken from commercial satellites show major new nuclear sites in Iran, facilities Iran had not reported to the IAEA and that were obviously constructed in a way to conceal their size and importance.
- ***November:*** The UN Security Council passes Resolution 1441, its purpose to disarm Iraq of its weapons of mass destruction.

2003

- ***February 5:*** U.S. secretary of state Colin Powell addresses the UN Security Council and presents evidence that Iraq is seeking to manufacture nuclear weapons.
- ***March 19:*** A U.S.-led coalition invades Iraq.

2004

- ***January 22:*** International Atomic Energy Agency (IAEA) director general Mohammed ElBaradei urges Iran to cooperate with inspections of its nuclear sites in order to prove that its facilities are not weapons related.
- ***January 28:*** David Kay, leader of the Iraq Survey Group charged with finding weapons of mass destruction in Iraq after the invasion, reports to the Senate Armed Services Committee. "We were almost all wrong," says Kay—Iraq did not have a viable weapons program at the time of the invasion.
- ***February 4:*** Abdul Qadeer Khan, the "father" of Pakistan's nuclear weapons program, signs a confession admitting that he provided Iran, North Korea, and Libya with the designs and technology to produce the fuel for nuclear weapons during the last 15 years.

2005

- ***March 16:*** The White House releases its National Security Strategy, which reaffirms President Bush's doctrine of preemptive war.

Chronology

2006

- ***January:*** Iran rejects a Russian offer to produce nuclear fuel in its plants for Iran.
- ***February 13:*** Iran says it has "resumed" its uranium enrichment.
- ***February 6:*** The International Atomic Energy Agency, citing Iran's obstructionist tactics and history of concealment, refers the case to the UN Security Council.
- ***July 31:*** The UN Security Council passes Resolution 1696, calling on Iran to suspend uranium enrichment by August 31, 2006, or face sanctions.
- ***December 23:*** The UN Security Council passes Resolution 1737, imposing sanctions on Iran.

2007

- ***February 13:*** U.S. secretary of state Condoleezza Rice announces that North Korea has agreed to take steps to dismantle its nuclear program in return for an aid package from the United States.
- ***March 24:*** The UN Security Council passes Resolution 1747, imposing additional sanctions on Iran.

Glossary

ABM Treaty (Anti-ballistic Missile Treaty) A 1972 U.S.-Russian treaty sharply limiting research and deployment of antiballistic MISSILES—defensive missiles whose purpose would be to disable or destroy incoming offensive nuclear-armed ballistic missiles.

arsenal A stock of weapons.

artillery shells MISSILES of caliber larger than 15 mm that are shot from big guns such as cannon, howitzers, and missile launchers. During the COLD WAR, the United States and the USSR deployed "tactical," or "battlefield," nuclear weapons in the form of artillery shells in Europe. In 1991, the United States unilaterally withdrew its nuclear artillery shells from service; the Soviets withdrew theirs the following year.

atmospheric testing Testing of nuclear weapons above ground.

atomic bomb An explosive weapon of great destructive power derived from the rapid release of energy in the fission of heavy atomic nuclei such as the isotope uranium 235 or plutonium.

Atoms for Peace An early NUCLEAR NONPROLIFERATION program proposed to the UN by U.S. president Dwight D. Eisenhower in the 1950s. Under Atoms for Peace, nuclear weapons states would share fissile material and nuclear energy technology with other countries if the countries receiving the assistance would accept curbs on their development of nuclear weapons technology. Unfortunately, the details of Atoms for Peace, as ultimately agreed on at the UN, made it ineffective as a tool of nuclear nonproliferation.

authoritarian A term referring to a government or country characterized by favoring absolute obedience to authority, not individual freedom. Authoritarian states are sometimes contrasted with "totalitarian states." Both sharply limit political freedom and dissent, but only totalitarian regimes attempt to regulate every aspect of life or practice "thought control."

ballistic missile A rocket that assumes a free-falling trajectory after an internally guided, self-powered ascent.

Ballistic Missile Early Warning System An electronic system to detect and provide early warning of attack by enemy INTERCONTINENTAL BALLISTIC MISSILES.

Bharatiya Janata Party (BJP) Ultranationalist Indian party.

bilateral Relating to agreements reached between two countries.

biological weapons Weapons that use disease-producing microorganisms or toxic biological products (such as botulism toxin, produced by bacteria) to cause death or injury to humans, animals, or plants.

Central Intelligence Agency (CIA) Agency of the U.S. government responsible for collecting and coordinating intelligence and counterintelligence activities abroad in the national interest.

chemical weapons Poisons, contaminants, and irritants used to cause death or injury in warfare. Horror at the casualties caused by the use of agents such as chlorine gas, hydrogen cyanide, and nerve gas in World War I led to the 1925 Geneva Protocol, which made it criminal under international law to use chemical weapons.

cold war A state of political tension and military rivalry between nations that stops short of full-scale war, especially the international rivalry that existed between the United States and the Soviet Union between 1945 and 1991.

Comprehensive Test Ban Treaty A treaty banning all tests of nuclear weapons.

conventional warfare Warfare that does not employ weapons of mass destruction, that is, that does not make use of nuclear, chemical, or biological weapons.

counterproliferation Actions taken to defeat the threat and/or use of weapons of mass destruction against the United States, its military forces, and its allies. Logically, then, counterproliferation includes nonproliferation—limiting the spread of nuclear weapons to states hostile to the United States—but it also includes actions that actually increase nuclear proliferation, such as giving nuclear weapons to U.S. allies.

CTBT *See* COMPREHENSIVE TEST BAN TREATY.

deploy To base a weapons system in the field, ready for use in combat.

Desert Fox The official name given to the December 1998 operation in which the United States and Britain bombed sites in Iraq suspected of being involved in weapons production.

deterrence *See* NUCLEAR DETERRENCE.

dictatorship A government in which the ruler is unconstrained by law.

Glossary

dirty bomb A bomb that uses high explosives to disperse toxic nuclear material, causing death, injury, and long-term contamination to people and property.

DMZ Demilitarized Zone, usually referring to neutral ground on the border between North Korea and South Korea—actually highly militarized, the most heavily armed border in the world.

enriched uranium Uranium containing a high concentration of U-235, the isotope needed for nuclear fission reactions.

escalation An increase, enlargement, or intensification; in warfare, an enlargement of the scope of hostilities or in the destructiveness of the weapons used by the parties to the war.

fireball A luminous, intensely hot spherical cloud of dust, gas, and vapor caused by a nuclear explosion.

first strike capability *See* NUCLEAR FIRST STRIKE CAPABILITY.

fissile material A substance capable of sustaining a chain reaction of NUCLEAR FISSION; with appropriate technology, the material used as the core of a nuclear fission bomb may be refined from fissile materials.

greenhouse gases Any of the atmospheric gases that contribute to the greenhouse effect, whereby solar radiation is trapped in the Earth's atmosphere; an increase in greenhouse gases may lead to average higher global temperatures.

HE *See* HIGH EXPLOSIVES.

HEU *See* HIGHLY ENRICHED URANIUM.

high explosives (HE) A material such as TNT that combusts instantaneously, causing a powerful and violent explosion.

highly enriched uranium (HEU) Uranium that has been processed until it contains 20 percent or more of the fissile isotope uranium-235. Weapons-grade HEU is generally enriched to 93 percent or more U-235.

Hiroshima A Japanese city on the coast of the Seto Inland Sea. On August 6, 1945, the first nuclear weapon used in war was dropped on Hiroshima, killing an estimated 80,000 people and destroying 68 percent of the city's buildings.

horizontal nuclear proliferation The spread of nuclear weapons and nuclear weapons technology to countries that do not already have them.

hydrogen bomb A bomb in which a fission reaction like that in an atomic bomb is used to trigger a far more potent explosion in which the nuclei of the hydrogen isotopes tritium or deuterium are fused; hydrogen bombs are the most powerful explosive devices ever invented. They can be made more powerful by adding to the amount of hydrogen isotopes they contain.

IAEA *See* INTERNATIONAL ATOMIC ENERGY AGENCY.

ICBM *See* INTERCONTINENTAL BALLISTIC MISSILE.

intercontinental ballistic missile A long-range ballistic missile that can travel from one continent to another.

International Atomic Energy Agency (IAEA) The UN agency concerned with nuclear energy. It was established on July 29, 1957, its mission to promote the peaceful use of nuclear energy while slowing the spread of nuclear weapons technology. The IAEA pursues its mission through three main functions: inspections of existing nuclear facilities to ensure peaceful use, information and standards to ensure the stability of nuclear facilities, and as a clearinghouse of information on the peaceful applications of nuclear technology.

Islamic fundamentalism An ideology among adherents of Islam that calls for a return to a supposed state of religious purity when all laws were promulgated and all governments run in accordance with the dictates of Islam. People called Islamic fundamentalists represent a wide range of views, belong to different sects of Islam, and differ in the methods they advocate for furthering their cause.

Joint Chiefs of Staff The executive body that advises the president of the United States on military questions; it is composed of the chiefs of the army, the navy, and the air force and the commandant of the marines.

KGB The Committee for State Security, the Soviet Union's main security, secret police, and intelligence agency from 1954 to 1991.

kiloton A measure used to express the explosive force of nuclear weapons, especially the earlier, less powerful examples; equals 1,000 tons of TNT.

limited nuclear war War in which nuclear weapons are used but that does not escalate to an uncontrolled nuclear exchange.

megaton A measure commonly used to express the explosive force of nuclear weapons; equals 1,000,000 tons of TNT.

military industrial complex A group of common interests formed by the mutual needs of a permanent military establishment and a large arms industry. The phrase was given currency by President Dwight D. Eisenhower in his farewell speech three days before the end of his presidency.

MIRVs (Multiple Independently Targeted Reentry Vehicles) Ballistic missiles having multiple, independently targeted warheads, so that a single booster rocket can ultimately send several nuclear bombs to several targets.

missile A rocket carrying a warhead or conventional or nuclear explosives; may be ballistic or directed by remote control.

missile defense technology Technology intended to disable or destroy enemy ballistic missiles before they reach their targets.

Missile Technology Control Regime (MTCR) Similar to the Nuclear Suppliers Group, the MTCR is an organization of technologically advanced states whose members agree to restrict their sales of missile technology.

mobilization The act of assembling or putting into readiness for a war or other emergency.

MTCR *See* MISSILE TECHNOLOGY CONTROL REGIME.

multilateral Relating to action taken in consultation or cooperation among three or more countries, as in action taken in cooperation with allies or through the UN.

Nagasaki A Japanese harbor city founded before 1500 that became a center of the shipbuilding industry during World War II. On August 9, 1945, the second atomic bomb used in warfare was dropped on Nagasaki. According to statistics presented at the Nagasaki Peace Park, the bomb killed 73,884, injured 74,909, and caused disease in 120,820 people.

National Security Council A group of advisers to the U.S. president on national security and foreign policy, usually including the president, vice president, several cabinet members, the Joint Chiefs of Staff, and the director of national intelligence. Many other countries have national security councils.

National Security Decision Directive (NSDD) An executive order on a subject related to national security issued by the president of the United States with the advice and consent of the NATIONAL SECURITY COUNCIL. Many NSDDs are classified, that is, secret.

NATO (North Atlantic Treaty Organization) An international COLD WAR alliance of Western European and North American countries established in April 1949 to counter the threat of aggression by the Soviet Union.

NGOs (nongovernmental organizations) Especially humanitarian organizations such as the Red Cross that are international in scope and not linked to one nation or its foreign policy. NGOs hope to provide assistance to people who need it with no strings attached. They attempt to avoid local and international political complications, not always with complete success.

no first use policy A pledge not to be the first to introduce nuclear weapons into a conflict, but only to use them in response to a nuclear attack.

NSG *See* NUCLEAR SUPPLIERS GROUP.

nuclear deterrence The deployment of nuclear weapons as a means of preventing enemy attack; nuclear deterrence depends on the enemy's belief that you have a credible "second strike" capability—that the defender's ability to inflict unacceptable damage cannot be destroyed by a sneak attack.

nuclear first strike capability The ability to destroy an enemy's fighting ability with a surprise nuclear attack.

nuclear fission A reaction in which neutrons collide with the nuclei of uranium-235 or plutonium atoms, causing them to become unstable and "split" into smaller elements, accompanied by a release of energy. This reaction is the source of the energy in nuclear power generators and atomic bombs.

nuclear fusion A process by which atomic nuclei fuse together to form a heavier nucleus; when the elements to be fused are light elements, as are the hydrogen isotopes fused in the reactions used in the hydrogen bomb, the results include a net release of energy.

nuclear nonproliferation The effort to combat the spread of nuclear weapons and nuclear weapons technology, usually linked to the effort to combat the spread of ballistic missile technology.

Nuclear Non-proliferation Treaty (NPT) An international treaty that seeks to limit the possession of nuclear weapons to the five states that already possessed them in 1968. The NPT struck a bargain with its nonnuclear-weapons-state signatories: They would forgo the acquisition or development of nuclear weapons, and in exchange they would receive assistance with the development of nuclear energy for peaceful purposes. Further, the nuclear weapons states would take steps toward disarmament.

nuclear proliferation The spread of nuclear weapons and nuclear weapons technology.

nuclear reactor A device in which nuclear chain reactions are initiated, controlled, and sustained at a steady rate.

nuclear second strike capability The ability to survive a surprise nuclear attack and to reply with a nuclear attack that will inflict unacceptable damage on the enemy.

Nuclear Suppliers Group (NSG) An organization of technologically advanced states created to hinder nuclear proliferation; its members agree to restrict their sales of nuclear technology to states that might use it to develop nuclear weapons capability.

nuclear weapons Weapons deriving their destructive force from the release of nuclear energy by means either of NUCLEAR FISSION (in atom bombs) or NUCLEAR FUSION (in hydrogen or thermonuclear bombs).

nuclear weapons state A state in possession of nuclear weapons; NUCLEAR NON-PROLIFERATION TREATY defines as those states detonating a nuclear explosive device before January 1967.

nuclear winter A worldwide darkening and cooling of the atmosphere leading to the extinction of many species believed by some to be a probable outcome of large-scale nuclear war.

Operation Enduring Freedom Official name of the U.S. military project to invade Afghanistan and topple the Taliban regime, accomplished in 2002.

Glossary

Operation Iraqi Freedom Official name given to the U.S. military project to invade Iraq and topple the regime of Saddam Hussein, accomplished in 2003.

Pelindaba Treaty A treaty signed in 1996 creating a nuclear weapon–free zone in Africa.

preemptive war War begun in expectation of an imminent attack by the enemy, as might be indicated in a time of crisis by a mobilization of an army or navy on one's borders.

preventive war War to disable an enemy who is expected to pose an eventual threat.

al-Qaeda An international organization of loosely affiliated groups that carry out attacks and bombings in an attempt to disrupt the economies and influence the policies of nations in the Middle East and the West in order to advance the cause of ISLAMIC FUNDAMENTALISM.

radiation A stream of particles or electromagnetic waves emitted by the atoms and molecules of a radioactive substance as a result of nuclear decay.

rogue state A term used primarily by American diplomats and politicians to describe states that support terrorism, are indifferent to international opinion, and/or seek to acquire nuclear weapons against the wishes of the United States. Critics of the term consider it unhelpful; during its last year in office the Clinton administration consciously dropped its use, suggesting the substitute "nation of concern."

Robust Nuclear Earth Penetrator A proposed low-yield, tactical, battlefield nuclear weapon that would be used to destroy hardened targets such as underground bunkers.

Russian Federation A federation in northeastern Europe and northern Asia, formerly the heart of the SOVIET UNION.

SAC *See* STRATEGIC AIR COMMAND.

sanction A penalty.

satellite state A country that is dependent on a more powerful country and that in return supports its patron's international policies; often used to describe the relationship between the states of Eastern Europe and the SOVIET UNION during the cold war.

second strike capability *See* NUCLEAR SECOND STRIKE CAPABILITY.

Security Council Resolution A decision of the UN Security Council binding upon all members of the UN.

silo Storage facility; in farming, a storehouse for grain; for nuclear weapons, a storehouse for ballistic missiles, often missiles ready to launch on short notice.

SLBM Submarine-launched ballistic missile.

SORT (Strategic Offensive Reduction Treaty) An arms agreement between the United States and the Russian Federation signed in 2002 by U.S. president George Bush and Russian president Vladimir Putin. Under the terms of the treaty, the United States and Russia will reduce their deployed offensive nuclear forces to 1,700 to 2,200 strategic warheads each by December 31, 2012.

Soviet Union The Union of Soviet Socialist Republics (USSR), in its time the largest country, in terms of area, on Earth, stretching from the Baltic and Black Seas to the Pacific Ocean. Established in 1922 by the union of Russia and various other Soviet republics, the USSR was a totalitarian society dedicated to communism, interpreted as state control of the economy and of many other aspects of public and private life. Its territory was the scene of the greatest battles of World War II, from which it emerged as a superpower, with its armed forces in control of Eastern Europe. It was officially dissolved on December 25, 1991, into 15 separate states: the Russian Federation, Armenia, Azerbaijan, Belarus, Estonia, the Republic of Georgia, Kazakhstan, Kyrgyzstan, Latvia, Lithuania, Moldova, Tajikistan, Turkmenistan, Ukraine, and Uzbekistan.

START I (Strategic Arms Reduction Treaty I) An arms agreement between the Soviet Union and the United States signed July 31, 1991.

START II (Strategic Arms Reduction Treaty II) an agreement between the United States and the Russian Federation which banned the use of MIRVs (multiple independently targeted reentry vehicles) on ICBMs (INTERCONTINENTAL BALLISTIC MISSILES). START II was signed on January 3, 1993, by Russian president Boris Yeltsin and U.S. president George H. W. Bush. It would have entered into force in December 2001. However, the Russian Federation withdrew from the treaty after the United States withdrew from the ABM Treaty, so START II never went into force.

stockpile A supply stored for future use.

Strategic Defense Initiative A missile defense program introduced in the 1980s by U.S. president Ronald Reagan; promoted to the American public as a "space shield" against nuclear armed INTERCONTINENTAL BALLISTIC MISSILES, it was popularly called "Star Wars."

strategic nuclear weapons While the term *strategic* sometimes alludes to nuclear weapons in general, strategic nuclear weapons target cities, in contrast to "tactical" nuclear weapons, which would be used on military targets.

superterrorism Terrorist acts that cause devastation on a large scale, such as the attacks of September 11, 2001, on the United States.

tactical nuclear weapons Nuclear weapons of relatively small energy for use against military targets; often used in contrast to "strategic" weapons, which target cities.

thermonuclear Of, relating to, or derived from the fusion of atomic nuclei at high temperatures; relating to the use of nuclear weapons based on fusion.

terrorism The calculated use of violence or the threat of violence against civilians in order to achieve political, religious, or ideological goals.

totalitarian Characterized by a government that exercises absolute and centralized political control and attempts to regulate all aspects of life, including "thought control." Often contrasted to "authoritarian" governments, which suppress political dissent but grant some freedom in private life.

Treaty of Rarotonga A treaty signed in 1985 establishing a nuclear-free zone in the South Pacific.

Treaty of Tlatelolco A treaty originally signed in 1967 making Latin America and the Caribbean a "nuclear-free zone."

UNAEC *See* UNITED NATIONS ATOMIC ENERGY COMMISSION.

underground testing Testing of nuclear weapons below ground.

unilateral Relating to action by one country on its own.

United Nations Atomic Energy Commission (UNAEC) An agency established by the UN General Assembly on January 24, 1946, just 14 days after the General Assembly's opening session. The UNAEC was later superseded by the UN International Atomic Energy Agency.

United Nations General Assembly A deliberative body consisting of representatives from all member nations of the UN. As the only UN organ in which all members are represented, the assembly serves as a forum for members to discuss issues of international law and to make decisions regarding the functioning of the organization.

United Nations Security Council An organ of the UN charged with maintaining international peace and security. The Security Council is made up of 15 member states consisting of five permanent members—China, France, Russia, the United Kingdom, and the United States—and 10 rotating members. Under the UN charter, UN member governments must carry out decisions of the UN Security Council embodied in UN Security Council Resolutions.

V-2 rocket An unmanned guided rocket developed by German scientists during World War II. It was the ancestor of the ballistic missile. It carried one ton of high explosives capable of destroying a large building. Since it was not very accurate, its primary military use was to inspire terror.

vertical nuclear proliferation The increase in the number of nuclear weapons in the arsenals of existing nuclear weapons states.

warhead The front part of a guided missile, rocket, or torpedo that carries the nuclear or explosive charge or the chemical or biological agents.

Warsaw Pact A military alliance of communist Eastern European nations formed in 1955 in response to the COLD WAR.

weapons grade uranium Uranium with a high enough concentration of the isotope Uranium-235 to be useable in the core of an atomic bomb.

weapons of mass destruction A term usually used to denote nuclear, biological, or chemical agents capable of inflicting death and property damage on a vast scale; radiological weapons are sometimes included among the list of weapons of mass destruction.

WMD *See* WEAPONS OF MASS DESTRUCTION.

World Health Organization The UN specialized agency for health established on April 7, 1948.

X-ray laser A device that uses the principle of amplification by the stimulated emission of radiation to produce an intense beam of coherent X-rays; the X-ray laser proposed by nuclear physicist Edward Teller for the Strategic Defense Initiative would have been deployed in space and powered by a thermonuclear explosion.

Zionism The movement to secure a homeland for the Jewish people; also the movement to establish Israel as a Jewish state.

Index

Note: page numbers in **boldface** indicate major treatment of a subject. Page numbers followed by *f* indicate figures. Page numbers followed by *b* indicate biographical entries. Page numbers followed by *c* indicate chronology entries. Page numbers followed by *g* indicate glossary entries.

A

Index

Index

Index

Index

Index

S

Index

V

W

Index